SCOTUS AMERICANUS

The title Scotus Americanus *was the* nom de plume *of the author of a pamphlet published in 1773 advocating emigration to America.*

. .
.

I conclude . . . if the scheme should be carried on and fixed on so firm a basis as that we might on it's faith venture to bring a man from his own country, it would be best for me to interest some person in Scotland to engage a good one. From that country we are surest of having sober attentive men.

THOMAS JEFFERSON to WILSON CARY NICHOLAS, 31 December 1783, on a proposal to found a school in Albermarle County, Virginia.

.

SCOTUS AMERICANUS

*A survey of the sources for links
between Scotland and America in
the eighteenth century*

. .

WILLIAM R. BROCK

*Professor emeritus of Modern History,
University of Glasgow*

*With a chapter on Scotland and
American medicine by*
DR C. HELEN BROCK

AT THE EDINBURGH UNIVERSITY PRESS

.

© W. R. Brock 1982
Edinburgh University Press
22 George Square, Edinburgh

Typeset by Image Services (Edinburgh) Ltd
Printed in Great Britain by
Redwood Burn Limited
Trowbridge

British Library Cataloguing in Publication Data

Brock, William R.
    Scotus Americanus: a survey of the sources
    for links between Scotland and America in
    the eighteenth century.
    1. Scotland – Foreign relations –
    United States – History – Sources
    I. Title
    941.107   DA948.AZ

ISBN 0-85224-420-7

PREFACE

This book is intended to serve a dual purpose. It offers a general survey and commentary on the Scottish links with the American colonies in the eighteenth century, illustrated by accounts of the fortunes, misfortunes, migrations, and business ventures of the many individuals whose papers have survived in British and American libraries. At the same time it offers an outline guide for those who wish to investigate more fully either the story as a whole, or the history of families, business partnerships, and American settlements. The first part of each chapter provides a general introduction and the second detailed information on the sources. If the hundreds of individuals, whose lives or momentary appearances are recorded, appear and disappear with sometimes bewildering rapidity this may give a better impression of eighteenth-century life than a structured narrative selecting only the information judged to be relevant. Those who have been engaged upon the search have become fascinated by the pursuit of wandering Scots, men on the make, successful merchants, hardworking factors, doctors, ministers of religion, soldiers, college teachers, and humble tutors. These brief lives, business ventures and professional skills fill the transatlantic panorama with real men, who contributed their mites to Scottish and American societies during a century that was vital for both.

The list of sources at the end of the volume is arranged by repository with holdings in chronological order. This will enable the researcher to see at a glance where the sources for his topic or period are to be found. In this way it is hoped that the lists will be useful for the novice as well as the professional, for the student in search of a dissertation topic as well as for scholars who wish to assess the bedrock of evidence on which generalisations must rest.

The work was undertaken by the Denis Brogan Centre at the University of Glasgow. Much of the material was surveyed by three research assistants who each spent a year in the Centre: David Cross, Graham Walker and Iain Russell. All three worked in the Scottish Record Office, the Scottish National Library, the Strathclyde Regional Archives, and the Mitchell Library in Glasgow. David Cross visited many American libraries not only in the eastern states but as far afield as Florida and Michigan. Graham Walker visited Aberdeen, Perth, Dumfries, and the Public Record Office in London. Iain Russell accompanied me on profitable visits to the Library of Congress, the Maryland Hall of Records, and the Historical Societies of Maryland, Massachusetts, and New York. I am grateful to all three not only for their industry, but for their company on many occasions.

My wife, Dr C. Helen Brock, has made a special study of Americans who received their medical education in Scotland, and of the influence of Scottish medicine in America. She is responsible for Chapter VI, Appendix A and Appendix B, and for help and advice on many matters affecting educational and scientific links between the two countries.

My special thanks are due to Dr Charles Ritcheson, American cultural attaché in London during the bicentennial year, without whose encouragement and help the work would have been impossible. It has also been supported by the University of Glasgow, the Ross Fund Committee of the University of Glasgow, and the Nuffield foundation.

The list of libraries visited will indicate the amount of help received from librarians and archivists, but special thanks are due to the staff of the Scottish Record Office in Edinburgh. This work would have been vastly more difficult without their *List of American Documents*, published in 1976, while the speed and courtesy with which requests are met make the Scottish Record Office a model of what a great archival collection should be.

My wife wishes to acknowledge the help of Dr Whitfield Bell of the American Philosophical Society, who most generously allowed her to draw upon his unrivalled knowledge of American medical and scientific history during the eighteenth century.

Abstracts and transcripts of the material surveyed have been deposited in the Glasgow University Library. Enquiries should be addressed to the Curator of Special Collections.

W.R.B., Glasgow, May 1981

ACKNOWLEDGEMENT

Mr Richard Dell, archivist of the Strathclyde Region, made a pioneer survey in 1970 of the sources in American archives for the study of the Glasgow tobacco trade. His report not only revealed the amount of material that awaited investigation but also set a high standard for all who wished to build upon his foundations. It is therefore appropriate to give special prominence to this acknowledgement. Mr Dell's visit to the United States was sponsored by the Committee of the Ross Fund of the University of Glasgow, and thanks to him must therefore be accompanied by an appreciation of the generous way in which the study of Scots overseas has been financed from this fund.

CONTENTS

ABBREVIATIONS

Archives and Libraries

CIW = Colonial Institute, Williamsburg, Virginia
DUL = Duke University Library, Durham, N.C.
LC = Library of Congress, Washington, D.C.
MASS HS = Massachusetts Historical Society, Boston
MD HR = Maryland Hall of Records, Annapolis
MD HS = Maryland Historical Society, Baltimore
MLG = Mitchell Library, Glasgow
NCSA = North Carolina State Archives, Raleigh
NLS = National Library of Scotland, Edinburgh
NYHS = New York Historical Society, New York
NYPL = New York Public Library, New York
PA HS = Pennsylvania Historical Society, Philadelphia
PRO = Public Record Office, London
PUL = Princeton University Library, Princeton
SCC = South Carolina Collection, Columbia
SCHS = South Carolina Historical Society, Charleston
SRA = Strathclyde Regional Archives, Glasgow
SRO = Scottish Record Office, Edinburgh
UNC = University of North Carolina (Southern
    Historical Collections), Chapel Hill
U VA = University of Virginia Library, Charlottesville
VA HS = Virginia Historical Society, Richmond
VA SL = Virginia State Library, Richmond
WMC = William and Mary College, Williamsburg
YUB = Yale University, Beinecke Library, New Haven
YUL = Yale University Library, New Haven

Periodicals

EC HR = Economic History Review
MD HIST M = Maryland Historical Magazine
NC HIST R = North Carolina Historical Review
PENN HIST M = Pennsylvania Historical Magazine
VA MHB = Virginia Magazine of History and Biography
WMQ = William and Mary Quarterly

Chapter One

BACKGROUND AND BEGINNINGS

During the eighteenth century the foundations of modern American civilisation were laid. A rapid growth in population, the rise of towns and commerce, experience in representative government, the revolution, independence, and new constitutions in states and the Union were symptoms of growth from small weak colonies to a new nation. In this great transformation men of English descent and honouring English traditions played the leading role in all fields. It would be idle to suggest otherwise; yet there is good ground for claiming that next to transplanted English the migrant Scots played the most important part.

Though less numerous than immigrants from Northern Ireland, lowland Scots came to occupy a significant place in colonial life. In the Glasgow tobacco trade they organised the most efficient business of the age and contributed greatly to the development of inland areas in Virginia and Maryland. Scots merchant communities were found in all the commercial cities, and played a part in the organisation of overseas trade. They permeated the official establishment, especially in the southern colonies, and provided several colonial governors. They supplied clergy for the episcopalian and presbyterian churches. They served as tutors in hundreds of colonial families, especially in the South, and many went on to establish schools. Above all they had a powerful influence upon medicine, philosophical ideas, and the struggling colonial colleges.

Highland Scots could not claim similar achievements, and their time would not come until their descendants entered into the main stream of American life. In the eighteenth century their settlements were poor – only in North Carolina did they achieve some modest prosperity – and they were cut off from fellow colonists by dress, custom, and often by the Gaelic language. Their settlements suffered disastrous blows during the Revolution, when so many became Loyalists. Nevertheless Highlanders crossed the Atlantic in considerable numbers, added a romantic element to a somewhat prosaic culture, and continued their migration into the nineteenth century. There are probably more descendants of the clans in modern America than in Scotland. The Highlands formed one of the population reserves upon which colonial legislators and land speculators drew to subdue the wilderness and civilize a continent. Offers of land on ostensibly attractive terms drew them to thinly populated frontier areas or neglected tracts in the older settled districts, to Georgia in its earliest days, to the great northern wilderness of New York, or to the Cape Fear valley of North Carolina.

If Scottish influences upon America are often elusive, the effects of the American connection upon Scotland are clear. Ventures in America formed an important part of the process by which the people of a small, poor, but vigorous country sought opportunity to prosper, and though America was not the only field for Scottish enterprise, it affected a wide range of people. Among those who sought their fortunes (or at least a competence) in the American colonies were the sons of lairds, young doctors, merchants of all descriptions, clergy, teachers, artisans and mechanics, indentured servants, hundreds of young men who went out as clerks or apprentice storekeepers, and thousands of Highland crofters rendered desperate in their original homes. The eighteenth century was the flowering time of Scottish universities, and the high reputation that they enjoyed in America – especially in philosophy and medicine – contributed to their success.

The economic consequences of the American connection are open to dispute. Some have argued that Scotland would have done better without the restraints of the imperial trading system, or the accumulation of wealth in the hands of merchants, and this view derives from Adam Smith who had unrivalled opportunities to observe the system at first-hand. Nevertheless the Glasgow tobacco trade was the first big business in Scotland, and the first to beat competitors by hard-driving efficiency. It stimulated the shipping, gave the Clyde a major interest in world-trade, encouraged manufacture for the colonial markets, and helped a potentially good banking system become one of the strongest in Europe. Scottish banking derived additional strength from association with the London money market where many Scottish merchants established branches that were part commercial and part financial, but this extension of the Scottish banking interest was partly a consequence of the American connection.

The influence of America upon Dumfries and Galloway was considerable, though in a minor key compared with the tremendous developments on the Clyde. In the early years of the century Dumfries enjoyed considerable trade with the American colonies, but this failed to develop. The facilities for handling large numbers of ocean-going vessels were much better on the Clyde than in the south-western ports, and a more vigorous merchant community with wide trading contacts was already established in Glasgow by the close of the seventeenth century. As a primarily agricultural region the south-west had little to export that the colonies required, and would-be travellers or emigrants were likely to find ships sailing more frequently from the Clyde ports. In addition Dumfries had to compete with the thriving port of Liverpool a hundred miles to the south. The south-west did however contribute to the transatlantic migration, and can claim distinction in American history as the native land of John Paul Jones. Dumfries and Galloway shared with many other parts of the United Kingdom the experience of emigration and consequent family connections, but there was no major movement of people to America comparable to that from the Highlands or Ulster.

The effects upon Aberdeen and the north-east are more difficult to summarise. The region contributed its share of humble emigrants, younger sons of lairds in search of prosperity, tutors, schoolmasters, and episcopal clergy. King's College, Aberdeen, had a direct effect upon American colleges through the work of William Smith as first provost of the University of Pennsylvania, but few American students found their way to the northern colleges and Aberdeen gave more than it received. Kirkwall enjoyed a spell of commercial prosperity from American trade, but this was caused by the accident of British law which made it compulsory for ships carrying the most valuable colonial commodities to pass through the customs at a British port. There were no long-term consequences in Orkney as on the Clyde. In the north-east the most important result of the American connection was the network of family relationships as Gordons, Duffs, Grants, McKays, Sinclairs and many others established themselves in the colonies.

In the middle years of the century and increasing number of Scots, mainly from the Highlands, entered the service of the Crown as soldiers. The lairds supplied the officers, while the sons of hundreds of crofters formed the rank and file. The most successful regiments were those recruited from single districts, in which men served under leaders of their own clan. During their tours of duty Highland officers joined the elites in colonial cities. Some regiments were disbanded in North America and the soldiers and non-commissioned officers were offered grants of land. Probably the most far-reaching effect of military service was to spread knowledge of the colonies in Scotland, and thus to stimulate trade, migration, and settlement.

The effects of American trade were not limited to the two-way traffic in tobacco and manufactured goods. Scottish merchants also handled some exports from the mainland colonies which did not play much part in the trade of the Clyde. They exported rice from South Carolina to English ports and, more especially, to the Mediterranean. Individual Scots in South Carolina were prominent in developing the cultivation and export of indigo, and with less success, tried to promote the production of silk and wine; but these activities had little effect upon Scotland which neither contributed to their development nor shared in the profits. However, in the export of wheat, timber, provisions and livestock from the mainland colonies, Norfolk, Virginia became an important entrepôt and the leading men were Scottish merchants who had originally gone out to engage upon the tobacco trade. Some timber and barrel staves went to Scotland – usually as deck cargoes on the tobacco ships – but their principal market was in the West Indies. Other reasons – principally the quest for sugar – attracted Scottish merchants to the Caribbean, but exports from the mainland colonies contributed to the build-up of Scottish interests in the British islands. The ships that carried exports to the West Indies usually picked up return cargoes of sugar or molasses, some for use in the American colonies and some for direct export to Scotland. Greenock became the major centre for importing, distributing and re-exporting of sugar.

Scottish enterprise and settlement flourished within the framework of imperial law. Trade conformed to regulations worked out during the seventeenth century, and the government of the colonies followed patterns which Scots had no hand in making. During the course of the century Scots abroad had to accept the consequences of decisions made at Westminster, but apart from a few grandees among the Scottish aristocracy, few attempted to participate in making policy. Though all of Scotland was affected by the rebellions of 1715 and 1745, only a minority saw great issues at stake. For the most part Scottish merchants, settlers, doctors, and even colonial office holders wanted to make their own way with little regard to politics. They were not a politically conscious people in a modern sense, and those who took the lead in commerce and the professions were not of the type whose names survive in the history of nations. Even the most influential men in the story are now almost forgotten, but it may be worthwhile to linger with the records of those that have no other memorial.

At the close of the seventeenth century Scots and English were subjects of the same sovereign, but belonged to separate nations. The colonies of North America belonged to the English Crown and the English Parliament sought to preserve a monopoly of their trade wherever it was practicable and profitable to do so. Several English colonies were governed by proprietors, under charters granted by the King, and they might have an added interest in excluding Scottish competition. Scottish merchants traded with the English colonies, but were not allowed to bring out the most valuable commodities, were excluded from the carrying trade between colonies, and could bring in only the produce of Scotland. A poor country had little to export save people, but the demand for servants in the colonies could make this a profitable business. Sometimes impoverished Scots were ready to sell themselves to merchants or masters of vessels, into virtual slavery for a term of years in exchange for their passage. Convicts or captured rebels were transported without even this semblance of voluntary consent. In this way hundreds of Scots arrived in North America but genealogical research has failed to reveal their descendants. No memorial records their arrival, and diligent research is unlikely to yield more than scattered and fragmentary evidence of their existence.

The first considerable number of Scots to reach the New World in this undistinguished way were prisoners captured by Cromwell at Dunbar and Worcester, and transported in 1651. Most of them were sent to New

England, but seem to have been treated well. In 1657 the establishment of a Scots Charitable Society in Boston suggests that some had prospered enough to care for their less fortunate countrymen. No early records have survived, but in the eighteenth century a few widows or sick persons were relieved by the charity.[1]

There had been much thought in Scotland of the need to found colonies, for the wisdom of the day held that this was the surest foundation for national prosperity and the best outlet for people who could not be supported at home.[2]

The disastrous failure of the Darien colony put an end to these plans, but for a short period in the late seventeenth century enthusiasm for colonisation ran high. It was reinforced amongst extreme presbyterians by the hope that a colony might provide a home for persecuted Covenanters. The outcome was the establishment of a settlement at Stewart's Town in Carolina in 1684.[3]

At this time the parent colony was less than twenty years old, and still under the control of proprietors. The Scottish scheme came about as the result of an agreement between them and a Scottish group headed by Sir John Cochrane of Ochiltree and Sir George Campbell of Cessnock. They were helped in their negotiations by Bishop Gilbert Burnet, a distinguished graduate of Glasgow University, who was close to the Whig leaders at a time when they were at the height of their power in London. For their part the proprietors welcomed the proposal for a settlement that would protect the southern flank of their colony against Spanish attack, and were prepared to grant freedom of worship to the intending colonists. The English colonists took a different view, but in 1682 the proprietors informed the Governor that they had agreed to the Scottish settlement and ordered him to give them what assistance he could.

In 1682 there was talk in Scotland of sending out a party of one thousand colonists and a thousand cows, but more cautious counsels prevailed and a single ship was sent out to inspect the land; it returned in the following year. The most active men in promoting the scheme were Principal William Dunlop of Glasgow University and Lord Cardross, who was to head the first party of colonists. In July 1684 a ship appropriately named *Carolina Merchant* sailed from Gourock with about 140 persons on board.

With so small a party, destined for so remote a settlement, help from the English colonists at Charleston was essential; but this was made unlikely when Cardross announced, on arrival, that he was not subject to the authority of the Governor. In May 1685 the Council of the colony issued a warrant for his arrest. This was countermanded by the proprietors, but by the time their decision was made known the tiny Scottish colony was in serious difficulties. The details are obscure but the Spanish alleged that the Scots had encouraged Indians to attack their mission of Santa Catalina and in 1686 had sent a party of 150 to attack Stewart's Town. The Scots had only 25 men fit to fight, and their settlement was completely destroyed. The survivors took refuge in Charleston, and no attempt was made to reestablish the settlement.

A better planned and more successful settlement in East New Jersey was inspired by Robert Barclay, a prominent Scottish Quaker, who hoped to emulate William Penn. A charter was obtained in 1683 and twenty-four proprietors, of whom half were prominent Englishmen, were named. The English proprietors were probably chosen to disarm opposition at court, and to suggest that the enterprise was neither exclusively Quaker nor predominantly Scottish. However the chief proprietor was the Earl of Perth, and in Scotland it was presented as a national enterprise. In 1684 there was published 'an advertisement to all tradesmen, husbandmen, servants and others who are willing to transport themselves to the province of New East Jersey in America, a great part of which belongs to Scotsmen, proprietors thereof'. It was said that several ships would be leaving in May, June and July from Leith, Montrose, Aberdeen and Glasgow. It was also hoped that the colony might become a haven for persecuted Covenanters. In 1685 George Scot of Pitlochrie published a *Model of the Government of the Province of East New Jersey in America*, compared the settlements in New Jersey and South Carolina, much to the disparagement of the latter, and concluded with a selection of letters from Scottish settlers already in the colony.[4]

In the same year the failure of Argyle's revolt against James VII and II left a large number of covenanting prisoners in the hands of the authorities, and Barclay applied to the Privy Council for some of them to be transported to East New Jersey. Lord Neil Campbell, brother of Argyle, but not directly implicated in the rebellion, had already considered moving to a colony, and joined with Barclay in seeking permission to take some of the prisoners with him. Some colonists were sent out and apparently arrived without incident, but tragedy attended a party gathered by George Scot of Pitlochrie himself. He had hoped for volunteers but attracted few, and most of those who set sail with him in the *Henry & Francis* had been imprisoned at Dunottar Castle. Disease, perhaps contracted in the prison, spread throughout the ship and more than sixty died including Pitlochrie and his wife. Many of the prisoners were released after arrival but the majority seem to have left for other colonies.

Lord Neil Campbell was appointed deputy governor in 1686, and came to East New Jersey in October of that year. He brought with him some immigrant settlers for whom he claimed headrights, but soon decided to return to Scotland. Andrew Hamilton, formerly an Edinburgh Merchant, was left as his substitute and subsequently as deputy governor, and carried out his duties with considerable success. In 1697 he was deprived of his office as a consequence of an Act of the English Parliament (retaliating against the Scottish Act of 1695 establishing the Company of Scotland trading to Africa and the Indies) which declared that no person not a natural born subject of England could hold 'a public post of trust or profit' in the colonies. Hamilton returned to England in 1697, obtained a ruling from the government that the Act did not exclude his Majesty's Scottish subjects from office, and returned triumphantly as Governor of both East and West New Jersey. This was a legal victory for the Scots but implicitly extinguished their hope for an independent colony. In the united province of New Jersey the Scottish settlement was indisputably part of the English colonial empire, and in 1702 the proprietors surrendered their charter to the Crown. English, Scottish, Dutch and Swedish were now all comprised in the crown colony of New Jersey.[5]

The Scottish settlement in New Jersey is of some significance in the history of Presbyterianism in America. It seems certain that the Covenanters formed congregations and local tradition maintains that the earliest site was some six miles north of the town of Freehold. The year 1692 is accepted, on not very good authority, as that in which the 'Old Scots' church at Freehold was built, but it was not until 1706 that the minister, John Boyd, was able to win official recognition under the terms of the Toleration Act of 1689. On 27 December 1706 John Boyd was ordained at Freehold with Francis McKemie as moderator, while Jezediah Andrews of Philadelphia and John Hampton of Maryland conducted the examination. In the words of the historian of the church:

> This memorable scene is the beginning of organic Presbyterian history in the New World. This is the first known presbytery meeting and the first known Presbyterian ordination. There may have been presbytery meetings and ordinations before this, and ordinations presuppose a presbytery to ordain. Yet in tracing back to its sources the wondrous course of the development of the church, history stops at John Boyd and the Old Scots' meeting house of Freehold. Back at this point lie the uncertainties of tradition or conjecture. Onward from this all is clear, cogent and connected.[6]

When the wheel of fortune in Scotland turned in favour of the Presbyterians it turned against the Episcopalians. No longer the chief recipients of official favour and, except around Aberdeen, a small minority of the population, the Episcopalians found themselves faced with the choice between obscurity at home without the prospects of advancement and seeking opportunities elsewhere. In English court circles there were several persons with obligations to Scottish friends, and the colonial church was an obvious way of rewarding faithful but disappointed adherents. The pioneer and subsequent architect of Scottish influence upon the colonial church was James Blair, a graduate of Aberdeen, who went out to Virginia in 1685 and became the Bishop of London's commissary in Virginia. This position gave him authority over the church in the largest and most influential of the colonies, and there are indications that he used his position to promote the fortunes of other Scottish episcopalians. On one occasion, during a visit to London in 1697 he was called upon to defend himself against the charge of having filled the Virginian church with dissolute Scottish clergy, but was exonerated by the Archbishop and the Bishop of London. He went on to fight with successive governors – winning most of his battles – and was for many years a member of the Council. At an advanced age, in 1740, he successfully defended his right, as senior member of the Council, to serve as acting governor during the appointed Governor's absence. In addition to his ecclesiastical and civilian duties he was the first president of William and Mary College, and nursed the infant institution through its early years of trial.[7]

During the later years of the seventeenth century Glasgow was growing rapidly. One historian has observed that Glasgow was the second city of Scotland by 1660, and for the next fifty years 'stood alone with Edinburgh, rightly famous for her pioneering enterprise on the admittedly narrow stage of the Scottish economy'.[8] The needs of Scotland were obvious – iron, hemp, sugar, and all kinds of tropical goods – yet there was little native produce to export in order to pay for these imports. The incentive to develop trade in valuable goods that could be re-exported at a profit was clear and accounts for determined efforts to break through the barriers imposed by the English laws of trade. There was considerable importation of tobacco into the Clyde, and Scottish officials were content to collect the duties and applaud the merchants for their success.[9]

This trade, carried on in defiance of English law, played an important part in the Scottish economy but was not an easily won prize. Each voyage had to be carefully planned, subterfuges and evasions adopted, bribes found for English officials, and many risks taken before the valuable product was safely home and ready for re-sale abroad. In addition there seems to have been a great deal of smuggling by small men operating in the lesser ports and this continued well into the eighteenth century. It has been suggested that smuggling and clandestine but officially recognised trade was so flourishing by 1707 that the English readily agreed to sacrifice protection of the laws of trade at the time of the Union. This seems improbable.

At the beginnings of the eighteenth century the links between Scotland and America were sporadic and uncertain. Planned settlement had either failed or been absorbed into the general pattern of English colonial development. There were religious connections, both presbyterian and episcopal, but these played a comparatively small role in the religious history of the colonies. Trade existed, but encumbered by the uncertainties of illegal operation, devious expedients, the possibility that English laws would be more strictly enforced, or that there would be reprisals against the Scots. The one point gained was that the King's Scottish subjects were no longer barred from official employment in the colonies. Apart from a little interest in the methods adopted in Scotland for the training of presbyterian ministers, cultural influences did not exist. There was indeed little to indicate that the coming century would see the emergence of Scotland as an important – perhaps a major – influence upon American civilization.

The sources for early Scottish attempts to settle in and trade with North America are meagre. The papers of the Scottish Privy Council to 1692 have been published, and the remainder (to 1708) which are now in the Scottish Record Office will be published in due course.[10] From 1666 the published register contains many references to transportation, shipping and trade and it is probable that similar references will be found in the unpublished sources. There is also some information about the Carolina and East New Jersey settlements. The records of the Exchequer of Scotland include the customs books, 1663–91, for Aberdeen, Leith, Port Glasgow and other ports. From these and other Exchequer papers information about the importation of tobacco can be gleaned.[11] The Court of Session was the supreme civil court in Scotland and its productions include business papers and accounts offered as exhibits in commerical suits or bankruptcies. However there appears to be only one such exhibit for the period prior to the Act of Union.[12]

Official records of the South Carolina grant were retained by the English Privy Council, but sources dealing with the plans, personal motives and experience in Carolina are very slight. The Hume of Marchmont muniments in the Scottish Record Office include some letters, of which the most important have been published by the Historical Manuscripts Commission.[13] The collection of the Society of Antiquaries of Scotland, now deposited in the Scottish record Office, includes an extract of a charter between Lord Cardross and ship's captain for a voyage from Charleston to Virginia.[14]

The official records of the East New Jersey proprietory grant must also be sought in the Public Record Office in London. The Scottish Record Office holds a printed advertisement of 1685 offering passages from Leith, Montrose, Aberdeen and Kirkwall for emigrants to New Jersey. From the same year there is also a letter addressed to the Earl of Perth stating that the writer had been unable to obtain possession of land in New Jersey, sold him by Lord Perth, because 'all the campions ground and riversids ar takin up alradie by Quakers, Independents, Presbiterians, Anabaptists, and in a word *by all the offscourings of hell*'. This has also been published.[15] The heirs of Lord Perth continued to hold Land in New Jersey, and this became involved in controversy during and after the revolution.[16] There are also two titles to land in East New Jersey, granted in 1683–5, in the Scottish Record Office.[17] There are probably more sources yet to be investigated in New Jersey. The records of the proprietory officer are at Perth Amboy and a register of land grants in the state archives.[18]

The papers of the Dunlop family contain a number of items dealing with Scottish enterprise in America before the Act of Union.[19] In March 1683 John Dunlop, who had been sent south to seek opportunities, wrote to his father, James, that he had been unable to find anything suitable and had therefore resolved 'to go to New York in ye West Indies'. Other letters described his preparation for the voyage and help received from Gavin Lawrie, a Scots Quaker whose son was Governor of West New Jersey. He sailed from Plymouth on 29 April 1683 and arrived in New York on 5 July. A letter of 7 August reported surprising good fortune:

> For I had not kept store heir above on weik till I had most partlie disposed of all for present money, and now not one farthing's worth to dispose of.

He had lost nothing by bad debts which was 'a great matter for a stranger in yˢ place', and reckoned a profit of 80 per cent. Encouraged by this success he collected a cargo of flour and bread, valued at nearly £200, and took ship to the West Indies – only to die there in November of a fever.

Before succumbing to fatal disease John wrote several informative letters about prospects in America. He repeatedly warned his father against any involvement in the Carolina scheme. In London he had taken the advice of a Mr Foulis and another who were:

> so far from counselling anie of yʳ friends to be Concerned in it they were shewr yᵗ anie people yᵗ should be transported into yᵗ place should ours then then who occasioned yᵗ transportation and should gladly wish to be at home to beg yʳ bread in yʳ native Countrie.

After arrival in New York he again warned against Carolina and thought that Delaware offered a much fairer prospect; but he did not expect to settle any where as a planter – 'for yʳ is no profit yʳ wᵗout hard labour' – and would not advise his brother to come out for more than a trading voyage. Nevertheless a William Dunlop, who may have been John's brother, was in South Carolina in 1688–9, and seems to have been employed by James Colleton, the Governor, on a mission to the Governor of Florida.[20] Two documents sent by a Samuel Williamson from Carolina in June 1689 refer to his 'beloved friend' Dunlop, and deal with matters concerning his will.

Archibald Dunlop, who was certainly a brother of John, wrote a letter from New York on 9 September 1701 to another brother, James.[21] He complained that none of his brothers had written since he left Scotland. He said that he had been successful in two trading voyages and had taken a quarter share in a ship bound for Curacao. At the time of writing he was uncertain whether to make the voyage himself; the profit would be greater, but there was risk of capture by the Spaniards and he had heard much of their 'barbarities' to prisoners. A good part of the letter was taken up with enquiries about remittance of bills.

These early letters establish that Scots were under no restraint when shipping goods to the English colonies or taking out shipments of non-enumerated products for the West Indies. It was a different story when they attempted to take part in the shipment of tobacco to the British Isles or engage in the carrying trade between mainland colonies. Here they encountered the full rigours of the English laws of trade. There survives a remarkably full letter written by Daniel Campbell of Glasgow in 1692.[22] He was one of the largest Scottish merchants of the day with interests in trade with the Baltic and other North European ports, was also sending ships to trade with North America as early as 1692, and for outward voyages sometimes sent shiploads of indentured servants, recruited from the poor of the Scottish lowlands. His problem was to find a profitable return cargo, and inevitably he thought of ways to get his hand on tobacco – a commodity for which there was an unlimited demand in his European markets.

The letter consists of secret instructions given to James Robison, who was to be in charge of one venture in 1696. Six or seven Scottish mechants had contributed £100 each; and some of this was to be invested in Scottish goods and taken south, clearing the English customs at Carlisle. He was then to go to London, buy more goods suitable for the New England market, and find a ship sailing for Boston or New York. On arrival he was to sell his goods and purchase a 'half-worn' ship, which could probably be obtained cheapest at Boston.

Robison was then to load this ship with goods suitable for Virginia – chiefly rum, sugar, and salt – and seek out a merchant prepared to lend his name to this incursion into the intercolonial trade from which the English sought to exclude their competitors. In Virginia he would sell his goods, purchase tobacco, and 'speak the Collector of Customs fair' until he could find an English merchant or Virginian planter to join his scheme and consign the tobacco to Bideford or some other English port. As the French and British were at war he would then have to join a convoy, for Daniel Campbell had already suffered losses from French privateers. When the ship reached a point that Robison judged to be far enough to the north, he would order the captain to break convoy and make for the Clyde to collect orders. To avoid French privateers and English revenue cutters the ship would head straight for the west coast of Scotland, pass through the sounds of Mull and Islay, and finally round Kintyre.

The instructions clearly drew upon previous experience, and suggest that a good deal of trade was carried on in this way; but subterfuge, bribes, and unwritten agreements were no substitute for open trade. So while the document suggests extensive illegal trade, it also provides evidence of good commercial reasons for supporting the Act of Union.

There is also some evidence of tobacco landed illegally in Dumfries and Galloway.[23] It would seem that some Dumfries merchants had a close working arrangement with those of Whitehaven. Tobacco consigned to the English port could be diverted to Scotland, thus avoiding payment of English import duties. If the matter were handled with care it would also be possible to avoid Scottish duties. This may have worked in some cases, but informal agreements are likely to fall apart and in 1696 a cargo of tobacco, brought direct from America to Annan, was subject to a long dispute over ownership during which its sale was prohibited by court injunction. No one profited, because the tobacco rotted in the cellars where it had been stored.

Finally, among these meagre records of early Scottish enterprise in America, there is fragmentary evidence of a proposed colony in Florida. This consists of a letter written in 1712 by George Bell to the Society in Scotland for the Propagation of Christian Knowledge.[24] He thought that Florida would offer fair prospects. 'This country is not lyk unto Darien wher they had not men to assist you against the Spaniards'. It was not surrounded by Spanish forts, and a new colony would have time to grow. Nothing more is heard of this scheme. Perhaps someone asked who was to pay the cost when the King of Spain sent the inevitable expedition to establish his sovereignty over Florida. In any case by 1712 Scottish merchants had unrestricted entry to British colonies, and would-be settlers would be welcome as subjects of the United Kingdom'

Chapter Two

GOING TO AMERICA

It has been estimated that in 1790 there were 260,322 people of Scottish birth or descent in the United States.[1] The total population of the United States was 3,929,000, so the proportion of Scots was 8.3 per cent. In the nation as a whole there were more of German descent, forming one third of the population of Pennsylvania, and they were also numerous in New York, New Jersey, Maryland, Kentucky, and Tennessee. In other colonies Scots were, next to the English, the largest group. The estimate attempted to avoid the confusion, so often apparent in older American works, between Scots and 'Scots-Irish', and corrects the common impression that far more of the latter joined the Atlantic migration of the eighteenth century. People from the present counties of Northern Ireland comprised 6 per cent of the population. A further 3.7 per cent came from the counties now included in the Republic of Ireland. A good many of those from the South were probably presbyterians, and so regarded as 'Scots-Irish', which would suggest that the numbers of Scots and Scots-Irish were approximately the same.

The distribution of Scots in 1790 was particularly interesting.

New England	*Number*	*Percentage of whole population*
Maine	4,325	4.47
New Hampshire	8,749	4.5
Vermont	4,339	5.1
Massachusetts	16,420	4.4
Rhode Island	3,751	5.8
Connecticut	5,109	2.2
Middle Atlantic		
New York	22,006	7.0
New Jersey	13,087	7.7
Pennsylvania	36,410	8.6
Delaware	3,705	8.0
The South		
Maryland	15,857	7.6
Virginia	45,096	10.2
North Carolina	42,799	14.8
South Carolina	21,167	15.1
Georgia	8,197	15.5

It will be observed that there were more Scots in Virginia than in all New England, and that South Carolina had almost as many as the much larger state of New York. North Carolina had almost as many as Virginia, and a larger proportion of the total population. Moreover it is possible that the method of calculation underestimates the number in Virginia, Maryland, and South Carolina.[2]

It is impossible to estimate the number who spent a term of years in the colonies, and then returned home. Many of the merchants prominent in Glasgow toward the end of the century had spent five, ten, or even twenty years in Virginia or Maryland. In other colonies this kind of movement out and back was less frequent but not uncommon. An estimate based on the 1790 census cannot take into account the large number of Scots who became Loyalist and left the colonies never to return. An analysis of loyalist claims show that 19 per cent were from Scotland, against 11.6 per cent of English and 11.3 of Irish birth, or respectively 470, 290 and 280,[3] but the number of Loyalists who entered claims were a very small proportion of those who left the United States. Only men who had lost sizeable property found it worthwhile to embark upon the long and possibly expensive process of lodging a claim and collecting the necessary evidence, and many of the Scottish Loyalists are known to have been poor Highlanders, recently arrived in the country. It is therefore likely that the proportion of Scots among the Loyalists was even higher than the claims suggest. A very tentative estimate places the number of all Loyalists who went into exile at 160,000, though the figure may have been considerably higher.[4] Taking the conservative estimate, and the Scottish share as 19 per cent, about 30,400 Scots may have left the colonies during and after the Revolution. What is certain is that the Loyalists included a majority of active Scottish leaders in commerce and most of those who were office holders.

It is not known how many Scots settled in America before the Act of Union. The abortive settlement in South Carolina and the more successful experiment in East New Jersey have already been noted, as has the considerable number accepting indentures that condemned them to virtual slavery for serveral years. After the rebellion of 1715 collapsed many prisoners were transported to the colonies. Some of the Jacobite exiles were tolerably well received and went on to prosper,[5] but among men forced to endure hard labour, short rations and an unfamiliar climate, mortality must have been high. The same is probably true of convicts transported in later years. Speculation must replace hard evidence but it is a reasonable surmise that few of the 260,322 Scots of 1790 can have been descended from men or women who arrived before 1707 or were transported for rebellion and crime. Voluntary migration during the sixty-eight years following the Act of Union, or the seven following the peace of 1783, must have accounted for the largest number.

These figures must be seen in the context of general population movements in eighteenth century Scotland. A guess that may not have been well-informed suggests 1,000,000 at the time of the Act of Union, but in 1755 a well-considered estimate by Dr Alexander Webster put the figure at over 1,265,000, and in 1801 the first census returned 1,608,000. In the next two censuses (1811 and 1821) the population climbed to 1,806,000 and 2,091,000.[5] The transatlantic migration must therefore be seen as a chapter in the tale of expanding population, and other parts of the overseas empire also attracted Scots emigrants to a greater or lesser extent – British North America, the West Indies, and India – and a still larger number moved south into England. In the last quarter of the century the loss was offset by immigration from Ireland. Just after the turn of the century there was another upward surge in migration to the United States. The conclusion is that rising population stimulated movement, and a vigorous people sought openings wherever circumstances allowed, and political accident and economic opportunity made the American colonies the most favoured destination of those who sought to improve their lot by leaving their ancestral homes.

Emigrants to American Colonies were drawn mainly from six social groups: landowning families, (particularly the smaller lairds of the Lowlands), professional men (especially doctors), merchants, skilled tradesmen, farming families, and crofters. The Highland migration is distinct from the other movements and will be dealt with in another chapter. Amongst the other groups there is overlap between the lairds, professional men, and merchants. Many of the sons of landowners trained as lawyers and doctors or sought commercial careers, while Glasgow merchants and Edinburgh lawyers bought country estates and assumed the rights and privileges of lairds. These literate groups contributed by far the largest body of source material for the study of migration. They wrote frequent letters, had the greatest incentive to keep in touch with the family at home, and addressed people who were accustomed to keeping business and family correspondence. In the course of time the muniments of many landed families ended up in public repositories, as did the papers of lawyers charged with executing wills, dealing with creditors, or presenting loyalist claims. By contrast only occasional and fragmentary evidence survives of the far more numerous passengers of modest or no means who crowded the ships bound for the New World.

From surviving records of landed, professional, and merchant families, it is possible to construct a composite picture of the upper-class emigrant. He might come from a family in comfortable circumstances, but if so he was probably a younger son with poor expectations at home. Though he might eventually hope to own land in the colonies, his first objective was normally to succeed in business or medicine. If a boy of slender means came from a merchant background, or managed to win the good will of one of the greater merchants, his usual aims were to learn the business, gain the confidence of his employers, trade a little on his own account, and eventually win his way to a partnership at home or abroad; but if his early education led him into the ministry of the Church of Scotland, it was not easy to persuade him to respond to a call from the colonies (except perhaps from congregations in commercial towns) because able young ministers (and many less gifted) had ample opportunities at home. Episcopalians had more limited prospects and many found their way into the colonial Anglican Church.

Colonial office was a frequent object of ambition, and several Scots reached the top of the ladder. The best known Scottish Governors were James Glen of South Carolina and Lawrence Dinwiddie of Virginia. Cadwallader Colden of New York did not rise higher than Lieutenant-Governor but acted as governor for long periods. Many Scots joined in the competition for lesser offices such as secretary of a colony, collector of customs, or surveyor of crown lands. Few Scottish lawyers made a career in the colonies, as knowledge of Scots law was no advantage in a country where the English common law reigned supreme.

Many Highland gentlemen and a few from the Lowlands spent some years in the colonies as army officers, and though transient visitors they gave an air of distinction to Scottish social life in the towns and to newly formed St Andrew's Societies. Scottish naval officers were less numerous, but masters of merchant vessels were frequent visitors; they traded on their own account in goods and indentured servants, executed commissions at home, and became respected and influential figures. Neil Jamieson, who became the wealthiest Scottish merchant in Virginia, first came to Norfolk in charge of a ship and was known as 'Captain' in his earlier years.

There are many success stories but few started from the lower rungs of the social ladder. They might begin with little money, but probably had education and friends. Scots of this class helped each other with employment, business introductions, and perhaps credit. The account books of successful Scottish merchants show how much of their business was done with fellow Scots, and even when their trade was with London rather than Glasgow, their correspondents in the capital were usually Scots who had taken the road south and established mercantile and banking businesses. In the coastal trade, they usually seemed to find Scots in other colonies with whom to conduct their business.

To some extent this fellow feeling crossed the Highland line as it seldom did at home. When Highlanders settled in numbers in North Carolina, it seemed natural that Lowland Scots from Charleston, South Carolina, should become their supply merchants, while Highland gentlemen who moved to Charleston, Savannah or New York associated with the merchants and doctors who formed the core of the resident Scottish community.

There is little direct evidence on small Lowland farmers, who sold up at home to invest in a passage to America and land in the colonies. The prospect of acquiring large tracts at what must have seemed to be very low prices, or paying the nominal rents demanded by some land speculators, must have attracted ambitious young men whose families had struggled along for generations on small holdings or poor soil, and to younger sons who had little to hope from their patrimony. It was said that they could do well if they were prepared to work hard, accept the prospect of lean years while the land was cleared, and nurse it carefully towards full production. With a little cash, prospects might be improved by the purchase of a slave.

Young men with no money were forced to other expedients if they wished to try their luck in America. For men with education a much favoured course was to seek employment as tutors in wealthy colonial households, or as schoolmasters, and young Scots seem to have acquired an unusually high reputation for diligence, sobriety, serious purpose, and skill in imparting knowledge to their pupils. Even after the Revolution Thomas Jefferson recommended that the managers of the new school in Albermarle County, Virginia, should seek a Scottish schoolmaster when no suitable American could be found at Princeton and none but Irish in Philadelphia.[6] A would-be tutor might pay his own passage, and then seek employment at an agreed wage. If he could not pay his passage he might enter into a contract before he left Britain, or after arrival in the colonies, with the employer exacting service for a term of years, and giving bed and board but no more than a nominal wage.

Many young men (or fathers acting on their behalf) took out indentures with merchants to serve for a period in the colonies as clerks, book-keepers, storekeepers, or assistants to factors. The wages offered were usually low, but sometimes a limited trade on their own account was allowed. Bed, board, and laundry were usually promised, and sometimes the merchant accepted responsibility for training the young man in business practices. A cash payment might be demanded before the apprenticeship began, for the merchant carried considerable risks and if the new recruit proved to be lazy, unreliable, incompetent, or dissolute there was little that could be done about it. On the other hand merchants with expanding interests relied upon this means to attract and train able young men who might eventually become key men in the operations at home or abroad. A good many notable fortunes were made from these humble beginnings.

The indenture system was widely used by other types of emigrant. At the bottom of the social ladder were men and women who virtually sold themselves to ships' captains in return for their passage, and were in turn sold by the captain to colonial planters whom they were bound to serve, usually for five or seven years. The full rigour of the law could be invoked against fugitives from labour and employers possessed ample powers of

punishment; but one enthusiast for emigration to North Carolina said that
the demand for labour was such that employers competed for the services of
immigrants, paid their passages, and offered good wages.[7] In Maryland an
observer took a much less favourable view of the prospects for penniless
families; young indentured servants might build for posterity, but men and
women of mature years could not hope to survive unscathed the years of
harsh treatment and poor food.[8]

Somewhat better off were men with skill or some education, who might
find colonial employment through the help of merchants or others at home.
There are no individual case histories, but correspondence from the
colonies is full of requests for gardeners, weavers, craftsmen of various
kinds, and men willing to train as overseers. When there was this demand a
shrewd man could presumably strike a good bargain.

Letters from men already established in the colonies invariably advised
would-be emigrants of the upper class not to trust to luck for a good start in
life, but to provide themselves with tangible assets or marketable skills. In
the early part of the century a typical stratagem was for a man to purchase
goods in Scotland or England (making sure that he first obtained advice
about the needs of the colonial market), bargain for freight and passage in a
ship, hope for a quick sale, and use the profits to launch himself in business.
By the middle of the century references to this kind of individual venture no
longer occur, and the typical aspiring merchant would seek employment
with an established firm, acquire experience in the colonies, put down the
money for partnership, or set up his own business. At some later stage in life
he would have to decide whether to invest in land and slaves, or continue to
work his way up the commercial ladder.

No skill was more in demand, or yielded better rewards, than that of
medicine. Unhealthy summers, over-indulgence, epidemic diseases, and
the normal incidents of birth, infant illness, and poor adult health made
doctors much in demand, and those trained in Edinburgh had an enormous
advantage. There were failures, as in every profession, but most surviving
sources record the success, wealth, and superior status of medical men. As
the century went on the advantages of an Edinburgh medical education
became more apparent.

Why did so many leave their homes to embark upon the uncertainties of
migration to lands of which they have no more than shadowy knowledge?
The simple answer is that Scotland was a poor country in which too many
competed for too few resources. At the bottom of the social scale many
normally lived on the margin of subsistence, and fell below it in bad years.
Among the gentry many had lands which yielded poor returns and no spare
income to bestow on younger sons. Trade, law, and the practice of medicine
provided outlets, but opportunities at home were restricted. Rising standards for those with a position to maintain, meant more pressure on rents

and heavier demands upon the poorer occupiers of the land. For them the future looked increasingly bleak, and the perils of the unknown seemed more inviting than the certain prospect of never making ends meet.

In retrospect we know that things would grow better. Agricultural improvement, the efforts of some paternalistic landowners, more demand from distant markets for cattle and sheep, and for all kinds of produce from growing towns, made the future for rural Scotland much better in the second half of the century. The increase in trade and manufactures would give the central belt a leading place in the first industrial revolution. Greater prosperity would provide more and better careers in the professions. This bright future was hidden from men in the early years of the century, and to many the only remedy seemed to be movement to another place where skill, hard work, and luck could bring better rewards. Many of the upper classes intended to make their fortunes and return; the poor or small property owners could have no such expectation.

For a country with so few opportunities Scotland had an unusually effective educational system. From parochial schools to high schools or academies, and then to the five ancient colleges, no other country in Europe offered so many openings for poor boys below the rank of gentlemen, and the intake of students from humble homes probably increased during the eighteenth century. The large number of bursaries, given by pious bene-factors to the ancient Scottish universities is testimony to the importance attached to the education of poor but meritorious young men. As four of the universities (including the two colleges of Aberdeen) were situated in cities it was also comparatively cheap for sons of craftsmen and shopkeepers to attend classes.[9] Men sought degrees primarily in order to qualify as ministers, doctors, or lawyers, but a great many attended classes to obtain what was described as a 'liberal education'. Of the 166 tobacco merchants in business between 1740 and 1790, who have been identified, 36 matri-culated at the University of Glasgow.[10] No other mercantile community of the eighteenth century could claim anything like so high a proportion of men receiving higher education. Nor does this complete the count, for matriculation was not compulsory except for men who wish to proceed to a degree (which few sons of merchants did), and many attended classes with no other object than award of the 'class ticket'. According to a contemporary 'it was usual for the sons of merchants to attend the College for one or two years".[11] Sons of the lowland lairds frequently attended one of the universities, as did the sons of ministers and lawyers.

One of the minor discoveries from reading the letters and papers of sources of merchants, factors, storekeepers and clerks is the high standard of literacy. They were no less immune than the majority of men to spelling errors or grammatical lapses, but the overall impression is clarity, precision, and workmanlike use of the language. In this there is a marked contrast between men educated in the first half of the eighteenth century and those who completed their education in earlier years.

The universities were at the top of an educational pyramid that was exceptionally broad based for the eighteenth century and rivalled only by New England, but all this would yield little profit if there were no rewards for the educated. Educational achievement increased the pressure upon the few opportunities that were available, and left a large number of young men with skill that could not be fully employed at home but with enough training in rational thought to calculate the chances of success elsewhere. It is also worth reflecting upon the fact that moral philosophy – mainly a study of the ethical principles upon which conduct should be based – was the distinctive feature of Scottish universities, and though young Scots of this generation were no more paragons of virtue than others of their kind, they were trained to perceive that honesty was the best policy. If these assets won meagre rewards at home, there was a wealth of opportunity in the empire of trade and settlement that Scotland joined in 1707.

The sources illustrating these themes fall into five categories. There are first the wandering traders, picking up a living as they moved from place to place; they bought cargoes, sold for profit, entered into partnerships, launched out once more on their own, and – unfortunately for our purpose – usually disappeared from the record at the moment of success or failure. Secondly, there are the men who went out with a fixed purpose of establishing themselves as merchants and later perhaps as landowners. Not all intended to remain permanently, but many of them ended by doing so. Allied with them were men with professional skills, especially medical skills that were in so much demand in colonies with growing populations and unhealthy climates. Other allied groups consisted of men who sought colonial office and ministers of religion. There was a good deal of overlap; some doctors got a start by investing in a cargo of goods for sale in the colonies, some merchants sought office, and some office holders speculated in trade. A minister usually started with land attached to his church and might become a substantial landowner as time went on. Thirdly, there were men who attached themselves to a going concern, and sought employment that took them to the colonies for a term of years. By far the most numerous in this category were the men employed by the Glasgow tobacco merchants, but not much is heard of them until the middle of the century. A fourth category consists of men with small property, which they sold up in order to pay their passages and purchase land and the equipment to start farming. Though men of this type were numerous, they left little trace in the surviving literary evidence. The most probable place to seek information would be amongst the records of land offices and local courts. A fifth category consisted of men without property, who were forced to mortgage the future by entering into indentures to continue in employment for a term of years.

One advantage, perhaps unexpected, accrued to Orkney as a result of union with England. The Acts of Trade and Navigation, which now became part of the law of Scotland, required amongst other things that certain 'enumerated' commodities could be shipped from the colonies only to British ports where they had to be landed and passed through the customs before being sent on to other destinations. The port of Kirkwall was convenient for ships sailing from America by the great circle route with cargoes destined for northern Europe, and the goods and formalities could probably be handled more expeditiously than in crowded southern ports. The route was particularly favoured by ships bringing rice from South Carolina, and for a period of forty years or more Kirkwall became one of the principal British ports handling that commodity.[12] In the colonies foreign goods could be imported directly only from the country or origin, and return cargoes picked up in Rotterdam, Amsterdam, or Hamburg, with items which came from other countries, had to be landed and British duties paid in the same way. Few goods in either direction were left in Kirkwall for re-sale elsewhere, but merchants must have made a modest profit from handling charges. American ships were the source of over 95 per cent of the customs' revenue from 1750 to 1764, and in the last five years of that period for 77 per cent of the ships using the port.

Thereafter there was a sharp drop and even before the Revolution this trade was of little account. It may have been hit by non-importation agreements in 1765 and after 1767, but it showed no signs of recovery. Rice could be shipped without restriction to ports south of Cape Finisterre, and it may have been more profitable to unload it in Spanish or Portuguese ports, and pick up return cargoes in England. One consequence of this intercourse was that Kirkwall was the port of departure for many emigrants from the northeast and for the greater part of the eighteenth century it was very easy for Orcadians to obtain passages to America.

The sources for all these activities are fragmentary and unevenly distributed. In some cases one or two letters illuminate an individual and his experience, but thereafter he disappears from view. In other cases there are letters widely separated by years, so that one catches momentary glimpses in youth and maturity. Or one may find sources covering intensively a few years in a man's working life, but nothing from earlier or later periods. A large amount of the evidence is derived from country houses, lawyers' offices, and commercial concerns. By the nature of things surviving evidence derives from men who were both literate and had an incentive to write things down. Poor farmer emigrants or indentured servants seldom wrote, and even if they did the chance that their letters have survived is remote. Even though letters from poor men, who had recently emigrated, may have been treasured by their families, time has borne them away beyond all hope of recovery. The evidence is therefore tilted towards landed families, businesses, and institutions with the habit of preserving records. A bias in the evidence toward the 'establishment' is familiar to all historians, and lamented by some; but it is all the evidence that exists, and from it historians must interpret the past in as many aspects and guises as they can imagine.

From the Act of Union to the Revolution a steady stream of Scots from upper-class families went to the American colonies. One can assume that the surviving sources provide information on no more than a small fraction of those who looked to the west to compensate for lack of opportunity at home; nevertheless the volume is considerable, and the sample large enough to identify the various types, enterprises, successes, and failures.

There were those who hoped for windfall profit from one or two trading voyages, and others who expected to stay longer and build up a colonial business. There were men who expected to remain for a few years, and those who did not expect to return. Several went out as doctors, though most of them hoped that professional success would enable them to purchase land. A number sought and obtained colonial office, and this in turn enabled them to promote the interests of their families and friends. Some were provident or lucky; others took the wrong risks or failed to cope with the complexity of unfamiliar problems.

An example of the wandering Scot in search of quick profits and a speedy return is found in James Clerk, son of Sir John Clerk of Penicuik.[13] In August 1716 he wrote that he had arrived in Boston, and that his goods were 'in order and well conditioned'. He regretted the fact that he had brought out Scotch goods as part of his cargo, 'they being seldom in demand, save in the Spring'. Nevertheless he hoped to get the best prices possible, and not to prolong his stay in America. This kind of sporadic trading expedition may have led, in other cases, to more permanent connections and eventually to settlement in a colony.

The life of the opportunist Scot is epitomised in a letter written by Simon Dunbar on 11 August 1748 to his sister, Mrs Gordon of Elgin:[14]

> I'm now on my journey to New York & from thence to New Providence, & so for South Carolina. If the War continues I shall return to Providence again as it is a money getting place, but at all events I'm determined to settle in some place being a little wearied of rambling tho' it has been much to my Advantage in every Respect.

The saga of the Dunbars, which took them to every part of the North Atlantic trading world, began early in the century. In February 1719/20 John Dunbar wrote from Newport, Rhode Island, that he had spent six months, 'altogether idle' in Virginia, and had then gone to Massachusetts where he met his brother James who had had a good business but 'being of too generous a disposition' failed and was forced to leave the colony.

John Dunbar then went into partnership with Captain J. Sellwood of Bristol on a trading voyage from New England to Virginia. They took out sugar, rum, molasses, Rhode Island cheese and madeira wine, and returned with tobacco, corn, wheat, pease, port, tallow, snake root, walnut wood, hides, bear skins, beaver skins, and fur of all kinds. This cargo sold well in Rhode Island and Boston, and John Dunbar's next voyage was in Bristol with barrel staves, planks, boards, and two large masts. In Bristol he met another brother, David, with whom he engaged on a slaving voyage to Guinea and Virginia.

John Dunbar's letters include an exciting account of the way in which David had quelled a slave mutiny. The ship arrived safely in Virginia, but peaceable trading evidently lacked excitement for David and when last heard of he was off to New Spain as quartermaster on a privateer. The youngest brother, Simon, whose letter of 1748 was quoted above, was also 'concerned in privateering.'

The life of another wandering Scot is illustrated by the letters of Roderick Gordon to his brother Arthur Gordon of Carnoustie.[15] Roderick was qualified as a doctor, and served at first as a ship's surgeon. The correspondence begins with a letter from London of 19 October 1728 saying that he had decided to go out to Virginia and to settle there. He wanted another brother, Charles, to go shares in a cargo for the colony, and also to make arrangements with a reliable merchant to whom tobacco might be consigned. As one gets to know Roderick from his letters, it seems likely that he expected Charles to put up the money and do the work; but in 1729 and 1730 his prospects in Virginia seemed good. He practised his profession and found the colony 'excellent for my employ'. He soon claimed to be earning £100 a year, by 1733 estimated his income at more than £300, and with such good prospects married a Virginian lady of Scottish descent; but the cost of living was high and by 1736 there are hints of financial embarrassment. Estates in the colony were precarious in value because they depended on slaves 'who are very mortal in this country', while men of his profession were 'obliged to live very high'.

In his early days in Virginia, Roderick Gordon was an enthusiast for the country and an ardent advocate of emigration. In a letter of June 1734 to William Duff, M.P. for Banffshire he wrote:

My situation in this Colony is tolerable & we live in the most plentiful Country in the world, for all the necessaries of life; for our Estates consist chiefly in land and nigros; which nigros make grain in plenty to raise all the necessary provisions within ourselves, as also a great deal for export; which returns as Rum, Sugar, Molasses from the Caribee Islands & Wine from other Islands: & the tobacco, made at the same time by these slaves, returns us from England all necessary appearall, for ourselves & slaves; not only at the cheapest rate but are likewise imported here freight free. I beg pardon for this tedious Description of our Country, but did thousands in Scotland know it they would desire banishment never to return . . . whereas there are vast tracts of unbounded land in this Colony free to any inhabitants of Great Britain, who will seat thereon, which is vast incouragement to labourers that cannot live at home.

In a similar letter to his brother George he added, 'Pity is that thousands of my Country people should stay starving at home, when they may live here in peace and plenty, as a great many who have been transported for a punishment, have found pleasure, profit, & ease, & would rather undergo any hardship than be forced back to their own Country'.

Despite this enthusiasm things did not go well. His brother George constantly ignored invitations to join in a trading venture and send out cargoes of suitable commodities, either because he had no inclination for trade or because he had no confidence in Roderick. In 1743 Roderick returned to Scotland; not a prosperous physician and planter but a prodigal with many debts on his hands. Nevertheless he persuaded George's son, James, to accompany him to Virginia.

Soon after Roderick's return to Virginia he joined a privateer as a surgeon, with a typically optimistic prospect of three shares in all prizes and right to claim all medicine and medical equipment seized. James Gordon wrote that his uncle had behaved very badly, left his estate in poor condition and burdened with numerous debts. In 1745 Roderick returned to Virginia, but the correspondence ceases with the suspicion that young James had a tough job on his hands.

Few of those who were transported have left records of the life in America, but one family enjoyed good fortune. On 13 October 1716 one hundred and twelve 'rebel prisoners' from Scotland were shipped to Virginia and among them was Francis Hume, younger brother of Sir George Hume of Wedderburn. Six years later he was joined by his nephew, George Hume, who had also been convicted for his part in the rebellion of 1715.[16] They were fortunate in being related to Governor Spotiswood who made Francis a factor for his Virginian estates. George Hume was less fortunate as Spotiswood was removed from office soon after his arrival, but he obtained employment as a surveyor – a lucrative and influential post in an expanding colony – and despite his record of service with the Jacobite army was commissioned in the colonial militia in 1729. In the preceding year he had been given a fourth share in a land grant of 10,000 acres and a third share in another of 6,000. He was also a Justice of the Peace, and his employment brought him into friendly relations with many eminent Virginians including George Washington. He died in 1760.

Further information about the Hume (or Home) family in Virginia is found in the Scottish Record Office.[17] Later in the century Patrick Home visited Rappahannock Forge, Virginia, to clear up the affairs of James Hume, his uncle and son of George. His uncle's estate was 'very extensive and consisted of a good many slaves" but was "much embarrassed'. In January 1801 James Home, a British naval officer, also visited his relations at Rappahannock Forge. Mr Francis Home, son of George, was 'a mild, sedate, placid old Gentleman, & very fond of talking about his Relations in Scotland'. But the Humes of Virginia were under a misapprehension which James does not seem to have dispelled. They thought that they were the heirs of Wedderburn through their father George, but James wrote that, 'Our American friends know nothing of their father's prior marriage, and it is justifiable in them to believe any story he may have told them about their right of succession to the estate of Wedderburn'; but this Virginia marriage was bigamous and they were all illegitimate.[18]

A member of another Scottish landed family who went to America was Sir Patrick Houston, an early landowner in Georgia.[19] He was given a substantial land grant, but by 1737 had cleared and planted not more than 30 acres. He also experimented with trading ventures, imported goods for sale to the Indians, and obtained a contract for supply of food to the military garrisons. He was quartermaster to General Oglethorpe's regiment in 1748, and began to prosper as a cotton and indigo planter. He married the sister of Captain Dunbar, an Inverness man who brought several shiploads of immigrants from Scotland to Georgia. The Houston family continued to accumulate land with grants to Sir Patrick in the parishes of Christ Church, St George, and St Patrick, to his wife in St David, and in various parts of the colony to his four sons.[20] John, the eldest, was Governor of Georgia for a short period during the Revolution and is said to have had property confiscated by both sides.[21]

South Carolina attracted many lowland Scots of the landed or professional classes. A few documents, preserved because of their relevance to later litigation, provide evidence of the career of Alexander Nisbet.[22] In 1721 an indenture was drawn up by which Robert Nisbet, advised by his brother, Sir John Nisbet of Dean, undertook to serve Alexander Nisbet for five years. This is followed in 1723 by an agreement between Alexander Nisbet and Alexander Kinloch to operate a store at Red Bank, South Carolina, in partnership for three years, and in the following year another member of the family, Walter Nisbet, was admitted as a co-partner and storekeeper.

One of the most successful Scottish emigrants of the early eighteenth century was Robert Pringle from Symington, who was born in 1702 and moved to South Carolina in 1725.[23] He acted first as agent for London and New England merchants, then tried his hand at the Indian and slave trades, but made his fortune as an exporter of rice and indigo. In 1734 he married Jane Allen, daughter of a wealthy planter and, after her death, Judith, widow of Stephen Bull, whose father was Lieutenant Governor. In this way wealth and connection brought Robert Pringle into the inner circle of Charleston society. He did little or no trade with Scotland but many of his business associates were Scots. His first partner in Charleston was James Reid, and he had a life-long business association with his brother, Andrew, who first acquired wealth as a sea captain trading between New York and Europe, and then set up on his own in London. The two brothers were never partners, but they corresponded frequently and helped each other in many ways.

Robert Pringle had a lively mind and wide interests. He was much concerned by the colony's too exclusive dependence upon rice, and was a pioneer in the commercial cultivation of indigo. In 1758 he wrote a long letter to the Royal Society of London in which he discussed the cultivation of log wood, white mulberry (for silk worms), grapes, help, oranges, olives, and cork trees, and put in a plea for a stronger defence against French or Spanish attacks or slave revolts.[24] Pringle also played his part in public life. He was a vestryman of St Philip's Church and from 1761 church warden of the new parish of St Michael. He served in the Commons House of Assembly from 1751 to 1762, and in 1761, though without legal training, was appointed an assistant judge of the Court of Common Pleas. In this situation he became the centre of controversy; during the Stamp Act crisis he ordered the clerk of the court to record decisions on unstamped paper, and in 1770 was dismissed because his judicial pronouncements were unacceptable to the government. One of his sons, John Julius, became Speaker of the Assembly and state Attorney General 1792–1808.

Robert Pringle was an outstanding example of a Scottish merchant who achieved prominence in a colony through close identification with its economic and political development. A less successful career was that of John Murray of Murraythwaite (or Murraywhat) near Ecclefechan, who inherited his Scottish estate in 1729 at the age of three.[25] His uncle, also called John Murray, was established in South Carolina by 1743 as a doctor and prospered in his profession. He said that he had brought out no money, but by 1747 had no difficulty in raising £1,000. He thought that a young doctor could earn £300 a year, as he himself got twice that in 1752 'tho' the town was not too sickly'. Referring to a younger member of the family he wrote, 'Cousin Billy was well-advised when he applied himself to Physick, it being absolutely the best travelling business in the World and one that will soon give him an Estate if you are liberal enough in his education'. Dr John Murray was joined by his nephew, William Murray, in 1750 and made him a partner in 1753.

Meanwhile the head of the family at Murraythwaite was struggling with an impoverished estate and an inescapable burden of debt. The good fortune of his uncle and brother in South Carolina naturally turned his thoughts to that colony and he first considered practising law, but his brother warned him that the province was already swarming with lawyers. His ambition then turned towards colonial office and in 1753 he purchased the Secretaryship of the colony from a Mr Hammerton, then resident in London, who nevertheless retained part of the official fees.

John Murray's first impressions of South Carolina were enthusiastic. He wrote to his mother that Charleston far exceeded his expectations 'We have all the Elegancys and Conveniencys of life in great variety and plenty, and people here seem to make the most of life.' Both brothers were on good terms with James Glen, the Scottish Governor, and the way ahead seemed clear for a prosperous career. In 1757 John wrote to James Oswald at the Board of Trade in London:

> This province is every day becoming of more and more consequence to Great Britain – and indeed if we consider with attention the many valuable articles of produce now exported from hence we will not scruple to pronounce this the most flourishing and most important of all the Colonies.

Nevertheless things went less well for the brothers than they hoped. They tried their luck as importers, but a cargo from the British Linen Company was a disaster as the goods were either unsuitable for the market or perished on arrival. The ensuing debt and dispute haunted them for many years. In 1757 they purchased an indigo plantation with thirty slaves, but it was never very profitable. Neither did things go smoothly in the Secretaryship. On arrival John found that, apart from Hammerton's share, another person acting as deputy had all fees, save £200, assigned to him for ten years. When Hammerton died John Murray failed to obtain outright possession of the office. In 1763 he told his mother that he was 'heartily tired of Carolina', and in 1765 returned to Britain with the confession that 'there is something in the air of Carolina that does not at all agree with my constitution'. He never returned, though he continued to own land on the Saluda river.

In 1771 James Simpson, a neighbour, wrote that John Murray's land was of little value. What he had seen was very poor, and settlers on the better land were too impoverished and lazy to raise the money for purchase. In 1798-1800 Murray's agent instituted proceedings to evict squatters, but seems to have had no success. William Murray returned to Murraythwaite some time after his elder brother, and managed the estate temporarily in 1778. He was short of money and nourished grievances. He had never received what he believed to be his share of his patrimony, wanted £2000 for having acting as deputy secretary during John's absence, and claimed that he was owed money from the sale of the plantation. John Murray of Murraythwaite lived on, unmarried, and died in 1823 in the house that he had owned for ninety-four years. There was probably no one then living in South Carolina who could recall his brief period as Secretary.

Another Scot in South Carolina worked his way up the social ladder from more humble beginnings. James Steuart was the son of a laird, John Steuart of Dalguise, near Dunkeld, but he worked in Charleston as a shipwright.[26] He went out to the colony in 1749, and early in 1751 was making about five shillings a day but could live more cheaply than in London, except for high house rent. He dropped a hint to his father that with a loan of £500 he could buy slaves and begin to show a profit; his last job had been acknowledged as the best in the country, but with hired labour there had been no profit in it. Later in the same year he was joined by a partner, John Rosse, with a valuable recommendation from the Surveyor General of the Navy to the senior captain on the Carolina station. Apparently he wanted further help of the same kind and asked his father to obtain, through influential friends, a recommendation from one of the Lords of the Admiralty; he suggested that the Duke of Atholl might be persuaded to approach Lord Sandwich. Work on ships of the Royal Navy, if he could get it, was 'verry beneficial and sure pay'. Apart from his business plans, he lamented that there was no one to look after him. He was unmarried and had not had a shirt or stocking mended but gave 'them always to the Nigroes when torn or holes in y^m'.

It was not clear whether he was successful in getting contracts to repair the naval ships, but by the end of 1752 he was doing reasonably well. By then he and his partner had seven slaves of their own, and were able to hire as many more as they wished; but he hoped to branch out into trading. With a large stock he could build a ship and either take freight or load it with his own purchase of rice.

By 1754 he was basking in the self-esteem of a self-made man. Hearing that his younger brother, Hew, was living a life of fashion, he wrote to his father:

> I know that if your had sent me up to Yorkshire about 20 years ago beruffled, besilked, and bepoudered it might have been the means of my being in Raggs at this day.

He went on to describe the rise to affluence of his partner and himself:

> We came in here with about £800, we put on our trousers went to work, by this way raised slaves by degrees, lived snug and untill of late nobody knew what we were worth. Now we have got experience and are known and respected by the first Rank and we wear Silk Jacketts and Ruffels.

He no longer did manual work himself, but was much occupied with business affairs. Despite his own success he thought that Hew would be well-advised to apprentice himself to a merchant rather than start out on his own. 'Often a Master takes his clerk or storekeeper into partnership with him, or he might wish to join with another – that would be the time to give him money'.

James Steuart intended to return home, but also considered staying in

South Carolina since he had accumulated enough money. It was 'good Old Man's Country' with 'all the necessarys of Life's abundance'. He was not destined to make the choice as he died in Charleston in 1755.

There were four brothers of the Fyffe family in South Carolina – William, Alexander, David and Charles – who came from Dron near Dundee. William was a doctor by profession, but found planting and trade were more profitable. Writing to his sister about his son's education he told her to 'cherish' any inclinations towards medicine, but added that he would 'hardly make a fortune at it except by marriage'. Trade was a much more lucrative prospect, and provided that 'his friends would support him with sufficient credit to commence business . . . he could hardly fail with a common share of Understanding and Industry to acquire an easy fortune in a short time'.

Alexander Fyffe died before his elder brother, but was possessed of considerable property. William had difficulty in collecting the debts that were owned to the estate, largely because there was no ready money to be had. 'There is such unlimited credit that we hardly feel the need of it in any other respect except where the merchant is push'd and they insist for cash from planters who are in their debt, some of whose negroes being sold for cash go off at half their value'. Charles Fyffe went to Norfolk, Virginia, where he practised as a doctor, engaged in trade and later moved to Charleston, South Carolina. He served with Loyalist forces until captured by the Americans and was later granted an annuity of £100 on account of property destroyed by British forces. He returned to South Carolina in 1784, but by 1786 was in New York.[27]

Another Scot who became a prominent merchant, first in Charleston and then in Wilmington, North Carolina, was Robert Hogg. There seems to be no information about his early days in America, but fragmentary business records show that he enjoyed substantial success. He imported goods from London and Bristol to Charleston, exported rice and other commodities, and supplied goods for his own store at Wilmington. He also set up a store at Cross Creek on the Cape Fear River, and his ledger book shows him to have been a principal supplier of goods to the Highland settlers in that district.[28] At the outbreak of the Revolution he was living in Wilmington, and was probably one of the richest men in North Carolina. He became a somewhat half-hearted Loyalist, and his misfortunes will be noted in a later chapter.

There are also some records of another Scottish merchant in Charleston, Alexander Fraser,[29] who survived the Revolution, but left no evidence of his early days in South Carolina. His principal business was the export of rice to London, and he also had a store at Goose Creek. Both he and his son, William, owned land and slaves in the later years of the century. Though there is no evidence of trade or continuing family links with Scotland, his papers provide an interesting illustration of the way in which Scottish merchants continued to associate with each other and provide useful contacts in various parts of America. The names of the men with whom Fraser had business contacts include Alexander, Anderson, Chisholm, Cameron, McAdam, McKenzie, McNeill, and Wyllie, while the captain of a ship chartered by him was called Hercules Angus.

The Cathcarts of Genoch had many connections with North Carolina.[30] In 1737 Dr William Cathcart set out for the colony with a cargo of 'goods and medicines' valued at £300. In 1742 he married the Governor's daughter-in-law, and, though he seems to have been financially distressed at one time, won his way to prosperity if not affluence. In 1758 a letter from North Carolina noted that he was in good health, and that 'by means of his vastly extensive business in the Phisical way, occasioned by the Small Pox in that country, he has greatly mended his fortune'. He bought a plantation, and seems to have been moderately successful. His son, Gabriel Cathcart, visited Scotland and apparently his father wished him to obtain a legal education, but there is no record of his having done so.

A letter of 1764 from Gabriel Cathcart, then returned to North Carolina, provides a rare insight into the way in which many Scots of humbler birth may have come to America. He recalled 'a young lad from about Ballantrae . . . that came to Genoch . . .' and wanted to come out to America as an overseer. If he was still available, and prepared to bind himself for four years, Gabriel would give him bed and board, and £7 sterling a year. His passage money would be deducted from his first year's pay. 'His business will be to look after a few Negroes under my father which will make it very easy for him, as he has been in the country service most of his life.' The ship which carried the letter would be returning direct from Port Glasgow to North Carolina, and the young man should take passage on her. 'If you cannot get him for 7 you can give 8 – you know the cheaper the better.'

The majority of Scots in Virginia were either men engaged in the tobacco trade or episcopalian clergymen, but the town of Norfolk attracted a good many men who hoped to establish themselves as general merchants. Tobacco might form a part but not the whole of their business. Charles Steuart, who came from an upper class Orkney family, was a good example, and his voluminous papers provide ample information about life at mid-century in the Virginian port.[31] He was established as a merchant in the late 1750s, but in 1762–3 he was given responsibility for handling an incident in which a Spanish admiral and his party were attacked while in Portsmouth, Virginia. The situation was delicate as negotiations for peace with Spain were proceeding at the time, and Steuart's success brought him to official notice and later to his appointment as Receiver-General of Customs with responsibilities from Quebec to Florida. The later volumes of his correspondence contain much information about disturbances in Norfolk from 1769 onwards and about Scottish Loyalists. They will be described in their appropriate place.

After his appointment to office Charles Steuart continued to correspond frequently with two Scottish associates in Norfolk, William Aitchison and James Parker. Parker was a particularly interesting correspondent, whose letters contain much of personal and topical information. Writing in December 1770 he recalled that he had once been a factor to a Glasgow merchant, and had he been related to one of the principals and had 'a patient, diligent, saving, and subservient disposition' he might have 'jogged on in a state of dependence to this day'. Clearly he had quarrelled with 'Spiers, the Mercantile God of Glasgow', and this had led to establishing his own business with fortunate results. In 1771 he was still optimistic about the prospects of a young man in America, and urged Steuart to send out his nephew.

> The business of this country is very soon acquired, if he is disposed to push for himself, he'll not want chances. I have just been thinking of the people in my remembrance who have done anything for themselves in this place. . . . Of our countrymen, there are some who have made fortunes, others who have got a sufficiency with prudent management to get easily through life and a great many of the rising generation in a very thriving way. They had generally speaking little or nothing to begin with.

The number of Scottish episcopal clergy who obtained parishes in Virginia is partly explained by the early influence of James Blair, as the Bishop of London's commissary in the colony. His career will be noted at greater length in Chapter V. A clergyman who achieved some eminence in Virginia was the Rev. Robert Rose, who was born in Scotland in 1705.[32] He was rector of St. Anne, Essex county, 1727–48, and then of St. Anne, Albermarle country. He seems to have been a close friend of Lieutenant Governor Spotiswood, and in addition to his clerical duties was a planter, surveyor, amateur lawyer, and part-time physician. Most entries in his diary are brief, but in 1750 he committed to paper a long essay on curing tobacco. He left four sons, all of whom actively supported the Revolution.

Robert Rose's brother, Charles, was also a clergyman in Virginia from about 1736 to his death in 1761. One of his sons, also called Robert, matriculated at Glasgow University in 1762, and was a surgeon with the Continental Line during the Revolution. The Scottish connection was maintained when a grandson of Charles married a daughter of William Allason, who had come out to Virginia as a tobacco factor, and whose rise to independence and affluence will be noted in the next chapter.

The Scotts of Dipple in Moray had connections with Virginia for almost a century, and maintained long-standing and close ties with King's College, Aberdeen. The Rev. John Scott, born about 1650, was rector of Dipple in

Moray. His son Alexander went to Virginia as rector of Overwharton, and on his death in 1738 was succeeded by his half-brother James, who was probably educated at King's College and whose eldest son, Alexander, was said to have been lost at sea when returning after graduation. James's second son, also James, married Elizabeth Harrison, became a captain of militia, a member of the House of Burgesses and of the Virginia Convention 1775-6. He died during the war. His third son, John, graduated M.A. at King's College in 1768, and his youngest son, Gustavus, studied at Aberdeen and the Middle Temple. Another son, Robert, was lost at sea, and there is no record of a sixth son, William. Gustavus was a member of the Continental Congress 1784-5. James Scott's eldest daughter married Cuthbert Bullitt who belonged to a prominent Virginian family.

Most of the papers concern John Scott and his family.[33] His career started inauspiciously with a duel which his second and brother-in-law, Cuthbert Bullitt, tried to stop on conscientious grounds. In doing so he became involved in a quarrel with a Mr Bayliss, John's opponent, and killed him. Bullitt was acquitted of murder, but the case became so notorious that John and his younger brother thought it prudent to leave Virginia. They went to Scotland and entered King's College. John graduated in 1768, was ordained in 1769, and went to a parish in Maryland. In spite of his connection with leading Virginian families he was accused of loyalism during the war, and his movements were restricted. After a time he was allowed to go to Virginia, where he died in 1784 at the age of thirty-seven.

During his residence in Aberdeen, John Scott, married Elizabeth, daughter of Thomas Gordon, professor of Moral Philosophy and Provost of King's College. The bulk of the correspondence in the Peyton family papers consists of letters from Thomas Gordon to his daughter, son-in-law, and grandson, Robert Eden Scott. There are also letters from other relatives and friends. Apparently Mrs Scott was left in straightened circumstances and in 1786 her father was trying to obtain money for her from the funds for the relief of Loyalists. This was of no avail and she was advised to apply to the authorities at Halifax. Robert Eden Scott came to Scotland in 1787 and was employed as tutor in Lady Errol's family, but Thomas Gordon wanted him to study at the university – either law or medicine – 'for this kind of knowledge can easily be carried about with him; and may be useful as nobody can say what Providence has in view for him. If he were proposing to travel with this or any other pupil a decent knowledge in Medicine is now held to be a necessary requisite'. Robert Eden Scott them moved to Glasgow as tutor in the Oswald family, and his pupil was studying at Glasgow College. Gordon thought that this would be 'very beneficial to him as it will lead to an acquaintance with Dr Reid and many worthy professors there'. Gordon then employed him as his assistant; he did not really need one but this step gave Robert 'a relation to the society in which his Ancestors have served reputably for ages'. After this he returned to Virginia, studied medicine for a short while at the University of Pennsylvania, and then studied law under Bushrod Washington. He returned to Aberdeen in 1794, where fortune smiled on him. Thomas Gordon died in 1797 and Robert Eden Scott succeeded him as professor of moral philosophy and then, in 1800, as provost. His qualifications for teaching philosophy do not appear obvious, but it seemed that he acquitted himself creditably and acquired a reputation that survived. He died in 1811 at the age of forty-two. Meanwhile his sister had married into the influential Virginian family of Peyton.[34]

In the preceding pages there have been several references to opportunities in the colonies for Scots with medical skill. The qualifications of some who went out were probably dubious, but as more locally trained men entered the profession a sound education in Scotland became highly advantageous to would-be migrants. The situation was explained in an interesting letter of 1772 from John Campbell of Bladensburg, Maryland.[35]

You desire my Sentiments on the practice of Physic in this part of the world. You shall have it, & of those I have conversed with on the subject. There is not any business followed in this Continent, which in the end would prove more advantageous, than the practice of Physic and Surgery, but you must take this along with you that like all other Employments, it must be attended with the utmost care, diligence, & attention. A regular Education is necessary so as to be the master of the Theoretical [? – letter torn] this you already have. In this [and?] the Neighbouring Colony of Virginia, it will amaze you how few of those who pretend to the Practice of Physic, and are dignified with the name of Doctor deserve the appellation – mere Smatterers who found their Skill wholly on spending about 2 years in the Philadelphia or Jersey College, where perhaps they may learn enough of cramp technical terms, to give the ignorant a great opinion of their knowledge, & themselves the power of making out an unintelligible & enormous high charged Bill . . . You must at once see the advantage one who has enjoyed a liberal education must have over this class, expecially when attended with abilities, attention, and an engaging, insinuating behaviour.

On the eve of the Revolution there must have been hundreds of Scottish doctors practising in the American colonies, and the influence of Scotland on American medicine is given extended treatment in chapter VI.

When East Florida came under British rule in 1763 it was inevitable that some Scots should contemplate this new land of opportunity. The Earl of Casillis acquired land in the colony and in June 1767 received a long letter about the prospects from William Stork of London.[36] He proposed to start on a modest scale with five white male servants and ten Negroes. 'I have procured the Servants', he wrote, 'and on account of their industry and sobriety, I have preferred Scotch to English.' They were indentured for eight years, and then each was to receive £20 and 50 acres. However it seems that not all accepted the eight years bond for in 1769 there is reference to the dismissal of two carpenters 'in order to get rid of their claim for twenty pounds a piece when their time was elapsed which only extended till next October'. Stork estimated the costs of establishing the plantation at £36 to £40 for slaves, £50 for equipping and transporting the five whites, and £70 for tools and equipment. A further £100 would be spent on surveying land, and £500 for cattle and more slaves.

A great deal more information about East Florida comes from John Ross of Leith, who was in the colony from 1768 to 1785.[37] In 1776 he had joined a Mr Gray at a salary of £50 a year, and wanted his father to advance him £70 to purchase a slave woman and her children. 'I wonder you should suspect me of any other connexion with such a Wench than that of having got some children by her'. Six years later he sent two mulattos (presumably his children) to Britain with certificates of freedom, intending that they should go to Leith 'if the old gentleman allows it'. In 1782 he was thinking of exporting turpentine and wrote to Sir Robert Herries (an old family friend) with a request for information about prices and markets. He apologised for troubling Sir Robert, but having left Britain fourteen years before there was no one else to whom he could turn for advice. In 1782 he learned with dismay that the British intended to abandon Florida, but evidently decided to stay. In April 1783 he obtained a grant of 500 acres, but in 1785, after Spanish power had been re-established, he decided to leave and moved to Dominica where he died in the following year.

A much more important speculator in Florida lands was General James Robertson. Between 1763 and 1786 he acquired 15,000 acres, but the Spanish refused to recognise his titles. This led to lengthy and probably fruitless litigation, but the papers generated by the case contain much information on Florida and its climate, soil, and people. General Robertson also speculated heavily in land in other colonies. He had a grant of 5,000 acres in Cumberland County, New York, in 1767, and in 1775 leased two 2,000 acre lots in Charlotte County. He purchased land west of Broadway in New York city, and further land in Vermont. When he left America in April 1783 he left in the hands of his attorney a long list of securities for debts owing to him.[38]

Not all emigrants from Scottish landed families made good or behaved well. James Freeman, who probably came from Aberdeen, owned a plantation in Virginia, but in 1742 and 1743 he was in London – for reasons which are not explained – and imprisoned for debt.[39] His father-in-law, William Wallace, wrote to him from Virginia about plantation affairs, shipments of tobacco, and the health of slaves. The difficulty of sending tobacco home during war, with the Spanish taking a toll of British merchant ships, may explain Freeman's financial misfortunes. He was released from prison, and announced his intention of returning to Virginia, but other evidence makes clear that all was not well.

Freeman had paid James Duncan, a merchant in Perth, with a bill drawn on Roger Hog and Samuel Hyde, two London merchants; but Roger Hog had never heard of him and was amazed at his impudence. His lawyer concluded that 'Freeman must be some worthless fellow'. He had, in fact, forged the bill of credit, and Duncan was advised 'to secure Freeman for I am afraid he will make an elopement, as soon as you show him the bill and protest'. Duncan learned from Roger Hog that Freeman had been banished from Virginia for horse-stealing. A warrant was issued by Sheriff of Perthshire, but there, as often happens in these tantalisingly incomplete records, the story ends.

Two brothers of Donald McLeod of Geanies, James and William, were in America between 1770 and 1776.[40] William was employed by Alexander Speirs of Glasgow, but James may have been trading on his own account. He frequently complained that he was short of money and that trade was bad. At one time he had an ambitious scheme which was to involve his brother Donald, and two Scottish acquaintances in Virginia, Dr James Davidson and Dr Eric Pirie from Aberdeen. This came to nothing and by the end of 1774 he had enough of Virginia and was preparing to leave. Political troubles made business impossible, and though he stayed on in 1775 he wrote that he was 'very firmly of opinion that trade will never flourish again in this country to the same extent as it formerly has done'. By July 1776 he was in St Vincent and learning to be a sugar planter.

William McLeod led a more settled existence at Oxford and, for a short while, at Queenstown in Maryland where he was a storekeeper for Speirs, French & Co. His letters comment on the political situation, though in a superficial way, and, in common with other Scots in Maryland, he was subject to suspicion and abuse. His opinion would certainly have made him a Loyalist, but it seems unlikely that he was able to afford the gesture of defiance or flight.

Surprisingly few of the sources deal with lowland Scots who went to the northern colonies. This may, in part, be explained by a social differentiation. The southern colonies attracted the sons of lairds, and in course of time their letters came to rest in family muniments or lawyers' offices. Emigrants to the northern colonies came mainly from lower middle-class families, who were not in the habit of keeping estate records, or were small farmers, penniless tutors, or artisans. Though there were many Scottish merchants in Philadelphia and New York it seems that few came from families who kept 'muniments', and their letters home went the way of all waste paper. Some of the Glasgow merchants had collateral interests in the northern commercial cities, and these will be mentioned in the chapter on the tobacco trade.

The letters from Charles Mercer of Pittendreich to his brother Robert in New York, and the latter's diary for 1770–74 are therefore rare survivors from what must have been a much larger body of evidence.[41] Robert Mercer was a partner in Mercer and Ramsay of New York. He relied upon his brother to raise money as required from Edinburgh bankers. In 1769 Charles reported that the bankers were calling in all their cash advances, and borrowing themselves at five per cent. Apparently Mercer and Ramsay had been on the brink of failure, and Charles warned his brother to be 'careful, diligent and active, and not so ready as you have been hitherto in trusting persons you know nothing of'. He was also told to give ample notice of drafts drawn on merchants or bankers in Scotland.

Robert Mercer engaged in varied enterprises. In 1769 he mentions a cargo sent to Mobile, and in 1772 an 'adventure to New Orleans'. He also owned a tobacco and snuff manufactory in New York. His diary mentions the arrival of ships, the purchase of slaves, other business transactions, and convivial parties. On 1 March 1772 he dined at Captain Tolmies with Dr Middleton, Dr Stewart, Captain Grant, Walter Buchanan, Will Pagan, Mr Lowther, Archibald Currie, and Lawyer Woods–'All Scotch except Woods'. There are also political comments, which will be noted in a later chapter. Unfortunately the diary is scrappy, and the letters few. Relations between the brothers became strained and in 1772 Charles submitted a legal claim for money owed to him by Mercer and Ramsay, and the debt was still outstanding at the close of 1774. This may account for the absence of letters from Robert in the Pittendriech muniments, though his diary must have found its way there by some means.

A man who achieved some prominence in New York was John Lindsay, brother of the Laird of Wormistone, who arrived in Philadelphia in August 1729.[42] His first impressions of the new country were enthusiastic, but he soon found that the goods in which he had invested would not yield enough to start profitable trading. Accordingly he moved to New York and set out to win the favour of Governor Tryon and obtain official employment. He was successful in getting the post of naval officer at New York with a salary of £200 a year. With a secure income it seems that he was able to set himself up as a merchant in the city.

Lindsay was also successful in obtaining two grants of land west of the town of Schnectady and south of the Mohawk river, and in 1738 he decided to give up trade and farm his land 'which I think a much surer way of life and much more innocent'. He proposed to settle a hundred families on his land and seems to have had some plan to bring over colonists from Scotland. This went forward very slowly, but in 1742 six families and a minister arrived. He was also engaged in military affairs, with a commission in the New York forces, and in 1748 was appointed lieutenant governor of a new fort at Oswego. He died suddenly in 1751.

Years later John Bethune (formerly Lindsay) tried to establish a claim to the Lindsay estate in New York. Though his two patents were shown on a map, made in 1790, definitive evidence of the original grant was lacking and the land had long since been settled by others. Late in the nineteenth century the Earl of Lindsay was still trying to establish the claim.

Public office was a legitimate object of ambition for men who regarded themselves as gentlemen. Naturally office in the colonies was less sought after than office at home, but the Scottish gentry, who lacked the influence of their English counterparts, hoped to gather colonial crumbs from the patronage plate. It was also easier for a minister to reward Scottish supporters by appointing their dependants to America than by finding posts in the home establishment. As a result a considerable number of Scots held colonial office in the eighteenth century, and some rose to the highest positions. The best known are Cadwallader Colden, lieutenant and acting governor of New York, Alexander Spotswood and Robert Dinwiddie, governors of Virginia, James Glen, governor of South Carolina, Gabriel Johnstone and Thomas Pollock, both governors of North Carolina, and John Murray, Earl of Dunmore, governor of New York and Virginia 1770-6.

Few office holders expected to remain more than a few years in the colonies. The salaries were usually low, but the income from fees and perquisites could be considerable. Official positions also provided good opportunities for acquiring land or profiting from trading ventures. The story of the Murrays of Murraythwaite has already been told, and though John Murray made little or nothing from his secretaryship, he was able to speculate in imported linen and land purchase. It was bad luck or bad judgment which prevented him from making his fortune in a situation that others found lucrative. An office holder could not hope for wealth that could compare with that of a successful merchant or large landowner, but he could make enough to live better than on an impoverished Scottish estate.

An unexpected seeker after colonial office was James Macpherson, the translator and perhaps fabricator of *Ossian*. In 1763 he was living in London, at the height of his reputation, but he decided nevertheless to seek office under George Johnstone, another Scot who had been appointed Governor of West Florida with headquarters at Pensacola. Macpherson became his secretary, together with sinecure offices as president of the Council and Surveyor General. He did not stay long in Florida, as he quarrelled with Johnstone and preferred to visit other provinces rather than perform his duties. He returned to London in 1764, but was allowed to retain for life a salary of £200 a year as Surveyor General. This he earned by writing pamphlets supporting the Government, including a very successful defence of its American policy in 1775.

Scots who attained high positions in the colonial administration often promoted the interests of their fellow countrymen. Eighteenth century practice condoned the use of official patronage to serve friends and men recommended by them. The rewards might take the form of appointments or land grants, but a colonial governor's freedom of action was severely limited; appointments might be made without reference to him, and his own recommendations were often ignored. Much of the patronage was kept in the hands of the government at Westminster, while other posts were at the disposal of the holders. John Murray obtained the secretaryship of South Carolina by negotiating with Mr Hammerton, the absentee Secretary who lived in London. James Macpherson received his salary as Surveyor of West Florida because the ministers wished to secure his support as a writer. The Governor had some control over appointments in the established Church of England in his colony, but patronage was in the hands of the Bishop of London, often acting on the advice of his commissaries in the colonies. The Society for the Propagation of the Gospel in London was the major influence in selecting 'missionaries' for colonial parishes. After 1763 Governors lost the right to approve land grants and control over this valuable species of patronage was transferred to London.

When a governor had conformed to the wishes of London he had still to reckon with the colonial legislature representing principally the wealthier landowners, with their own claims on colonial patronage and power to control taxation and expenditure (including the Governor's salary). There were also appointments, such as those to the magistracy, which could go only to men with local influence. The parish vestries, composed of prominent local men, exerted considerable influence, expected the commissaries to defer to their wishes in the appointment of clergy and civil authorities to respect their views on minor local posts. Given all these limitations a Scottish Governor had little opportunity for filling the colonial administration with young men from his native land. The road to colonial office was routed through London.

It would be possible to find out more about the work of Scottish colonial administrators from the records of government departments in London; but this would illuminate the general problem of British government of colonies rather than to the specific issue of Scottish influence upon colonial life. The survey of official correspondence has therefore been limited to that in repositories other than the public records.

James Glen, Governor of South Carolina for an unusually long period, 1738–65, was probably the best known Scottish office holder. The early years of his tenure were full of promise.[43] The colony prospered, Indian threats were successfully resisted, and the Governor appeared to be in full control. His later years were troubled by disputes with the legislature and the waning of his personal authority. In his early days Glen was not restrained by false modesty. He found the province 'in ashes, defenceless and declining'; he would leave it 'fortified and flourishing'. The advantages of South Carolina encouraged him to believe that it could become the greatest province in the British dominions. He frequently expressed the view that constitutional change was necessary in order to produce a better balance between the component parts of the government. Not unnaturally this included a substantial increase in executive power.

Many of Glen's letters dealt with Indian affairs. He stressed his own success in promoting peaceful relations, and made several personal visits to Indian chiefs with gifts of goods and money. With his eye firmly set upon goal of economic development, he deplored Indian wars which entailed high taxation, lack of security for the settlements, and opportunity for French or Spanish intrigue.

Glen was not slow to draw the attention of the government at Westminister to his unremitting and unselfish labour for the good of the colony. He disclaimed any personal financial interest, and though he became a substantial property owner there is no reason to question his integrity. He certainly worked hard, and his record for efficiency was far above that of most colonial administrators. However his letters also illlustrate the difficulty experienced by a colonial governor in trying to build up a personal following; there were a great many recommendations of individuals to colonial office but only a few were successful.[44]

A different picture of Glen emerges from the letters of Alexander Gordon, who went to South Carolina as his secretary, and also became clerk of the Council.[45] Perhaps the appointments were forced upon Glen, for he seems to have ignored Gordon who complained, 'Have I not a Governor that never has befriended me, nor supported me, notwithstanding the Many repeated Obligations he lay under to me in London'. Gordon was well connected. In Scotland he had been secretary for 'The Society for the Encouragement of Learning', and had extravagant hopes of bettering himself abroad. He confessed that he had met a few men of culture with whom he could converse; but there were many of whom he became heartily sick. 'Some of them even attempt to take away my place for me, for not going into some dirty Jobs and for having done my duty according to Truth or Conscience'. He intended to remove from 'this den of thieves' as soon as he could sell or farm out his office, but found time to write a *Complete History of the Ancient Egyptians* which friends urged him to publish.

Thomas Pollock was governor of North Carolina 1712–4 and again in 1722. Only two of his letters related to Scottish affairs.[46] On 3 April 1717 he wrote to Sir Robert Pollok, ostensibly to enquire after the health and fortunes of his relatives, but with the real purpose of locating a Robert Hamilton who had defrauded him. Twenty years later he wrote to James

Pollok of Balgray complaining that Sir Robert had answered none of his letters, and that Robert Hamilton still owed him money.

A more considerable figure was Robert Dinwiddie, Lieutenant Governor of Virginia 1751–7. As the actual Governor was an absentee earl, Dinwiddie was, in effect, Governor and normally addressed as such.[47] The Dinwiddie family had come originally from the south-west but his father had made a fortune in Glasgow. His brother Lawrence remained in charge of the business and was twice provost, 1724–4. Robert had had a varied career before he came to Virginia: merchant, member of council, and then collector of customs in Bermuda; 'Surveyor General of the Southern part of the continent of North America' in 1738 with oversight of the customs from Philadelphia to Jamaica; and in 1743 commissioned to investigate frauds in the West India customs service. From 1746 to 1751 he was back in London and Glasgow, and amongst other business interests was a partner with his brother in the Delftfield pottery.

His tenure as governor was troubled by French and Indian wars and by disputes with the Virginian assembly over taxation. He was an early advocate of Parliamentary taxation of the colonies. Nevertheless he won some respect, and was an active patron of William and Mary College and a benefactor of its library. In this indirect way he may have assisted the diffusion of Scottish philosophy in America.

There is no evidence that he used his official position to promote the interests of his native city, but Glasgow merchants were probably helped in many ways by the fact that a man from one of their leading families held this post during a critical period for the establishment of Scottish dominance in Virginian trade. In 1754 the University of Glasgow gave him an honorary degree with the citation that as a native of the city and graduate of the University 'he does honour to both, and may have occasion to promote their interest'. He died in 1770 – too early to comment upon the development of colonial resistance which would have horrified him.

Many of the sources contain examples of Scots petitioning for colonial patronage. There are some typical examples in the papers of Sir Hew Dalrymple.[48] In July 1749 his cousin, John Dalrymple, wrote that he was leaving the army and intended to settle in North Carolina, where he already had a plantation. 'It would be of great service to me there', he said, 'if I were made one of the King's Counsel'. In January 1754 George Warrender wrote at the request of Mr Pyott, a local parson. Pyott's son John, who had taken the name of Graham, had gone out to Savannah and wished to have a recommendation to the new Governor. Warrender suggested that Sir Hew Dalrymple might approach Mr Oswald of the Board of Trade. Further letters from Mr Pyott requested a colonial appointment for his son and asked for him to be made a member of the Council. There must be hundreds of similar letters in the papers of all public men who had, or were thought to have, influence with the government, and in the papers of all the great departments preserved in the Public Record Office. In some respects the problems of patronage were less difficult to solve in Scotland than in England, as the men who had influence with the government were easily identified and few in number. There may not have been much merit in the system, but it served well the interests of young men bred in a country where aspirations were high, education good, and opportunities limited. A full survey of these long forgotten letters could furnish a remarkable insight into the aspirations and problems of the upper and middle classes in eighteenth-century Scotland.

Even those who obtained office were not always satisfied. John Drummond of Quarrell was a director of the East India Company and a man of influence in government circles.[49] He was probably instrumental in obtaining appointments in South Carolina for two who had applied to him, George Morley and James Wedderburn. The former wrote a letter of complaint in October 1733. He was, he said, 'not the first Gentleman that had been deceived in the Account of this country'. The precise nature of his dissatisfaction is not clear, but he had sold his office – though he might have done better by farming it out – and intended to return home as soon as possible. James Wedderburn, writing later in the same year was more cheerful. He thanked Drummond for obtaining for him the office of clerk of the Common Pleas. He hoped to make a good living, but solicited further favours. Drummond's correspondence included many other letters from men whom he had helped to emigrate but only one more from America;[50] he may have been dissatisfied with outcome of business speculations in the colonies and decided to concentrate his attention upon other parts of the world. In October 1733 he received a letter from a Mr D. Gordon in Philadelphia about debts owed to himself and Lord Morton. Gordon explained that there would be no money forthcoming because of difficulties 'occasioned by our unlucky circumstances in this place . . . owing chiefly to the great debts we contract for British goods'.

The eighteenth-century tutor normally had a professional training and never imagined himself as a candidate for office. Socially he was on the same level as white servants or craftsmen and might indeed have come as an indentured servant and been sold to an employer. Yet in their humble way tutors played an important part in the diffusion of Scottish culture. Literally hundreds must have been in service with wealthy colonial families by the middle of the century, and many Americans, especially in the South, were said to carry with them through life ineradicable traces of a Scottish accent acquired from their earliest preceptors. For the most part their reputation stood high, for, as Jefferson wrote, 'From that country we are surest of having sober attentive men'.[51]

Not all tutors started from the bottom rung. George Panton had been in charge of the school at Jedburgh, obtained a degree from Marischal, and exerted great efforts to get himself ordained as a clergyman of the Church of England before setting out for America to take employment as tutor with the family of a wealthy New Yorker.[52] Others with less impressive credentials emigrated independently and sought employment as tutors as the first step towards setting themselves up as schoolmasters. Others again can have been little more than employed to keep the children out of mischief rather than impart learning to them.

One unhappy story appears in the papers of John Drummond of Quarrel.[53] A man called John Borthwick had been convicted, perhaps of fraud or theft, and sentenced to death. From the way in which he wrote English he must have been an educated man, but had been saved from the gallows by Drummond's intervention, and the sentence commuted to one of transportation and seven years service in Virginia. His labour was purchased by Colonel Charles Grymes, who held a post in the customs. Considering his crime (whatever it was) Borthwick seems to have done as well as he could expect, but this did not prevent him from pouring out complaints to Drummond.

The first letter from Borthwick gives a description of the voyage and arrival in Virginia. It may be typical of the way in which hundreds of unhappy men were sent to the colonies. The voyage took ten weeks.

> After . . . much ill usage, many Hardships and Perils at sea, we arrived in this river [the Rappahannock], and of upwards of 200 transports, 100 died in the voyage, the first four weeks we were at sea. . . . The ships provisions being very bad, especially water, was the occasion that most of the Transports died in the voyage of a Flux.

In Virginia Borthwick performed 'the tedious office of schoolmaster' for the children of Colonel Grymes and others. He was also 'a Book keeper and waiting servant'. The prospect of seven years in this employment appalled him, and he pleaded with Drummond to secure his release.

> I am your honour's by Redemption and Purchase. It was you, Sir, that Redeemed me from the immediate stroke of a shameful and ignominious death. Oh, take some compassion on me in the present Woeful and sad Extremity and deliver me from this ignominious servitude.

It was, he said, a life of 'meanest servitude'. If freed there were abundant opportunities for acquiring wealth in Virginia by hard work, and he would soon be able to recompense those whom he had wronged. There is no indication of Drummond's response but one can only record that many humble immigrants, who had committed no crime, would have been happy to obtain employment as schoolmaster, book keeper, asnd waiting servant, with a prospect of freedom when indentures had been worked out.

One such man was the engaging John Harrower, whose journal has been published.[54] Harrower was a Shetlander, and in 1773 he left his wife and children in Lerwick to make his fortune – or, at least, to better himself. The diary records his failure to find work in London where he 'was like a blind man without a guide', and on 26 January 1774, after only a week, he wrote, 'this day I being reduced to the last shilling I have was obliged to engage to go to Virginia for four years as a schoolmaster for Bedd, Board, Washing and five pounds during the whole time'. Without pretensions to literary elegance he had a lively style, some telling phrases, and a good eye for detail. He was employed by Colonel William Dangerfield, of Belvidere, near Fredericksburg, and told his wife, 'I am obliged to speak English as best I can, for Lady Dangerfield speaks nothing but high english and the Colonel has his education in England'. Clearly however, employment became friendship and his employer helped him to find other pupils, earn money and put away some savings. There were lively descriptions of difficulties with the children, and a skirmish with the Indians. He also made arrangements for receiving his wife's letters, and commented on the effects of non-importation.

On 10 July 1776 he wrote to his wife, 'I hope (please God) if I am spared to make you a Virginian Lady among the woods of America which is far more pleasant than the roaring of the raging seas around Zetland'. By this time no reader could help wishing that the hope would be fulfilled; but there the diary stops, and a sad sequel is found in a letter from his wife to Colonel Dangerfield. Her husband had died in April 1777, but she knew nothing of it until she received letters from his employer a year later. He had written in highly appreciative terms, and offered to remit the £70 which Harrower had saved. By this time war raged between Britain and the colonies, and Mrs Harrower's postscript tells an eloquent story.

> If this letter comes to the hands of any British Officer it is humbly hoped that in Compation to a poor Widdow He will forward it as directed.

It certainly reached Dangerfield as it is with his papers in the Virginia State Library, and, if it was in his power, she must surely have received the seventy pounds.

Another young Scot seeking scholastic employment was David Duff, a protégé of Sir James Grant, who arrived at Port Tobacco, Maryland in 1772.[55] He seems to have been prone to accident, for he had missed by four hours a ship sailing direct from the Clyde to Maryland, and had had to travel by way of Norfolk, Virginia. In Maryland he refused one good offer, tried for employment in a school, but found that the position had been filled a few days previously. He settled instead for employment as a tutor at £16 sterling a year, with permission to take other pupils and reckoned that he would clear £40 or £50 a year 'which is here reckoned very handsome'.

However as this failed to meet his 'most moderate expectations', he obtained a post in a large school and lived 'much more comfortably', though still dissatisfied.

He then confided to his patron the real reason for having chosen Maryland. This was the hope of obtaining 'one of those lucrative parishes' in the established church; but these were much sought after and their value had induced 'so many of the natives to make their sons clergymen'. Moreover he confessed that he could not 'speak even nonsense fluently and the people in this part of the country in my opinion prefer pleasing the ear to mending the heart'. With ecclesiastical prospects dim, he thought of trying to be a physician; they 'seldom fail of making money'. One suspects that he had to settle for a career as a humble schoolmaster, or that he decided to try to satisfy his somewhat erratic ambitions elsewhere.

A more orthodox start to a teaching career appears in a note sent in 1774 to George McMurdo of Dumfries who had numerous connections in Virginia.[56] He had apparently consulted a schoolmaster in Dumfries about finding a suitable tutor to serve in the colony, and a letter recommended a young man called William Hepburn, a former pupil at the school with some teaching experience. He was 'a young man of a good natural temper, had had a good classical education . . . and would answer for all the branches that your friend requires'. He was willing to go to Virginia as a tutor on a four year contract at £30 sterling a year, his passage paid, and a small advance to cover expenses. This is probably more typical of the way in which hundreds of young Scots became tutors, than those who went as reprieved convicts, indentured servants, destitute men who sold themselves to ship's captains and were ready to take anything, or others with extravagant hopes of rich colonial parishes.[57]

Chapter Three

THE GLASGOW TOBACCO TRADE

Tobacco was an ideal commodity for accumulating profit at a nodal point of international commerce. It was high in value in proportion to bulk, served markets with few or no alternative sources of supply, and, within limits, could be held in store for sale at the most advantageous price. There were risks which meant that it was not a trade for novices or mere speculators, as the crop was uncertain, the quality variable, and sales much affected by general economic conditions. In this difficult trade Glasgow merchants proved their mastery. Unlike their London competitors, who sold tobacco consigned to them by the planters, the Glasgow men purchased in Maryland and Virginia, accepting the risk from the moment it entered their warehouses in the colonies. Their storekeepers could pay cash, but it was more profitable to supply goods in return for tobacco, which meant getting the right articles to the right place and the right time. A successful store was stocked with goods from England, Scotland, and imports from Europe or the East. The business of supply had therefore to be mastered before the merchant could obtain tobacco for sale, and this meant much skill and delicate negotiation, through agents in London, Ireland, France, Holland, Sweden, and other north European countries.

In the early days most tobacco was grown on large plantations with easy access to navigable water, but during the first half of the eighteenth century cultivation was moving inland, where the plantations were smaller and the producers less affluent than the great landowners of the tidewater. The role of the Glasgow merchant in this expansion was crucial. They established stores at the head of navigation; at Piscataway and Bladensburg in Maryland, at Alexandria and Dumfries on tributaries of the Potomac, at Fredericksburg and Falmouth just below the falls of the Rappahannock, at Manchester, Rockyridge, Warwick and Shockoes near Richmond.[1] At the entrance to the Chesapeake the port of Norfolk, Virginia, served planters in the Albermarle district of North Carolina and an entrepôt for local and West Indian trade. On the eve of the Revolution it was said to be predominantly a Scottish town.

Most of the store trade depended upon credit rather than cash. Surviving ledgers show planters debiting supplies from the stores against tobacco brought in at the end of the season. Purchases often outweighed the sales, and the planter would enter the new year in debt. Interest might be charged on overdue debts, but the Glasgow merchants were usually content to let the debit balance run on from year to year. In effect they supplied the working capital which enabled planters to stay in business, expand in good times, and maintain the standard of life to which they aspired. When bad times came, and debts had to be called in, this essential economic function was likely to cause resentment rather than gratitude.

The business of buying tobacco and selling imported goods to the planters generated secondary activities. Staves and timber were often carried as deck cargo by the homeward bound tobacco ships. Trade with the West Indies and coasting trade with the lesser Atlantic ports were profitable sidelines. Neil Jamieson, Glassford's principal factor at Norfolk became the acknowledged master of these complex commercial operations.

The key man in the operation was the factor. Though in law no more than an agent for his principal in Glasgow, he had to be a man of wide experience, sound judgment, and quick decision. Most factors were salaried servants of a Glasgow partnership, but some of the older and more successful were partners in the home concern.[2] In some cases the factor was senior partner in a company trading in the colonies with Glasgow associates as other partners. The leading factors spent many years in the colonies, but were frequently joined for shorter periods by younger members or friends of the Glasgow merchant families, who came out to learn the business. Alexander Speirs, who ended his career as head of the largest of all the tobacco companies, said in 1775 that he had spent twenty years of his life in Virginia. In addition there was frequent movement between the Clyde and the colonies, with some on short visits, some intending to take up subordinate positions, and others returning home.

The factor had to know every detail of his district, and all the planters with whom he might hope to trade. He had to judge who was worth a gamble, and who should be kept on a tight rein. A major objective in all his operations was to get a quick turn-round of ships at the tobacco port. Time spent tied up at the wharves was money ill-spent, while a stock of good tobacco ready for immediate loading meant more time to play the market at the other end, with the prospect of a second profitable trip within the year. It was also essential to study the needs of the planter and ensure that the store was stocked accordingly.

The complexities of the trade meant that the head of a Glasgow firm had to be a man of exceptional experience. If the partnership was wealthy it might own ships, and this meant responsibility for their fitting and manning. If not, they would have to charter ships, while smaller firms negotiated for the purchase of cargo space. Probably even the largest men in the business had occasion, from time to time, to ship goods in vessels belonging to other owners. Selection of the cargoes had to be done with care. Naturally, it was cheapest to buy as much as possible for shipment from the Clyde, but it was often necessary to arrange for articles to be picked up in English or European ports.

Despite their affluence the tobacco merchants carried on their business with the minimum of overheads. They bought land and built themselves fine houses, but continued to operate from cramped offices with no more than two or threee clerks. Most of the important letters were written in their own hands, although the second copy, usually sent by a different route, and the letterbook copy might be entrusted to a clerk.[3] Complicated trans- actions, which began in the colonies and ended with sale to a European buyer, were carried in the heads of single men or two or three close asso- ciates. The reputation of a partner was all important, as each was jointly responsible for liabilities. The banker who loaned money, or the merchant who supplied goods on credit, had to be sure that there was no weak link in the chain. A partner who was incompetent, extravagant, untrustworthy, or senile had to be dropped before he could do harm, and the frequent changes in the style of partnerships make it difficult to trace them from year to year.[4]

The tobacco merchants sold principally to foreign buyers, and a contract to supply the French farmers-general played a significant part in the rise of the Glasgow tobacco empire.[5] However the competitive advantage gained by the Glasgow merchants was such that some undercut English merchants with shipments direct from the Chesapeke to London, Liverpool, or Bristol.[6]

A sophisticated banking system was required to finance long distance trades. Producers wanted payment or goods on credit, manufactuers or other suppliers had to be paid, ships fitted, and salaries found, while returns from sales of tobacco overseas might be slow to come in. The international trading system depended upon extended credit, ability to advance large sums on bills of exchange, and willingness to take calculated risks. The operations of Glasgow merchants and bankers was facilitated by the number of Scottish banking and mercantile houses established in London during the first half of the century.

It has been argued that efficiency in mobilising credit and raising capital was an important factor in lowering costs,[7] but the major source of capital was always investment by partners, personal loans, or ploughed back profits. Banks supplied short-term credit that gave the merchants sufficient elasticity in their operation, but did not generate capital for long-term investment.[8]

The present survey has not covered official records. Loyalist claims have been sampled and their detailed analysis would yield much more information about asserts held in Virginia and Maryland at the outbreak of the Revolution.[9] All known collections of letters, ledgers, and journals relating to operations in the colonies have been surveyed, though it is always possible that further major collections will come to light. There are, for instance, no papers yet located belonging to Buchanan, Hastie & Co., or their associated partnerships. Some of the smaller firms are noted only in single references, and others seem to have left no trace.

There are some major gaps revealed by the survey. The paucity of evidence prior to 1707 was noted in chapter I, but there is also surprisingly little on development between 1707 and 1750.[10] The major collections begin with a fully-fledged organisation without specific information about the establishment of the store system or the replacement of supercargoes by resident factors.

A major gap is the lack of evidence about the private lives of the factors and their subordinates in the colonies. They were encouraged to establish good relations with the local planters, but their allegiance was always to their principals at home rather than to the community in which they lived. Glasgow merchants did not take kindly to marriage into colonial families, and this explained the dismissal of one storekeeper of William Cunninghame & Co. 'They cannot agree to be served by a married man, if a single man can be got, thinking the former must often be necessarily called from their business affairs.[11] They would have been equally displeased to learn that one of their factors was living as a Virginian gentleman and enjoying the pleasures of a dissipated life. Nevertheless the young Scotsmen who served the tobacco lords cannot have been indifferent to female charms, and must have enjoyed some social pleasures outside the counting house. When congregated in towns they may have created their own social life, but when serving in more isolated stores it seems unlikely that they did not mix with the local planters and merchants. All this must remain as conjecture until more personal accounts come to light. One would willingly exchange several volumes of accounts for the scribblings of one gossipy letter-writer with an eye for the significance of minor events.

This gap in the sources accounts for what may seem to be some imbalance in the survey. The difficulties or misfortunes of some small concerns are given considerably more space than the operations of the great companies. The affairs of the unsuccessful partnership between James Lawson and John Semple were insignificant compared with the business conducted by John Glassford, William Cunninghame, or the other tobacco lords; Alexander Hamilton of Piscataway was a lively and voluminous correspondent but he was never in the same class as Neil Jamieson of Norfolk or John Robinson of Falmouth; but these records, left by lesser men in the trade, throw some light on human aspects of the great Glasgow enterprise. Hundreds of young men went out with high hopes. A few succeeded, some failed, most had to be content with modest rewards; but the experience of minor participants may do more than the records of success to illuminate what can only be described, in a trite phrase, as 'the romance of trade'.

The unpopularity of the Scots factors has been accepted by many historians, but most of the evidence comes from after 1772 – when a financial crisis at home caused many merchants to take urgent steps to call in their debts – or from the period of the Revolution when several of the wealthiest factors became open Loyalists.[12] By a contemporary estimate there were 2,000 factors in Virginia on the eve of the Revolution, and most of them must have been Scottish.[13] This is probably an overestimate if applied to factors strictly defined, but an underestimate if intended to include storekeepers and assistants. In addition there were clerks, men employed in the warehouses, and other subordinates. Loyalist claims account for only a fraction of this number; the majority of resident Scots laid low, while a minority gave active support to the 'patriots'. There is some indication that younger men took the opportunity of promoting themselves when experienced factors returned home or withdrew into neutral obscurity.[14] A large number must have stayed on, and either established themselves in Virginian society or moved to other parts of the United States.

The tobacco companies became considerable property owners before the Revolution, though merchants did not welcome mortgages in place of good bills. In a few instances factors may have purchased land for themselves, but in most cases land came into the hands of the companies as settlement for debt. Most of this property was sequestrated during the Revolution. Many factors probably owned a few slaves for domestic service or unskilled labour on wharves or in warehouses; and some may have engaged in slave trading as a sideline; but this was a specialised occupation and participation was probably limited to local sales or purchases.

Salaries for young men were low, and even older men were not well paid. There was therefore a strong incentive for them to trade on their own account, and this was often allowed for and defined in the terms of agreement. A storekeeper was also in a good position to profit from his situation, for though he relied for the bulk of his stock on what the Glasgow company chose to send, he could also make independent purchases of local or imported commodities, and might engage in private trading ventures. Neil Jamieson at Norfolk established a thriving trade with the West Indies, especially Antigua.

Though Glasgow merchants often complained that the remittances home were disappointingly small, and factors frequently found it necessary to explain that tobacco had not been brought in, that store goods lay unsold, or that debts were impossible to collect; but accusations of dishonesty were infrequent. Indeed the business could not be conducted at all without mutual trust, which helps to explain the preference shown by Glasgow merchants for younger relations or members of families well-known to them. In a country where opportunities for educated young men were still very limited there was never any difficulty in filling posts in the colonies even when the financial terms and conditions of service seem harsh by modern standards.

The ramifications of the tobacco trade led Glasgow merchants into other commercial enterprises. They consigned some goods to New York, Philadelphia, and other Atlantic ports; sent some of their ships direct from colonial to English ports; imported staves and timber, and exported an increasing variety of goods, not all for sale in the tobacco colonies. Trade with the West Indies has an independent history, but several tobacco merchants were involved in it.

Finally the store trade stimulated production of manufactured goods in Scotland. Dr Devine has demonstrated the extent to which the tobacco merchants financed tanneries, sugar refining, linen, iron, and – towards the end of the century – cotton.[15] There were old-established ropeworks and bottleworks which flourished on the colonial trade. An interesting example of specialised industry was the Delftfield pottery near Broomielaw which made high quality china, mainly for the American market.[16]

The bulk of the sources surveyed in this chapter deal with the tobacco trade at its zenith, from 1750 to 1775. Subsequent chapters will deal with the effects of the Revolution, and later attempts to restore trade between Scotland and the United States; but at this stage a few comments on the closing years of the 'golden age' are appropriate. There are signs that by 1770 the dominance of Glasgow merchants was being threatened. The number competing in the field may have been disadvantageous; for though Glasgow men made some effort to fix prices and avoid cut-throat competition, there was no control over separate transactions. London and Bristol merchants were anxious to win back a larger share, and Whitehaven was still a serious competitor. Apart from the need to offer an attractive price for tobacco there was keen competition among the stores, and the less efficient suffered. Planters learned to play off store against store, English against Scottish merchant, and consignments on their own account against sales to storekeepers. They could also plant wheat or other food crops if tobacco profits fell. Many of the inland planters, who had been struggling to gain a foothold twenty years before, became men of substance and could afford to take risks.

Several of the Glasgow merchants foresaw the difficulties which might arise if they continued to depend on tobacco, and began to diversify their activities before the Revolution. Their experience in international trade suggested openings which could be exploited as separate ventures or in combination with tobacco. Several became alarmed at the extent and doubtful security of their colonial debts, which might be regarded as investments which would bring returns by ensuring an increased supply of tobacco, but became less defensible as probit margins narrowed.

The difficulties – real or imagined – became more pronounced in 1772 when the Scottish credit system experienced a severe shock. The crisis began with the Scottish banking houses in London, and the belief that large amounts of Edinburgh and Glasgow money were deposited with them spread the effects to Scotland. It caught the largest private banking partnership – Douglas, Heron & Co., known as the Ayr bank – at a particularly unfortunate time and brought about its failure.[17] 114 of the bank's 226 partners became insolvent and other banks experienced a time of great difficulty. In America bills on Glasgow became suspect, and planters demanded cash for their tobacco if they could not get goods at low prices.

There is therefore ground for believing that even without the Revolution the emphasis and character of the tobacco trade would have changed. This is not to say that the Glasgow men would have abandoned Virginia and Maryland. Even though prospects for tobacco were slightly dimmed they were still very good, and the base of operations was strong enough to allow for experiment and diversification. Experience of trade between the Chesapeke and the Clyde was an asset which would not evaporate because of stiffening competition or a few bad debts. Though change was in the air before 1775, only the upheaval of Revolution could break down the bastions of economic strength which had been erected during the preceding half century.

Amongst the few surviving records of the Glasgow tobacco trade before 1750 the most important are those of the Bogle family[18] These illustrate the unsuccessful attempts of an important family to gain a footing in the trade. By implication they suggest the devices which led other companies to success.

The first important group of letters is from George Bogle, whilst a student at Leiden, to his father, Robert, in Glasgow. It seems that he kept a close eye on the commercial situation in Rotterdam, where his father sent most of his tobacco. Their agents in that city were Alexander and John Carstairs, sometimes referred to as 'factors', though confined to handling goods for sale on commission.

George Bogle was keenly critical of the business in Holland. Tobacco sent by the English merchants arrived two or three months earlier than the Scots and was of much better quality. In August 1726 he remarked that 'Good tobacco will help to raise the sinking credit as well as the low price of Scots tobacco in Holland'. From 1727 he was in charge of most of the company operations in Glasgow, but does not seem to have the right blend of imagination and practical ability to develop trade on successful lines. His brother, Matthew, moved between Glasgow and Virginia, acting as more than supercargo but never setting up a permanent establishment in the colony. He was in Virginia before 1729, but returned to Glasgow in that year. In 1730 he wrote to his friend and agent in Virginia, Norman

Brockenborough, that he hoped to return but had been forced to remain in Scotland longer than expected in order to dispose of his tobacco. He asked Brockenborough to send the rest of his tobacco, collect his outstanding debts, and persuade 'good friends' to send their tobacco to him for sale on commission.

In November 1730 George Bogle wrote to John Govan, a Scots merchant in London, asking him to buy and ship goods to Virginia on his account. They were to be sent to Colonel McKenzie at Hampton, Thomas Neilson at Yorktown, or James Reid at Urbana, and await collection by Matthew. By September 1731 Matthew was back in Virginia and George wrote that he had received a consignment of tobacco, but that the goods for sale had not yet been sent. In the same year George expressed his intention of getting out of the trade, but suggested that Matthew might settle on the Rappahannock, act as an agent for local planters, and sell their tobacco on commission. Matthew may have been little more than a broker, taking in tobacco and selling to buyers on the spot, but George Bogle was also hoping for tobacco to sell on commission from his headquarters in Glasgow. He sent Matthew some cases of claret so that 'You may drink a Bottle with the Gentlemen of your acquaintance and see if you can Engage them to give us Consignments'.

This looks like haphazard organisation compared with either the London merchants of the day or with the operations of the later tobacco lords of Glasgow. The Bogles had no standing arrangements with large planters for sales on commission; they sometimes purchased in Virginia on their own account but established no permanent stores in the colony; they also touted for consignments, and maintained an irregular supply of exported goods. It is no wonder that in 1731 George lamented that 'we are following a Losing Trade – which will be heavy on us this same year', and that he told John Carstairs in Rotterdam that tobacco was 'the most vile losing Trade that was ever invented'.

There are hints of more stable operations when George asked Matthew to look out for a store where another agent, John Graham, could establish himself. He was to assist Matthew in the purchase of tobacco, and £1,146 of exported goods were on the way; but at the same time George advised Matthew to get clear of the business, leaving no debts unpaid or goods unsold when he left Virginia.

Worse was to follow. The ship on which John Graham travelled hit a storm on 1 January 1732. Some of the goods were jettisoned, others damaged, and none were insured. This disaster may have persuaded George Bogle to cut his losses, and by 1736 the family business was concerned almost exclusively with the West Indies, especially Jamaica. Matthew Bogle returned to Glasgow and set up business as a tobacco importer.

Other Glasgow merchants importing tobacco before 1750 have been identified, but the details of their operations remain obscure. The list includes several commemorated in the street names of the modern city: William Anderson; James Baird; Walter Brock; James Brown; Andrew, Archibald and George Buchanan; Daniel Campbell; Lawrence Dinwiddie; Colin Dunlop; William Gray; James Hastie; Archibald Ingram; John Jamieson; John McCall; George and John Murdock; Alexander and Richard Oswald; Andrew Ramsay; John Ritchie; John Robertson; James Simson; James Smellie; Alexander Speirs; John Thompson; William Wallace; and Thomas Youille. There were several James Dunlops active during the eighteenth century, and one was certainly importing tobacco in the first half of the century.[19]

Despite George Bogle's lack of success, it is clear that someone made money out of business, and the earliest records of large companies after 1750 – John Glassford and William Cunninghame – show the factor and store system fully organised and profitable. It seems probable that Glasgow merchants continued to take a little tobacco for sale on commission, but apart from the Bogle records there is evidence of but a single transactions of this kind. This consists of two letters, both written on 26 February 1733 by Richard Oswald of Glasgow to the executors of the estate of Robert Carter of Virginia. The first records of sale of tobacco sent by Carter 1731, and the second acknowledges receipt of another consignment.[20]

In these early years it was by no means certain that Glasgow would win ascendancy in the tobacco trade. Not only was there competition from established English competitors, but also a vigorous bid from the merchants of Dumfries, where the leading merchants were Hugh Lawson & Co., Benjamin, George and William Bell, Alexander Fergusson, Robert and Edward Maxwell & Co., James Corbet, and Charles Kirkpatrick. Most of them were able to handle 150 tons of cargo single-handed, though there was co-operation in particularly ambitious ventures. They may have anticipated the Glasgow merchants by maintaining permanent establishments in Virginia – the town of Alexandria in Virginia was a centre for settlement from this part of Scotland.[21] It appears that one, sometimes two, ships sailed from Dumfries every three or four months, returning with tobacco. The picture is incomplete, and it is estimated that more tobacco came ashore illegally than was passed through His Majesty's custom houses. The south-west coastline, with its many inlets and fishing villages, was ideal for a flourishing smuggling business. This may have depressed legitimate business, and the Dumfries trade never developed a strong back-up of banking and manufacturing establishments.

Between 1750 and 1765 Glasgow merchants took the giant steps forward which gave their city dominance in the tobacco trade and a leading position among the commercial cities of Europe. In his study of the tobacco merchants Thomas Devine indentifies three major groups led by William Cunninghame, Alexander Speirs, and John Glassford; and three others in which the leading partnerships were Buchanan, Hastie & Co., Thomson, Snodgras & Co., and T & A. Donald & Co.[22] There is abundant information about the Glassford group, consisting of Glassford & Co., Glassford, Gordon, Monteith & Co., Henderson, McCall & Co., and George Kippen & Co., which was probably the most sophisticated in its organisation. In the Cunninghame group were William Cunninghame & Co., Cunninghame, Findlay & Co., and Cunninghame, Brown & Co.; in the Speirs group, Speirs, Bowman & Co., Speirs, French & Co., and Patrick Colquhoun & Co. There were a number of independent merchants who carried on a substantial trade – John Alston, James Baird, James and John Ballantine, Colin Dunlop, Cuming, McKenzie & Co., William Gray, John McCall, James Ritchie, Hugh Wyllie, and members of the Oswald family. There were many others with smaller businesses, who survived for a time before failing or being absorbed by one of the more powerful companies.

The statistical history of the Glasgow tobacco trade has been pieced together by Professor Price and Dr Devine from material in the Public Record Office and the Scottish Record Office.[23] The Exchequer Records in the Scottish Record Office contain accounts of the trade of all Scottish ports, with lists of all goods imported and exported or carried in the coast trade but liable to duty. There are accounts of all money received and interest due, and details of all sailings or entries. The quantities of tobacco and the goods exported by individual merchants and partnerships are also recorded. In addition to tobacco, imports included sugar, rice, rum, spices, and 'general goods'. Frequent items among the exports are woollens, linen, flax, haberdashery, hats, shoes, and pipes.[24]

The Exchequer Records in the Scottish Record Office also include the 'Inquisitions and Extents' on goods subject to seizure, and the property of Crown debtors, and proceedings consequent upon writes of extent, or *Diem clausit extremum*.[25] In addition to Port Glasgow and Greenock, imports were recorded for Ayr, Aberdeen, Anstruther, Bo'ness, Dumfries, Dundee, Inverness, Kirkcudbright, Leith, Montrose and Perth.[26] It is probable that the accounts were prepared to help the government reckon the effects of American non-exportation agreements. The Melville Castle muniments include amounts of tobacco imported into Scotland between 1752 and 1775.

Under a Maryland Act of 1745 all tobacco was inspected for quality, and stored in an official warehouse, while the planters were given 'crop notes'. The exporters took these 'crop notes' and gave cash, credit, or goods in exchange. Unfortunately the records are confined to salaries of the officials and warehouse expenses and do not indicate the owners or exporters of tobacco.[27] Scattered in the surviving records of the tobacco merchants and their factors are hundreds of account books, some well-kept and well-preserved, some fragmentary, and many details of transactions hastily recorded in daybooks or wastebooks for future reference.[28]

Many of the surviving business records were gathered together by the owners or their agents after the war to provide evidence for recovery of debts or loyalist claims. The records of Maryland are particularly well preserved, and as the state pursued a drastic policy of sequestration, confiscation, and forced sales of Loyalist property, they shed much light on the complex trading system.[29] There is also much information about the Virginian claims of William Cunninghame & Co. in the accounts and papers of John Turner, their factor and storekeeper at Rockyridge, Virginia.[30]

This survey of the sources will not cover the organization of the trade in Scotland, but focus on their activities in the colonies.[31] The hundreds of young men who went out to learn the business, remained as factors, store-keepers, assistants, clerks, and bookkeepers, left voluminous but uneven evidence of their work and problems. There is little before 1760, and after that very little about private lives. Letters must have been sent home to parents, benefactors, or friends – indeed the business letters sometimes refer to such enclosures and request that they should be forwarded – but few survive. In most cases it is not possible to do more than guess at the personal relationship between Scots merchants and local planters. There are but fleeting references to their social life, and none to attendance at churches or social gatherings.

A good start for an analysis of this evidence is a memorial prepared in January 1766 for Charles Townshend, Paymaster General, by one of the most experienced men in the business, Archibald Henderson, former factor for John Glassford & Co. at Colchester, Virginia.[32] He began by sketching the outlines of the trade. Factors were established throughout the colonies; their stores sold manufactures, European and East Indian goods, they took tobacco in payment, and this was exported in ships sent out from Glasgow. Much of the store trade was with young men who had bought or rented cheap land, had no capital, and depended for success upon their own labour. It was the normal practice to let men of this type take goods on credit, in the hope that they would develop their farms, acquire resources, and pay their debts.

The risks inherent in this kind of business could be carried only if the courts were impartial and efficient when dealing with claims for debt. Whether they liked it or not, men from Britain in Virginia and Maryland had to adapt themselves to local legal practice. In Virginia, wrote Henderson, there were courts in every county with unlimited jurisdiction in civil cases, in which all claims for sums over twenty-five shillings were heard. The presiding magistrates were appointed by the Governor, were unpaid, could not be forced to hear a case or be punished for refusing to act. Proceedings were very slow and simple cases might take over two years. In the supreme court judges received 'a trifling allowance' and 'nothing like a regular appointment for judges', and though Henderson did not infer that the judges were open to bribery, they had an incentive to prolong cases and exact the maximum fee. In Maryland the judges were also poorly paid, and legal costs prevented many people from taking legitimate claims to court. For 'any administration of justice at all' a 'total alteration' of the constitution of Virginia and Maryland was required. The present situation was a dreadful one for men who have a 'large proportion of their fortune depending on debts'. On the other hand Henderson argued that it would be folly for the British government to enforce the Stamp Act which would alienate the colonists, increase the difficulty of debt recovery, and perhaps prompt the seizure of British property. He believed that the Glasgow merchants wished the British government to pursue a conciliatory course, restore tranquility, allow the people to pursue their 'labour and industry', and repay their debts. A reform of the judicial system could then go forward, to ensure the regular administration of justice so that 'those who are indebted . . . may not have it in their power to leave the country'.

Archibald Henderson's brother, Alexander, was also a Glassford factor whose letterbook for 1758–65 has been preserved.[33] The first letter records that he had taken over the Colchester store from his brother, but that prospects were less favourable than he had hoped. There were four competitors nearby, all with well-stocked stores. In August 1760, 3,300 hogsheads were brought in for inspection, 500 shipped by the planters themselves, and fifteen large stores with four or five smaller ones competed for the remaining 2,800. Stores run by a Mr Grayson and a Mr Ross, backed by a 'large concern' were the most dangerous.

Alexander Henderson was critical of the quantity and quality of goods supplied by John Glassford, which were also badly packed and often damaged on arrival. The goods sent in convict ships were particularly liable to damage or delays. These ship often waited in a home port until they had a full load, and might call elsewhere in America before arriving in Virginia. In addition to pilfering from cargoes the convicts carried jail fever, which was infectious, usually 'fatal to those seized by it', and communicated 'by means of books or any commodity coming from on board an unclean ship'.[34] Galssford & Co. had employed London agents for those unsatisfactory shipments, perhaps because the freight charges were low.

Again and again Henderson reported complaints about the poor quality of the goods received as an explanation for the poor remittances that he was able to send. In February 1759 he reported that he had obtained 864 hogsheads, which does not seem to be bad going, if the other stores had to share out 2,000 between them. Perhaps Henderson was a sharper business-

man than his many excuses suggest, or he may have relied much upon the
advice of his elder brother, Archibald, who was Glassford's chief factor. He
wrote in 1762 that business had not been extensive, 'but it affords me
particular satisfaction that it has not been a losing Trade'; there was not
much capital locked up in the business, and Glassford made a profit as a
result of Henderson's management.

Nevertheless Alexander Henderson's relations with Glassford were often
strained. In 1759 he had wanted to trade on his own account with the back
country, but this brought a warning from Glassford against risky trade and
an offer of a six year contract. This Henderson refused because he wanted to
be free to engage on any profitable venture that came his way. The contract
would have limited him to £100 worth of goods imported on his own
account which was 'really too hard' and would 'put it out of my power to
acquire a livelihood, before I am so far advanced in life as to lose a relish for
the enjoyments of it.' In the following year he agreed to give Glassford two
years' notice before leaving his employment, but rejected a wage increase of
£10 a year and asked instead for freedom to import more goods. In February
1762 Glassford offered him what seems to have been a commission on his
transactions – 'My wages should be more or less, as the Trade turned out at
the Place in that Period' – but in September of that year he delivered an
ultimatum. He had been offered £100 a year to manage another store, and
would accept unless Glassford matched the offer. He must have won his
point, and in 1763, with the return of his brother to Glasgow, he took on
wider responsibilities in Quantico and Alexandria as well as Colchester.

It is ironical, in view of his earlier arguments with Glassford, that
Henderson was soon reprimanding a junior storekeeper for becoming
involved in 'a Wholesale Trade with the back people'. He asked Glassford
to order its discontinuance 'but for ready pay', though four years earlier he
had complained bitterly when Glassford pressed for speedier payments and
no risky debts, which were 'next to impossibilities'. Greatly to his satisfaction the offending storekeeper was removed in 1764 and replaced by one
in whom he had more condfidence. In 1765 there were still debts valued at
£541, unsettled as a result of trade with the 'back people'.[35] Alexander
Henderson, though sometimes querulous, was also a forthright and lively
letter-writer. One must regret that 'a Chit Chat Epistle' to John Campbell,
mentioned in the letter of November 1762, has not survived.

Archibald Henderson was succeeded as Glassford's chief factor by Neil
Jamieson, who came to Virginia in 1760. Norfolk became his home, a base
for his commercial operations and headquarters for the Glassford interests
in Virginia and Maryland. Unlike less important factors he does not seem to
have been fettered by limits on his private trading. He exported Virginian
and North Carolinian produce to the West Indies, established personal
links with merchants in Antigua, imported sugar from the West Indies,

wine from the Azores and the Mediterranean, and salt from Bordeaux. He acquired a partnership in John Glassford & Co., and was senior partner in Jamieson, Campbell, Calvert & Co., a Virginian distillery. His legal affairs were handled by two Virginians at the head of their profession, George Wythe and Robert Carter Nicholas. He was acquainted with Thomas Jefferson, though the evidence for this rests upon a single letter of a mutual friend. He married a daughter of Colonel John Thoroughgood, who was prominent in Virginian life.[36]

A very large collection of Neil Jamieson's papers is held by the Library of Congress.[37] There is a smaller collection, relating mainly to his later years, in the New York Historical Society. Associated with the Library of Congress collection are journals, ledgers, inventories and letterbooks relating to fifteen stores operated by John Glassford & Co. or other companies under their control.

The Library of Congress collection of Jamieson papers is in twenty-two volumes containing about 5,300 items. The most interesting are a very large number of letters from John Glassford. It is clear that in the early years Glassford kept a tight control of operations. For instance, in 1761 he wrote long and detailed letters to Jamieson on 17 and 31 March, 21 April, 9, 18 and 23 May, 4 June, 6 and 16 July, 10 and 27 August, and 10 October; but their voluminous nature raises one question – could Neil Jamieson read them well enough to act upon all their detailed instructions? Glassford's handwriting was so bad, that even a man with experience and a strong incentive to give them close reading may have been baffled.

The Jamieson collection also includes letters from Arthur Morsom, factor at Falmouth, dealing with many aspects of the trade. The letters run from 1764 to 1772, and there is probably no other series containing quite so much information about the business problems of an important factor. There are also letters from Alexander Henderson and other Glassford factors.[38]

Another major tobacco company well represented in the sources is William Cunninghame & Co.[39] Papers in the Scottish Record Office include the correspondence of John Chalmers of Edinburgh who dealt with Cunninghame's legal affairs from 1767 to 1774, and many of the materials refer to a long-running dispute between Cunninghame and James Dougall, a former partner. There are also letters and papers relating to partnerships allied with William Cunninghame & Co., including Alexander Cunninghame & Co. (subsequently styled Cunninghame, Findlay & Co.), letters from Alexander Speirs, and from persons handling William Cunninghame's affairs in America after independence.

The most important items in the collection are copies of letters from William Cunninghame to John Robinson, his chief factor at Falmouth, Virginia, and Robinson's letterbooks. Cunninghame's letters were numerous, long, and while crammed with advice and instructions about specific items of business also kept Robinson informed of the movements of ships and the freights they carried. In July 1772 Cunninghame sent letters to all his factors, rebuking them for extravagance and laxity in the conduct of business.

One of John Robinson's letterbooks contains letters addressed to the subordinate factors and storekeepers who worked under his direction. The factors were kept informed of prices, market conditions, and the movement of ships; they received instructions about the quantities of tobacco to be purchased and the maximum prices to be offered; and in return they reported sales from their stores and goods required. The other letterbook contains Robinson's letters to William Cunninghame, with much information about debts, bills, shipments, the conduct of factors and competition from other firms. Though strictly confined to business matters, this collection is an unrivalled source for information on the changes and chances of the tobacco trade.

Unfortunately no comparable body of evidence has survived for the operations of other large companies. The papers of Alexander Speirs refer mainly to the period of the war and after, though material collected to substantiate claims for debt illustrate the company's extensive interests in Virginia.[40] Colin Dunlop was major figure in Glasgow commercial life, and was Provost in 1770; but neither his papers nor those of his brothers, Robert and Thomas, both of whom were prominent in the American trade, seem to have survived. There are papers of Colin's nephew, James Dunlop – who remained in America during the war and became prosperous after the peace – which will be considered in chapters VI and VIII.

James and Henry Ritchie operated a successful family partnership, though their operations were not on the same scale as Glassford, Cunninghame, or Speirs. They owned a store at Hobshole in Virginia, and when they decided to suspend trading in August 1775 were owed a total of over £3,000 by local planters; even in Virginian currency this was a considerable sum and illustrates the way in which the stable Glasgow firms helped to finance colonial enterprise.[41]

A historian is fortunate when he discovers a correspondent who writes voluminously, displays an unusual range of experience, and is also a lively letter-writer. Such was Alexander Hamilton, who started his American career as factor for the small and unsuccesful partnership of John Semple and James Lawson and whose early correspondence gives a rare insight into the kind of difficulties that more successful men encountered.

Hamilton was the younger son of a lawyer at Mauchline in Ayrshire who had, at some time, advanced considerable sums to John Semple, perhaps to launch him upon what all had hoped would be a successful business career in America. Semple went into partnership with his brother-in-law, James

Lawson, and kinship may explain why two men so obviously incompatible came to be associated with each other.[42] Alexander Hamilton became their factor at Port Tobacco, Maryland, and Semple also came out to the colony.

Semple was clearly a man of imagination, who believed that he could spot a winner, In 1763 he had almost persuaded Hamilton to join with him in opening a Maryland store for the purchase of grain and its shipment to the West Indies, when James Lawson wrote to say that Semple had drawn heavily on the company but failed to send home enough tobacco to cover his debts. Lawson would neither support his speculative ventures, nor send more goods unless some remittances were sent. A letter then followed saying that nevertheless Hamilton's father wished him to take a sixteenth share in Semple's speculation, but in September 1764 Lawson wrote again to say that he had heard nothing from Semple, warned Hamilton not to purchase 'anything new tho' ever so profitable', and above all not to draw bills on the company payable in Glasgow because they could not raise more than £5,000. In the following month things were even worse, with Lawson declaring himself caught between two fires, 'Maryland creditors and John Semple's debts'. He also took the occasion to warn Hamilton against speculating in the grain trade with the West Indies or allowing Maryland planters to run up long-standing debts.

In July 1765 Lawson issued an ultimatum: he required full accounts and told Semple to seek new partners in Glasgow. Meanwhile Semple had continued his own speculative career and acquired an iron foundry and house in Virginia which he named Keep Triste (the Semple family motto). James Lawson then came out to Maryland himself to take personal charge of his concerns, and dispensed with Hamilton's services as factor. There is another glimpse of Semple in 1769. He had been ill but had recovered. Twenty-six of his slaves had been 'executed' (i.e. impounded for debt). Lawson paid up the debts but took in return a mortgage on the Virginia property. Later Francis Hamilton, elder brother of Alexander, was able to get a share of the property as security for debts owed to his father, and Keep Triste was to provide a quiet haven for Alexander Hamilton during the troubled years of war.

In 1768 Alexander Hamilton obtained employment as assistant factor for another small company, Simson, Baird & Co., in a store at Piscataway. His superior was James Brown with whom he was to be associated for many years. Brown returned to Glasgow, formed his own company with five other partners, and took over Simson, Baird & Co. Henceforward Hamilton was factor for James Brown & Co., and his letterbooks provide a splendid source for the operations of one of the smaller tobacco companies.[43] His most frequent complaint was that the wrong goods, of the wrong quality, were sent out at the wrong time. 'It is true', he wrote in May 1774, 'that I have a great many Goods on hand, but they are not such as I can sell at this time'. In October of the same year he wrote that 'the small quantity of goods you have sent will not preserve the Custom of this store, if you continue it'. James Brown had sent out hoes 'which I did not write for, and which you must have seen by my Inventory were not wanted', and had not sent Irish linen or dunlaps which were much in demand. It was particularly frustrating as there had never been so much tobacco on offer, and Congress had agreed to enforce non-importation on 1 December.

The Hamilton letters also contain much information about the way in which tobacco was acquired, ships loaded, and money remitted to Glasgow. Unlike the letters of most factors they also contain extensive comments on political events, but these will be reserved for later examination.

Men who engaged in the tobacco trade without previous connection with one of the established companies might find the going hard. In 1764 Robert Reid set up in partnership in Virginia with Robert Woddrop.[44] He was friendly with a young Glasgow merchant, James McCall, and wished him to join this partnership. McCall refused for reasons wich are not apparent in the correspondence, but probably because he preferred to use his capital to develop a business in Glasgow. However McCall helped Reid to raise money and his letters reveal the extent to which young merchants relied on family loans or friends for gifts. Reid's father had already advanced his son some money (which McCall considered generous), but was reluctant to call upon other members of the family. McCall wrote that he had sought Mr Reid's permission 'in proposing to your Grandmother and Miss Eliza to give you a handsome Compliment at your first set out, but his delicacy would not consent to allow me to urge it'. However in March 1765 McCall was able to tell Robert Reid that his Aunt Eliza had made him a 'Compliment' of £100. The money had been lodged with McCall who would pay interest on it.

Attempting to trade on small capital made things difficult for the two young men in Virginia, and Robert Reid soon expressed dissatisfaction with his partner. In March 1765 McCall, who had already got a firm footing in Glasgow, wrote, 'I have only to assure you if you think your partner weak in money affairs and that such a small trade will not answer, if you will come home this winter I will take you in as a partner with me in my Northumberland Store and you shall be Factor & go out early in the Spring with goods to begin on a new foundation'. To avoid unpleasantness he might offer Woddrop a share, but only in proportion to the money he contributed. He hinted that Reid might raise more money from family or friends to purchase a larger share. It would be a condition of the new partnership that Reid would trade in Virginia only in McCall's account.

This proposal hung fire, either because Reid felt an obligation to Woddrop or wished to retain his independence. In February 1766 he wrote to his father that he had been unable to accept McCall's offer, but still wished to quit his present trade, 'the smallness of which and not having a substantial partner at home is my objection to it'. If he joined McCall he would be in a more advantageous and secure footing. He probably intended to drop a broad hint that a substantial loan from his father would enable him to join McCall on better terms than those proposed. So far as he was concerned the Stamp Act disturbance had put an end to any hope of sufficient profits to purchase a partnership at home.

Robert Reid could at least draw on some capital from home, but the majority of young men who went out to Virginia had to accept whatever terms the Glasgow merchant offered. Neill Campbell belonged to a family in comfortable circumstances—his father was supervisor of excise in Glasgow – but the indenture made in January 1758, between himself on the one part and Archibald Ingram and John Glassford on the other, looks severe.[45] With his father's consent he was bound to serve John Glassford & Co. in Virginia for five years as an apprentice. He would work under the direction of the company's factors. His salary would rise for each year of service, from £5 to £20, and he was allowed to trade on his own account to the value of £20 a year.

Daniel Campbell, sone of Alexander Campbell of Kilbride, secured slightly better terms from Glassford in 1770. He may have been more experienced or his father may have been willing to pay a larger premium. He was to serve Glassford for four years as an assistant factor in Maryland, with bed and board, and wages of £30 a year to be paid at the conclusion of his service. He was allowed each year to import goods valued at £20 to trade on his own account. In addition he was given a free passage out and back.[46]

For a young man who succeeded the rewards were considerable. Favourable reports on his progress might bring an offer of promotion within the company; if he lived frugally and traded wisely he might make substantial profits from goods imported on his own account; and long service as a factor or store keeper might put him in a position to purchase a partnership. Even without this a man who knew the business could command a good wage, either at home or in the colony. Even so, there was a long way to go from apprenticeship with a £5 wage in the first year to affluence as a successful Glasgow merchant or chief factor for a large company. A good many young men who went out in the flush times before 1772 were probably caught with little cash and no prospects when engulfed in the time of troubles. They had little option but to accept the situation, declare their support for the United States, and seek whatever employment they could find. Some may have found themselves as unwilling volunteers in the Continental or state forces.

In a competitive society many would fail, or be content with modest success, and there were rules which the novice in the tobacco trade neglected at his cost. When Robert Reid began to trade in Virginia in January 1764 James McCall wrote that he should be much on his guard when giving credit, especially to those from whom he was not certain of annual payments:[47]

> You should also be attentive to that great point, the price of tob° & not run headlong in giving high prices when tob° is low in Britain or when you are not on an absolute certainty of selling yr Tob° for cash at or near the price you give for it.

This was a council of perfection, but perhaps over-cautious when the most profitable transactions required a willingness to take risks. In practice the savings achieved by efficient management often enabled the Glasgow factors to go above the current price. As William Lee, a member of a distinguished Virginian family, who was for a time in London handling tobacco shipments on commission, complained:

> There seems to be something very mysterious in the Glasgow trade; their factors raise the price nominally in Virginia and their principals always begin to lower it here in Britain.[48]

The answer was that Glasgow factors almost always paid for tobacco in goods from their stores with a large margin of profit. The book values attached to tobacco and to goods could be adjusted to win the best custom while appearing to outbid their rivals.

Things did not always go smoothly. In March 1770 Thomas Adams, agent for the London firm of Perkins, Buchanan, Brown & Co. wrote that the planters had been getting very high prices, were entirely out of debt, and chose to be their own bankers, or deposit money with substantial local concerns, rather than leave credit balances at the stores:

> The Virginians seem to be gaining ground fast on the Glasgow men in the Tobacco Trade; the latter were never in such low Credit since their first settlement in this Country – their Notes which formerly passed Current in payment are now not looked at.[49]

Virginian gentlemen were themselves entering the trade, and tobacco could only be obtained by sending out carefully chosen cargoes.

This was too early to sound the death knell of the Glasgow tobacco trade, and in the following year William Lee wrote to Landon Carter, 'I think it self evident, that Glasgow has almost monopolized Virginia and its inhabitants'.[50] Indeed some of the large Glasgow companies were doing very well in 1770 and 1771; but the conflict of evidence highlights the fact that success was not easily won and could be patchy. Men went to the wall who got their equations wrong, filled their stores with unsuitable goods or overstocked with suitable ones, offered prices too low or bought too high, allowed insufficient credit or permitted bad debts to accumulate. It was equally important that ships were ready to load when required, and were not left idle for weeks while awaiting deliveries at the wharf.

The Glasgow merchants often had difficulty in remitting money, particularly when they wished to get advances in London. The William Lee Letterbooks contain advice to Robert Carter Nicholas that bills payable in Glasgow at thirty days sight were marked down by 2½ per cent in London; this made them just equal in value to sixty day bills drawn on London.[51] In April 1772 he wrote to Francis Lightfoot Lee:

> I would request you never to buy for me a bill drawn upon any merchant in Scotland . . . for you may depend upon it there is a real difference between bills on London & Scotland, tho I can't persuade Mr. Treasurer Nicholas of this who has it more in his power than any other man to rectify this abuse & impositions of the Scottish Factors by which the country loses some thousands every year to the emolument of Glasgow.[52]

In other words Virginian officials should set an example by refusing to accept bills payable in Glasgow and insist that they should be paid from funds available in London. This would put Glasgow merchants to the inconvenience and expense of maintaining large balances in London.

Further light is thrown on trading difficulties in the papers of Francis Jerdone, factor for Alexander Speirs and Hugh Brown of Glasgow.[53] As early as 1757 he pointed out that agents for Glasgow companies were at a disadvantage if they could pay only in bills drawn on Glasgow merchants and not payable in London, and that planters played off Glasgow against Bristol and London. They would hardly ever sell tobacco before the Bristol ships came in, and as these sailed late there was little point in sending a Glasgow ship before May. In 1758 there was no trade between the York River and Glasgow, except that shipped by one factor, Robert Donald, who always seemed to have ships at his disposal. The London merchants sent out ships to load the tobacco they wanted, but ships from Bristol often wanted assurance of a return freight before accepting tobacco. In other words the prime concern of the London merchants was to get tobacco, while those of Bristol were more concerned with outlets for exports and re-exports. The challenge for Glasgow merchants was to beat both at their chosen games.

A good deal of business transacted by Glasgow merchants was handled by Scottish banking houses in London. In June 1772 disaster struck when Fordyce, a Scottish banker in the capital, absconded with a large sum of money; his bank stopped payment and was forced into bankruptcy. In William Lee's words, 'This House stopping like Wildfire ran thro' all the Scottish Connections & produced a Bankruptcy, or stopping of payments, of all the capital Scotch Houses, except two or three, among the rest.'[54] He reckoned that twenty-four Scottish banking partnerships had gone down. The infection spread to Scotland and brought down the Ayr Bank, which was heavily involved in tobacco transactions. The shock wave spread throughout the whole commercial empire of Glasgow, producing effects which were still felt when overtaken by political convulsion.

The Glasgow merchants did not aspire to be great landowners in Virginia and Maryland. They bought the land on which to build stores, warehouses, wharves, and domestic buildings. Some of the larger companies acquired land incidentally, as payment for debt or by establishing claims to the property of insolvent debtors. There seems to be no record of a Glasgow-owned estate producing tobacco for the market. There are however records of two factors who bought plantations and established landowning families in Virginia. It is perhaps significant that neither was linked by family ties with any of the leading merchants and both carried on a good deal of independent trading even while serving as factors. Francis Jerdone came from Jedburgh.[55] He was born in 1730 and was factor for Alexander Speirs and Hugh Brown while still in his twenties. In 1760 he quarrelled with Speirs and Brown because they alleged that he had disobeyed instructions and insisted on treating half the tobacco as shipped on his own account. Speirs and Brown then protested a bill of exchange sent by him. He continued as an active merchant, but did little further business with Scotland. However, in common with other Scottish merchants, the names of compatriots in America continue to figure prominently in his business correspondence.[56] In 1771 he bought a plantation at Providence Forge, Virginia. He supported the Revolution and by the time of his death in 1791 was firmly established as a Virginian landowner.

William Allason was born in the Gorbals, then a small village south of the Clyde.[57] He established himself as a merchant at Falmouth, Virginia, and bills of exchange drawn in 1759 show him doing business with Robert Arthur of Crawfordsdyke, Richard Oswald & Co., a Scottish company operating in London, and John Barns & Co. of Glasgow, names which demonstrated strong commercial ties with Scotland.[58] He was also agent for Baird & Walker, a small Glasgow tobacco firm, but this was only a minor part of his growing business. Baird & Walker ceased trading in 1774, and John Baird wrote to ask Allason whether he had any further claims on the partnership. Allason also carried on a business correspondence with William Homer, a Virginian then at Liverpool. He became very wealthy – in 1792 a letter from his brother David refers to the purchase of two estates for the large sum of £20,000.

The tobacco trade stimulated a lively export trade to America, and several of the larger merchants acquired interests in manufactories. Most of the exports came from very small factories and workshops; but there were some larger establishments producing rope, bottles, and ironware. Some of the shipments to Virginia and Maryland had to be obtained in London or elsewhere, but Scottish-made goods predominated and increased during the century. There is abundant evidence from the papers of Glasgow merchants, colonial merchants, and planters to illustrate the range of goods supplied. For the economic historian there is also much evidence on prices.

A small collection of the papers of one planter, John Smith of Pocket Plantation, Virginia, provide some insights into the Glasgow export trade. Smith dealt with Alexander Banks, factor for Alexander Speirs & Co., at Manchester, Virginia.[59] In 1772 he purchased a total of £300 7s. 1¾d. and was credited with £284 2s. 11d. on account of tobacco purchased by Banks. His purchases included all kinds of textiles, yarn, thread, silk, hats, cutlery, and books. From the range and quantity it seems likely that John Smith kept a store as well as running a plantation.

There is one intersting example of Virginian merchants ordering direct from Glasgow. They were Briggs and Blow of Southampton, Virginia, who dealt with William and Alexander Cunninghame, with Hugh Warden of Glasgow as their purchasing agent.[60] Briggs and Blow imported textiles of all kinds, small quanitities of silk, stockings, cloaks, gloves, ivory combs, ribbon, shoes, hardware, nails, rope, and many small articles from Glasgow. Hugh Warden seems also to have ordered from London on their behalf. A separate invoice must surely relate to an order placed with Briggs and Blow by a schoolmaster since it included writing paper, blank books, pocket books, wafers in boxes, and ink powder; also one dozen Dilworth's spelling books, one dozen prayer books, six Bibles, six Salmon's Grammar, three Gazetteers, three *Whole Duty of Man*, three *Young Men's Companions*, six Watt's hymn books, and '1 doz. histories'. In 1771 William Cunninghame received no remittances, and reacted unfavourably to the suggestion that he should receive payment by tobacco sent for sale on commission: Briggs and Blow owed £760 5s. 0d., and the commission business required large advances from which Cunninghame would receive 'no adequate advantage'. He declined doing further business with them, but it seems that the firm managed to find some money, reduced the debit balance to £342 15s. 2d., and was allowed to order more goods. The incident illustrates the extent to which limited resources in the colonies restrained growth of exports from the Clyde.

Further light on exports from the Clyde to Virginia is found in the Lockhart family papers.[61] Many letters deal with the ship *Blandford*, which was normally used for direct trade between Virginia and Fort Glasgow. The owners were represented at Port Glasgow by James King, and there are references to the companies which supplied the ship with stores, provisions, and equipment.[62] The owners were concerned exclusively with the ship, and accepted and freight consigned to Virginia. Presumably the return cargo to Port Glasgow was tobacco.

The famous Carron Iron Company supplied iron manufactures for John Glassford, George Kippen (one of Glassford's associates) and Alexander Speirs.[63] In 1760 the company wrote to John Glassford soliciting his custom for ironware supplied to North America and the West Indies, and stating that they could supply metalware for sugar grinding, 'dogs for N. American fireplaces', irons, and many articles of cast metal, on terms as good as any in England. In another letter the company asked Glassford to tell his friends that the blast furnace at Carron was in operation and they were ready to take orders for blast iron goods. It seems that Glassford recommended Carron to Bogle, Cross & Munroe, and George Kippen. This was the beginning of what became a mutually profitable association with Glasgow firms which exported to America.[64]

Much of the import and export business generated by John Glassford, but not concerned directly with the tobacco trade, was handled by a separate partnership, George Kippen, John Glassford & Co.[65] Their principal business was the importation of American flax seed and linseed, and the export of linen; but Kippen also handled a large volume of exports to America supplied by Scottish merchants or manufacturers, while corespondents in Bristol handled shipments from that port. Most of the American importers were in New York.

Another Glasgow merchant with wide-ranging interests was George Oswald of Scotstoun, but the surviving records of Oswald, Dennistoun & Co. consist of no more than an incomplete cash book and journal for 1763-7.[66] Oswald imported tobacco, sugar and wine, owned ships and conducted a marine insurance business. He invested in the Glasgow Bottleworks Company which was an important by-product of the export trade.

In addition to the collections – major in bulk or significant in content – which have been surveyed in this chapter there are a large number of partnerships or individuals known only from single or fragmentary sources. There are also several companies which were active before the Revolution, but with records that deal only with the revolutionary or post-war periods; these will be noticed in later chapters.

In concluding this survey of sources for the Glasgow trade it is necessary to emphasise once more how little they reveal about the personal lives of those involved. Alexander Hamilton and the querulous James Lawson come to life, but most corespondents are known only as men who kept accounts and wrote business letters. What cannot be recovered is the optimism, imagination, and energy which drove young men to distant shores in search of fortune if not fame.

Chapter Four

THE HIGHLAND MIGRATION

During the half century preceding the Revolution there was a steady flow of Highlanders to the American colonies. A few may have moved before 1730, but the surviving evidence indicates that migration began about 1732. There was an upsurge, beginning in the late 1760s, and reaching its greatest volume in 1774 and 1775; but for the Revolution this flood of migrants would probably have continued unless the British government had decided to check it. After independence migration resumed, reaching another peak in the early years of the nineteenth century, but in this phase a considerable number, perhaps a majority, went to British North America.[1]

It is a persistent myth that the Highland migration was caused by the failure of the Jacobite risings in 1715 and 1745. The evidence for transportation after 1715 is fragmentary and confined to a few individuals. Most of the prisoners sentenced to transportation were probably sent to the West Indies. The evidence for transportation after 1745 has been more fully investigated, and an estimate that 936 were sentenced to transportation is not likely to be far from the truth.[2] Of these some may have been pardoned after sentence, some lost at sea, and some, in a ship captured by the French, set free in Martinique. Others are known to have been sent to the Bahamas. An estimate that 610 arrived in the American colonies is therefore credible.[3] These were scattered over the several colonies, and the effect in any one of them was slight.

A variation on this fallacy that has commanded more support is that the defeat of the rising in 1745 was the immediate cause of a great voluntary exodus in the following years.[4] The rebellion was not a rising of 'the Highlands', but of some Highland clans. The larger part part, perhaps two-thirds, of the Jacobite army came from areas around Dundee, Kincardine, Aberdeen, and the north-east from Aberdeen to Inverness, while the chieftains of some clans supporting the Pretender had considerable difficulty in raising men for his army, and the rate of desertion was high.[5] Nor do the clans that contributed the largest contingents figure most frequently in the history of Highland settlement in the colonies.[6] Eye witness estimates of numbers are notoriously unreliable, and contemporary stories of a Highland horde have to be discounted. The list of rebels compiled by officials shortly after the event contains 2,590 names. Cumberland claimed to hold 3,471 prisoners in all parts of Scotland after Culloden. The army that had invaded England was not larger than 7,000 and may have been as small as 5,000. Some Jacobite forces had remained in

Scotland. A possible total for the Pretender's army is therefore 9,000.[7]

Whatever the degree of popular enthusiasm for the Stuart cause the initiative came from the chiefs, but in migration they played an inactive part. At the best they were indifferent; at the worst they provided an incentive by raising rents. The decision to emigrate was taken at a much lower level, by individuals, heads of families, or by the small gentry or 'tacksmen'. The tacksmen had originally held land from the chiefs with an obligation to provide men and arms when required for the clan army. As the Highlands became more peaceful this military function became obsolete and the tacksmen contracted with large landowners to provide an annual income in rents; they could be respected local figures and natural leaders of a small community, or distrusted middlemen solely concerned with getting the largest income from rents. The tacksman himself might be dissatisfied with a position which required him to take responsibility for the least satisfactory aspect of clan relationship, while an absentee landlord enjoyed traditional respect and a lion's share of the income. If a tacksman could organise a migration to one of the colonies, he might take with him the labour force and receive the land that would enable him to set up as an independent gentleman.

The determined pacification of the Highlands after the rebellion accentuated established trends. The maintenance of private armies became not only economically burdensome, but positively illegal. The recruitment of Highland gentry into the British army brought them into closer contact, and social competition, with their Lowland and English counterparts. Income was wanted to improve standards of life, and to match the comforts of English country houses. At the same time the vogue for agricultural improvement opened prospects for greater yield with less labour, and often provided a sound reason for getting men to give up uneconomic small crofts. There was a demand for higher income from rents, but also, in many instances, a good price for the crofter who was prepared to move.

There were other long-term forces at work. The Highlands and islands were thinly populated, but the amount of arable land was very limited. Even if crops or livestock could be raised the distance from markets made operations difficult. Traditionally the majority of the people had lived close to subsistence level, and in the eighteenth century their number was increasing.[8] Even without rising rents there would have been an incentive for younger sons, who could see no future on the family croft, to move. What the rent question did was to add to their number many heads of families who could see no hope of providing for their children or even keeping themselves.

Finally it may be noticed that the movement to America was only a part of the Highland migration. A great many moved to the Lowlands, especially Edinburgh and Glasgow; some found their way to England and other

British possessions. The disadvantage of moving to a distant land was that the conditions were often unknown, and a permanent break with the old home was necessary but this was offset during the eighteenth century by an increasing volume of information about life in the colonies, the very advantageous conditions on which land could be obtained, and the knowledge that earlier Highland settlements would provide a familiar environment. After 1745, when Highland dress was forbidden, the colonies offered the additional attraction of a place where this prohibition did not apply. In addition there was the knowledge that Highland immigrants would receive a positive welcome, not only from their own kin, but also from colonial authorities and landowners. The early records of attempts to recruit colonists for Georgia demonstrate that there was sufficient *cause* for Highland crofters to emigrate as early as 1735; what was lacking was information, leadership, and willingness to break traditional ties. During the next forty years these deficiences were made up. Information became widely disseminated, and greater contact with the colonies meant that there was usually at least one local family able to supply a first-hand account of conditions. At an early stage it was observed that if a substantial number from one clan moved, others would follow. Increased information meant that more men of local influence were prepared to take the lead. The contrast between between accounts of prosperity in the colonies and deepening poverty at home, was sufficient to weaken traditional ties.

It is therefore possible to summarise briefly the causes of migration. The Highlands formed a region with poor or undeveloped resources. The people themselves were unable to increase production, and initiative from above – in the form of agricultural improvement or the encouragement of fisheries – came too late, was effective only in limited areas and might reduce the demand for labour. Nevertheless population increased (thanks, perhaps, to a more nutritious diet), while chiefs lost the incentive to subsidise the poor in order to maintain a fighting force. Stories of a country in which land was abundant and poor men could prosper had obvious attractions, and attachment to traditional leaders weakened as the latter showed less and less will or capacity to help their humbler clansmen. These causes operated independently of political events in 1715 and 1745, and the picture might not have been greatly altered if they had not occurred.

The Highlander who decided, or was persuaded, to emigrate, had several courses open to him. If he was lucky enough to have some cash, he could go as an individual or in a family group, pay his own passage, and seek land on arrival. If he had little or no money he might enter into an arrangement with a man of property who intended to emigrate. There were always men anxious to recruit servants to obtain the fifty acres of land often granted for each able-bodied man brought to a colony. The terms of the contract depended upon how much money a man could put towards his passage.

A penniless man would have to accept indentures that bound him to serve for up to seven years. Alternatively the penniless migrant might mortgage himself to the captain of the immigrant ship, who would make his profit by selling their labour to the highest bidder on arrival. This usually meant that the immigrant was bound to service for a term of years, because the employer paid his passage money; but when the demand for labour was acute he might find himself able to contract to work as a normal hired labourer.

Hector St John Crèvecouer described an immigrant from Barra. He arrived without money or friends, without knowledge of the new country, and without experience of farming in a land of woods and trees. He made a good personal impression, and soon after arrival he obtained employment from a prosperous farmer. As he learned the ways of his new environment, his wages were increased and he was able to save. After a few years he acquired land of his own and, when last heard of, enjoyed a modest prosperity.[9]

An anonymous pamphleteer, 'Scotus-Americanus', who wrote from Islay but had spent several years in North Carolina, extolled the benefits of migration.[10] Even those who arrived without money did well, provided that they were ready to work. Their labour was much in demand, and they could make good terms for themselves. Tales of long years spent in virtual slavery were untrue, and very few failed to establish themselves as independent farmers. Other observers were less optimistic; almost all agreed that America offered the best hope for the next generation, but parents who migrated must expect to sacrifice themselves to hard work and penury for the sake of the children. There is however one powerful argument to support the view that a majority of Highlanders found life to their liking. A conservative people, tenaciously attached to the land, could have been easily dissuaded by bad reports from men and women of their own clan who had gone ahead. The very fact the migration continued, increased and was higher than ever before on the eve of the Revolution, is proof that news was encouraging.

One agency which helped to scatter Highlanders to far corners of the world was the British army. As a deliberate policy the British government recruited Highland regiments, and allayed the discontent of the gentry by offering them honourable careers in the service of the crown. A well-known case is that of Allan MacDonald, husband of Flora MacDonald whose fame rested upon assistance rendered to Charles Edward in his escape after Culloden. Allan MacDonald was pardoned for his part in the rebellion, and subsequently accepted a commission in the British army. On retirement, though still a young man, he migrated to North Carolina, became a loyalist leader during the Revolution, and a second exile took his wife and himself back to Scotland. At first the Highland regiments were raised only for service in Scotland, but later service abroad became normal although often accepted unwillingly. However, once introduced to the prospects of a new life many soldiers were ready to accept their discharge and a grant of land in one of the American colonies. Men of the 42nd Highlanders (the Black Watch) received several grants of land in New York between 1765 and 1775. Others may have deserted and found themselves new homes in the wilderness, for the Highland regiments (with the notable exception of the 42nd) became notorious for mutinies when they served abroad under officers not of their own clan.

Much information about the Highland migration was collected by John Maclean and published in 1900.[11] His robust American patriotism prevented him from appreciating why so many Highlanders became Loyalist, and he was apt to treat those who did as knaves or dupes. He identified three periods of migration to North Carolina. The first led to the small settlement at Cross Creek district, which was renamed Campbelltown and is now Fayetteville. Some may have been there by 1729. The second period was during the government of Gabriel Johnston, 1734-52, who was a Scot, educated at St Andrews where he became professor of oriental languages, before embarking on a career as politician and office-seeker. He was an able but unpopular Governor, and among the charges lodged against him was that of showing too great a partiality for Scotsmen, including Jacobite rebels. In 1745 he appointed William McGregor, a rebel of 1715, as a J.P. It was probably with his encouragement that more immigrants came from the Highlands, including a shipload of 350, mainly from Argyll, who arrived in 1739 under the leadership of Neil McNeil. In 1740 Johnston appointed several J.P.s from among the Highlanders at Cross Creek, and more of their relations and friends began to arrive. The legislature assisted emigration by exempting settlers from taxes for ten years and granted £1000 for distribution among needy families. This period of settlement continued until 1747. In the last two years pardoned Jacobites may have been included, but the majority continued to come from Argyll where Jacobitism was unpopular.

The third major movement began in 1769 and continued to 1775. During these years Scottish newspapers and periodicals reported emigration from Argyll, Skye, Sutherland, Ross-shire, and Caithness.[12] The allocation of land was usually on a straight count of heads, including children. The largest grant was 640 acres to a family including three males, wives and children, and the most frequent were grants of 100 acres to single individuals (thirteen males and five females). In 1770 the most common name was McNeil, but in 1774 a large number of MacDonalds came from Raasay and Skye. There is no record of a minister among the Highlanders until the Revd. James Campbell began work in 1757, though he had already been several years in the colony.

In New York the first settlement identified by Maclean was that organised and led by Lachlan Campbell between 1737 and 1739, and recruited mainly from Islay. Campbell had been offered generous terms by the Crown – 200 acres for each family, and exemption from taxes except for a quit rent of 1s. 9¼d. per 100 acres, and 1,000 acres for himself for each family brought over – but the government refused to honour the bargain, and he and his followers had to do their best to acquire private land. He returned to Scotland and served under Cumberland in 1745, but returned to America in 1747 where he died of 'a broken heart'.[13] Finally the Campbell sons got a huge grant of 47,450 acres, known as the Argyll patent, and some survivors of the original party also got land. The settlers were supplemented by disbanded soldiers of the 77th Regiment.

Sir William Johnson received a very large grant of 100,000 acres north of the Mohawk, and large number of Highlanders came from Glengarry, Glenmoriston, Glen Urquhart and Strathglass. Most of them were Catholics. William Johnson died in 1774 and his two sons, John and Guy, became prominent Loyalists during the Revolution, and most Highlanders took the same side. About 600 were disarmed in February 1776, and many – including six chiefs of the McDonnells – were taken prisoner. John Johnson took a party of 130 Highlanders and 120 others to Canada, and they were followed in March 1777 by another party under John McDonnell. Many of these catholic Highlanders served under John Johnson in the Royal Highland Emigrant Regiment and in the King's Royal Regiment of New York, in which all the officers were named McDonnell. Many of their descendants now live at Glengarry in Quebec.

Maclean gave currency to a story well-known among the Glengarry Highlanders. Donald Grant of Moriston, who had served under Prince Charles, led one party on the flight to Canada. In old age he liked to tell of his exploits, and the number under his command increased with repetition. A visitor, wishing to flatter him, said that his leadership had equalled that of Moses himself. To which Grant replied, "Compare *me* to MOSES! Why Moses took forty years in his vain attempts to lead his men over a much shorter distance, and through a mere trifling wilderness in comparison with mine, and he never did reach his destination, and lost half his army in the Red Sea. I brought my people here without the loss of a single man."

The historian who embarks upon the study of emigration and expects to find an abundance of sources is likely to be disappointed. There must have been hundreds of letters from colonists to families and friends at home; few have survived. There must have been correspondence about intending moves, planned or unplanned, but nearly all has disappeared with the passage of time. There are few surviving lists for eighteenth century sailings. The *Scots Magazine* contains occasional references to emigration, but there is no systematic account. To this sparsity of information there is one exception which proves the rule. In 1773 the British government became alarmed by reports of excess migration and instituted an enquiry. For two years therefore there is a large amount of information about sailings, passengers, their place of origin, their destination, and their reasons for emigration.

The results of this enquiry are preserved in the Treasury records.[14] So far as Scotland is concerned the lists are probably far from complete. Many parties sailed from small harbours and escaped investigation by customs officers, and when a ship called at several ports the less active officials were likely to assume that someone else had done the work. Only at Lerwick and for one shipload did the customs officers describe at length the reasons given for emigration. Nevertheless the lists probably provide a fair sample of the emigrants and their motives.

All the emigrants questioned at Lerwick came from Sutherland or Caithness. Several seem to have been farmers of some substance who had seen better days, and included some men of advanced years – four of sixty, one seventy one, and one seventy five – but there were also several young single men. Most of the farmers gave hard times, rising prices, oppressive demands for services from the landlords, and a rapid increase in rents as their reasons for migration. Not all were agriculturalists; three were shoemakers, one a shopkeeper, and two tailors. One had been a schoolmaster, and another, having education, hoped for a position in Carolina as a teacher or clerk. Almost all those questioned said that they had been encouraged to go by good reports from friends or relations in America. Typical was the comment of one farmer that 'he was induced to emigrate by advices received from his friends in America, that provisions are extremely plenty and cheap, and the price of labour very high, so that People who are temperate and laborious have every chance of bettering their circumstances.' Another said that he had 'very promising prospects by advices from his Friends in Carolina, as they had bettered their circumstances greatly since they went there.' The schoolmaster had been assured that he could find a more profitable school, while a shoemaker had heard that 'tradesmen of all kinds will find large encouragement.'

A lengthy report from an unnamed port summarised the reasons given for emigrating from parts of Argyll as advanced rents, and the conversion of arable land and cattle pastures to sheep walks. Labourers declared that they could not support their families, and that it was from no other motive that 'they quit a Country which above all others they would wish to live in.' All in this shipload came from Glenorchy or Appin except two families from Lismore. At Greenock the reporting officers failed to make full enquiry into the reason for leaving; having ascertained that one phrase seemed to suit all cases, they used it for each individual, even the wives and children – 'For

High Rents and better Encouragement'. Another Greenock list varied the causes between 'High rents and oppression' and 'Poverty occasioned by want of work.'

A few of the emigrants came from the upper ranks of society. There was a 'gentleman' of twenty who went out to be a merchant, a young man of twenty-one to follow his trade as a surgeon, some weavers from Glasgow, a merchant from Edinburgh, and his wife who went 'to comfort her husband.' The large party from Glenorchy included one gentleman, who was probably a tacksman, and his family. The party from Appin included one former army officer with a servant and illegitimate daughter, one 'gentleman farmer' with his son, and one former ship master with his wife and son.

The general impression given by the result of this enquiry is confirmed by an unpublished and unsigned letter from Harris written in 1772.[15] The writer said that the people had formerly been docile and much attached to their chiefs; but recently high rents, hard labour, and absentee landlords had changed all this.

> They were roused from their servile state and former dependence on those who seemed no longer to treat them with lenity and attachments. That Spirit of Emigration has now got in among them which in a few years will carry the Inhabitants of the Highlands and Islands of Scotland into North America.

They had no wish to move to the lowlands, to work amongst a people whom they despised.

> They launched out into a new World breathing a Spirit of Liberty and a Desire of every individual becoming a Proprietor.

They believed that they could buy land cheaply, or rent it at trifling rates, or dreamed 'of conquering it from the Indians with the Sword – the most desirable way of holding any for a Highlander.'

Church records may supply further information. Unfortunately the Church of Scotland General Assembly papers have not been catalogued after 1741, and a large collection in the Scottish Catholic Archives have not been catalogued at all.[16] The main concern of the Churches was, of course, with affairs in Scotland, but there may have been requests for ministers or priests and these would include information about the number, clan, and religious affiliation of settlers. The correspondence of Catholic priests in the islands and catholic districts on the mainland, may include information about individual or collective plans to emigrate.

Information about what the emigrants did on arrival may be easier to gather. Land grants are recorded, wills are preserved, and evidence of litigation survive. These sources may be easy to locate, but are laborious to work. Literary evidence of settler experiences in the colonists is available but limited. Colonists who were anxious to preserve their separate identity, and whose native tongue was not English, left few letters and no reminiscences.

The path of the historians of eighteenth-century Highland emigration cannot therefore be easy. At the outset he will encounter a host of deeply-rooted misconceptions; in mid-course he will discover that the readily available sources are meagre and unevenly distributed; before the end of the road he may find himself immersed in the task of tracking obscure individuals through the voluminous records of land offices and colonial courts. When the task is complete he may be doubtful of what he has achieved. The volume of Highland migration was not comparable to that from contemporary Protestant Ireland or the later migration from Catholic Ireland and insignificant when compared with the great tide of Italian and Slav migration early in this century. It left a less distinctive mark than the German migration to Pennsylvania and the mid-west, or the Scandinavian settlement in Minnesota. Moreover, except in the enthusiastic claims of St Andrew Societies, little survives in oral tradition. Nevertheless it was an important event in Scottish history, and today Americans of Highland descent far outnumber those who remain in the homeland.

The transportation of prisoners.

The Scottish Record Office has but one certificate, dated 17 October 1716 and signed at Williamsburg, Virginia, stating that Robert Stewart, a jacobite prisoner taken at Preston, was to be bound to serve Captain Edward Trafford for seven years.[17]

For the aftermath of the '45 the evidence in the Scottish Record Office is almost as meagre but of greater importance.[18] The first document, dated 31 March 1746, contains the signatures of 125 Highland prisoners. The second, of the same date, is an indenture between these signatories and Samuel Smith of London, binding them to serve him for life. In the same document Smith assigned the prisoners to John Hanbury for shipment to the American colonies, to serve him there for seven years, and then to remain in America 'according to the express condition and terms of His Majesty's most gracious pardon'.

There are a number of points of interest about this document. Samuel Smith of London and Richard Gildart of Liverpool obtained the contract for the transportation of prisoners. They received £5 a head, and expected to make a profit by selling them in the colonies. The royal pardon for the crime of high treason was given on condition that the persons pardoned should bind themselves by indentures for life to Gildart or Smith to serve them or their assignees in the colonies. This would allow Gildart or Smith to prescribe the actual terms of service, but the document strengthens the supposition of Sir Bruce Seton and Jean Arnot that the normal term served was seven years.[19] Of more puzzling significance is the date – two weeks before Culloden, and six weeks before the first official record of a government decision on the treatment of prisoners. In their study Seton and Arnot depended mainly upon the State Papers Domestic, supplemented by jail books of various towns and court records, but unfortunately these sources do not reveal the destination of those sentenced to transportation.

Recruiting colonists for Georgia.

It seems likely that the first Highlanders in Georgia were three Mackay brothers who arrived in 1734. The eldest, Patrick, had lost money by speculation, and had been forced to sell his estates in Sutherland. It is not known whether the Mackay brothers brought servants with them, but it is unlikely that Highland gentlemen travelled without some humbler members of their clan. Later they claimed 640 acres on account of thirty white servants imported in 1736.[20] It was probably at the suggestion of the Mackays that General Oglethorpe decided to recruit more Highland colonists to defend his southern frontier, and on 16 July 1735 the council of trustees approved instructions to another brother, Lieutenant Hugh Mackay, to agree with and assemble for shipment 110 freemen and servants, together with fifty women and children. The trustees agreed to pay for their passages and apportion land among them. Another Scotsman, Captain George Dunbar, who had already been in Georgia, was to make arrangements for their passage in his ship.[21]

On 24 July 1735 Hugh Mackay wrote to the trustees.[22] He had met some gentry in Ross-shire who seemed who seemed to be 'very hearty in the affair I am employ'd in', but in Sutherland he had found Lord Sutherland and other gentlemen 'not so very favourable for fear of losing those poor creatures, who they look on to be their property as Much as their Cattle'. He had yet to get among his own tribe; but his general impression was that it would be unwise 'to send so large a Ship as that in which Capt Dunbar came from Georgia'.

> A Damnable Practise has prevailed and been carry'd on for Some time past, and us'd at this very time, Viz. Bind Servants by their indentures for Georgia and Ship them off for Jamaica, this practice, which I am credibly informed is carryed on in most of the Seaports of Scotland, frightens the Vulgar from treating w^t or coming near any person that design to carry them to a better place.

On 1 September Mackay was more optimistic. 'Notwithstanding of the Strongest opposition, and carried on the Vilest Manner, that is by under hand Agents instilling terrible apprehensions in the people's minds' he had made some headway, and believed that but for want of cash many would be prepared to 'embrace this opportunity'.[23] If those willing to depart could be got away, and 'accounts transmitted here of their being happily settled' the trustees would be able to obtain all the settlers they wanted from Scotland.

He acknowledged his debt to the clergy for help, and particularly to one minister from Inverness whose goodwill proceeded 'from a principle of Humanity Christian Charity'.

> Shocked to see his fellow creatures in the utmost Slavery and endeavour'd to be condemned so by their Masters by false aspersions against the scheme of settling the Colony, he did his utmost to open their eyes.

Mackay's own family responded, and he requested that two nephews and a brother might be included in his grant. One nephew was on military service in Holland but 'will be an American if I live two years'. Indeed he was 'fully persuaded that if the Colony subsists but three years there will be more Mackays in America than in the Highlands.' On 21 October Captain Dunbar reported that the ship was now overfull, and that he might have to turn some back. He was very pleased with a minister, Mr John McLeod, who had joined them and 'with respect to most of our embarcation Ile venture to say they do not leave cleverer fellows behind them'.[24]

A letter of 26 February 1736/7 to the trustees from Daniel McLachlan reveals so much about conditions in Highlands, and the obstacles to emigration, that it deserves a lengthy extract. He had been travelling among the clans:

> and as I am intimately acquainted with, and nearly related to, the most of 'em; I cant be a Stranger to their Temper and Disposition. . . . Our clans are so very attached to their Chieftains and Heads of Tribes, that no considerable Number of them can ever be prevailed upon to leave their Country without their Leaders. – And those Leaders again, as they have never been from Home are afraid to venture into any foreign Country; but at the same time they put so much Confidence in, and have such affection for one another, that they would go in Shoals to any Colony in America, provided there was a Sufficient Detachment of their own people planted there before 'em; and if they were sure to raise from the Produce of their Labour and a Comfortable Subsistence. – In short, there only wants Some one of the Highland Clans to lead the way, and all the rest may easily be prevailed upon to follow.[25]

He proposed that he should be commissioned to raise a contingent, beginning with his own clan, and 'Such members of leading Families as would be considerable enough to pave the way, and Decoy the rest into happiness and plenty'. The project would be a countinuing one and 'I believe in my Conscience, was this plan vigorously pursued, we should have in a very few years as many trussed up Plaids in Georgia as in the Highlands of Scotland'. These, he said, were the very people to succeed in a new colony: familiar with hardship, simple in their needs but 'withall a Set of bold, Courageous, Nervous, able-bodied Men'. In 1737 he proposed to bring out one hundred men, without expense to the trustees, if they were promised land. If not they would go elsewhere, and 'wherever they plant themselves the rest of the clans will follow 'em'.

Apparently the trustees did not take up McLachlan's proposal, but his observations have the ring of authenticity, and his forecast of the snowball effect of successful settlement was borne out by events.[26] The next forty years did not see more Highlanders established in America than in Scotland, but their number was considerable.

Highlanders in Georgia participated in the unsuccessful attack on St Augustine in 1740, and distinguished themselves at the battle of Bloody Marsh on St Simon's Island in 1742. There were two Highland military units at this time – the Highland Troop of Rangers and a Highland Independent Company raised by John Mackintosh – but by 1743 it was becoming difficult to find enough volunteers.[27] This was not because men were in short supply but because their success as settlers made them reluctant to leave their farms. For this reason Oglethorpe welcomed thirty-eight members of the 43rd Highland Regiment who were sent to Georgia as a punishment for mutiny and eventually disbanded in 1749.[28]

The state of Georgia has published the records of early land grants, and from them it is possible to derive much information about the settlement and progress of the Highlanders.[29] The entry claims for 1733-50 include a number of Scottish names, including ten called Mackintosh and eight Mackays. Others included McBean, Munro, McLeod, McDonald, Baillie, Dunbar, and Cuthbert. Sir Patrick Houston (noted in chapter II) and two members of his families received grants. Seven who received small grants were disbanded soldiers.

The Crown grants of 1755-75 show that some Highlanders had become very large landowners. Lachlan Mackintosh had 8,512 acres in St Andrew, 2,300 in St David, 900 on St Simon's Island, 500 in St Matthew, and 200 on Cumberland Island. George Mackintosh had a principal holding of 6,588 acres in St Andrew; and other grants in St Thomas, St Patrick, St Mary, and Sapello Island. Several other Highlanders had grants of comparable size. In addition to the grantees most of the tenants and servants would be Scots, many of the same clan as the owner.

The first major Highland settlement was on the north bank of the Altamaha River, and later many settled on the islands and in other parishes. General Oglethorpe's first intention was to provide for frontier defence by settling warlike Highlanders on the colonial frontier, but he was also impressed by their success as farmers. He seems to have developed a strong respect for them, and on one occasion demonstrated his pleasure by wearing Highland dress during a visit to one of their settlements. His interest probably explains the rapid progress of Highland leaders into the ranks of the colony's greater landowners.

The area north of the Altamaha River became St Andrew Parish (now McIntosh County), and remained the principal centre of Highland settlement, but the land grants show substantial holdings in St John (now Liberty County), to the north, and St David and St Patrick (Glynn County), and St Thomas and St Mary (Camden County) to the south. They were also much in evidence on St Simon's and Sapello Islands, and on other small offshore islands.

The success and wealth of the larger Highland landowners, and the continued respect they enjoyed, probably explains why there were few Loyalists among the Highlanders of Georgia. By the time of the Revolution they were fully assimilated, and the oldest were amongst the 'founding fathers' of the colony. It is also probable that the passage of time had weakened ties with the home country as Georgia does not seem to have had a large share in the Highland migration of later years. By then North Carolina and New York beckoned to the impoverished crofter.

No colony was more attractive to the Highlanders than North Carolina, and none has received more attention from scholars.[30] Local tradition maintains that Highlanders first settled in 1729, but no documentary evidence has been found for earlier than 1732, when grants of land were made to John Innes, Hugh Campbell, and William Forbes. The law of North Carolina stipulated fifty acres for each person brought into the colony and the total grants received by these three indicates that they were responsible for seventy-six people. Some indentured servants may have been among the large number of grants of Highlanders in 1734-7; but as many grants were for large tracts over 400 acres this probably indicates the arrival of more men of substance with followers. They settled on the Cape Fear River, about 100 miles north of Wilmington, and established a small trading centre at Cross Creek. Innes came from Caithness, but most of the others from Islay, Jura, Kintyre and other mainland parts of Argyll. When it became necessary to find a name for their county capital they called it Campbelltown while the country itself became Cumberland.[31] In all 691 people with Highland names received land grants between 1732 and 1775, while many who came out as indentured servants or penniless immigrants saved enough to buy from private owners.[32]

One surviving indenture for service in Carolina is on a printed sheet, which suggests that the practice was so widespread that a standard form was used, with only the names, date, and other specific information filled in by hand.[33] This indenture, was dated 31 January 1737, records a contract between John McLeod, 'indweller in Edinburgh', and William Campbell, who was sixteen years of age and was to be apprentice and servant to McLeod, for four years in Carolina 'or any other of his Majesty's Plantations'. Young Campbell got his fare to America, clothes, meat, drink, washing, lodging, and all other 'necessaries' during his period of service.

It is probable that McLeod made a business of providing servants for employers in the colonies to whom he would sell his rights, or perhaps to men who were collecting parties for emigration to America.

There is a good deal of information about migration to North Carolina in the papers of the MacAlester family.[34] Alexander MacAlester came to North Carolina from Islay in 1736, settled near Campbelltown, and was a member of the Provincial Congress in 1775 and 1776. He was married three times, and had four surviving children by his second and as many as eleven by his third wife. His brother, Hector, spent some time in North Carolina, and then returned to live at Monyquill on the Isle of Arran. The most interesting part of the MacAlester papers consists of letters from Hector to Alexander.

In the first letter, 26 June 1754, Hector declared his intention of returning to Carolina after his long absence, and described his efforts to gather and despatch a party of emigrants. Having learned that a Captain Neill Campbell had failed to find passengers awaiting him in Jura, he had sent a message offering to get him his full complement. Meanwhile the owners of a snow, the *Argyll,* had promised to have the vessel ready for him between March and July of the following year and 'on that I have fixed since I can do no better and have gott all my people settled for this year'. He then says that Mr Neill McLeod 'whome the Colloney wanted over to be their Minister was to goe with me & as he is a very popular man amongst the Commonality, would incourage numbers to leave this County so youll not fail to advise to write preferringly for him again, he is a good preacher and full master of the highland tongue & am sure w'd please all partys'.

In 1766 or 1767 Alexander wrote to Hector, giving news of friends in North Carolina. One was a commander of a snow, and another was working as a saddle-maker. On 15th March 1769 Hector wrote of his plans to return to North Carolina as 'their are some hundreds of famylies in this Island, and our neighbouring County Argyleshire, determined to leave their Country, and have applyd to me to goe with them to Carolina'. He had intended to send his nineteen year old son to Norfolk in Virginia 'alongst with a friend of his that is going there to keep Store', but this fell through because the owners of the store made a deal with another lad. On 21st June 1770 a man called John Boyd wrote to Alexander from Balnakile recommending three young men who were bound for the Cape Fear district. They were 'clever pretty lads . . . fit for Sea or Land . . . and would pass for Gentlemen'.

There is a fragment of a letter dated 26 July 1770 from Angus McCuaig of Assobos in Islay, and a full letter from him dated 22 August 1771. In the latter he makes enquiries about North Carolina—how cattle were reared, the means by which the land was cultivated for grain. The bearer of the letter was Allan Dugald (or McDugald) 'a good Scoller and a worthy man'. He also said that Hector intended to go to America the following Spring.

On 29 November 1770 Alexander wrote a letter addressed to 'Der Cusin' comparing conditions in Scotland unfavourably with those in America. On the same day he also wrote to Hector lamenting the fact that he had not fulfilled his intention of coming over. Again he extolled the virtues of North Carolina, but doubted whether he would see his brother again 'as you have not given me any mor ashurance than you did Eight and twenty years ago'. It was probably in reply to this letter that Hector wrote on 12 September 1771, 'some hundred famylies goeing this year from the Island of Skye, and added, 'a few goes from this Island'.

On 15 November 1771 John Boyd wrote from Balnakile an unpunctuated letter to be delivered by 'a friend . . . who with his Father and a Large Family is Going from the Isle of Skye to Settle in North Carolina the Father is bred a Surgeon I need not recommend him to you as his Qualification in that Business will do for him but the young Gentleman I am so anxious about his name is Dugald Campbell who is I have reason to believe a good Classical scholar writes a Good hand and understands figures'.

In October 1771 a James McAlester wrote to Alexander. 'I would wish to here in General how the poore people that went from this Country last year is Satled'. He gave the names of thirteen from his locality of whom he would particularly welcome news.

An undated letter from Alexander is perhaps a reply as he reports that the people who had come over in the previous year are all doing well 'but as you observe they are the poorest Sort that comes & no Dout meet with some Difficulty be fore they can fix themselves'. On 22 January 1774 he wrote to Hector that 'we have had com this year upwards of Seven hundred Soles from Skaye and the Neburing Isles & a great many Expected nixt year'.

In the last letter in the series, undated, Alexander writes to Hector of alarm in the colonies over the 'pernicious acts [of parliament] which will bring america to mear Slavery if they should be put into execution'. He served in the Provincial Congress 1775 and 1776. His son, Alexander jr, had ten children, and the family continued to play a prominent part in North Carolina.

The anonymous pamphlet, published in Glasgow in 1773 by 'Scotus Americanus', provides an insight into the arguments and inducements offered to highlanders.[35] It began with a strong attack upon landlords, especially those who were absentees. In the Highlands and Isles thousands of men and women 'without means, without encouragement, at a distance from market, against climate, and soil too, in many places' were expected to 'cultivate and enclose wide extended heaths, rugged mountains, and large barren morasses'. Ignoring these handicaps the owners raised rents, and then complained of emigration.

For those who decided to leave the country North Carolina was 'of all our colonies – the most proper for Highlanders of any degree to remove to, if they want to live in s state of health, ease, and independence'. Many from Argyll and the western isles had already settled at Cross Creek, known as New Campbelltown. There were also Highlanders in Anson County. The would-be settler was advised to seek out a portion of crown land or unpatented land, or secure an order from the governor. The order would be delivered to the surveyor, and when he had made a survey the patent would be registered. The cost of taking up 640 acres would be £10, with a quit rent of 2s. 6d. for 100 acres. A man who arrived with £500 in his pocket, could live as well as men with £500 a year in Scotland. There were many cattle, larger than those in the Highlands, Slaves cost from £25 to £40 and were well-treated.

Poor men, without passage money, could nevertheless better themselves. They would arrive in the colony as 'redemptioners' at the disposal of the captain who would sell them to cover his costs. But the demand for labour was so great that the poor immigrant would be almost certain to find someone prepared to pay their passage money. They would then be under contract to an employer, but as free men. The author concluded that 'Upon the whole . . . the best country in the world for a poor man to go to, and do well'.

While the opportunities for crofters received most emphasis and space, the pamphlet noted that there were also much demand for men with professional skills. The Church of England was the established religion, but Presbyterians were most numerous. 'Devines . . . might here find decent livings; lawyers and physicians are here respected; professors of science are as yet few; teachers of youth are much carressed and wanted'.

Robert Hogg was a Scottish merchant who became prominent in North Carolina. His original business was in Charleston, South Carolina, but his main field of activity was supply of the Highland settlers in North Carolina through stores at Wilmington and Cross Creek. He took up permanent residence at Wilmington, and became one of the wealthiest men in the colony.[36] His success inspired his brother, James, to bring a party of Highlanders to the colony, and his papers provide useful information about the way in which emigration could be planned.[37]

James Hogg was born in East Lothian but became a tacksman in the parish of Borlum, near Thurso. He does not seem to have been popular locally, as many papers deal with the eviction of sub-tenants and disputes arising over objects impounded after the wreck of a ship. In 1773 he formed a plan to take two hundred emigrants to North Carolina. He made a contract with James Inglis of Edinburgh to provide a ship, and the terms offered to the emigrants were reasonable. Unfortunately the ship ran aground off the Shetlands and put into Lerwick. A long delay ensued, and James Hogg sued the captain of the ship for refusing to feed the passengers.

He handled the case for himself and the emigrants, but seems to have left alone for America before it was settled. The subsequent history of the emigrants does not appear in the papers, but it is probable that they eventually reached North Carolina.[38] Other items in the James Hogg papers deal with the business that he established in North Carolina. His brother became a Loyalist, and some papers deal with his attempts to return from New York and acquire North Carolinian citizenship.[39]

There are a few surviving letters addressed to Colin Shaw, who emigrated from Jura at some time before 1764, and became a merchant with a business in Cumberland County.[40] These include two from Donald Campbell, and one each from Duncan and Angus Shaw. They give information about emigration from Jura, and also served as letters of introduction for immigrants travelling to North Carolina.[41]

Despite the participation of many North Carolina Highlanders on the Loyalist side during the Revolution, their settlements survived. Lady Liston, wife of Sir Robert Liston, British minister in Washington 1796-1800, kept a diary and visited a Scottish district about twenty miles from Fayetteville:

> The Gallic language is still prevalent amongst them, their Negroes speak it, and they have a clergyman who preaches in it.[42]

Between 1821 and 1824 an anonymous Scottish traveller and diarist also visited the Highland settlements, met a dozen or more of the original settlers (probably survivors of the 1770–75 migration) who still spoke Gaelic or broken English, and attended a service 'performed in the Scottish Presbyterian form'.[43]

In 1851 the *Raleigh Register* reprinted from the *Inverness Courier* a letter from a minister who had served in the region settled by the Highlanders. He said that the Gaelic language was still spoken 'in all its purity by many in these counties'. On a recent Sabbath he had assisted at a service four miles from his own home at which over 150 had taken their seats at the communion table. He was able to preach in the language of their childhood which many had not heard from the pulpit for ten years. Before his own arrival in the state, the Revd. Colin Maciver from Stornoway had preached in Gaelic, but he had been infirm for many years and died in 1850. Though it is clear from this account that Gaelic was a dying language in North Carolina, Scottish traditions were still very much alive. The *North Carolina Presbyterian*, a religious newspaper, had over 800 'Macs' on its list of subscribers, and the presbytery of Fayetteville had thirteen 'Macs' and seven others of Highland descent among its clerical members. It was known in the Synod of North Carolina as 'the Scotch Presbytery'.[44]

While this evidence shows the tenaciousness of Highland speech and custom in North Carolina, it also suggests that the descendants of the Highland settlers had not played a prominent part in the state outside the counties in which they had settled.[45] If their presence had been more familiar, the *Raleigh Register* would hardly have thought it worthwhile to draw the attention of their readers to its existence. Moreover oral traditions seem to have been weak. According to the minister's letter the first recorded immigration was in 1749, when Neil NacNeil brought a large party from Kintyre, but this was at least fifteen and perhaps twenty years after the earliest settlement.

The great uninhabited tracts of northern New York offered opportunities for adventurous settlers. Much of the land had been distributed in huge grants, and the owners were anxious to increase its value by attracting settlers. Highlanders seemed to be the ideal colonists to endure the hardships of winter and to cultivate a wilderness. On 20 December 1749 Robert Livingston and Julian Verplanck drew up an advertisement, which they endorsed 'to be sent to Scotland'.[46] They would 'grant lands to People that will come over to the Province within one year after the date for settling two or three hundred families'. Each family would have as many acres of new upland as they required, rent free for ten years, and thereafter to pay a peck of wheat a year for each acre. The leases would be granted for the natural lives of any two persons named by the lessee.

Attractive terms did not always mean that the land would live up to expectations, or that the agreement would be honoured once the settlers were secured. In 1733 General Sir John Reid described an experience which may have not have been untypical. On arrival a party of Highlanders had been offered inferior land on less advantageous terms that those which they had accepted before sailing. He hoped to get them the land and terms originally promised, but failing that he intended to grant them land on Otter Creek near Crown Point. This he would offer for ten years rent free and a cash advance of £200 per family; thereafter they would pay an annual rent of sixpence (New York currency) a year for each acre.[47]

These misfortunes were less likely to befall immigrants whose terms were nogotiated by a Highland chief, or who held land on lease from him. There are several examples of large grants of this kind. An undated draft of a grant of 47,450 acres to Donald Campbell, adjoining 10,000 acres already granted to him.[48] The grant was to be administered by trustees – named as Duncan Reid, Alexander Montgomery, Alexander MacNachten, Neil Shaw, Henry Van Vleck, Archibald Campbell, George Campbell, Neil Gillespie, Alexander MacLean and Ennis Graham. One of the conditions was that the trustees should hold 500 acres for the support of a minister and a schoolmaster.

Further study of the Highlanders in New York demands intensive work on the records preserved in the New York State Archives at Albany, and in county archives. Information about land grants can be found in the State Archives, and there is also a large collection of the manuscripts of Sir

William Johnson, supplementing those already published. These include a
rent roll of the Kingsborough patent on which the catholic Highlanders
were settled. There is further information about this patent in the
Montgomery County Archives, Fonda, New York. These archives hold
biographical notes on 125 settlers – many of them Highlanders – on the
Kingsborough patent prepared in 1959 by Mr Duncan Fraser. The names
were identified from a ledger of 1774 at Johnston Hall, Johnston, New
York, and the biographical information obtained from a wide variety
of sources.[49] The standard grant to individuals was 100 acres, not freehold
but with a low annual rent. As the majority of Highlanders on the
Kingsborough patent went to Canada during the Revolution, a search for
information about individuals will take the enquirer to the archives of
Ontario and Quebec.

Chapter Five

FAITH, EDUCATIO N AND INTELLECT

At the beginning of the eighteenth century Scotland commanded respect from those American churches which took their theology from Calvin. The Church of Scotland was, wrote Cotton Mather, 'of all God's churches, anywhere under heaven, the dearest unto Him'; it was 'fine gold', and the purity of its discipline endeared it 'to all lovers of goodness'.[1] The Scottish presbyterians had triumphed over both Catholic plots and royal attempts to force episcopacy upon the people. This record of 'dissent' did not endear Scottish presbyterianism to the anglican upper class of the southern colonies, but for this very reason it was admired by other denominations seeking legal equality.

Given this good opinion the Scottish Church missed an opportunity. There was no great enthusiasm on the part of ministers, whether of moderate or evangelical persuasion, to cross the Atlantic and plant the good seed in new soil. The Church offered abundant opportunities at home for both the ambitious and the idealistic. There were few better lives for a man with some learning, and a wish to do well, than that of a parochial minister in Scotland. If there were no splendid rewards comparable to English bishoprics, there were professorships at universities and calls to influential city parishes. Many did cross the Atlantic before the Revolution, but of them all only John Witherspoon was a man of distinction and he required much persuasion before agreeing to go.

The triumph of presbyterianism in Scotland made the colonies attractive to Scottish episcopalians, who now found the prospects of advancement in their own country severely limited. James Blair, graduate of Marischal College, Aberdeen, led the way to Virginia in 1685. He became president of the yet unbuilt William and Mary College, and the Bishop of London's commissary.[2] He held both positions into extreme old age, until his death fifty-eight years later. In 1697 Blair was summoned to Lambeth to answer charges levied against him by Governor Andros. He was alleged to have packed the colonial ministry with Scottish clergy who troubled the Council 'with complaints about their salaries'. There were also specific charges against individuals and an accusation that Blair had misappropriated funds subscribed for the college. The meeting was attended by Bishop Compton of London and Archbishop Tenison.[3]

In the ensuing argument Blair counterattacked, accused Governor Andros of obstructing progress on the college, and presumably defended the Scottish clergy. Bishop Compton asserted that 'if anyone was responsible for the presence of Scottish clergy he was', and Blair was cleared of all the charges against him. This triumph, and Blair's many influential years in Virginia, ensured a strong Scottish element in the Church of England in Virginia. It also led to close personal ties, continued in one well-documented case for several generations, with King's and Marischal Colleges at Aberdeen.[4]

Scottish episcopalians also played an important part in the middle colonies. The Revd. Charles Inglis was the major figure in the Church of England in New York, and in 1754 a young episcopalian called William Smith began a career at the College of Philadelphia (later the University of Pennsylvania) which was to be of great consequence in the history of American higher education.

Whatever the influence of individual episcopalians, the great majority of Scots in the colonies were presbyterians and the influence of the Kirk was widely diffused even where no congregations were formed. It is impossible to measure or even to guess at the influence of individuals, but it must have been significant that so many colonial children first learned their letters from Scottish tutors. Some wealthy colonial families could afford to engage a young man recommended by a minister or professor; others had to be content with an indentured servant with enough basic knowledge to pass it on to children.[5] It may be that the American reputation of Scottish philosophy owed something to the pride of young tutors who knew nothing of what Hutcheson, Reid, or Adam Smith taught, but were keen to extol their native country as a land of learning.

Scottish presbyterianism had its controversies, and these were reflected in the colonies. The moderates, who had adopted a relaxed form of Calvinist theology, fought for control of the church with the evangelical or popular party. In America the 'old side' and 'new side' represented a different division of opinion. "Old side" presbyterians stressed church discipline, the authority of Synods, and doctrinal uniformity; the 'new side', responding to evangelical enthusiasm, stressed personal relationship with God, the freedom of ministers and congregations to respond to the Spirit, and pastors who were dedicated rather than learned. In Scotland both parties required an educated ministry, but the moderates were strongly entrenched in the upper and professional classes and respected leadership by a social élite, while the evangelicals were more likely to detect evidence of grace in those of humble origin. The leaders of the Scottish enlightenment were pre-eminently moderates, but paradoxically John Witherspoon, who was so important in the diffusion of enlightenment thought in America, was brought over to save the College of New Jersey from capture by the 'old side'.

The disputes between the moderates and the evangelical or popular party did not produce a formal division of the Church of Scotland, but in 1773 a serious split developed over the right of the patron (usually the crown or a local laird) to appoint ministers to parishes. This led to a secession and the formation of the Associate Presbytery in 1733 and an Associate Synod in 1744.[6] In 1747 the seceders split over the oath required from burgesses of Edinburgh, Glasgow and Perth, which was introduced in 1745 as a means of detecting rebels and ensuring that others affirmed their loyalty. It included the sentence: 'I profess and allow with all my heart, the true religion presently professed within this realm, and authorised by the laws thereof'. For some secessionists this meant no more than the exclusion of Roman Catholics, but for the majority it was taken to mean recognition of the authority of the established Church of Scotland over all congregations. This in turn involved the much more serious issue of separation between church and state. The Burghers, as the minority were styled, saw obedience to civil authority as a Christian duty; their opponents, or Anti-Burghers, proclaiming the entire separation of church and state, insisted that the civil power need not be obeyed in ecclesiastical matters if it confliected with the claims of conscience. The original secession had been a plea for liberty, but rival seceders showed no tolerance for each others' views. Both groups were vigourous and anxious to propagate their views, including missionary efforts in the colonies.

Some Scots migrating to America in the middle years of the century carried with them secession views and soon wished to form their own congregations. In other instances some of the established congregations may have been convinced by secession arguments. In the colonies little significance was attached to the patronage controversy, but the secessionists included in their appeal a strong attack upon the moral laxity tolerated by the established churches in Scotland and England. In 1774 the Associate Presbytery declared that:

> All ranks of persons have corrupted their Ways. Our Nobility and Gentry have, for the most part, burst the Lord's Bonds assunder, and Cast away his Cords from them. Our Ministers, Burgesses, and Commons of all sorts have turned away backward, and foresaken the Holy One of Israel. The whole Head is sick, and the whole Heart is faint.[7]

From these causes had flowed a 'flood of errors', including Deism, Arianism, Arminianism, and Latitudinarian, Independent, and Sectarian extremes. It may be far-fetched to attribute much influence to the small and largely obscure congregations of the secession in America. Nevertheless it is a matter of record that there is a close correspondence between this picture of corruption in Great Britain and a persistent theme in Revolutionary rhetoric which argued for separation from a decadent and morally contaminated society. The arguments of the Anti-Burghers against the recognition of civil authority in matters of conscience had an even stronger appeal in the colonies as they began to question British rule.[8]

The account of secession in Scotland is further complicated by the appearance of yet one more seceding group. This was the Relief Church formed in 1773, which like the seceders repudiated civil authority in ecclesiastical affairs, but went further to question the right of assemblies and synods to bind their members in matters of faith. Each congregation was a church in itself and could make its own decisions, but further fragmentation was avoided by adopting a relaxed view of the requirements for church membership. While the Church of Scotland and both secession churches accepted the Solemn League and Covenant as a declaration of faith and principles to which all must adhere (even if interpretations differed), the Relief Church denied the right to insist upon acceptance of any man-made covenant as a test of faith. All believing Christians were welcome and would not be examined rigorously on the precise way in which they understood the faith. The Relief secession came somewhat too late to effect argument during the Revolution, but an American Reform synod adopted very similar ideas.

Many of the Highland emigrants, expecially to New York, were Catholic. A good deal is known about one group, the Glengarry Highlanders, who settled shortly before the Revolution, became Loyalists, and migrated to the province of Quebec, where their descendents still live. Links with the catholic church in Scotland remained close, but at present little is known of the details or personalities.[9] The protestant domination in all colonies was such that catholics could not expect to occupy more than a place on the sidelines of developing American society.

The record of Scottish influence upon American university education has recently been thoroughly explored.[10] The story begins with James Blair, although he did not aspire to be an educational innovator. William and Mary was an anglican foundation, but Oxford and Cambridge were unsuitable models for a tiny institution in a society without traditions of higher education, and it seems that Blair adopted the methods and curriculum that he had known at Aberdeen. Students attended lectures, and were examined on them. The curriculum included familiar grounding in Latin language and literature, but its distinctive characteristic was the inclusion of moral philosophy as a compulsory class for senior students. This was hardly philosophy as understood by either Schoolmen or Cartesians, but rather an examination of the ethical implications of individual and collective action. Its range was wide, but its essential element was a rigorous analysis of the motives and consequences of social behaviour. Moral philosophy assumed the truths of the Christian religion, but taught students to explain or justify human action on rational grounds. Francis Hutcheson, whom so many Americans came to regarded as their philosophic mentor, began his *Short Introduction to Moral Philosophy*, addressed to 'the Students in Universities', by pointing out that moral philosophy taught men how to live and not merely how to sharpen their wits:

> Look not upon this part of philosophy as a matter of ostentation, or show of knowledge, but as the most sacred law of life and conduct, which none can despise with impunity, or without impiety towards God.

In a more indirect way the example of the Scottish universities influenced American development. Oxford and Cambridge were under anglican influence and the majority of students went there as a preparation for holy orders. The Scottish universities trained an educated ministry, but also attracted a wide variety of lay students. The sons of lairds, merchants, even of weavers and carpenters, attended classes without specific vocational objectives and, following this example, many of the Virginian gentry (including Thomas Jefferson) attended William and Mary. When Benjamin Franklin set in motion the events that led to the foundation of the University of Peensylvania he also had the Scottish model in mind. The first president William Smith, had studied at Aberdeen, and had already shown himself to be an advocate of university reform by proposing a curriculum based on that recently adopted at his old college. A later president of the university, Edgar F. Smith, was perhaps a partial witness, but there is force in his comment that:

> There is not the slightest doubt that the Scottish imprint upon American collegiate training is the only imprint worth talking about. If Cambridge and Oxford had influenced Harvard very profoundly, it is not likely that Harvard, William and Mary, Yale, Princeton and Columbia would have accepted the Plan that William Smith put into operation here.[11]

Equally important were the number of students from the colonies who attended Scottish universities. They did so for many reasons. Only members of the Church of England could take degrees at Oxford and Cambridge, and even for anglicans the Scottish universities were cheaper and had a reputation for serious study. In every field of learning – but especially in philosophy, science, and medicine – they could attend the classes of professors whose reputations had crossed the Atlantic. Above all the fame of Edinburgh as a medical school attracted Americans, especially from Virginia, South Carolina, and Pennsylvania. The Scottish influence upon the development of American medicine was so important that a separate chapter is devoted to it.

There has been controversy over the contribution of Scottish philosophy to American though in the revolutionary era. Many of the older works ignore the Scottish enlightenment, placing most emphasis on Locke and Montesquieu and adding some comment on Sidney, Harrington, and traditions of the seventeenth-century constitutional struggles in England.

Attention has also been drawn to the popularity, in the colonies, of John Trenchard and Thomas Gordon, the English eighteenth-century writers who voiced radical criticism of aristocratic and anglican dominance. Henry May was the first writer to draw attention to Scottish influences upon eighteenth century thought and stress the importance of Thomas Reid's 'common sense' philosophy. He noted that the 'common sense' school had begun its conquests just before and during the American Revolution, but concluded that 'it was in the 1790s and under moderately conservative auspices that the Scottish authors really moved into positions of great strength in America'.[12] This late date for the significant influence of Scottish thought has been vigorously challenged by Garry Wills, who claims proof that ideas derived from Francis Hutcheson and Thomas Reid inspired the Declaration of Independence.[13]

Francis Alison, who attended Hutcheson's lectures at Glasgow, delivered lectures at Philadelphia in words taken almost verbatim from the master. Alison's principal reputation was as a classical scholar, and he made no claim to originality as a philosopher. The faithfulness with which he followed Hutcheson is attested by surviving lectures notes, but it is not clear whether he dictated from Hutcheson's *Short Introduction to Moral Philosophy,* usually known as the *Compend,* or merely told students to copy from the book itself.[14] Whatever the reason the notes are positive proof that Hutcheson dominated philosophical teaching at Benjamin Franklin's new university. In the order of study drawn up by William Smith, works by Hutcheson figured in two successive years. He was also included in the curriculum at the new King's College in New York, and introduced at Princeton by John Witherspoon. Jefferson was probably introduced to Hutcheson by his much admired Scottish teacher at William and Mary, William Small.

This is important, for no one who reads the political section in Hutcheson's *System of Moral Philosophy* can fail to be struck by a close correspondence between his ideas and those of so many Revolutionary writers. There were other sources for American ideas, but there seems to be a good ground for raising the stock of Hutcheson as a source of American political theory, though not perhaps for lowering that of Locke.

The notes on Alison's lectures repeat most of Hutcheson's remarks on political authority, including the statement that 'civil power can scarce be constituted justly in any other way than by the consent of the people', which clearly anticipates a famous phrase from the Declaration of Independence. The notes omitted the following passage from Hutcheson:

> If any citizens, with permission of the government, and at their own expense find new habitations; they may justly constitute themselves into an independent state in unity with their mother country. If any are sent off at the publick charge as a colony, to make settlements

subject to the state, for augmenting its commerce and power; such persons should hold all the rights of other subjects; and whatever grants are made to them should be faithfully observed. If the mother country attempts anything oppressive toward a colony, and the colony be able to subsist as a sovereign state by itself; or if the mother country lose its liberty, or have its plan of polity miserably changed to the worse; the colony is not bound to remain subject any longer; 'tis enough that it remains in a friendly state.

There could hardly be found a better summary of justifications for colonial independence: no acknowledgement of hereditary authority; the equality of colonies and mother country; the inviolability of charters; and oppression or a departure from the original constitution as ground for separation provided that the colony can maintain indpendence. It is not known why this significant passage was omitted from Alison's notes, but Hutcheson's book was widely circulated and found in both private and college libraries.

Garry Wills claims that Thomas Reid must be regarded as the principal begetter of 'self-evident truths' in the Declaration of Independence. This depends upon inference rather than upon positive proof. It was John Locke who first argued that some ideas did not require rational proof because denial would involve a logical absurdity. Reid broadened this concept to include moral propositions which were universally accepted by the 'common sense' of mankind. Reid would certainly have agreed that the right to live was self-evident and could not be alienated; whether he would have agreed that liberty and the pursuit of happiness belonged to the same category is doubtful. He might have accepted equality as self-evident in the limited sense that all men were born with the same faculties and instincts. John Witherspoon accepted Reid's theory of common sense, because it could easily be reconciled with Calvinist theology. Man's moral character was implanted by the Creator, and it was not necessary to begin the destructive process of trying to explain moral sense by rational process which might end in reasoning away all certainty. Witherspoon taught several leaders in Revolutionary thought and action, including James Madison. Another Revolutionary intellectual, James Wilson, who was born in Scotland, shows the imprint of the common sense philosophy and quoted Hutcheson verbatim though with acknowledgement.[15] There is also evidence that John Adams read Hutcheson's *Short Introduction to Moral Philosophy* as early as 1756.[16]

The argument will continue amongst intellectual historians, but it seems clear that future accounts of Revolutionary thought will give more prominence to the Scottish writers. None will deny that after independence they were firmly established in the mainstream of American philosophical teaching, or that for a majority of educated Americans in the first half of the nineteenth century, 'philosophy' meant 'Scottish philosophy' and little else.

The works of Lord Kames are seldom read today, and it is worth while to note briefly some of his leading ideas. Eighteenth century Americans were impressed by his treatment of human law and institutions as the product of historical circumstances, providing stability yet nevertheless subject to change in accordance with needs. There was also his insistence that man was a social being:

> A man is made to purchase the means of life by the help of others in society. Why? Because from the constitution of both his body and his mind, he cannot live comfortably but in society.

Man was a 'complex machine' and might be thought of 'as so many springs and weights counteracting and balancing one another'. When properly adjusted 'the movement of life was beautiful, because regular and uniform'; once disturbed, disorder and derangement would result; but such disturbance was not accidental and had ascertainable causes. 'There is nothing in the whole universe than can properly be called contingent'.[17]

It might follow that when disturbances arose in social and political affairs, the causes must be sought in the nature of man, the character of society, and the factors which had disturbed the harmonious operation of both. This was, at least, a possible line of thought for those who were puzzled or exasperated by the changes in British policy after 1763.

In the earlier part of *Essays upon Several Subjects concerning British Antiquities* the historical approach was evident, but the meat for an American reader lies in the Appendix upon hereditary and indefeasible right, particularly as the author explained that it was written in 1745 'amidst the calamities of a Civil War'.

In this Appendix Kames argued that there was nothing in man's nature 'to subject him to the power of any, his Creator and his Parents excepted'. Government was a necessity, but 'like all other Arts, being invented for the Good of Mankind, it must be the Privilege of every Society to improve upon it, as well as upon Manufacturers and Husbandry'. No form of government was preferable to any other, except so far as it promoted the good of society:

> We may therefore conclude, with the Highest Degree of Assurance, that Kings have no other Commission from God, but what every Magistrate has, supreme and subordinate, who is legally elected according to the standing laws of the Society to which he belongs.[18]

Could man change society as he wished? As a good Calvinist Kames believed that man was powerless to alter his destiny; but he also believed that in order to inspire men to do good God had implanted in them the illusion of free will. The appearance of choice existed, but the necessary choice was predestined. This could be a comforting argument for men caught up in events which seemed to depend upon personal judgement of right and wrong.

Kames was not a major social or political philosopher, but the popularity of his works in America and the frequency with which they appear in colonial library lists suggests the need for serious consideration of his arguments and of their possible effect upon the generation which came to maturity between 1760 and 1776.

Intellectual history depends upon an understanding of what passed from mind to mind. This is a process that does not lend itself readily to documentary evidence, and the controversy over Scottish influence on Revolutionary thought, summarised in the preceding pages, is a good illustration of the way that historians may be forced to argue from inference rather than evidence. The argument that Thomas Jefferson must have read and assimilated Thomas Reid's early published work, as presented by Garry Wills, is strong but cannot be proved. Even when surviving literary evidence appears to bear testimony to the influence of a particular writer it may still remain uncertain whether the case has been proved. Indeed, as men are prone to claim authority for their statements without reading the original, the acknowledgement of an intellectual debt may well be misleading.

One is on firmer ground in religious history. If the study of doctrine suffers from the same handicaps as general intellectual history, it is at least possible to count ministers, congregations, or church members, provided that the records are accurate and have been preserved. Unfortunately this all-important condition does not apply to most Scots churches in the colonies. Knowledge may be enlarged when the church archives in the Scottish Record Office have been fully catalogued, but even then one cannot expect a sudden flood of exact knowledge. Presbyterian organisation meant that most matters were settled on the spot, and there was no need for reference to Edinburgh. Consequently there is no great body of detailed record such as exists for more centralised churches.

Despite the large number of presbyterian Scots in Virginia and Maryland on the eve of the Revolution, there is no satisfactory evidence of their churches. Probably many Scottish factors conformed to the practice of their anglican neighbours. Even in Norfolk where so many of the merchants were Scots, it is not clear whether a church building existed before the Revolution.[19] We know that there were substantial kirks in Charleston and Alexandria, because they still exist. There are references to pre-Revolutionary Scots churches in Philadelphia and New York, but there is no body of records.

There is evidence of the difficulty in getting ministers to go to more remote parts of the colonies, but most of it comes from the early part of the century. It seems likely that as colonial population grew, enough native-born men presented themselves for ordination by colonial presbyteries and the need for recruitment in Scotland diminished. Perhaps searches in American county archives will yet yield information about these churches and the people who worshipped them.

By contrast there is far more documentation about episcopal clergy. The authority of the Bishop of London meant active supervision over the colonial church, and every man seeking ordination was required to come to England. The records in Lambeth Palace are therefore voluminous. They have been catalogued and abstracts made of the most important papers.[20]

The Society for the Propagation of the Gospel in London maintained many 'missionaries' in America. Most of them served as parish priests in stable christian communities, and only a few were engaged in converting the heathen. They included several Scottish episcopalians.[21]

The records of Scottish Catholicism are meagre. Reference has already been made to the Glengarry Highlanders, who settled in northern New York, but migrated to Canada during the Revolution. So far no information has come to light about the church life of Catholics who migrated from Barra, South Uist, other catholic islands and mainland districts. It seems likely that the collections of various Catholic dioseces and societies will yield information about Highland Catholicism in America, but prospects for the eighteenth century are not promising. It is possible that they found priests to provide for their spiritual needs among the Irish and English catholics already settled in the colonies. Whatever the full story may be it must be accepted that Scottish catholicism left little or no mark upon the history of the church in America.

There were links between Scottish and Pennsylvanian Quakers. John Pemberton, a devout Philadelphia Quaker, conducted a missionary visit to Scotland in 1787. The Edinburgh Quakers were a small but active group, and the number of students from Philadelphia at the university gave them a special responsibility for seeing that discipline was observed. Their records are in the Scottish Record Office.

It is easier to discover sources for Scottish influences upon American university education. Most of them have already been surveyed and used in histories of William and Mary, Pennsylvania, and Princeton Universities. Moreover one returns to the problem of what was actually transmitted, and here the notes of Francis Alison's lectures at Philadelphia are important. Not that Alison was an original or perceptive philosopher. Indeed his very lack or originality, as witnessed by his notes, provides evidence that he handed out undiluted Hutcheson to generations of Pennsylvanian students. The evidence for Scottish influence at Princeton is also clear.

The wider influence of Scottish learning and educational method is more difficult to document or prove. The pre-eminent position of Thomas Reid and Dugald Stewart in the teaching of philosophy in American colleges at the close of the eighteenth, and far into the nineteenth century, is well known. The precise steps by which they achieved this influence had not been thoroughly explored. Perhaps the safest generalisation is that of all philosophic writings they seemed best fitted to provide the moral reassurance, confidence in rational discussion, and optimism that a new nation required.

With these disclaimers it remains to survey some of the evidence, albeit fragmentary, for Scottish contributions to American religion, education and intellect. There is however one major exception to deficiency in the sources. Abundant letters, lecture notes, and other materials illustrate the influence of Scottish medicine, and these are surveyed in a separate chapter.

The Church of Scotland and American Presbyterianism

The letters of Cotton Mather provide much evidence of his admiration for the Church of Scotland. He was given a D.D. by the University of Glasgow in 1710, and from 1712 to the end of his life corresponded with Principal John Stirling and with Robert Wodrow, historian of the Church of Scotland. They were, he wrote in 1723, 'some of the most valuable friends I have in the world'. There is no doubt that he came to prefer the discipline of presbyterianism to the looser organisation of congregationalism, but was unsuccessful in his attempts to bring the two denominations into close relations with each other.

Most of the original letters are in the National Library of Scotland, though there are some drafts with the American Antiquarian Society, Worcester, Mass, which do not appear in the National Library collection.[22] A large selection of the letters has been published.[23]

The designs of the Church of England were frequently mentioned in Mather's letters to Stirling and Wodrow. On 16 September 1715 he was disturbed by news from 'the miserable colony of Carolina' brought by three Scottish ministers 'refugees from thence now sojourning in my next neighbourhood'. Under their influence it had been 'in a hopeful way to be a religious country', but Church of England ministers had no sooner arrived 'than a torrent of wickedness broke in with them, and carried all before it'. The wrath of God had been made manifest when the savages 'destroyed multitudes of people, with such barbarities as no Myrmidons before them have ever perpetuated'. His fear of Anglican aggression in New England was a major reason for seeking close alliance with the Calvinists of the Scottish church. But in November 1716 he was happy to report that 'their attempts to disturb our Churches is come to nothing', and they had converted none but 'ignorant and vicious wretches'.

Security from these dangers demanded close friendship with a church which was 'fine gold' and endeared itself 'to all lovers of goodnes'. The University of Glasgow was much praised; it had 'excellent professors', and trained men fitted in all respects for the ministry.

What the Church of Scotland did not do was to send out a constant supply of ministers to the colonies. In 1704 there was an appeal from South Carolina for a minister, perhaps from survivors of the ill-fated Stewart's Town settlement. In 1712 another appeal was sent to the presbytery of Edinburgh asking for more ministers to be sent to that 'remote corner of the globe'. Presbyterians on James Island also asked for a continuance of the work 'so happily begun amongst us in this wildnerness'. Archibald Stobo, the leading minister in South Carolina, enclosed this with a personal appeal for a 'pious sober young man' to be sent out; there were but three Presbyterian ministers in the colony and though 'sound and able men', were much in need of assistance.[24]

The call was answered by a young minister called John Squyre who arrived in South Carolina in 1714. He began his ministry on James Island but found the situation unpropitious. The presbyterian community, small as it was, was divided into quarrelling factions. The people were 'rude and ignorant', and would not accept the kind of catechising he wished to employ. This might have been endured and remedied, but Indian raids made life hazardous. In 1715 Squyre, Stobo, and another minister named Traill decided to leave South Carolina, and took ship to Boston. There they found a welcome which soon brought embarrassment.

Cotton Mather wrote to his friend John Stirling that the arrival of the three Scottish ministers provided an opportunity 'to express our communion with the dear Church of Scotland'. To his dismay the Presbyterians refused communion with Congregationalists, and to make matter worse held private meetings, baptised in private houses, attempted to show discord, and attracted to their cause 'some of the more loose and profane sort'. He was particularly bitter against Squyre, and reported that he had cast 'scurvy reflections on the College of Glasgow, asserting it to be no university'. This was, perhaps, particularly galling to Cotton Mather who had recently received a D.D. from Glasgow.[25]

Reading between the lines one can see that members of the small Scottish community in Boston were dissatisfied with Congregationalism and wanted a minister of their own. This interpretation is confirmed by the fact that a petition was soon on the way from Boston to the Society in Scotland for the Propagation of Christian Knowledge, asking it to support Squyre as a minister in Boston.[26] The Society replied that it had insufficient funds for its needs in Scotland, but that a request for a minister had been received by the General Assembly. The General Assembly papers contain no such petition, but in 1725 Squyre's reasons for leaving South Carolina were approved.

Meanwhile there is evidence of early Scottish influences in the Presbyterian Church in other colonies. Some of the evidence is found in nineteenth-century histories, and the sources upon which they relied may have disappeared. Francis Mackemie, the father of the church in the American colonies, came from Ireland but was educated at Glasgow University. He began his work in Maryland and by 1705 it was said that there were five congregations with churches in Somerset county.[26] In a letter dated 1 August 1716 the Revd. James Anderson of Delaware wrote to Principal Stirling of Glasgow.[27]

> In this country there are since I came here [1709] settled three other Presbyterian ministers, two of which are from your city of Glasgow. There are, in all, of ministers who meet in Presbytery once a year, sometimes in Philadelphia, sometimes here in Newcastle, seventeen; and two probationers from the west of Ireland, whom we have under trial for ordination; twelve of which have had the most and best of their education at your famous University of Glasgow.... We make it our business to follow the Directory of the Church of Scotland, which, as well we may, we owe as our mother church.

Similar references to the 'mother church' are frequent in the early years of American Presbyterianism and in 1741, when the separation occurred between the 'new side' and 'old side', the former stressed their relationship with the Church of Scotland. An appeal to the General Assembly in Scotland, soliciting aid, proclaimed that:

> The young daughter of the Church of Scotland, helpless and exposed in this foreign land, cries to her tender and powerful mother for relief.

When Samuel Davies visited Great Britain to appeal for funds on behalf of the New Side College of New Jersey (Princeton), he was particularly well received in Edinburgh and Glasgow, and his visit was financially rewarding.[28]

There is an interesting sequel to the early and apparently discouraging links between the Presbyterians in South Carolina and the 'mother church'. While most Scottish presbyteries came to look for ministers amongst those who had been born and educated in America, or who had already spent some years in the country, the church in Charleston continued to send to Scotland for ministers. Though records have not survived, a letter written in 1857 by an elder of the Church, Judge Mitchell King, has the ring of authentic oral tradition:[29]

> The first Presbyterian Church in Charleston, from the time of the Rev. Archibald Stobo – a survivor of the ministers who accompanied the Scottish adventurers to the unfortunate colony of New Caledonia, had usually been supplied with pastors from Scotland. ... When the church required a minister, the congregation usually remitted funds to some friends in Scotland, to defray expenses, and solicited some distinguished gentlemen to select and send an eligible pastor to them.

The practice continued after the Revolution, and in 1792 the 'distinguished gentlemen' in Edinburgh were assured that:

> He will preach to a polite, well-informed congregation, and . . . will appear at the head of the Presbyterian interest in the state.

The largest Presbyterian church in Charleston – a fine nineteenth century building – is still known as the First (Scots) Presbyterian Church.

A struggling presbyterian congregation in New York also appealed for help from Scotland. In 1724 a minister named John Nicol presented "The Case of the presbyterian congregation at New York, humbly laid before charitable Christians in Scotland".[30] He described the distressed condition of the congregation with heavy debts incurred to purchase land and build a church. He asked for financial aid, more ministers, and closer ties between the presbyterians in New York and the 'Church of Scotland, our Mother Church'. In addition to his appeal there was an address from the presbytery of Long Island, and a historical account by Nicol of the presbytery of New York. The Revd. James Anderson was described by the presbytery of Long Island and by Nicol as the man most active in establishing presbyterianism in the colony.

Men were more difficult to obtain than money. In April 1746 Francis Hutcheson received a letter from a presbytery in Pennsylvania regretting 'their want of proper Ministers and Books'.[31] There was little hope of doing anything for them in Glasgow:

> I shall speak to some wise men here. but would as soon speak to the Roman conclave as to our presbytery.

Writing to a friend in Belfast, Hutcheson hoped that it might be possible to send over some ministers from Ireland. He said that the preaching of Whitfield had promoted a contempt for literature, and books were difficult to obtain, but that he would send them his 'best advice about Books and Philosophy', and hoped to buy them books 'cheaper than they can be got anywhere'. His Pennsylvania correspondents were also 'bewailing some wretched contentions among themselves'. This may refer either to the split between 'old side' and 'new side' presbyterians, or to the secession of the Associate Presbyteries.

Although the Society in Scotland for the Propagation of Christian Knowledge had refused to support a minister in Boston, it had an early and coninuing interest in the conversion of the American Indians. The society's main field of activity was in the Highlands, but interest in America was aroused by a letter from Eleazor Wheelock of Lebanon, Connecticut.[32] He had taught English to Indian boys, and some had learned Latin and Greek. Two had even read the *Aeneid*, and he expected three to be fit for college (presumably Yale). He had also made progress in the education of five Indian girls and a son of the 'King of the Mohegans'. He observed that the colonists were very hostile to the Indians, but believed that it was a duty to bring Christianity to them.

A pamphlet printed by the society in 1763 contains further reference to this Indian mission.[33] It includes a letter from the Revd. David Borthwick of New York about Samuel Occum, a Mohegan Christian who became celebrated as a minister. He had been sent on a mission to the Oneydas Indians amongst whom he preached and baptised every Sunday. There are further references in the pamphlet to this missionary work in letters from the Revd. Samuel Mather and Dr Channey. The pamphlet concludes with an Act of the General Assembly of the Church of Scotland dated 31 May 1762 authorising a plan to educate Indians, train them in language and religion, and then send missionaries in pairs, one English and one Indian, to 'propagate Christian knowledge among some other of the Indian tribes'.

The society's report for 1774 contained a full account of activities among the Penobscot Indians of New England, the Delawares of Pennsylvania, the Oneydas, and the Indians in Connecticut and around Albany. Missionaries singled out for special praise were Azariah Horton, David and John Brainerd, Samuel Kirkland, Nathanial Whitaker, and Eleazor Wheelock. It is clear that none of these missionaries came from Scotland, though the society raised funds for their support.

One can infer that the Revolution imposed great difficulties in pursuing this grand design, and in the later records of the S.S.P.C.K. there are only occasional references to America. However there is evidence of continued interest in a journal from 1809 to 1817 kept by John Sargent, missionary at New Stockbridge in Connecticut, who was supported by the society. The journal which consists mainly of a formal record of services, communicants, and baptisms was kept 'for the information of the Society'. It is preserved in the New York Historical Society.[34]

In the middle years of the nineteenth century William D. Sprague compiled a multi-volume work entitled *Annals of the American Pulpit*. He conducted an assiduous correspondence with elderly men, whose recollections went back into the eighteenth century, and drew upon oral traditions that have since been lost. The work may therefore be treated as a historical source, though not a reliable one. Volumes III and IV, published in 1860, are devoted to the Presbyterian clergy. It is not a complete record – Sprague provided biographies only for those who had achieved some distinction – but the sample is large and provides the basis for some tentative generalisations. A very large majority of the presbyterian clergy who served during the eighteenth century had been born in the colonies and were of English or Irish descent, or migrated from Northern Ireland during the course of the century. Scottish born ministers were a minority, and most of them came to America at an early age as individual migrants or with their parents. With the single exception of Charleston,

South Carolina, there is no record of a presbytery applying to Scotland for a supply of ministers. In the Associate presbyteries things may have been different; in the later years of the eighteenth century most of their congregations were small, isolated, and anxious to keep alive their ties with the secession churches in Scotland. They sought to raise funds and may sometimes have tried to recruit ministers.

The best way to document the argument that the Church of Scotland ceased to act as the 'mother church' – in the sense that sons of the church were not sent out as ministers in the new world – is to summarise the information collected by Sprague about ministers born in Scotland. The list is given in the approximate chronological order in which they began their ministry. It does not include John Witherspoon and Charles Nisbet, whose careers and papers are described elsewhere:

George Gillespie, b. 1683 in Glasgow, educated Glasgow University, University, recommended to Cotton Mather by Principal Stirling, ordained 1713 and served in New Jersey until his death in 1760.

James Anderson, b. 1678 in Scotland, emigrated to Virginia in 1709, moved to Delaware, and then to New York where he was minister to the first presbyterian congregation, d. 1740.

Alexander Boyd, date of birth unknown, educated Glasgow University, emigrated to America in 1743 and settled in Maine. Difficulties arose over reports received from Scotland about his conduct there, but he ministered at Newcastle, Maine, 'constantly involved in difficulties, and labouring to very little advantage, until the latter part of the year 1758, when his demission was finally effected.[35]

Samuel Kennedy, b. 1720 in Scotland. At Edinburgh University and moved to America some time after 1740. He was minister of Basking Ridge, N.J. Unlike most of the Scottish and Northern Irish clergy he favoured the new side.

Henry Pattullo, b. 1757 in Scotland, came to America as a child, ministered first in Virginia but from 1765 in North Carolina. Played an active part in movement for independence. Teacher and a self-taught scholar. d. 1801.

John Carmichael, b. Target, Argyll, 1728. Parents emigrated 1737. Attended Princeton and settled at the Forks of Brandywine, Pennsylvania. Active in promoting the cause of independence, d. 1785.

Alexander Hewat, b. 1733, educated at Kelso and Edinburgh University. Made his mark in Edinburgh, and in 1763 accepted a call to Charleston. He became a close friend of Governor Bull, and prepared a history of South Carolina published in London in 1779. He is not recorded as an active Loyalist, but probably left South Carolina in 1776. He lived subsequently in London and Edinburgh but continued to correspond with members of his old congregation. Their respect for him was witnessed in 1792 when he was asked to participate in the selection of a new minister. He died in 1828 or 1829.

Archibald Scott, b. 1745 in Scotland. Migrated as a boy and alone to Pennsylvania. Educated thanks to the generosity of friends. In 1777 he accepted a call to a scattered district in Prince Edward County, Virginia. Active supporter of the Revolution, d. 1799.

William Morrison, b. Perthshire 1748. His parents were very poor and he migrated as a young man in order to earn enough to educate himself for the ministry. From 1783 he was pastor of Londonderry, New Hampshire where lived 'a great number of his own countrymen and their descendents'.[36]

James Muir, b. 1757 at Cumnock, the son and grandson of ministers. Graduated at Glasgow in 1776 but completed his theological studies in London, and accepted a call from a congregation in Bermuda. In 1778 he had decided to return to Scotland, but the ship in which he had taken passage was driven back by storms, and took refuge in New York. There he remained until 1791 when he accepted a call to Alexandria, Virginia, where he served until his death in 1820. A friend of John Witherspoon, he was the author of several books including (1795) an answer to Tom Paine's *Age of Reason,* and received a D.D. from Yale in 1791. A reminisence of his pulpit manner says that 'his sermons were always full of vigorous and condensed thought, and in point of style very much of the Addisonian school . . . (but) delivered in an accent so intensely Scotch that it seemed to an unpractised ear not only strange but ludicrous'.

John Mason came to New York from Scotland in 1761 and took charge of the "old secession" Scottish presbyterian church in Cedar Street. He died suddenly in 1792.

John Mitchell Mason, son and successor of John Mason, was born in 1770. He was at Edinburgh University in 1791, but cut short his studies on his father's death, and though no more than twenty-three was invited to become pastor of the Cedar Street church in 1793. In 1812 he moved to a new church in Murray Street. He was also professor of theology at Columbia. In 1816 and 1817 he visited Britain, where one of his objects was 'to obtain a supply of ministers from Scotland for the destitute congregations of the Associate Reformed Church'. Unfortunately his health began to deteriorate – the description indicates a brain tumour – and he gradually lost control over his faculties. He was persuaded to accept the presidency of Dickinson College in 1821, but it quickly became apparent that he was too ill to carry out his duties. For many years he had been ill at ease with the narrow views of the Associate Reformed Church and in 1822 joined the Presbyterian Church. He died in 1829.

George Buist, b. 1778 in Fifeshire, and was at Edinburgh University in 1789. He published an abridged version of Hume's *History of England* and contributed to the *Encyclopaedia Britannica*. In 1793 he was offered and accepted charge of the Scots Presbyterian Church in Charleston, South Carolina. From 1805 he also acted as principal of Charleston College. He died prematurely in 1808. A memoir by Judge Mitchell King, written in July 1852, recalled that 'by great diligence and attention' Dr Buist 'had almost wholly overcome the Scottish peculiarities of pronounciation, and only a practised and acute ear could have discovered that he was once a native of Scotland.[37]

There are other scattered references in various archives to presbyterian churches in America. Dr John Rodgers, pastor of the first presbyterian church in New York, and Alexander Robertson, who was for many years a prominent member of the congregation, were the subjects of an unpublished a memoir by their great-grand-daughter, Mary Darden Rodgers.[38] Dr Rodgers was ordained before 1749, but did not move to New York and take charge of the first presbyterian church in Wall Street until shortly before the Revolution. This congregation adhered to the 'old secession'. His son, also called John, was born in 1757, served as an army surgeon with the continental army, and subsequently studied at London, Paris, and Edinburgh, where he obtained an M.D. Alexander Robertson was born at Polmont in 1743 and emigrated to America with his parents in 1751. Though only his earliest years were spent in Scotland he retained his Scottish accent, and was described in his later years as a typical Scottish merchant of the old school. He established himself in the linen trade, and owned mills and a farm near Greenwich Village. He was responsible for bringing over a party of Scottish weavers, but this enterprise did not prosper. During the British occupation of the city he withdrew to a country estate, where he demonstrated his sympathies by frequently entertaining officers of Washington's army. After the Revolution he became very prosperous and was for many years treasurer and benefactor of the Wall Street church.[39]

A brief record of one Scots church in Philadelphia survives.[40] In September 1778, after the British occupied the city, the congregation dispersed. When it gathered again a dispute arose, which probably developed from recriminations over attitudes during the occupation. The majority agreed to depose the minister, but the church had formerly adhered to the secession and the minority appealed to the Associate Synod in Scotland, which found in favour of the deposed minister. There followed an angry controversy challenging the jurisdiction of a foreign body, with a reply from the synod that its authority was purely spiritual. The outcome is not recorded, but it is inconceivable that the minority and synod were successful in maintaining a right to decide who should minister to an American congregation.

There is however some evidence of continuing links between the Associate Presbyteries in Scotland and America. There is a minute of the Associate Presbytery of Glasgow, dated February 1791, respecting the appointment of John Cree to the Presbytery of Pennsylvania, and a printed statement from the Associate Prestbytery of Glasgow about the use of an organ in St Andrew's church, Philadelphia.[41]

A curious offshoot of the links between American and Scottish Presbyterianism was the willingness of the Scottish universities to give Doctorates of Divinity to eminent American divines. Benjamin Franklin was instrumental in obtaining these degrees in several cases but whether from a disinterested desire to see his countrymen honoured, or, as was suspected, as part of intricate, personal and political calculation, cannot be known. In 1765 Ezra Stiles, then pastor of Newport, Rhode Island, and later president of Yale received a D.D. from Edinburgh. He had not solicited the honour and noted that 'I received it Nov. 22 1765 having not the least notice of it till it arrived in Newport'. He had apparently been awarded it as the result of a suggestion made by Benjamin Franklin to William Robertson, principal of Edinburgh.[42]

In May 1769 Stiles wrote as a private 'Memoir and Conjecture'.:

> How came Dr. Benj Franklin to procure several Doctorates for American Presbyterian Ministers, himself being an Episcopalian and a Crown Officer of £5 or 600 Ster. yearly?

He noticed that his own doctorate coincided with the passage of the Stamp Act and that Dr Cooper of Boston and Dr Rodgers wre honoured in 1767 and 1768, when opposition to the 'Townshead Acts' mounted in the colonies. He concluded that by these means Franklin:

> Reduced the opposition to him among the clergy of Pennsylvania to but a third of the Synod. Pleased all New England Cong & whole Presby. interest except Dr. Alison & the Min. of Pennsylvania. These perhaps he will gratify also.

Stiles believed that Franklin knew of a design to do away with the charters of three New England colonies and the proprietory governments of Pennsylvania and Maryland. Stiles conjectured that though opposed to these measures, Franklin believed that they would shortly be effected and that his own influence in Pennsylvania would suffer. Compliments to the Pennsylvania clergy might ward off criticism, while friends won in New England might secure an untroubled retirement and old age in one of those colonies.[43]

The Church of England in America

The history of the Rose and Scott families in Virginia was noticed in Chapter II. There are glimpses of the church in Virginia in a long letter from John Lang in the Scottish Record Office.[44] He was writing to an unidentified peer who had recommended him for ordination and preferment in Virginia; he also had a recommendation from the Earl of Orkney, and had been commended by the Bishop of London and Norwich, and thus began his colonial career in 1725 with all possible advantages. Indeed the Governor offered him the choice of all vacant parishes, and then allowed him to change to a better one which had become vacant. The new parish, St Peter' at New Kent, was 'judged one of the very best in the colony'; its salary was 16,000 pounds of sweet scented tobacco, and:

> The people of the best sort . . . abundantly civil and courteous, although the Common rank be very ignorant, opinionative and unmannerly.

But Lang was disturbed by the moral state of the colony, and thought that 'a Spiritual Jurisdiction' ought to be established 'for the Suppression of Vice even in the Clergy as well as the laity'. There had been no commission in the colony since the death of the former Bishop of London in 1723, but he anticipated that one would be sent as soon as the new Bishop had had his ecclesiastical jurisdiction over the colonies confirmed.[45] There was an implication that the previous commissary, James Blair, had been lax as 'all manner of crimes were overlok't so that Incestuous Marriages, as well as other Vices not to be named among people professing Christianity were tolerated'. Though new to the colony and but recently ordained, he modestly proposed himself for the vacant office.

Concurrently Lang wrote to the Bishop of London about the moral state of the colony. The people, he said, were ignorant and morally lax, many of the clergy were drunkards and the sober were lazy; negroes were bought for baptism but allowed to live thereafter without Christian discipline; one parishoner lived with his brother's widow and another with his deceased wife's sister; adultery and fornication was very general. Despite this show of zeal his hopes were disappointed, and James Blair was reappointed. Lang was next heard from in 1731, when he had moved to Maryland, was in bad health, and asked the Bishop of London for a position in England. His appeal was renewed in 1773, and again in four separate letters in 1735 and 1736.[46] It is not known whether his appeals succeeded or whether the unhappy man died, as he had predicted, in the heat of a Maryland summer.

Unfortunately Lang's accusation of drunkenness amongst the colonial parish clergy is amply supported by other evidence. The correspondence of the Bishops of London contains numerous complaints and accusations. There is no reason to suppose that the Scottish clergy were more guilty than the rest, but there are a number of complaints about their conduct and quality. In 1749 commissary William Dawson wrote to the Bishop of London that 'Northern Gentlemen having been bred as Presbyterians, did not have the necessary high regard for the Church'. Thomas Dawson, who succeeded his brother as commissary, made a similar complaint. This was during the governorship of Robert Dinwiddie and the Dawsons may have feared the growth of Scottish influences. More circumstantial is the observation of one Virginian clergyman (of English stock) in 1764, that there was a good deal of carelessness in giving titles for ordination and, in consequence, a good many unworthy persons, notably Scots, came to the colony as indentured schoolmasters, and got into the ministry. Governor Francis Fauquier agreed that many of those who applied for ordination were Scots who had come out as tutors and applied for ordination after three or four years residence.[47]

Such accusations are not heard from the Church of England in New York, where the Revd. Charles Inglis, was leader of the clergy in the years preceding the Revolution. He was a close but deferential friend of Sir William Johnston, a fellow Scot and the dominant personality in the interior of the colony. His letters to Johnson express frequent apprehensions about the designs of 'dissenters' and papists. He hoped that Johnson would use his influence with the government and with the Society for the Propagation of the Gospel to send out more missionaries; it was important to bring home the danger of popish conversion, and to stress the argument that true Christianity would produce a sober and industrious people well-suited for commerce. The independents were perhaps more dangerous, though less obviously so, than the catholics. One of them, a Mr Wheelock, seemed to have ample funds for missionary work. On 21 June 1770 he wrote 'I think we have as much reason to be apprehensive of Wheelock's converts as of those made by the Infallible Church, tho' it will not do to tell the Public so'.[48]

An analysis of the reasons for migration made by Inglis is perhaps worthy of quotation. The 'dissenters' all claimed that they had been driven abroad by Anglican persecution. It was rather:

> The passion for adventuring, or prospect of Gain, Want of Property, Inconstancy of Disposition, and some other circumstances that need not be mentioned, brought together a majority of [America's] inhabitants, to which Wars and Commerce have added a considerable number since.

Yale University holds a collection of papers that illustrate the way in which several young Scottish episcopalians came to serve the church in America.[49] George Panton was rector of the Grammar School at Jedburgh in 1769, but was dissatisfied with his situation. The school was in cramped quarters, and stood to the windward of a dunghill. His house was too small to take boarders, an incentive which might have attracted 'the ablest and

most experienced teacher'. Fortunately he had influential friends who
included the Revd. J. Macknight of Maybole, George Srewart, professor
of Humanity at Edinburgh, Professor R. Traill, and David Hume. He
planned to go out to America as a tutor, but believed that his prospects
would be greatly improved if he could first be ordained in the Church of
England. There were difficulties to be overcome. First he had to have a
university degree, but this was obtained from Marischal College,
Aberdeen, after paying a fee of £2 10s. 0d. It is not clear whether he had
attended classes at Marischal or Edinburgh. Marischal was notoriously lax
in its requirements for a D.D., but may have had stricter rules for an M.A.
The Bishop of Down and Connor, who frequently visited Edinburgh, was
willing to ordain him but doubted his authority for doing so. There was no
diocese of the Church of England in Scotland, but it was generally believed
that it came under the episcopal direction of the Bishop of London. This
point was settled satisfactorily, Panton received his ordination, and by June
1773 was in New York as tutor to the children of a Colonel Philips.

It is not clear who had paid for Panton's passage to America, but the
Society for the Propagation of the Gospel probably welcomed an
application from a man on the spot, who would cost them nothing, and in
December 1772 he was appointed to a 'missionary' post at Trenton, N.J. In
this situation he was soon involved in the problem of divided loyalties. In
October 1775 his name appears with other signatories of a letter from clergy
gathered at Philadelphia to the Bishop of London. They had felt obliged to
comply with the direction from Congress that 20 July should be a day of
humiliation, fasting and prayer, but 'we did surreptiously conduct
ourselves consistently with our duty as loyal subjects'.[50]

In 1779 Panton proposed to return to England, but was persuaded not to
do so by the secretary of the S.P.G., T.B. Chandler, who wrote that 'many of
the most respectable clergy from America have made the trial and none of
them can get anything but Good Words and Kind Wishes for their speedy
and safe return to their own country'. A friend, D. Batwell, did go to
England, and there are many letters from him – mainly relating to the non-
payment of Panton's salary – in the collection.[51] In August 1780 a letter was
addressed to Panton at New York as 'Chaplain of Prinvincial Forces'. The
papers end at this point and do not reveal whether he left New York after the
peace, returned to Scotland, went to England, or found preferment in
another British colony.

The Fettercairn Papers, now lodged in the Natural Library of Scotland,
contain a large number of letters written from America to Dr Myles Cooper.
He was a Church of England clergyman who had been president of King's
College, New York. Following a politically-inspired student rebellion, he
was forced to abandon his post at the end of 1774. He arrived in England in
1775. His only connection with Scotland (a country which he seems to have

disliked) was that he went to live in Edinburgh in 1778 and was there appointed chaplain of King's Chapel; but his correspondence includes many letters from Scottish clergy serving the Church of England in America. These include Charles Inglis, Dr Samuel Auchmuty, and Samuel Seabury.[52] Apart from this the letters include much information about the trials of churchmen during the time of troubles.

There are also some interesting letters condemning Dr William Smith at Pennsylvania who had trimmed his sails to the storm and published a sermon which Samuel Seabury considered 'most flaming patriotic' and John Milner 'a sacrifice to the prejudices of the times'. In a letter dated August 1775 Smith defended his sermon by saying that England could not expect to govern the colonies without granting constitutional liberties, and that it was the duty of the church to promote an honourable settlement. He urged Cooper to 'judge candidly of the part we find it necessary to act here for the preservation of our church and our own usefulness in the advancement of Religion. Peace, and Order.'

The Society of Friends in Edinburgh.

The Friends in Edinburgh assumed responsibility for young Quaker students from America.[53] For instance in November 1768 they received a letter of recommendation from Dr John Fothergill on behalf of John Coakley Letsome, and in April 1769 gave him a certificate to be presented to Friends in Holland. William Logan jr was also received in 1768 with a certificate of removal from the meeting in London, saying he had been sober and orderly during his residence there. In April 1770 the same William Logan and his wife made humble supplication to the Edinburgh meeting. Their offence was to have been married by a priest, 'which erroneous conduct we are now sincerely sorry for'. The meeting accepted this apology, believing it to be sincere, and so in October 1770 granted the couple certificates of removal.

In 1785 the Edinburgh meeting received a certificate on behalf of Caspar Wister, who was later to become eminent among Philadelphia physicians, and in the same year welcomed Thomas Ross and John Pemberton from America. Caspar Wister was given a certificate of removal in June 1786. There are further references in 1786 to the visit of John Pemberton, who had come to win converts by a preaching tour in England and Scotland.[54] There was also an exchange of greetings with the women's yearly meeting in Philadelphia.

In 1790 the Edinburgh meeting was much troubled by the conduct of John Pennington, who had come from Philadelphia to study medicine. He appeared to be 'much deficient in the knowledge of our principles, as also inconsistent in practice', and Alexander Cruikshank, appointed to visit and counsel him, made an unfavourable report in May 1791. But in August, after much anxious enquiry, the meeting signed a certificate of removal for Pennington addressed to Friends in London. Still more disturbing was the conduct of Andrew Gilchrist from Philadelphia. He robbed a Friend's shop, was found guilty of other 'fraudulent and dishonourable practices', and then absconded. The meeting formally disowned him.

The records contain several other references to the arrival of medical students from Philadelphia, and it is interesting to observe that their solicitious care for young Americans was not interrupted by the independence of the United States. Unfortunately there are no records from 1770 to 1785 so it is not possible to trace the response to political discontent and revolution. There are no relevant records after 1793.

Philosophy and Higher Education.

It would be inappropriate in a study of sources to pursue the controversy over the extent of Scottish influence upon American thought in the eighteenth century. The outline of the debate has already been sketched. Mention has also been made of the student notes which prove that Francis Alison was giving his students undiluted Hutcheson befor 1760. The note-taker, Jasper Yeates, belonged to a wealthy family, and was himself of considerable influence in Pennsylvania during the Revolutionary period.

There is further information about Francis Alison in the papers of Ezra Stiles, with whom he was on friendly terms.[55] These display a more lively mind than his derivative lectures might suggest. In May 1757 he was full of a proposal to launch a monthly magazine in Philadelpia:

> It may engage our young Students to become literary adventurers . . . promote a friendly intercourse among men of learning in our different Colonies, and possibly produce some papers worthy of approbation in Great Britain.

In March 1764 he wrote that he would advise students to aim at useful publications 'and trouble their heads no further to collect theses'. He approved 'the study of Natural Philosophy':

> We can know nothing of nature but by experience and plain, certain inferences from them; but our Philosophers are too sanguine and draw universal conclusions from their experiments that are too few to sustain their Fabricks.[56]

There was considerable interest in the best way of approaching higher education. The Library of Congress contains a brief account of the plan of education at the University of Glasgow dated 1759.[57] It was clearly in answer to enquiries, but there is no indication of the author or for whom it was intended. It begins by saying that the system of education in Scotland was so deficient that the students had to spend their first two years studying Latin and Greek. In their third year they studied Logic, Ontology, and Pneumatology; in their fourth Natural and Moral Philosophy; and in their fifth continued with Natural Philosophy. No Scottish student could be excused the classes in Logic, but they were not compulsory for students from England, Ireland, or foreign countries. There were no religious tests for admission.

Details were supplied on the number of hours allocated each week for lectures, but there are obvious omissions. There is no mention of mathematics, and other subjects were studied in final year besides natural philosophy.

Cotton Mather's admiration for the University of Glasgow derived from its contribution to Calvinist theology, but as the century wore on more secular themes predominated in the reputation of Scottish universities. It was not until after 1750 that the great names of the Scottish enlightenment became familiar in America, but there was considerable interest in the ecucational system. The project to found the Edinburgh Royal Infirmary attracted interest, and as early as 1742 Alexander Hamilton (a former Edinburgh student) wrote to commend a scheme which combined relief for the poor and destitute with opportunities for young men to study 'physic and surgery'.[58] Joshua Crosby of Philadelphia also hoped to raise money for the Edinburgbh Infirmary in 1748, and wrote that he always encouraged young Americans to go to Edinburgh, not only on account of its fame in science but also because it was 'less vicious and corrupt than ye South'.[59]

William Smith, first provost of the College of Philadelphia and University of Pennsylvania, was an important figure in the development of American higher education and a link between the new educational method of the Scottish universities and American colleges in the formative years. He was born near Aberdeen in 1727 and attended the university, though without graduating. He was an episcopalian and his first post was in London as 'Commissioner for the Established or Parochial Schoolmasters in Scotland'; he may also have been clerk to the Society for the Propagation of the Gospel. He then became a tutor to the children of Josiah Martin, with whom he arrived in New York in May 1751.[60]

During the next twelve months he wrote an anonymous pamphlet advocating the foundation of King's College in New York, and began a correspondence with Benjamin Franklin which was to be of great importance in his career. He returned to England to seek anglican orders, and was ordained at the same time as Samuel Seabury, a future leader of the American episcopal church. It was during this year that he revisited Aberdeen, and may have obtained a copy of the new regulations for King's College, Aberdeen, influenced by Thomas Reid, which reduced the time spent on logic and metaphysics and increased that devoted to natural history and philosophy. Machines had been acquired for practical work in natural philosophy and a chemistry laboratory had been established. These principles were elaborated in a pamphlet which Smith published on his return to New York. It was the first attempt in America to present a systematic analysis of the aim and methods of higher education.

The plan began with secondary education in Latin and Greek, to be covered in three or four years and serve as a qualification for entry to the College, where the curriculum could concentrate on other branches of knowledge. The college curriculum was:

First Year   Latin and English exercises continued
                  Mathematics
                  Logic with Metaphysics
Second Year Logic
                  Advanced Mathematics
                  Moral Philosophy
                  Natural Philosophy
Third Year Hutcheson's *Ethics*
                  Natural Law (Burlamequi)
                  Introduction to Civil History, Laws,
                      Government, Trade and Commerce
                  Astronomy
                  Natural History of Vegetables and Animals
                  Option
                  Chemistry

The study of classical literature continued in both the second and third years. The modern books prescribed for private study included Locke's *Essay on Human Understanding*, Hutcheson's *Metaphysics*, works by Puffendorf, Hooker, Selden, Montesquieu, Newton, and many others on science.

In 1754 Smith was appointed to teach logic, rhetoric, ethics, and natural philosophy at Franklin's new College of Philadelphia. In the following year he became provost and professor of natural philosophy and for a time also edited and published the *American Magazine*.[61] The curriculum adopted at Philadelphia (a somewhat modified version of the intensive instruction first proposed by Smith) had a great influence upon the newly founded colleges and inspired changes in the old. It represented a decisive departure from curricula based upon classical learning and formal philosophy, and established a claim for the sciences as an essential part of 'liberal education'.

In 1767, following the premature death of Jonathan Edwards, the trustees of the College of New Jersey at Princeton sought a new president. The college was under the control of 'new side' Presbyterians, and the trustees decided to look to a man from the evangelical or popular party in Scotland. Their choice fell upon John Witherspoon, minister of Paisley. Richard Stockton, a trustee and later to be a signer of the Declaration of Independence, went to Britain to obtain Witherspoon's acceptance, but could not stay long enough to receive it. Witherspoon had doubts about going to America – his wife was at first unwilling – and he began by suggesting other names, including that of Charles Nesbit, minister of Montrose, and later president of Dickinson College. The negotiations were then left in the hands of a young alumnus of Princeton destined to a career of distinction, Benjamin Rush, who was studying medicine at Edinburgh. A situation in which a young graduate student is entrusted with the task of persuading a distinguished divine to accept the presidency of his *alma mater* is hardly likely to occur in the twentieth century. In 1768, after much correspondence and doubt, Witherspoon accepted the post.[62]

John Witherspoon was a masterful college president and imposed his own ideas upon the curriculum. He too was influenced by Thomas Reid, both as philosopher and educator, and, as at Philadelphia, Scottish philosophy and scientific studies bulked large in the curriculum. A list of volumes from his library, purchased for Princeton after his death, includes no works of the Scottish enlightenment except Lord Kames' *Essays on the Principles of Morality and Natural Religion* (Edinburgh 1751) an an abridged (six sketches from Book I) *Sketches on the History of Man* (Philadelphia 1776). The few other works by Scottish authors were sermons, theological treatises and church histories. Hutcheson and Reid were certainly on the curriculum at Princeton so perhaps Witherspoon's copies were too worn to be purchased, and there would have been many duplicates available.[63]

The later history of the diffusion of Scottish educational ideas among American colleges has been studied elsewhere.[64] In the present context it is sufficient to observe that both the principal centres for the dissemination of Scottish ideas – Philadelphia and Princeton – survived the Revolution with enhanced reputations. This made their example of much greater importance than the newly founded King's College in New York, which would revive as Columbia University but shorn of its English and Anglican character.

Though William Smith's conduct during the Revolution aroused criticism from both Loyalists and patriots, the University of Pennsylvania grew in strength and reputation, while the support of many eminent Pennsylvanians ensured its future success. John Witherspoon's early support for the American cause, his membership of the Continental Congress, and signature on the Declaration of Independence, assured his reputation and that of his college. In this way the contribution of the Scottish enlightenment to American culture had more permanent consequences than the resistance of so many Scots to the principles of the Revolution.

Chapter Six

SCOTLAND AND AMERICAN MEDICINE

Above the entrance to the medical school of the University of Pennsylvania is carved the thistle of Scotland, a tribute to the great influence of Scotland not only on medicine in Philadelphia but also on medicine throughout North America. This influence was in part exerted through Scots doctors who had emigrated to America, but mainly through Americans who had sought their medical education at Edinburgh or, sometimes, Glasgow University.

Throughout the seventeenth century only a few doctors from Britain and the continent emigrated to the American colonies, for these offered little prospect of lucrative employment. In the eighteenth century, with an increase in urban populations and growing affluence, particularly in the southern colonies engaged in the tobacco trade, there were more opportunities for professional men such as doctors. A majority of these emigrating doctors came from Scotland.

The Edinburgh University medical faculty, established in 1726, offered the most comprehensive medical education available in Britain. It took the Leiden medical school as its model, and provided teaching in all the branches of medicine. Since all the first professors had spent some time at Leiden, the influence of Herman Boerhaave was paramount. An infirmary was established in 1729 partly to provide for clinical teaching. The teaching of practical surgery, first in the hands of Alexander Monro, *primus,* and then of his son, though neither of them was a practising surgeon, was rather neglected. About 1766 James Rae began private lectures in surgery, and after 1770 managed to organize surgery classes at the infirmary. The private classes of John Bell, started in 1790, were so successful that the university professors organized an embargo on his using the infirmary and his teaching came to an end. Benjamin Bell, a student intent on becoming a surgeon, left Edinburgh in 1771 because, he said, 'had I now been entering the world as a physician I should never have thought of going further than where I have been, but for a *Surgeon,* I assure you Edinburgh comes far short of either Paris of London'.[1] A ward for lying-in women was opened at the infirmary in 1756 so that students could have practical experience in midwifery.

Edinburgh attracted not only Scotsmen but also Englishmen who, through religion or poverty, were excluded from Oxford and Cambridge. Its reputation grew until, by the second half of the century, it was considered the most important medical school in Europe and attracted an

114

international body of students. Glasgow University started medical lectures in 1748 but, though its reputation grew, it never, in the eighteenth century, came to rival that of Edinburgh. Neither St. Andrews nor the colleges of Aberdeen offered any systematic medical education.

Scotland was a poor country and many of her doctors had no prospect of gainful employment in their native land. Some moved to England, others joined the armed forces or emigrated to British possessions overseas, including the American colonies. The chosen destinations in America were those colonies which, through emigration or trade, particularly the tobacco trade, already had Scottish settlements. The American colonies also offered a refuge to Scots doctors like Peter Middleton, Hugh Middleton and William Vans Murray who had supported the Stuart cause in 1715 or 1745 and found it politic to escape overseas.

It is impossible to give the total number of Scots doctors who emigrated to America in the eighteenth century. Those, like William Douglas in Boston, Alexander Garden and John Lining in South Carolina, and William Hunter in Rhode Island, who made their mark on American medicine are well known. Others served well a local community, but do not make the pages of American medical history. It is only in a little known local history of Dorchester County, Maryland,[2] that there is a record of William Vans Murray, cousin and ward of the Duke of Atholl, who escaped to Maryland after the 1715 uprising, settled in Cambridge, Dorchester County, and made a large fortune by the practice of medicine. Family papers on both sides of the Atlantic can sometimes help. John Murray, who emigrated to south Carolina about 1746, is nowhere recorded, except in the Murray of Murraythwaite Muniments at the Scottish Record Office[3], while knowledge of William Fyffe, also an emigrant doctor in South Carolina, comes from the Fyffe letters in the William L. Clements Library, University of Michigan.[4] There are certainly others of whom no record remains.

Incomplete as the records are, it is possible from them to sketch the pattern of emigration of Scottish doctors – how it was determined by previous emigration, family relationships and trade. Probably all the colonies received some Scottish doctors, but by far the largest number, at least forty-five, went to Virginia whilst nineteen went to Maryland: both were colonies connected with Scotland through the tobacco trade. At least nineteen, if not more, went to South Carolina which had a number of Scottish settlements. The medical histories of these three colonies have been studied in some detail, and this has led to the identification of many of these men. Massachusetts likewise has been investigated in this way and twelve Scots doctors have been identified in different parts of the colony, although it never received many Scots emigrants. Fifteen Scots doctors are known to have gone to North Carolina which had several Scottish settlements. In the remaining colonies where no particular study has been made of local records, nine are recorded in New York, seven in Pennsylvania, four in Rhode Island, three each in New Jersey and Georgia, two in Maine, one each in Connecticut, Florida and New Hampshire and none in Delaware,[5], but further research may well augment these numbers.

It is not possible to be certain of the medical education of these men. Those who emigrated before the Edinburgh medical school had been founded must have obtained their education either by apprenticeship or, like Cadwallader Colden or William Douglas, had gone abroad. Colden went to London and Paris and Douglas to Paris and Leiden, obtaining a medical degree from Utrecht in 1712, whilst Thomas Moffat graduated at Rheims. Some younger men certainly graduated at Edinburgh, but others, for whom an Edinburgh education is claimed, may well have attended lectures in years for which no medical class lists survive but never graduated.[6]

Whatever their education, a number of these men brought to America a knowledge of modern medicine and kept in touch with medical developments in Europe. Some were men of wide interests and aware of the new approach by observation and experiment to medical and general scientific problems. As yet there were no scientific or medical journals published in America, so some of their papers on the effect of climate on the incident and expression of diseases, on small pox, yellow fever and diptheria – which from time to time assumed epidemic proportions in American towns and local communities[7] – were sent back to Britain for publication. Outside medicine they contributed to the knowledge of the American fauna and flora.[8] Cadwallader Colden, venturing into pure physics, even attempted to explain the causes of gravity.[9] These Scotsmen provided not all but a considerable amount of the medical and scientific writing to come out of America in the first half of the eighteenth century. William Hunter in Rhode Island and Peter Middleton in association with John Bard in New York provided early classes in anatomy. Though Cadwallader Colden was unsuccessful in founding an intercolonial scientific society,[10] William Douglas founded the first American medical society in Boston in 1736.[11] Nor was it only in medicine and science that they played a part, for a number of them entered into the artistic life and politics of the country.

But these Scotsmen were not the only way by which America kept in touch with European medicine. From the earliest days of the colonies, the sons of the wealthier colonists were sent back to Europe for their education. In the seventeenth century a few had studied medicine in England or on the continent. Various factors contributed to the growing numbers who, after the middle of the eighteenth century, sought their medical education in Britain. There was growing affluence in the colonies, particularly in those engaged in the tobacco trade. Undoubtedly, some, through contact with emigrant doctors, became aware of the limitations of the local apprenticeship system of medical education. Emigrant doctors tended to send their sons back to Scotland for their education. And, in addition, the cessation of hostilities between Britain and France in 1748 made passage across the Atlantic safer.

When in 1760 Arthur Lee from Virginia discussed with Dr Samuel Johnson where he should study medicine, he was told:

> that at Cambridge or Oxford, they never permit the students to attempt Physic till seven years study there has enabled them to take a Degree of Master of Arts. 'Therefore' says he 'if you have a large fortune and time enough to spare, go to either of these. If you would choose immediately to enter upon Physic and to attain sufficient knowledge Therein to carry you through life, at a small expense and in a short time, by all means go to Edinburgh or Leyden. . .'[12]

No Americans had the time or money during the eighteenth century to take their whole medical education at either Cambridge or Oxford, though a few like Charles Drayton from Virginia took some classes at Oxford[13] before moving to Edinburgh to complete his education. Others attended the hospitals and private medical and anatomical lectures in London, but these did not lead to a degree. A number therefore applied to either St Andrews or the colleges of Aberdeen for an M.D. which could be acquired on recommendation without attending the university. But the medical school at Edinburgh, with its comprehensive medical education and its certificate of competence in the form of an M.D. degree, attracted ever increasing numbers of Americans.

Again it is impossible to be sure that all those who studied in Scotland have been recorded. Those who graduated at Edinburgh or Glasgow appear in published lists,[14] but more than half who attended lectures did not take a degree. From the matriculation books of Edinburgh University from 1762 onwards and the class lists they contain it is possible to indentify many American students as their birthplace is recorded. The professors sometimes kept their own class lists to check on the payment of class dues, which were their only salary; but these class lists are neither complete nor cover the whole period from 1726 to the end of the century,[15] so failure to find the name of someone said by tradition to have studied at Edinburgh is not absolute proof that he was not there. If any studied at Glasgow without taking degrees there is no way of being certain, for, except for anatomy from 1790, no medical class lists survive.[16]

Only five Americans are recorded definitely as studying at Edinburgh before 1750; Phineas Bond in 1742, John Redman in 1746 and Charles Moore and Benjamin Morris arrived there in 1748, all from Philadelphia. John Moultrie, from South Carolina, son of an emigrant Scots doctor of the same name, in 1749, was the first American to take an Edinburgh M.D. Some others, like John Jones of New York and John Cumming of Boston, also may have been there around 1750. From 1750 onwards till the end of the century a hundred and six Virginians, forty-nine South Carolinians and twenty-four Marylanders were there, of whom thirty-seven Virginians, twenty-one from South Carolina and ten from Maryland graduated. These men came from affluent regions with strong family or trade connections with Scotland. Some of the Virginians also attended lectures and hospitals

Table I. The numbers of Americans from the different colonies or states who were in Scotland for each five-year period between 1740 and 1800.

	Connecticut	Delaware	Florida	Georgia	Kentucky	Maryland	Massachusetts	New Hampshire	New Jersey	New York	N. Carolina	Pennsylvania	Rhode Island	S. Carolina	Virginia	Americans	Total
1745								1				1					2
1750							1			1		2		1			5
1755	1				1	1				1		1					5
1760	1						2				1	3		1	5		13
1765	1					1	3			4		5	1	4	10	4	33
1770							3		1	1		3		6	11		25
1775		1					1					6		6	5		19
1780		1				3	1			2		2	1	3	8		21
1785	1	1				3	2			4		3		1	9		24
1790	1		2	1		4				2		3		5	11		29
1795	1			1	1	6				4	5	11		9	21	1	60
1800		1		1	1	3	2	1		3	1	1	1	13	26	1	54
Total	4	4	–	6	3	24	12	1	2	22	7	41	3	49	106	6	290

in London, but those from South Carolina and Maryland studied almost exclusively at Edinburgh.

Pennsylvania also sent a considerable number to Edinburgh. Through Benjamin Franklin, they were advised on their medical studies by Dr John Fothergill, an eminent London physician and himself a graduate of Edinburgh. Two Philadelphians who profited from his advice to 'lay a foundation of practice before entering upon theory'[17] spent a winter in London studying anatomy with William Hunter and attending the hospitals, and then went to Edinburgh to learn the more theoretical aspects of medicine. William Shippen graduated there in 1761. So inspired was he by the medical education he had received that he started providing anatomy lectures in Philadelphia. When John Morgan, who had graduated in 1763, returned in 1764 he and Shippen put into effect plans they had been maturing for establishing in Philadelphia the first American medical school. It opened in 1765. Founded on the pattern of Edinburgh, the first and all the succeeding professors until the end of the century, except Thomas Bond, professor of clinical medicine, were all Edinburgh-trained and even some of the lectures were based on notes taken at Edinburgh. Philadelphia had already imitated Edinburgh by establishing a hospital in 1752. Undoubtedly these professors encouraged some of their students to take the same road to medical proficiency as they had themselves taken, for as yet Philadelphia could not provide all that could be obtained at Edinburgh or London. In all, forty-one Philadelphians studied at Edinburgh, of whom seventeen also studied at London. Fourteen took degrees, but some came to Edinburgh having already obtained medical degrees from Philadelphia.

Samuel Bard from New York, who had known John Morgan at Edinburgh, heard about the plans for a Philadelphia medical school and was fired by ambition to found something similar in New York.[18] In 1768, together with James Smith and John van Brugh Tennent, both Edinburgh graduates, and the Scotsman Peter Middleton, he was instrumental in the founding of the medical school of King's College. A hospital had been opened in New York in 1767.

While the medical school of Philadelphia survived the Revolution eventually to amalgamate with the University of Pennsylvania in 1791, the medical school of King's College was disrupted and was only re-established in 1792 by the trustees of Columbia University, which replaced King's College. Of the twenty-three New Yorkers who went to Edinburgh, seven went before the founding of King's College and sixteen between 1780 and 1800, of whom nine proceeded to a degree there while one graduated at Glasgow and two at Leiden.

Georgia and North Carolina, which had a number of Scottish settlements but were poor colonies, sent only one student to Edinburgh before the Revolution. After 1776 Georgia sent five and North Carolina six, of whom three from Georgia but none from North Carolina graduated. Massachusetts, though comparatively wealthy, traded mainly with London and this is where most from that state chose to study, only twelve going to Edinburgh, two of whom were sons of Scottish emigrants, and of all those only three graduated. From Connecticut and Delaware four, from Rhode Island three, from New Jersey two, from New Hampshire one, and from Maine none, were at Edinburgh, and of all these only one, George Monro from Delaware, graduated in 1786.

Harvard opened its medical school in 1783. This differed from the Philadelphia and King's College medical schools in that only one of its first professors, Banjamin Waterhouse, had been at Edinburgh, a reflection of the limited attraction Edinburgh had for Massachusetts medical students.

The last medical school to open in the eighteenth century was at Dartmouth, New Hampshire, in 1798, mainly through the activities of Nathan Smith who had been at both Glasgow and Edinburgh.

It was thought that the establishment of American medical schools would reduce the numbers coming to Edinburgh, though this did not happen until

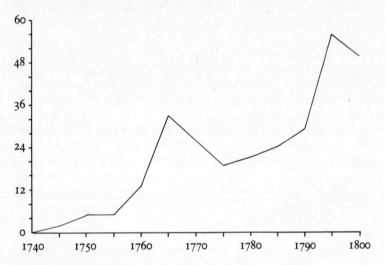

Graph I. American medical students in Scotland 1740–1800

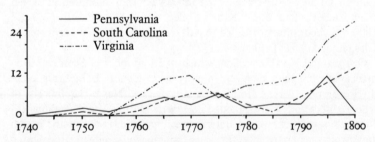

Graph II. American medical students from Pennsylvania, South Carolina and Virginia in Scotland 1740–1800

right at the end of the century. Between 1745 and 1755 the numbers rose slowly and between 1755 and 1765 much more steeply. Between 1765 and 1775 they did fall, but this is much more likely to have resulted not from the establishment of the Philadelphia and New York schools but from the contentions and trade disputes between America and Britain that brought about a shortage of ready money in America, which made people reluctant to buy bills of exchange from American students abroad. Surprisingly between 1775 and 1780 the numbers fell only very slightly. From 1780, even before the end of the Revolution, the numbers started to climb steeply until 1795 (see Graph I). ough after 1795 the number from Virginia and South Carolina continued to increase, only one Philadelphian was at Edinburgh during the last five years of the century (see Graph II).

Some who studied at Edinburgh chose to graduate at Glasgow.[19] Within the century Edinburgh several times tightened up the regulations for graduating, demanding attendance at a full range of courses at the university and at least two years attendance at the university, unless evidence was forthcoming that studies had been pursued at some other institution of similar standing. Before graduation a thesis had to be presented and defended in Latin. Some, like Benjamin Rush, found themselves 'less acquainted with classical and philosophical learning than was necessary to comprehend all that was taught in Medicine',[20] and not all repaired the deficiency, as did Rush by taking coaching in Latin from Dr John Brown, promoter of the Brunonian theory of disease, who maintained himself and family by teaching and translating theses into Latin. Glasgow, therefore, offered an escape for those weak in Latin, as it neither required a Latin thesis nor any residential qualification, only evidence of an adequate medical education. It was a help as well to those who could afford only a limited time in Scotland. It was also cheaper. A few, like George Glentworth and Ralph Ashton, applied to St Andrews or to one of the Aberdeen colleges for degrees, where again no thesis or residence was required. Others, like Benjamin Smith Barton and Benjamin Waterhouse, went on to graduate at continental universities.

Outside the medical lectures there were student medical societies where they discussed amongst themselves, sometimes in Latin, the medical problems of the day. The most famous was the Medical, later the Royal Medical Society, still in existence, to which many of the Americans were elected and in which Casper Wistar, Benjamin Smith Barton and George Logan all served as president.[21] The Chirurgo-Physical Society attracted few Americans and only John Pennington read them a paper.[22] The Physical, later the Royal Physical Society, founded in 1771, had many American members;[23] this society absorbed the American Physical Society which existed from 1794 to 1797, its membership being mainly, but not exclusively, American.[24] An early association of Virginian students aimed at mutual improvement in anatomy and the improvement of medicine back home.[25]

Outside the field of medical studies, some, like John Morgan, attended other univesity lectures such as those in rhetoric, philosophy or mathematics.[26] Professor John Walker's natural history lectures attracted a large American following,[27] and many also joined the Edinburgh Natural History Society[28] and read papers to it.[29] Others, like Benjamin Smith

Barton, Thomas Caw, William Charles Wells and James McClurg, became members of the prestigious Speculative Society,[30] discussing and
debating historical, literary and political subjects.

Some had opportunities of meeting the leaders of the enlightenment.
Arthur Lee, on a visit to Glasgow, spent a whole day with Adam Smith.[31]
John Morgan was introduced by Benjamin Franklin to Sir Alexander Dick,
President of the Royal College of Physicians,[32] whom Benjamin Rush also
met and was introduced by him to David Hume.[33] Morgan's introduction
to Dick and also to Lord Provost Drummond served him well as he was
elected a Fellow of the College of Physicians and was made a burgess of the
city of Edinburgh, as were Benjamin Rush and Samuel Bard. Friendships
were established with some of the 'best' families. William Hogg, the
banker, introduced Rush to Lord Leven, and Rush established friendship
with the whole family. When the second son was killed in the Battle of
Princeton during the Revolution, Rush was able to arrange his decent
burial and the erection of a memorial to him.[34]

They mostly lived with private families, were entertained by various
citizens and, as far as time would permit, entered into the social life of the
city, attending the churches, theatres, concerts and assemblies. Quakers
came with a certificate to the Edinburgh Society of Friends,[35] though
Caspar Wistar had difficulty in obtaining one as he had fallen 'into the
scandalous & alarming temptation of being engaged in a duel'.[36] Benjamin
Rush was a regular attender at the High Church of Edinburgh to hear Mr
Walker preach.[37] John Ravenscroft's accounts record frequent purchases of
theatre tickets.[38] Thomas Parke was also a theatre-goer.[39] John Morgan,
with good introductions, thoroughly enjoyed the assemblies.[40]

The students' reactions to their time in Edinburgh are recorded in letters
home to relations and friends, and in the diaries some of them kept. Thomas
Bulfinch, who left London in 1756 much to the surprise of his friends there,
found to his 'no small satisfaction that in the character I had of this place in
respect of the physical advantages it has over London, is true. . . and I am
well assured that if I had come here as soon as I arrived in England I should
have made much greater progress in the knowledge of my business than I
did in London'.[41] Thomas Bond, in 1771, considering European schools of
medicine for his son, Richard, wrote of the Edinburgh school, with which
he was not personally acquainted but knew many of the young men who had
studied there, 'it seems at this time to be better calculated to please the fancy
than to form the judgement and indeed the many extraordinary novelties
inculated there would be a Barr to public confidence in this part of the
world'.[42] This opinion of an elder statesman of medicine was not shared by
the younger generation, for as Franklin replied to him, 'the general run' of
American students was to Edinburgh.[43] William Quynn, in 1783,
commented on the 'Spirit of controversy amongst our Professors new

theories appear daily'.[44] This was at the time of the dispute between William Cullen and Dr John Brown who, in 1780 in his Elementa Medicinae, attempted to demolish the system of physic as taught at Edinburgh by Dr Cullen with his own Brunonian System, attributing all disease to over-excitement or debility of the nervous system, to be cured by treatment with opium or alcohol. His system owed much to Cullen's own ideas on disturbances of the nervous system in causing disease. Cullen's method of teaching, however, left students well aware of the tentative nature of many medical theories and encouraged them to subject all medical opinions to critical analysis and free discussion. It was this that his students found so stimulating.

By the end of the century, with William Cullen dead and Alexander Monro *secundas* having given the same lectures for nearly forty years, perhaps Edinburgh no longer shone so brightly. Nathan Smith, for instance, complained that having 'attended the medical and surgical operations in Glasgow, Edinburgh and London' he was 'disappointed to find them faulty in this country who have been so much looked up to by our own country and so little real merit'.[45]

As the individual professors, almost without exception it was William Cullen who won the admiration and affection of the Americans, 'The great, the unrivaled Dr Cullen',[46] 'that shining oracle of physic',[47] 'certainly one of the greatest men that ever lived, his method in arrangement and his perspicuity in argument as astonishingly true and convincing'.[48] He invited second year students to his house, gave them extra lectures and opportunities for discussion.[49] Many were welcomed as friends of the family and remained so for the rest of their lives.

Of the other professors, the anatomy lectures of Alexander Monro *secundus* rarely met with much approbation:

He is too much of a Philosopher to enter so minutely into his subject as the demonstrative part of it requires, on which account students may attend him three or four years without gaining a proper knowledge of this kind. But in his physiology perhaps no person is equal to him in perspicuity and strength of argument. A large fortune has lulled his genius to sleep; he therefore does not fatigue himself in making new discoveries but contents himself with delivering his lectures nearly verbatim as he did fifteen years ago.[50]

Moreover, the teaching of anatomy was hampered by 'the prejudices of the Scots', which made difficult the procuring of bodies for dissection.[51]

Thomas Parke's enthusiasm for Cullen did not extend to other professors. Of Francis Home he feared that 'Materia Medica will gain little improvements under his efforts'.[52] His was an uninformed criticism, for Home made substantial contributions to medical knowledge. As for Joseph Black, Parke cannot have been ignorant of his achievements in chemistry, but 'blushed for his delivery',[53] and according to another student his lectures were 'more suited to the Philosopher than the Practitioner'.[54] Dr Gregory, in 1778, 'was a young man and would shine but his state of health will not allow him to pay that attention to his studies which may perhaps be necessary. . . While Dr Duncan makes the greatest figure amongst these but he has nothing except his indefatigable industry to recommend him'.[55] Other students held quite different opinions, certainly about Joseph Black. Charles Minor of Virginia wrote from Edinburgh to Dr Augustus Smith in December 1790:

> The Professor of Chemistry possess the power of communicating his thoughts with ease and clearness in a more eminant degree than any man I ever heard. . . but Dr. Monro is not bless'd with that fluency and perspicuity of language for which Dr. Black is so remarkable. . . the excellence and sound judgement evident in the remarks will certainly compensate. . . I have added Materia Medica. . . of Dr. Home I will say nothing, indeed his documents are too sublime for my comprehension. . . I can no more understand them than a Hottentot would an Italian.[56]

William Quynn of Maryland, in 1783, wrote that 'there seems to be a great spirit of Emulation prevailing here amongst the students, who will excell in medical research, they seem to be indefatigable'.[57] But except for John Leigh of Virginia who, in 1786, won the Harveian prize for his essay *An experimental Inquiry into the properties of Opium,* and Benjamin Smith Barton, who also won the Harveian prize for his essay on *hyosciamus niger,* or black henbane, none of the Americans showed much interest in research. Their theses were digests of published work and other people's opinions. Back in America the climate was not yet ripe for experimental medicine. The practice of medicine, which generally involved surgery and dispensing as well as the normal work of the physician, was too demanding and too unrewarding to provide the leisure that was necessary for medical research. Benjamin Rush, stimulated by the ideas of William Cullen and John Brown, went on to postulate his own theory, without any experimental backing, that all disease was due to disturbances of the arterial system, to be cured by massive bleeding, treatment that was to be so disastrous in epidemics of yellow fever in Philadphia.

As to students' opinion of the city of Edinburgh and their fellow students, Arthur Lee wrote to his brother 'Nothing can be more disagreeable to me than this town and the manners of the people in it'.[58] The native students were also looked on with disfavour, 'more licentious youths are hardly to be found anywhere than I remember to have seen in Edinburgh'.[59] And George Logan told his brother that out of Monro's class of 300 there were not twenty he would wish to associate with.[60]

One common complaint in students' letters was shortage of money.

Delays in the mail, letters that went astray, a fall in the price of tobacco all produced their problems and left them dangerously short of cash. Thomas Ruston was driven almost to despair through shortage of money.[61] Nor was it always bills of exchange that were sent. Thomas Quynn wrote to his father that 'the young gentlemen who are here from Virginia are supplied with to-bacco, which I imagine would be a more profitable remittance than bills'.[62]

The students received various commissions from home. Arthur Lee looked for suitable tutors for the children of his brother and other friends.[63] As mentioned earlier, Benjamin Rush negotiated with John Witherspoon on behalf of the College of New Jersey, persuading him to accept the principalship of the College.[64] He also solicited gifts of books for the college from various bodies in Scotland. Benevolence did not flow only one way. Alexander Hamilton in Annapolis, in 1741, sent a contribution to the Edinburgh infirmary but could not get anyone else to contribute because trade was so bad.[65] And contributions to the infirmary also came from Philadelphia.

Their time in Edinburgh coming to an end, they invested any remaining money in books, surgical instruments and drugs and returned home, many of them to be, as Benjamin Franklin predicted of John Morgan, 'of great use to their country as well as an honour to the Medical School of Edinburgh'.[66]

Most of them were sound and careful physicians, and in spite of the 'novelties' that they had been subjected to most of them were conservative in their practice, guided more by common sense than speculation. So much so that one apprentice-trained practitioner described his Edinburgh-trained colleague as:

> Those self swolen sons of pedantic absurdity fresh and raw from that universal asylum of medical perfection Edinburgh. . . (who) enter with obstinate assurance the old round of obsolete prescriptions, which their infallible masters taught them, and like the mule that turns aside for no man, push on in their bloody career till the surrounding mortality but more especially the danger of their own thick skulls, bring them to a pause and works in them a new conviction.[67]

Indeed, for many years, except for a few physicians who attempted to put John Brown's ideas into practice, theory had little effect on the treatment of patients. Beyond the specific action of a few drugs like bark, mercury, digitalis and accepted purges and emetics, and recourse to bleeding, the physician had no tools at his command and practice varied according to the readiness with which doctors resorted to purges and bleeding. Edinburgh-trained doctors did not introduce any new methods of practice into America, though most of them set an example of reasonable practice by the standards of the day. In the northern regions the Edinburgh-trained doctors were so few that they can have little personal influence, except very locally, either through an example of how they went about their business or as a source of new medical knowledge.

Improvements in midwifery and surgery did not come to America through Edinburgh. No man trained only at Edinburgh made a name for himself as a man-midwife. Ephraim McDowell, a Virginian who moved to Kentucky, became famous for ovariotomies. He did study at Edinburgh, but he is the only American known to have attended John Bell's private surgery classes. Philip Syng Physic, sometimes called the father of American surgery, graduated at Edinburgh in 1792 but learnt his surgery from John Hunter in London.

Men who had been at Edinburgh joined the ranks of American medical authors, and in 1797 Samuel Latham Mitchell founded the *Medical Repository*, the first American medical journal. The botany and natural history lectures at the university stimulated interest in these subjects. George Logan was known as a keen amateur botanist, and John Mitchell was not only a botanist but also a mapmaker.[68] Adam Kuhn, who had also studied in Sweden with Linnaeus, was the first professor of botany and materia medica at Philadelphia, and Benjamin Smith Barton the first botany professor at the University of Pennsylvania. Benjamin Waterhouse, appointed professor of natural history at the College of Rhode Island in 1782, went on to give lectures in natural history at Harvard in 1783. Samuel Latham Mitchell was the first active professor of natural history at Colombia.

But Scotland's, and in particular Edinburgh's, greatest contribution to American medicine was in the inspiration that it gave to William Shippen, John Morgan and Samuel Board and their associates to set up in Philadelphia and New York the first medical schools in America. Though professional medical education was bound to start in America some time, that it started at that particular time and was organised in that particular way was due to the satisfaction and inspiration that Edinburgh gave to those students, which made them determined that America herself should have medical schools in the same style. George Buchanan attempted but failed to found a medical school in Baltimore, though he gave private medical lectures on diseases of woman and the Brunonian system. Many other Edinburgh-trained men passed on the benefits of their training to their apprentices. That the Philadelphian school achieved a good reputation there is little doubt. Perhaps it was not entirely chauvinism which prompted Benjamin Smith Barton to write to Benjamin Rush in 1787 that he was 'convinced by experience that little was wanting in Philadphia to make that school one of the first seats of medicine in the world'.[69] In 1791 Daniel Coxe proposed sending his son from England to study medicine not in Edinburgh but with Dr Rush in Philadelphia.[70] Inspired by Edinburgh, America was set on the path which has led to the high reputation that she now possesses in medical education and research.

Chapter Seven

DISCORD AND DISRUPTION

The accession of George III is an appropriate point from which to survey a half-century of expansion. In sacrificing indpendence Scotland had gained an empire. It is true that this expansion took place under the flag of the United Kingdom, but Scots could regard it as a national achievement. At the close of the sevententh century they had been unsuccessful competitors in the contest for overseas trade and possessions, but sixty years later they could compare their fortunes favourably with those of Denmark, Sweden, and the German states. Scots were established in all the commercial centres of North America and the Caribbean, the Clyde was a focal point in the Atlantic trading system, and substantial numbers from both Highlands and Lowlands had found new homes abroad.

Commercial profits had accumulated, the trade in re-exported tobacco had reached enormous proportions, and the export trade had given a great stimulus to manufactures. The benefits were unevenly distributed, but prosperity filtered down and the whole country had moved from the shadow of poverty which had darkened enterprise. Increased opportunity had fostered social mobility, while emigration had provided a safety valve both for the ambitious and the depressed. Building upon the foundations of a sound educational system, medicine, history, and philosophy had attained international statute.

In the light of this achievement, Scottish alarm at colonial unrest and revolution hardly requires explanation. Fifty years of enterprise and effort were placed in jeopardy. The loyalism of Scots in America was not perverse allegiance to an alien king, but a determination to preserve national interests that had been so greatly advanced under the descendents of James VI and I.

There was however another component in Scottish attitudes to the American Revolution. Moral philosophy, as expounded by Francis Hutcheson and his pupils, provided a battery of arguments for resistance to British authority, and the extent of this influence upon Thomas Jefferson has been persuasively argued. Two leading intellectuals of the Revolution – James Wilson and John Witherspoon – expressed ideas that had become common currency in the Scottish universities. Witherspoon also expressed an older tradition in calvinist thought which sanctioned resistance when rulers departed from the ways of the Lord and prophets were raised up to rebuke them. Thus the Revolution that threatened material achievement also vindicated an intellectual tradition that Scots had done so much to transmit to America.

These subtleties were of little significance to Scottish merchants resident in America, who saw only an immediate threat to their interests if the authority of the crown and the supremacy of Parliament were challenged. In the tobacco trade the conflict of interest was clear. The structure of the business was determined by the British laws of trade and navigation. Glasgow had succeeded in competition with the English ports, but the future was uncertain if the Americans could trade direct with Europe in foreign ships. The business dependended much upon the willingness of Glasgow merchants to allow the planters to take goods on credit and, however much relations between individuals depended upon mutual confidence, the sanction behind the system was the ability to recover debts in courts where judges acted in the King's name. Moreover the whole investment would be imperilled if colonial legislature won the right to issue legal tender paper money.

In commercial centres away from the Chesapeke the issues were less clearcut. Scottish merchants and professional men were divided in their attitude toward the dispute with Britain, but when finally men had to take a stand Scots everywhere contributed more than their proportionate share to Loyalism.[1] Nor do the numbers of professed Loyalists tell the whole story; many who secretly deplored revolution could not afford to make their gesture, were terrorised into compliance, or chose acquiescence as the most prudent course. In the tobacco colonies there are records of several factors who tried to ride out the storm as the best way of serving their employers and salvaging the losses inflicted by civil disturbance.

In the early stages of the dispute there were few overt expressions of support for British government. Indeed no commercial interest benefited from the Stamp Act and many endorsed the principle of no taxation with representation. The situation changed when popular protest threatened property and the normal work of the courts was disrupted. Nor were merchants likely to welcome the Townshend Acts, and several gave assurance that they would do nothing to infringe non-importation agreements. Nevertheless men whose livelihood depended upon importing from Britain were certain to incur suspicion, and many would observe the letter rather the spirit of colonial measures. Inasmuch as so many Scots merchants depended upon the direct trade with Britain they had every incentive to co-operate with the authorities wherever British troops or a resolute Governor afforded protection for legal trade.

Scots were also victims of the pseudo-radicalism associated with John Wilkes, for whom the Americans had an exaggerated respect. Wilkes had made alleged Scottish influence at Court a main (sometimes the only) item in his attack on the government, and in America Scottish merchants shared in the opprobrium when they seemed to seek the favour of royal officials. To this was added the poor reputation that traders and monied men always enjoy in a society dominated by upper-class landowners. It has been suggested in a previous chapter that the unpopularity of the Scots in Virginia may have been exaggerated and that the benefits of the economic relationship bred mutual understanding. Nevertheless tension existed and the strain became severe in difficult times. It was also unfortunate that the crisis of the Revolution followed hard upon the heels of a major economic crisis, which had forced the Scots to appear as grasping and unsympathetic creditors.[2]

Highlanders provide the best known example of Scottish loyalism, and to many its cause is bewildering. Wallace Brown, a historian of loyalism, asks 'why should these traditional opponents of the House of Hanover, with bitter memories of 1715 and 1745, fight for their erstwhile enemy?'[3] He suggests that many were recent immigrants and had had little chance of 'becoming Americanized'. Further reasons, adduced from Duane Meyer's work of Highlanders in North Carolina, are British successes in conciliating former opponents, service by many Highland gentlemen in the British army, generous land grants, fear of losing property, the natural conservatism of their leaders, and the traditional allegiance of Campbells to the Crown.

Both the question and the answer must be qualified. The Highland settlers were not uniformly Loyalist. In Georgia they supported the Revolution, and Lachlan McIntosh was prominent in state politics. In the Carolinas Highlanders were divided, though it is true that the majority were Loyalist. In New York an added factor was that many of the Highlanders were Catholic, so generalisations based on protestants in North Carolina may not apply. Nor is it true that all Highlanders were traditional enemies of the House of Hanover, though a minority had fought for the Pretender in 1715 and rather more in 1745. The Campbells were the best known but not the only clan opposed to the Stuarts and in favour of the Protestant succession.

Most Highlanders had left Scotland because of high rents and oppressive treatment by landlords. They did not associate these misfortunes with the King, and had no wish to see the colonial upper class given the same opportunity of exploitation. In Scotland Highland dress had been forbidden, but in the colonies it was permitted. The Catholic Highlanders had suffered from discrimination at home, but in America had land of their own and freedom to worship as they chose. To win these privileges they had sworn an oath of allegiance to the King, and a bond of honour was not to be lightly cast aside.

Highlanders remained a race apart and wished to preserve their independence. The means depended upon local circumstances. In Georgia they were well-established, did not feel threatened by other Georgians, and were prepared to defend the autonomy of the colony they had helped to build. In North Carolina some enjoyed a modest prosperity, but others were still poor and insecure with the threat to their independence coming from landowners, land speculators, and Wilmington merchants. Catholic Highlanders in New York had even clearer reasons for fearing the ascendency of the 'patriots'. The Quebec Act had aroused exaggerated fears, and abuse of Catholicism was a part of the stock-in-trade of anti-British rhetoric. It does not seem that other Highlanders in New York were moved by hostility to their landlords, who appear to have observed the generous terms on which they had offered land, but folk memory may have taught the tenants to regard with suspicion all invisible owners of large estates.

Perhaps the most potent factor in Highland loyalism was not material calculation or suspicions of the colonial upper class, but a strong attachment to their clan and country. Separation from Britain was not merely renunciation of allegiance to a distant king; it would snap the cords that bound together Highland people on both sides of the Atlantic.

The Revolution caused a radical change in the relationship between Scotland and America. Trade would revive, migration would resume and the reputation of Scottish learning and science would reach new heights; but all this would be seen as an aspect of relations between Great Britain and the United States rather than as a specific contribution by Scotland to American society. The reputation of Scotland would re-emerge in romantic guise, and lowland members of St Andrew's societies would be eager to adopt the symbols of Highland dress. But apart from occasional indulgence in ethnic nostalgia, lowland Scots and many of the Highlanders became invisible men in the later story of migration and settlement. The Scottish merchants who had acted as coherent and self-conscious groups in the colonial towns were split apart by the Revolution. If loyalist they lost all; if supporters of the Revolution they became part of a larger movement. They ceased to be Scots resident in America, and became Americans of Scottish descent.

It has been argued that the Glasgow companies suffered less damage than has sometimes been supposed.[4] Seven failed between 1775 and 1785, but the rate of failure in eighteenth-century business was always high and seven in ten years was not unusual. The bankrupt companies had imported only a small proportion of tobacco landed in the Clyde, lacked the resouces to hold large stocks and could not profit from the rise in prices once the exceptionally heavy imports of 1775 were depleted. The more successful firms were able to make windfall profits which more than offset the loss of assets in America.[5] One crash which attracted much attention and inflicted losses upon a considerable number of creditors was the failure of Buchanan, Hastie, & Co., with its associated companies of Bogle, Jamieson & Co. and

James Jamieson & Co., in December 1977. Buchanan, Hastie & Co. may have lost more in proportion to other tobacco companies, because they owned land in Virginia, but their losses there probably did not exceed £13,000 though they failed for over £62,000. The bulk of their creditors were not firms who had supplied goods, but those who had deposited money on loan. Difficulties arising from war and the interruption of trade created alarm and a shortage of credit, but the root cause was unwise management in relying too heavily on borrowed funds.[6]

However valid the argument that Glasgow commerce was able to stand the shock, one cannot alter the fact that irreparable damage was done to Scottish enterprise in Virginia and Maryland. Even if the losses by individuals were not significantly large in proportion to their total assets, they could not be ignored. In Maryland the confiscation of loyalist property was drastic, and much of it passed into the hands of local buyers. Attempts by factors who remained to protect the property of their employers by fictitious sales were usually unsuccessful. In Virginia the authorities acted more slowly, and with greater regard for property rights. Estates were sequestered and placed under administrators, but the legal title of former owners was not extinguished and land was not auctioned. Factors who wished to wind up their affairs and leave were allowed to do so. In 1776 the *Virginia Gazette* carried many advertisements of impending departure with a request for all claims to be submitted and debts settled. Nevertheless the large concerns which had dominated the trade were forced to dismantle their organisations, and most factors who remained ceased to trade actively. The few exceptions were men who had cut adrift from the parent company some time before the Revolution, and now traded on their own account.

Some firms made an effort to re-establish themselves after the war but the going was not easy, and the burden of unpaid debt hung heavily over the enterprise and discouraged new ventures. Moreover the Virginian courts proved to be notoriously unsympathetic to creditors, and the state failed to enforce obligations accepted in 1783 and renewed in 1794. Not until 1802 was there anything approaching a final settlement, and then only on a greatly reduced scale of payment. These delays also meant that the British government took many years to investigate and settle the loyalist claims for compensation. Some of these claims were grossly inflated, but there were many families in Scotland of moderate means who struggled on into the nineteenth century in the hope that something would be recovered from the wreck of their American fortunes.

Thus the Revolutions closed a chapter in Scottish-American relations. The seventy years after the Union had seen Scotland develop a reputation for business success, medical science, philosophic thought, and academic excellence. The new relationship had fostered the idea that, consciously or unconsciously, Scotland was making a distinct contribution to American progress. After independence Americans remained aware of Scottish characteristics, but Scottish enterprise was seen as a component part of British power rather than as the thrust of a small nation seeking influence and wealth. In America those who remained accepted a new allegiance and retained only sentimental ties with the old country.

Tobacco merchants and factors were normally reticent about political events but some letters from John Reid comment freely upon disturbances during the Stamp Act crisis.[7] On 13 February 1766 he wrote that little business had been done since the act came into force, and that the consequences if it were not suspended could not be foreseen. He did not believe that Parliament would give up the right to tax the colonies, but the situation of men who tried to comply with the law was intolerable. One distributor of stamps had been compelled to resign and Reid had been 'really surprised at the behaviour of some of my acquaintances.' Closure of the courts meant that legal obligations were ignored and 'even the Negroes begin to be of opinion that Law is at an end and think that they are liberty to act and do accordingly.'

On 1 March 1766 Reid sent James McCall of Glasgow a description of the 'anarchy and confusion.' He said that some Scottish merchants had received threatening letters, while others were openly threatened with violence. 'In this the common people are not only concerned but most of the better sort are at their head.' Trade was in disarray and the most fortunate merchants were those with the smallest property in the colony.[8] At the close of this letter he added a long postscript describing the ordeal of Archibald Ritchie of Hobshole who had been compelled to take an oath, presumably to comply with the resolution not to use stamps.[9] Refusal would have meant that he would have 'been dragged at the tail of a cart,' placed in pillory at several places, and finally released in the county most distant from his home.

> The Essex rabble is headed by Warren, Upshaw, the Roans, etc. and your old acquaintances Merry Smith who shines in the Court Houses as a friend of liberty in epistolary addresses to his countrymen exhorting them against the Scotts merchants and the abolition of the Stamp Act.

The correspondence of Charles Steuart contains many letters describing discontent, protest and violence in the city of Norfolk.[10] In May 1769 his friend, James Parker, expressed the hope that 'in time the people of Norfolk will be convinced that we are all bound by the same laws, and that the people they are pleased to call foreigners have as good a claim to protection and justice as if any of their ancestors had first settled this colony.' In February 1773 Andrew Donald reported that 'the patriotic magistrates of Amherst County have resolved not to do business more than twice in the year until all the inhabitants were clear of debt,' and James Parker concluded that

> Generally speaking the more a man is in debt the greater Patriot he is, in short the meaning of words like Tyrant is greatly altered and calling a man a patriot here is saying he is in bad circumstances.

However he did not think that all the wrong was on one side. No settlement would be possible so long as the government insisted upon taxation without consent or representation. 'It was no part of the original plan of settlement that a Briton should lose his liberty by moving to any part of the Empire.'

In 1774 Parker described the coercion of Scottish merchants. James Dunlop had been given the choice between being hung and signing the Association; he had signed. In Maryland a Mr Stewart had been presented with the still more distressing choice between summary execution and setting fire to one of his own vessels which had carried proscribed goods. After 1774 information peters out. Regular sailings from Norfolk ceased, letters sent out of the colony were likely to be intercepted, and resident merchants became increasingly apprehensive. In 1776 their world literally went up in smoke as Norfolk was burnt, partly by British troops under Lord Dunmore and partly by retreating patriots. When the British fleet withdrew it carried many Scottish merchants to New York, while others took refuge in the country. James Parker escaped but it was six years before his wife learned that he was still alive.

Whatever the private opinions of the Scottish merchants most of them were circumspect in their dealings and tried to avoid giving offence. In 1770 William Cunninghame told Richard Blow, a Virginian merchant, that 'we shall take particular care that your Association is not infringed in any of the articles we ship you as we are determined to pay the strictest regard to it, where we are concerned ourselves.'[11]

The fullest account of the tribulations of Scottish factors in the period immediately preceding the final break is found in the letters of Alexander Hamilton of Piscataway in Maryland. They are preserved with the Glassford collection in the Library of Congress and have been published.[12] In May 1774 he wrote that the planters were withholding payment of their debts in order 'to terrify the trade of Glasgow and force them to petition Parliament for a repeal of the Tea Act, well knowing that they have very considerable property in this part of the continent'. Merchants were placed in serious difficulties if the courts were not open for the recovery of debts, and by 1775 Hamilton reported that they were virtually closed – at least for suits of this kind – by popular pressure. Merchants were being required to sign the Association, and the able-bodied were threatened with forced service in the militia. Hamilton had no sympathy with the colonial protests, but decided that the best way he could serve his own and his employers' interests would be by remaining in America. There is evidence in the

Maryland state records of his attempts to save property from confiscation by fictitious sales to residents, and after the war he seems to have bought in property of James Brown & Co. to prevent it being sold by public auction.[13] These kind of manoeuvres could not be executed while tempers ran high, and as tension increased the best that he could do was to make arrangements to ride out the storm.

In December 1774 Hamilton wrote 'I can do no more until an alteration of times, and this Anarchy and Confusion subsides;' in April 1775 'Good order, Regularity and Justice seem to be declining fast, and very unpopular they are, and I am afraid will be more so, if affairs do not take a turn soon'; and in August 1775, 'the most unexceptionable Conduct will not screen any man. The cry is now if they will not fight for us, they are against us, no neutrality now. I sincerely wish for an accommodation and peace lasting and agreeable to both parties'. In the same month he was confronted with a demand to sign the Association and hold himself for military service. By his own account he declared that he would not take up arms against his king and country, though it is not clear whether this defiance was open or privately expressed. To settle his personal problem he transferred the store to Mr Hoggan, a subordinate who was very lame, required him to sign the Association, and then removed himself to Virginia where the pressure was less intense. He spent the rest of the war on a Virginian estate that his brother, Francis, had obtained as security for debts owed by John Semple to the Hamilton family.[14] After peace he returned to Maryland and engaged in efforts to recover the debts and property of his employers.[15]

The Maryland authorities were particularly severe in their treatment of Loyalists. In 1775 two factors, Archibald Campbell and William Lilburn, petitioned the Provincial Convention against their condemnation for refusing to sell linen at their store.[16] They claimed that they were bound to put their regular customers first and intended to dispose of their effects to those with whom they constantly traded. British manufactures were scarce, and without them they had nothing with which to pay for tobacco. They had been censured in accordance with the resolution that 'no merchant or other person ought to ingross any Goods, Wares, or Merchandise whatsoever', but they were not hoarding for speculation. It is not recorded whether the authorities took a lenient view.

Another Scottish factor in Maryland, John Campbell, at first sympathised with the colonists. In June 1774 he wrote that 'the Americans are making a just and proper struggle for their Liberties and to prevent them and their posterity falling a Victim to the oppressive hand of arbitrary power.'[17] But he disapproved of the Boston 'tea party', and thought that his views were shared in the South by others, who regarded New Englanders as 'hypocritical, designing, and fanatical'. Things grew worse, tar and feathers awaited anyone who spoke out, and 'We poor Scotch factors are looked upon here in general, with a very jealous eye as Enemies to the Country; & indeed by their Conduct they would endeavour to render us so, however we may be otherwise inclined.' By October 1775 he would express his views only in a letter entrusted to a friend, because correspondence was intercepted and 'it is even dangerous to communicate one's sentiments to paper, unless wholly coinciding with the ideas of our Western *Patriots,* who wish what is impossible, a universal Unanimity of Sentiment.'

In August 1776 John Campbell returned to Glasgow. With great difficulty he had obtained permission to leave Maryland, and once home he wrote that for six months past he had been 'deprived of every sense of the smallest freedom of action or even sentiment, amidst a constant bawling for Liberty & execration of arbitrary measures.' He and others had been 'in a state of slavish bondage to the most tyrannical Despotic & persecuting system ever produced from illegal usurpation or misguided enthusiastic zeal.'

Another example of the harrassment of suspected Scottish Loyalists in Maryland is provided by the case of the Revd. John Patterson.[18] He was summoned for having spoken words 'which reflected upon the Convention'. He defended himself by saying that 'the multitude was deluded, that he did not see why he should not judge upon the proceedings of the Convention . . . and that there was more liberty in Turkey than in this Province.' His case was remitted to the Council of Safety and he was then imprisoned. The Maryland records contain several letters of protest and requests for habeas corpus from Patterson. He was released but died soon after.

Several Maryland records deal with the confiscation of British property and its subsequent sale,[19] and others with events after the peace, when the state authorities refused to return Loyalist property or compensate the owners. These entries also provide valuable evidence for the extent of Scottish property in Maryland. James Dunlop & Co. lost 'a very valuable and finely situated house and lot' in Georgetown. John Glassford, Alexander Cunninghame & Co., and James Jamieson & Co. all lost houses and land in Port Tobacco. Other prominent Glasgow men whose property was confiscated included James Buchanan, Dr Henry Stevenson, Alexander Hamilton, Cunninghame, Findlay & Co., but it was John Glassford who sustained by far the greatest losses.

There is an interesting sidelight on Alexander Hamilton's attempts to salvage his employer's and his own proprty. After the peace in July 1785 the Intendant, Daniel of St Thomas Jennifer, wrote to Hamilton saying that he had learned that he had made a fictitious sale of property belonging to James Brown & Co. in Bladensburg. A deed had been executed transferring it to a Mr Redgate, but no price had been agreed or paid. Under these circumstances the Intendant proposed to sell the property by auction.

However Hamilton was not completely outflanked; he bought in the house one month before the auction though it cost him over £300. Nevertheless the picture of universal loyalism amongst Scots in Maryland is destroyed by one piece of evidence: many of those who bought confiscated property had unmistakably Scottish names. In some cases these purchases, like Hamilton's, may have been made to preserve property for their former owners. For instance, the list includes the name of Robert Henderson, a Glassford factor; but there is no reason to believe that all Scots names could be explained in this way. Perhaps it provided an economic opportunity for young men who were stranded by the high tide of political events.

There is also information about the Maryland confiscation in the papers of Daniel of St Thomas Jennifer.[20] These contain a report to the Maryland assembly on confiscation, while the whole policy is questioned in an interesting letter from Charles Carroll written in June 1781: 'I think with you and always thought so, that we have been too hasty in confiscating. We ought to have killed the bear before we divided his skin.'

Proceedings in Virginia were more leisurely and more considerate of commercial interests. The Council of state considered cases on their merits, often took extenuating circumstances into account, and did not require public affirmation of support for the Revolution. Resident factors were given permission to leave, if they wished to do so, once they had settled all claims upon them. Property was sequestered (though some was later confiscated) and placed under the administration of comissioners appointed by the Council.[21]

Despite wartime difficulties the planters were eager to sell tobacco and merchants to trade. The Gist Family papers[22] contain letters on this topic from John McLane and John Sterratt of Baltimore in 1776 and 1777. The latter wrote in November 1777 that 'trade now begins to be brisque here, many vessels loading out (chiefly with tobacco) although several of the Enemy ships at our Capes. I think there will be a great deal of business done this winter.' In September 1778 Sterratt reported a great demand for tobacco, and is a fair supposition that a good deal found its way to the Clyde.

There is indeed much evidence of attempts by Glasgow merchants to trade during the war. An active partnership in this endeavour was that of Henry and James Ritchie with their nephew, James Dunlop, who was in Philadelphia during the British occupation, as their principal agent.[23] In March 1777 the Ritchies instructed all their factors to purchase tobacco wherever possible. If the British troops entered Virginia, Dunlop was to accompany them, purchase tobacco and slaves, and send the latter to Jamaica. In Virginia Dunlop was not to give old customers the same credit they had once enjoyed, but might give them some 'favours'. When Philadelphia was evacuated by the British, Dunlop moved to New York, but the Ritchies still urged him to buy tobacco as great quantities were being exported from Virginia. In January 1779 he told Dunlop that as the war was going to be a long one 'speculations are safer than they were when Peace was expected', and that the best tobacco available should be purchased regardless of price. London merchants were getting tobacco by way of St Eustace and St Kitts.

Hopes had been raised in 1782 with the prospect of peace, but David Buchanan, a friend of Dunlop in Glasgow, took a pessimistic and prophetic view of the situation: 'The present talk of a peace has made our Merchants here look on their Virginian Debts as already in their pockets, I think however if they get 5/- in the £ out of these they will be well off and I should suppose that it will take a long time to collect even that.' Things became even worse when real peace was in sight. In 1783 Dunlop was rebuked by the Ritchies for buying too much tobacco at a time when prices were falling sharply and importers going bankrupt. 'It has indeed been an unfortunate year', wrote Henry Ritchie on 4 July, 'as the end of a war generally is, but scarcely anybody here has lost so much by tobacco as we have done.' They had also done badly in marine insurance, though paying out more from wrecks than captures. 'We seem to have lost our Trade', he wrote, and in August 'this last year has been the worst this town ever saw.'

Early in 1782 James Dunlop established contact with Neil McCoul, a factor at Rappahannock who had remained in Virginia though little to his profit. McCoul had withdrawn to a plantation that he had bought to save the expense of living in town when little or no business was to be done. His company's property had been sequestered, then confiscated and sold. What business could be done was 'more like Gaming than Trading from the many captures of our vessels, the interference of our legislature by taking the goods when wanted by the Army at their own price, and the instability of our paper currency.' Nothing could be purchased except for commodities or specie, which was used as soon as it appeared 'to pay for goods from Philadelphia or Boston.' His plantation was in debt and becoming less profitable every year. Nevertheless there were people ready to take any opportunity that offered and in July 1783 McCoul reported that Morsom and Lawson had opened a store at Falmouth stocked from New York. A note of ominous significance for the Glasgow trade came from James Anderson in Virginia, who said that France was the best market for tobacco and that he would prefer to ship directly to that country.

James Dunlop's brother George had little luck during the war. In August 1775 he wrote that he was thinking of coming out to Virginia in the Ritchies' employment, but when he eventually got to America he was in the army. On 15 July he wrote from prison at Yorktown.

One interesting aspect of the Dunlop papers is the way in which James was able to make use of Scottish connections in other colonies even before the peace. In 1782 he was busy trading with Scots merchants in Charleston,

South Carolina, when occupied by the British, and in 1783, in addition to McCoul, he was in touch with other Scots who had remained in Virginia. James Dunlop himself moved to Petersburg, Virginia, and then to Georgetown in Maryland. He became an American citizen and a wealthy man. The greatest of the Glasgow tobacco factors was less fortunate. Neil Jamieson left Norfolk with the British forces, abandoning much property, and made his way to New York.

One of the great tobacco merchants, Alexander Speirs, made known his own views to the British government in a memorandum dated November 1775.[24] He said that he had lived for twenty years in the colonies and had had extensive dealings with America. He believed that conciliation would be interpreted as weakness, strengthen the idea of independence, and force Britain to negotiate on American terms. Men who had once experienced power in the colonies would not readily abandon it and to these should be added 'the force and influence of all who are embarrassed in their circumstances, and feel themselves easy in being freed from the clamours of creditors and distresses of the law. . . They will wish for a revolution that the energy of the old laws may never be restored and the mortgages and securities upon their Estates in the hands of British subjects may be rendered ineffectual.' His remedy was drastic: twenty thousand Russian mercenaries should be employed because they would inspire more fear than British troops, while Indians on the frontier should also be stirred into action.

The papers of Alexander Speirs also illustrate the way in which the war forced one 'tobacco lord' to extend and diversify his interests.[25] Before the war the mainstay of his business was importing and re-exporting tobacco, but he was also concerned in other enterprises. In partnership with John Robertson he re-exported sugar, rice, and coffee to Europe. As Speirs, French & Co. he exported to Virginia and the West Indies, while as Speirs, Murdoch & Co. he was engaged in banking. He was associated with James Crawford & Co., merchants of Rotterdam, and imported wine, with a connoisseur's appreciation of sherry and madeira. In Virginia he also traded as Speirs, Bowman & Co. At home he was a shareholder in the Tanwork Company, the Port Glasgow Ropeworks, the West Sugar house, and the Printfield and Smithfield manufacturers.

In Virginia the chief factor for Speirs, French & Co. was Robert Burton, but when war came he moved his headquarters to the West Indies. Though Virginian property continued to be shown as assets in the accounts, it is clear that the major thrust of the company's operations shifted to the Caribbean. In 1781 Burton was sent £50,000 to be spent on commodities suitable for shipment to Europe. This, Speirs told him, 'will make you one of the most considerable merchants in the West Indies,' and his letters included a comprehensive 'scheme' of goods for shipment to the West Indies and many instructions on shipments to European ports.

After Speirs' death trustees took over his estate. Speirs, French & Co. were owed a total of £46,510 in the American colonies, and the trustees decided to wind up operations. The factors were ordered to sell the goods which remained on hand and remit the proceeds as soon as possible, though haste did not imply that they should sell below the market price. One cargo of rum was sent from the West Indies to exchange for tobacco, but there does not seem to have been a serious attempt to resume the trade. The collection of debts was left in the hands of the company's lawyers. Similar action was taken by Patrick Colquhoun & Co. in which Speirs had been a partner and major stockholder. Undoubtedly the death of Speirs precipitated action which might have been delayed, but there is evidence that he had left instructions for his Virginian interests to be liquidated, so there was no sudden reversal of company policy.

The scale of Scottish losses is illustrated by two items in the papers of Neil Jamieson.[26] In 1786 he prepared a statement of his personal losses for presentation to the commissioners at Nova Scotia. He valued his claim for property lost at £2,159 in Norfolk, £560 in Portsmouth, and £2,146 for a one-fifth share in a ship captured by an American privateer. A distillery owned by Jamieson, Campbell, Calvert & Co., with himself as senior partner was valued at £1,720, and he also claimed that British forces had destroyed £1,866 of his tobacco. These were large sums for the eighteenth century, and do not include the large amounts which he was probably owed by debtors, or assets which he had been able to move to New York. Another paper was one prepared for his principals in Glasgow, John Glassford & Co., listing debts owed to them in stores at Boyd's Hole, Colchester, Alexandria, and Dumfries. The majority of the debts were for small sums, but there were an enormous number of them.

A letter to Jamieson from Virginia in 1783 illustrates the accidental circumstances which might hinder the resumption of trade. John Lawrence asked whether he had in his possession any record of the company for which a Mr Corbet had been factor. According to a note left by Corbet, he had handed over to Jamieson his wastebooks for 1766 and 1768-74. 'A little time before Mr. Corbet died, I am informed that in one of his drunken fits he burnt the Books and Accounts that he had kept of his transactions on our account.' Lawrence was unable to discover what Corbet had sold, or what he had done with the cash received, and when he died 'not a single Dollar was found in his possession'.[27]

Many sources illustrate the efforts of the Glasgow companies to recover their debts or obtain compensation for lost property. A well-documented and wearisome case concerns the estate of William Gray who had operated a store at Port Royal, Virginia.[28] The case was handled in Virginia by Daniel Grinnan, a Virginian attorney, and Walter Colquhoun, a Glasgow-born merchant of Falmouth. Grinnan was also employed in winding up the

Virginian estates of McCall, Smellie & Co. and Gorge McCall & Co. and corresponded with Walter Fleming of Glasgow. On one occasion he put the claims before the commissioner for British debts at Philadphia, but the matter dragged on and an account prepared in May 1800 showed £1,936 still owing to Glasgow creditors.

Under the Anglo-American agreement of 1802 Congress assumed responsibility for £600,000 of outstanding debts, but the Glasgow creditors thought this insufficient to meet the many claims from the city. In March 1802 Walter Colquhoun went to Glasgow to negotiate settlements, apparently with some success, and returned to Virginia, but in October of the same year was back in Glasgow. His letters to Grinnan were frequent and contained much information about the city and its commerce during the Napoleonic wars. Grinnan must have won the confidence of his Glasgow clients, for James Robieson, acting for the trustees of William Cunninghame & Co., wrote several equally informative letters. Still the question of the debts remained unsettled, and disputes followed by war between the United States and Great Britain caused further delay. In 1816 Walter Fleming referred to accounts presented in 1810 but not yet paid.

Another example comes from the papers of James Ritchie & Co.[29] In 1789 Robert Ritchie sent instructions to a Colonel Abraham Maury who was commissioned to collect debts on behalf of the company. Maury could accept bonds in payment, and was allowed 'to give some indulgence' in order to obtain them. If the debtors would not give a bond, he should endeavour to get some written acknowledgement of the debt, or failing that verbal admission before a witness. If there was no witness Maury would get no commission – because an interested party would not have his evidence admitted in court – but in this event Ritchie promised him compensation if the debt was subsequently paid. Court action would be necessary if a debtor refused to pay without good reason, but prior assent should be obtained from the company before beginning suit. In reckoning up the debts Ritchie deducted seven years' interest as he believed that it was customary to impose no such charges during time of war.

There is much information about the debts and losses of Glasgow merchants in the records of loyalist claims.[30] Major claims were presented by John Glassford & Co., Neil Jamieson, Speirs, French & Co., James and Robert Dunlop, and James Ritchie. Ritchie's claim, dated 31st August 1798 was one of the largest and most detailed, with debts divided into seven classes: 'A' and 'B' consisted of debts on open account barred by the Act of Limitations; 'C' listed debts due from persons solvent at the time of the peace, but now believed to be insolvent; 'D', debts due from solvent persons who should pay in full except for interest during the war years; 'E' bonds given by persons from whom recovery was now doubtful; 'F', bonds or vouchers given by persons now deceased, whose property had been divided or squandered, on persons whose whereabouts was unknown; and 'G' – debts due from persons who were insolvent before the peace, did not become American citizens, or disputed the sum owed. The Ritchie claims were still unsettled in 1809.

In addition to claims by major companies there are many from individuals for whom recovery may well have made the difference between comfort and penury. For instance Bruce Campbell, surviving partner of William Patterson, Bruce Campbell and John Gemmell of Kilmarnock, claimed for small sums owed in Virginia by debtors believed solvent. Mrs Amelia Ballatine, sister of Hector MacAlister, formerly of Norfolk, Virginia, claimed for property abandoned by him. James Ravenscroft of Calvinsmoor in Kirkcudbright had been a physician in Virginia for many years and had acquired land; because of his loyalism he had been forced to leave his estate in the care of trustees who had sold it for below its real value. He claimed just over £7,000 sterling. James Brown, Robert Dreghorn, Mathew Orr, and James Corbet claimed for money owed to James Brown & Co. at Bladensburg and Piscataway, totalling almost £15,000. James Brown had previously employed Alexander Hamilton, the garrulous and likeable factor at Piscataway, to collect his debts, and Hamilton's comment, in a letter to Matthew Blair on 21 October 1784, is perhaps a fitting comment with which to close this review of Glasgow debts:

> I am trying to collect money but get none. Interest is the cry, they will not pay. It is a damned business for an old grey hair'd man to be pestered with.[31]

This survey of sources for the Glasgow debts has extended far into the post-war years, and it is now necessary to return to the period of the Revolution for material on Scots in other colonies. They are far less abundant, and in many cases one must be content with straws in the wind rather than the solid foundation of a factual edifice.

There is an interesting example of divided family allegiance in North Carolina. Robert Hogg had been long established as a merchant in Wilmington, and was probably one of the richest men in this poor colony. He became a Loyalist, though a somewhat doubtful one. His brother James, who had but recently arrived in the colony, became prominent as a patriot. It seems that Robert soon repented, and the state records contain several references to his application for permission to return and acquire state citizenship.[32] The story beings in 1778 with reference to a letter from Robert to James expressing his wish to return and a comment by Colonel Thomas Clark that he 'never considered him as an enemy to this country'. Robert Hogg made a formal petition for citizenship in 1779. This was approved by the legislature, but then deferred after an objection had been made that when he left 'he was generally deemed unfriendly to the public measures of this and the United States', and that he had voluntarily placed himself under the protection of the King of Great Britain. However a committee appointed to consider his petition reported that he left instructions for one half of his property to be used in defence of the American cause. Permission to return and acquire citizenship was finally granted, but Robert Hogg died before he could take advantage of it. In 1786 it was agreed to pay the executors of Hogg and Campbell £896 on account of supplies seized for public use in 1776.

Loyalist material in the North Carolina Department of Archives and History includes many references to men with Scottish names. Some of these are copies of records held elsewhere. These include (from the Colonial Office papers in the Public Record Office in London) letters from the royal governors of the Carolinas and Georgia, papers on the Loyalist volunteers, a 'form of association for Loyalists in North Carolina', and many petitions and memorials from Loyalists to the British government. Of particular interest in connection with the loyalist Highlanders is a list of prisoners who had served under Donald McDonald at Moore's Creek.[33]

There is a diary in the William L. Clements Library, University of Michigan, of an unidentified North Carolina Highland Loyalist Officer who took part in the battle of Moore's Creek Bridge, and was captured by Revolutionary forces. The diary ends with the arrival of his party of prisoners in Philadelphia. It gives a very detailed description both of the role of the North Carolina Scottish Loyalists in the Revolutionary war and of the sequence of events in this theatre of the conflict. The author also lists a number of the most active rebels, so 'that when justice and equity sitts triumphant these miscreants receive their just reward'.

In South Carolina the Scottish merchant community was divided by the Revolution. The St Andrews Society of Charleston may not be entirely typical as it included a high proportion of wealthy merchants and successful doctors but 32 of the 107 members in 1776 can be identified as Loyalists and only 15 as Whigs. An indication of the strength of loyalist sympathy is that meetings lapsed between 1776 and 1780, but revived when British troops occupied Charleston. In November 1780 20 old and 64 new members were present, but of the latter at least 20 were officers with the British army. After the British evacuation in December 1784 the society again lapsed. When it was revived in 1787 it is pleasant to record that both Whigs and former Loyalists were among its members.[34]

The Houghton Library of Harvard University contains much material collected by Mrs L. A. Parrish on southern Loyalists who took refuge in the West Indies and particularly in the Bahamas. Most of those whom she traced came from the Carolinas and the Floridas. The collection contains material on Scots in West Florida, where a Scottish regiment was stationed at Pensacola in 1764, and on Adam Chrystie, a wealthy planter who raised and led the West Florida Rangers on the loyalist side during the Revolution. When the war ended many of the Scots settlers moved at first to East Florida, until they learned that this colony was to be ceded to Spain. Some then went to Canada, but a considerable number arrived in the Bahamas in financial distress. One whose career is well documented was John Falconer, who opened a store in Nassau, prospered, and died in 1793.

In the northern colonies the evidence of Scottish response to the Revolution is more scattered. In New York the division amongst the wealthy was similar to that in Charleston. The St Andrew's Society was smaller, and only 21 members are identified as active in 1776. Of them 11 became Loyalist, and 10 supported the Revolution. The figures are slightly misleading because the Loyalists included three or four serving soldiers, whilst the Whigs included several second or third generation New Yorkers, including two Livingstone brothers, Robert Morris, and John Morrin Scott.[35]

During the long period that New York was occupied by British troops it became a refuge for many Loyalists, and the principal port of entry for imports from the British Isles. The efforts of Neil Jamieson, to recoup his fortunes has been described above. Other Scots, either refugees from other colonies, old residents, or newcomers, seem to have used the opportunity to establish themselves in the city. James Dunlop, a junior member of an extended family, moved from Petersburg, Virginia, to Philadelphia and then to New York, before returning to Virginia as factor for James Ritchie & Co. Robert Henderson, another Scottish merchant, may have arrived in New York before moving to Philadelphia after the peace. During the war Scottish merchants tried to use New York as a base while seeking new outlets for exports, while remaining poised for an assault on any part of the former colonies occupied by British troops.

In Boston the Scottish merchants were far less numerous, and most of them seem to have left when the British evacuated the city. At that time the treasurer of the Scots Charitable Society was William Cunningham, who took its books and bonds with him to New York. After the peace he was asked to return them to Boston, but refused to do so on the ground that 'the Scotch Society's Books and securities (but no cash) were legally in my hands, as an officer, and almost the whole of the members then quitted the Town and ordered me to take care of them.' However, it seems that enough members remained in Boston to obtain an Act of incorporation from the state legislature. Indeed it seems that the few who remained won a grudging degree of acceptance hitherto denied to them. Alexander Canning, their principal representatives, observed that the society had not been able to obtain incorporation before, and that even under the new Act they were restricted to on hundred members and an annual corporate income of £200. This was 'a convincing proof of their fears of the Scotch nation'.[36]

There are interesting sidelights on the war in the Campbell of Barcaldine Muniments.[37] Alexander Campbell arrived in Boston to set up a grocery business early in 1775, which was not perhaps the best time for a young man to make his fortune in that city. He had a taste of military life at Bunker's Hill, where he fought as a volunteer and was wounded. This turned his thoughts to office, and he wrote to his father to obtain a letter of recommendation from the Duke of Argyll to General Gage. He was optimistic about the future.

> I'm pretty sure they will soon be forced to submit. The Natives of this New England were always reckoned a barbarous cruel set . . . they even poison their balls with arsenick & they are a cowardly set that will not fight but when fenced by Trees, Houses or Trenches.

By 1777 he had done well for himself, with a captaincy in McLean's Regiment, a contract for the supply of wood to the army, a purchased lieutenancy for his son (which was an investment for the future as the child was only four years old), one house in New York, another on Long Island, and an income of £1,000 or more a year. 'All this,' wrote a cousin, 'owing to his own merit & spirited behaviour on Bunker's Hill.' But in 1778 it was reported by another relation that he was on the point of departure for home with numerous children and a drunken, deranged wife.

Another Campbell, also called Alexander, was a merchant in Greenock and kept in close touch with American affairs. In August 1775 he wrote that thirty or forty people had just arrived from Boston. He had 'often seen and heard of Scots Emigrants to America, but never untill now of American Emigrants to Scotland.' He thought this sufficiently important to add a postscript.

> For God's sake make the news of the arrival of Emigrants from America as Publick as possible, to . . . prevent our deluded Country Men from emigrating to a country where nothing but Anarchy and Confusion reigns.[38]

There is a good deal of information about events in Boston, seen through the eyes of a Scottish loyalist, in the papers of James Murray.[39] He had emigrated to North Carolina about 1735 where he prospered as a planter and merchant. He returned to Scotland in 1774, but in 1749 was back in North Carolina. He brought out his sister Elizabeth with him; but she remained in Boston and married first Thomas Campbell, a Scottish merchant, and after his death another Scot, James Smith, who was a wealthy sugar boiler. This gave John Murray a permanent attachment to Boston, and he moved there in 1765. Letters to his sister, who returned to Scotland after the death of her husband in 1769, conveyed his growing alarm at the course of events. In 1770 he wrote that 'it would give you pain to be in or near the turbulent town of Boston.' Later he wrote

> The factious spirit is now at a great height here, indeed it cannot rise

much higher without the poor people, many of whom seem almost starving for want of employment, going to plunder the rich and then cutting their throats.

After moving to Boston Murray had obtained office as Cashier and Paymaster of the customs in North America, and in 1773 was appointed to the normally lucrative post of Collector of the port of Boston. It was perhaps the most inauspicious moment in history to assume this responsiblity. With a long record of public support for the royal government he had no choice but to leave Boston when the British troops evacuated the city. He died in Nova Scotia, embittered and supported only by the small official salary which he continued to receive. His sister had returned to Boston while it was still in British hands, married Ralph Inman of Cambridge, lived out the troubles, and died in 1785.

Probably no Loyalists suffered more than Highlanders settled in New York state. Many were recent arrivals and, as noted in an earlier chapter, had settled in consequence of attractive terms offered by the owners of land. Property in the city was protected from confiscation by the terms of the 1783 treaty, but in the countryside the Americans had been severe with loyalist sympathisers. Papers on forfeited estates held by the New York Historical Society include the names of a number of Scots who had previously acquired land.[40] The Catholic or Glengarry Highlanders, many of clan McDonnell, migrated through the northern wilderness to Canada under the leadership of Sir John Johnson.[41]

A major source for the military activities of the Highland Loyalists is the letterbook of Captain Alexander McDonald of the Royal Highland Emigrants held by the New York Historical Society.[42] It reveals so much about the trials and tribulations of a Highland leader that extracts deserve quotation. He had left the army after the end of the Seven Years War, and settled in New York where he engaged in a curious assortment of trading activities – chandler, wine merchant, and organ seller. In a letter to General Howe dated 30 October 1775 he revealed that in the previous year he had secretly raised 100 men on Staten Island to fight for the King if it became necessary to do so. He then went to the settlement on the Mohawk river where there were two hundred MacDonalds 'who had fled from the Severity of their Landlords in the Highlands of Scotland, the Leading Men of whom most cheerfully agreed to be ready at a Call.' He thought that he could have raised 500 if it had not been advisable to act secretly. While he was engaged in this personal recruiting drive, a Colonel McLean arrived with authority from the government to collect together all the Highlanders in one place, offer each man 200 acres, and, if necessary, give arms to every man capable of fighting in His Majesty's service.

The state authorities must have heard reports of McDonald's activities. Asked to sign the Association, he refused and was forced to leave his home.

After his departure 'a parcel of fellows went to my house with more than Savage rudeness, rummaged the house, as they pretended, for arms, swore they would have me dead or alive and frightened her [his wife] out of her senses.' Later he lamented that his wife and children were destitute, that she had had a miscarriage brought on by distress, threats, and the burning of their house. He himself had been sentenced to death and could not return.

Nor were his hopes of the clan fulfilled. 'I wish with all my heart', he wrote, 'we could bring together the Number that was proposed by them'. But those who had responded suffered enough. 'As for all the McDonalds in America they may Curse the day that I was born as being the means of Leading them to ruin for my Zeal and attachment for government.'

In spite of these difficulties McDonald was still struggling in 1776 to find money to keep a son at Princeton under John Witherspoon, but by December 1777 had decided to send both his sons back to Scotland for their education. There is much more information in the McDonald letterbook about the trials and disappointments of Highland Loyalists, but one further quotation may suffice as a note *in memoriam* of those whose courage and dedication has seldom received due praise. On hearing that sentence of death had been passed upon him, he asked rhetorically:

> Is it because I would not offer such violence to my honour and Conscience as to falsify my oath of fidelity and allegiance, and take up arms against a Master whom I have served for thirty years and in a Cause of which I always entertained a bad opinion.

It is perhaps inevitable that sources provide abundant evidence for the views and activities of those who had most reason to complain. In the new United States the men who supported the Revolution, accepted independence, or merely laid low were the conformists. Apart from a few well-known names, they were less likely to appear in the records – they presented no loyalist claims, and debts owed to them did not accumulate throughout the war period or become the cause of endless litigation.

It may be accepted that a majority of Scots who were recently arrived in the colonies, or regarded themselves as no more than temporary residents, became loyalists. Evidence from the loyalist claims may be somewhat inflated by the large number of Glasgow merchants who lost property in Virginia and Maryland, but there is also evidence that in South Carolina, Philadelphia, New York, and Boston the majority of Scots merchants were loyalist. John Witherspoon was sufficiently alarmed by the fact and by its possible repercussions, that he wrote a pamphlet addressed to Scots resident in the colonies pleading with them to support or at least to abandon their opposition to the Revolution.

There are however straws in the wind which indicate the presence of a powerful minority of Scots on the 'patriot' side. Nearly all the Scottish presbyterian clergy whose biographies appeared in William B. Sprague's *Annals of the American Pulpit or Commemorative Notices of Distinguished American Clergymen* supported the Revolution.[43] This is not a representative list, for to a nineteenth-century American author 'patriotism' was itself a major criterion for inclusion. However the number so recorded was significant. It has already been noted that although majorities in the St Andrew's Societies of Charleston, Philadelphia and New York were loyalist, a substantial minority was neutral or supported the Revolution.

The sources for the life and actions of such eminent Scots as John Witherspoon and James Wilson are well-known.[44] The records of revolutionary Georgia contain many references to Lachlan McIntosh, whose influence kept most of the Highlanders of Georgia on the revolutionary side.[45] If men of more remote Scottish ancestry are included, the Livingstons of New York and Alexander Hamilton, the statesman, could be added.

A rare example of anti-British sentiment is found in the papers of Alexander Speirs.[46] He himself was bitter against the rebellion, but his sister, Judith, had married David Bell, a factor who also managed the Speir's estate in Virginia. On 16 February 1776 she wrote that she hoped that her brother would not think her a 'rebel'. Everyone, she argued, was obliged to take up arms in their own defence. The Americans wished to be dutiful subjects, but would not be treated as slaves. Judith Bell blamed Lord Dunmore for much of the trouble in Virginia; he was a 'tyrant' who appeared 'to take pleasure in killing his fellow men', and his attempt to free slaves was dangerous and vindictive.

How many others were persuaded by circumstances, interest, sentiment, or conviction to cast their lot with the movement for resistance and independence? Where the records are silent, the answer cannot be known; but it is a reasonable surmise that for every man or woman who left the rebellious colonies three or four remained.

Chapter Eight

SURVIVORS AND NEW BEGINNINGS

In the last chapter attention was focused on the emigrés, but concluded that Scots who remained comprised a majority of those in America at the outbreak of the Revolution. In the first place were those who remained voluntarily and enthusiastically; in the second those who remained under protest but preferred not to abandon families, homes and property; in the third were those who could afford no gesture and accepted the fact that they must obey the dictates of those who now controlled the colony in which they had settled. This last category probably included a large majority of the Lowland craftsmen, clerks, tutors, schoolmasters, and small farmers who had migrated during the preceding twenty years.

So far as trade was concerned it was those in the second category who were likely to bear the principal burden of renewed Scottish trade in the years following independence. Some experienced factors, such as Alexander Hamilton of Piscataway, remained; others, such as James Dunlop of Petersburg, had taken refuge in British-controlled cities, but were ready to launch a commercial offensive as soon as peace was restored. Many who had occupied subordinate positions in the tobacco hierarchy had remained in the colonies and were now anxious to establish themselves as principal factors or merchants on their own account.

What was true on a large scale of the tobacco trade also applied to other commercial centres. Divided by the Revolution, and with a majority of the leading and wealthy men disqualified by Loyalism, the Scottish communities still included enough younger men to take the lead in reviving old trading links or forging new ones.

A spectre haunting men who hoped to revive trade was the pre-war debt. On the one hand a commission to collect debts was the easiest way to re-establish a connection with home-based merchants, obtain supplies of sorely needed goods, and enjoy the benefits of long credit. On the other debt collection was not the best way of winning the goodwill of American customers upon whom their prosperity must ultimately depend. In addition to personal animosities and misunderstandings, the collectors of debts might incur disfavour from state authorities and find the scales weighted against them in the courts.

The preceding chapter showed how long drawn out these proceedings could be. The refusal of the British to negotiate a commercial treaty was responsible for the lack of enthusiasm with which the states aided the recovery of pre-war debts, and compensation for confiscated property was out of the question. The Constitution of 1787 gave the federal courts power to enforce treaty obligations, but there was no international agreement on Loyalist claims. The Jay Treaty of 1794 made the settlement of debts and the arbitration of claims a *quid pro quo* for British evacuation of the north-western forts, but disputes still lingered on. Not until 1802 was a definitive agreement reached, and even then many of the British creditors believed that they had been cheated and claims for confiscated property were satisfied only in part. These long drawn out disputes over debts and claims were of little interest to men making a fresh start or encumbered by dubious pre-war assets.

The concentration of loyalist merchants in New York during the war made this city a major base for new trade offensives, but the sources illustrate the extent to which Scottish merchants relied upon country-men stranded elsewhere by the tides of war. Virginia and Maryland, with many resident Scots anxious to repair broken ties, were obvious hunting grounds. Charleston, also occupied by the British at the close of war, was the home or refuge of many Scottish merchants. But Philadelphia offered the most tempting opportunities with its ocean trade, estab-lished coastal and West Indian trade, and access to new markets in the West.

Scottish merchants had to learn to live without protection from the British laws of trade. The only way in which American commerce could be drawn to the Clyde was by offering the right goods at the right prices, knowing the markets, and extending credit facilities. They were threatened by an American navigation law which might discriminate against British ships and would certainly nip in the bud the development of a carrying trade by Scottish ships between America, West India, and European ports. All British shippers were vulnerable, but particularly so the Scottish; with earlier endeavours so committed to American and entrepôt trades, they had to struggle harder to maintain their competitive advantages in the new situation. One result was to make the Scottish merchants decidedly pro-American in their public attitudes whatever their private feelings. Possibilities of a rupture in 1794 were regarded with dismay by Scots on both sides of the Atlantic, and their relief was considerable when Jay's Treaty drew the United States into the British orbit.

Migration to the United States resumed soon after the peace, but details remain obscure. There are indications that more men from lower middle-class and artisan families set out. Lean years after the outbreak of war with France persuaded many skilled men and their families to emigrate, despite attempts to prevent by law the loss of useful citizens. Highland migration resumed, reaching a peak after the turn of the century. The Earl of Selkirk proposed assisted emigration to British North America in order to divert the stream from the United states. The original causes of Highland emigration were reinforced as landowners grasped more eagerly the commercial possibilities of sheep rearing.

The years after indpendence saw a strengthening of intellectual links, as Scottish philosophy carried all before it in American colleges, and Adam Smith, whose *Wealth of Nations* appeared in the year of independence, became the acknowledged master of a new school of political economists. At the same time a small but influential group of Scots, mainly drawn from the professional class, became ardent admirers of America, while, in early years of the new century, the fame of the Scottish intellect was everywhere acknowledged in the United States. In 1802 was founded the *Edinburgh Review* which was to become an arbiter of American opinion. In its early years the *Review* was a literary rather than a political journal, but its popularity in America opened a new phase in Scottish-American intellectual history. Building upon a tradition established by Hugh Blair in his *Lectures on Rhetoric and Belles Lettres*, the Scottish critics guided literary taste.

The reputation of Scottish men of letters takes us far into the nineteenth century. So do the careers of several whom decision or chance took to America in these later years. In economics the world was changing as Scotland went through the experience of industrial revolution; the days of tobacco lords and Scottish factors were no more; cotton, textiles, iron manufacturers, and capital investment took their place. Scottish learning and medicine retained their reputation, but a growing number of American institutions advanced equal claims. Scottish philosophy ceased to be seen as an exciting new way of studying man in society, and became domesticated as a safe support for the protestant establishment. A century of massive achievement lay ahead, but the novelty of enterprise that had given Scottish culture a special place in American evolution lay behind.

Reviving trade with Virginia and Maryland

In July 1785 Patrick Colquhoun, the Glasgow merchant who was to become a London stipendiary magistrate and a notable writer on social topics, wrote an analysis of the prospects in tobacco for Henry Dundas who was close to the new prime minister, William Pitt.[1] Colquhoun pointed out the importance of tobacco for British prosperity but expressed alarm over the future of the trade: 'In America the British merchants are distressed beyond measure by the interference of smugglers in raising the price of tobacco greatly beyond its intrinsic value.' The illicit traders were smuggling directly to Britain and Ireland where they evaded payment of duty and thus undercut the legitimate merchants. He had had certain information of nearly a thousand hogsheads being landed in this way, and believed that the amount would increase. The real difficulty lay in America where 'a spirit appears to be rising . . . hostile to British commerce'. In the northern states this feeling was intense and 'should the contagion spread to the Southern provinces the situation of British property and British merchants would be truly deplorable'.[2] If the local authorities would not co-operate debts would not be paid, property would not be recovered, and there would be no co-operation in efforts to curb the activities of those who were known to be smuggling tobacco into Britain.

The merchants who were in the best position to re-open the trade were those who had taken refuge in New York during the war and had developed the substantial import trade in that city. Of them the most prominent was Neil Jamieson, former factor of John Glassford at Norfolk and in his own right a major strategist in the development of pre-war commerce. Trading during the war as a partner in Glassford, Gordon, Montieth & Co., he had been moderately succesful as an importer, and after the conclusion of peace he opened correspondence with Scottish merchants and factors who had remained in Virginia and Maryland. The names of the correspondents were not those familiar in earlier days and suggest that younger storekeepers or book keepers had stepped into the shoes of their earlier superiors.[3]

In August John Bayne wrote from Piscataway that 'all the old Traders are afraid to Trade any more of their property here until the Definite Treaty is settled'. He also reported the the Governor of Virginia had ordered four persons, who had returned prematurely, to leave the state.[4] A more enterprising young man, Daniel McCallum was keener to take advantage of the situation. 'It will probably occur to you', he wrote, 'that the few of us who remained here during the War will, for some time, possess great advantages over any new adventurers that may come here from Great Britain.' He himself had no connection with anyone in the trade, except for a commission for T. & R. Donald & Co. to safeguard their interests, and had opened a store 'in order to be ready for the reception of any Goods that may be sent me in the Fall, on consignment or otherwise'. He had 'as good a set of customers as any in the country, waiting to take their dealings with me in case I am as well supplied as my neighbour'. He had not heard from former correspondents in Glasgow and did not know their intentions, but it was, in any case, not his design to confine his connections to them but 'to have it in my power to serve as many of my friends as may incline to make use of me'.[4]

Jamieson received another hopeful letter from R. Donald at Petersburg, Virginia, dated 18 July 1783. 'The openings for Business both here & at Manchester', he said 'is so promising at present that we are desirous of availing ourselves of it.' He asked Jamieson to supply him with goods as he feared that the fall shipment from Britain would arrive too late, and assured him that payment would be made as soon as the crop came in. He and his partner, Simon Fraser, were no speculators and traded 'entirely on certainties – giving no Credit'.

Another Scottish trader who hoped for Jamieson's support was James Buchan of Richmond, who observed:

> Our experience in the Virg[a] Trade and our acquaintance with the people gives us all the advantage over the modern adventurers, who now crowd every house and shed within this Metropolis, tho' we may have suffered something by the War and remain in the situation of every other older trader, who has his former subject of Debts still at risk.

Probably the 'modern adventurers' included some of the smugglers Colquhoun condemned, and every Scottish commercial establishment laboured under the burden of unpaid debts. They faced the alternative between cutting their losses or risking unpopularity and years of litigation in unsympathetic courts.[5]

This was the preoccupation of J. Lyle, writing from Manchester, Virginia, on 16 October 1783. He hoped that the British government would make good these debts and had heard that Loyalists were to be indemnified for losses. He pointed out that generosity would be in the national interest, for if the government did not 'take care of their Merchants' interests Britain cannot long be powerful or rich'.

It is possible that Neil Jamieson distrusted assurances, foresaw too many difficulties, or felt that he was too old to venture on uncharted seas. In 1783 he decided to give up his New York business, abandoned attempts to re-open trade in Virginia and Maryland, and returned to Britain. His former employers, John Glassford & Co., did succeed in recovering a part of their former trade, but it would seem that their main objective was to recover debts and dispose of assets as profitably as they could.

One of the former Glassford factors, Robert Henderson, had remained in Virginia, trading from 1776 as Glassford & Henderson, and after the war re-opened stores at Boyd's Hole, Alexandria, and Port Tobacco. By 1790 Henderson was the dominant figure in the business, and the trustees of Glassford's estate were anxious to withdraw. By 1800 the controlling company was Vincent & Ferguson, operating exclusively in America, and in the following years almost all the former Glassford stores came under the control of Edelen, Thompson & Co. In 1795 the familiar name of John Glassford & Co. re-appears briefly as claimant for pre-war debts.

The change from Glasgow to American control is illustrated by the letterbook of Robert Ferguson, beginning in July 1787.[6] In the early years there are numerous letters to John Glassford & Co. and Maryland planters about the debts, but meanwhile he was planning a different strategy for his own operations. He wrote to Thomas Mundell, a former Glassford factor at Dumfries, reproving him for being too anxious to seek customers by offering store goods on credit:

> I thought by this time you had understood our plan, which is not to

sink money in Debts to any great degree. By keeping ourselves free from a load of debts we shall always have the power over our Neighbours.

Even if some credit had to be given Mundell should be reluctant to trust any planters on the Patuxcant River. Their distance from his store would give them plenty of opportunity to dispose of their tobacco elsewhere, and it was 'the Principle of many People of that Neighbourhood not to pay debts.' They owed another trader £25,000, but 'they have carried their Tob° to you and laughed at him.'

Ferguson took advantage of the freedom allowed now that Great Britain no longer had a monopoly. By July 1787 he was sending tobacco direct to Bordeaux, with a request that the proceeds should be remitted to him in good bills payable in the West Indies. By this time he was ordering most of his store goods from London and trading directly with Rotterdam. In Maryland he found a conservative spirit in the tobacco business – 'Our planters must have it bought from them in their old accustomed way let the Price be large or small' – but in Virginia there was more room for innovation. He instructed one of his store keepers, Colonel Jeremiah Jordan, that he should give cash for tobacco provided that the sellers agreed to make future purchases at his store but should offer a higher price if part of it were taken in goods.

Ferguson was also diversifying his interests, and in December 1787 was corresponding with Colonel John Stewart about shipping pig iron to Britain. He had two ships loading, but neither would go to Britain because of restrictions imposed by both countries. The British would not admit a ship if the master and two-thirds of the crew were American-born or had remained in America when independence was recognised, but the Maryland authorities would not give a ship clearance for Europe unless the master and two-thirds of the crew were American. This was particularly awkward because few seamen were to be found in Maryland. Evidence of the decline in direct trade with the Clyde is in a letter to Colonel Jordan telling him that letters for Scotland should be sent by way of London.

A radical alteration in old trading methods was noted by Ferguson in August 1787 when he wrote:

> The business of importing cargoes for Merchants without capital to sell out here to planters on credit is at an end; and people who have done it are ruined and those who came after will profit by their misfortune, if they do not truly deserve a double worse fall.

On the other hand future goodwill could be jeopardised by harsh treatment of debtors. John Glassford & Co. might be in want of money, but it should be 'extracted in the easiest manner possible for the Debtors'. There was 'so great a desire to do justice we must be clement as far as consistently we can'.

Difficulties were made worse by unsound practice amongst leaders in the

American financial world. The failure of Robert Morris had many repercussions, and American credit abroad was badly damaged. Ferguson gave an account of Davie Ross of James River, who had raised £80,000 through an agent in London, giving his plantation as security, but had sent no interest payment when due. His agent was imprisoned for debt in King's Bench, where he died, and the creditors got nothing. Incidents such as this were 'sufficient to damn the credit of every American, and of every man whose connections are with men capable of such actions'.

Robert Ferguson also handled a debt problem of quite a different kind. John Witherspoon had not received payment from a Mrs Judith Chase on account of the education of her son by a previous marriage.[7] 'Almost every third or fourth post', he wrote to Mrs Chase on 6 August 1787, 'brings me a letter from the Rev. Doct' Witherspoon of Prince Town College respecting his claim against you for money advanced by him.' He thought that she ought to sell land and settle the debt, giving Witherspoon a bond in order to gain time for the proceeds of sale to be realised. The lady was evasive, and two months later he told Witherspoon that he had no chance of getting his money without instituting legal proceedings. Litigation between citizens of different states raised difficult procedural problems, and Ferguson advised Witherspoon on the steps to be taken before he could being the case to a Maryland court.

Another view of prospects in the tobacco colonies is provided by James Fairlie, whose letterbooks for 1783-1815 have survived.[8] The letters are addressed to Robert Findlay & Co., Glasgow. He was in New York at the end of the war and his main interest was in trade with Jamiaca, but in October 1783 he decided to visit Virginia in order to assess the situation there. He met old friends who gave him a warm welcome, but was dismayed by the lawlessness of the country. A Mr Williamson had brought a cargo of goods to Hobshole, with the Governor's permission to stay for a limited period and sell his goods wholesale; but about five miles from Hobshole he had been attacked by solders, beaten, tarred and feathered. The soldiers (probably local militia) then descended on Hobshole, attacked the ship, beat the captain, and threatened to hang him. They were eventually restrained by 'some moderate and sensible people in the Neighbourhood'.

Fairlie had the usual trouble with debts. One debtor had removed to North Carolina, and while it would be difficult enough to get payment in Virginia to pursue a debtor into a neighbouring state was impossible. On 16 October he said that most people were anxious for the British merchants to return; but there was opposition from those with outstanding debts. He told Findlay & Co. that people were disappointed at seeing so few merchants and enclosed a list of goods in demand.[9]

James Dunlop, who has already been encountered as factor for James and Henry Ritchie at Petersburg, Virginia, and during the war in Philadelphia

and New York, returned to Virginia in 1785 and became a citizen of that
state. He then established himself at Georgetown, Maryland, and was
closely associated in business with another Scot, John Laird. In 1798 both
of them speculated in town lots in the new established national capital.[10]

Dunlop's first efforts after 1783 illustrate the difficulties created by the
new situation. In January 1784 John Laird & Co. deplored that his
operations had involved them in heavy losses, though satisfied that he had
acted according to his best judgement. In a further letter they added the now
familiar warning that he should be very careful about allowing credit or
taking bills for remittance. In March 1784 James Ritchie & Co. instructed
him to leave New York and go to Virginia:

> Inform yourself where you can bring a new business in the Tobacco
> line to most advantage, for we will have nothing to with grain.

They would give no credit, except a little between crops. European prices
were high but likely to drop, so there should be no delay, but their principal
motive for reopening former stores was to facilitate the collection of debts.
Tobacco prices were high in Virginia as well as in Europe, but trade was
brisk. Newcomers were trying to get into the business, and store rents
'amazingly high'. But no one was anxious to pay old debts.

James Ritchie was indeed one of the most active in trying to recover old
debts by new trading.[11] In March 1784 he sent out long instructions to his
factors. He insisted that the principal purpose was to recover old debts and
that fresh credit should not be given except a little between crops. Debtors
should be required to pay off debts with tobacco before they could be
supplied with goods. If judgement had been obtained from a court, or
covered by securities, these should not be surrendered unless the payment
of future interest was guaranteed. If they had nothing but a bond from the
debtor, they could renew it provided that interest was paid. He hoped that
few would seek to avoid payment of debts, and factors should work upon
men of honour, justice and influence to settle and set an example for their
neighbours. At first no goods were to be supplied except for cash or
produce, but after October 1784 they would extend credit to reliable
customers. Payments of debts in flour, corn, hemp, iron or provisions were
not to be accepted. Caution was necessary because no commercial treaty
had been signed and 'fears and jealousies and mistaken views of Interest on
both sides may prevent or retard that reconciliation which it is in the
interest of both Countries to cultivate'.

The factors were instructed to send monthly reports by the New York
packet, and information should be more exact than in the old days 'as the
Trade will in all probability take a new turn'. The Farmers General of
France had appointed William Alexander, formerly of Edinburgh and now
at Richmond, as their purchasing agent. They could safely sell to him
provided that payment was in bills drawn on London or Paris. They could

also ship tobacco directly to Rotterdam. Finally they were instructed to
board in lodgings and not set up houses of their own. 'We wish you to live
well and comfortably, but luxury and extravagance is inadmissable. The
frugal and economical Factor will succeed where others must fail – Send us
a yearly account of all expenses.'

Another company active at this time was Huie, Reid & Co., of Dumfries,
Virginia, whose parent company was Smith, Huie, & Alexander of Port
Glasgow.[12] Their manager was James Reid, probably the Reid whose early
papers are in Cunninghame Papers at Kilmarnock. In 1784 prospects were
uncertain but ended on an optimistic note. First a glut was forecast in the
European market, then the Port Glasgow company apologised for sending
unsuitable goods, prices improved, and finally they wished to expand
operations by opening a new store in Georgetown. In 1785 optimism
prevailed. 'Glasgow will have a large share of the American trade in future.
There have been more orders lodged this year for goods to go out to America
than Great Britain could execute in three years.' Nevertheless they believed
that the American trade was 'on a precarious footing'.

This prediction was fulfilled in 1789. The company was in dire need of
cash, threatened to bring legal action against one large debtor, and intended
'as soon as possible to bring our Business within a narrow compass.' Things
were worse in the following year. In Dumfries James Reid was nervous of
trading at the current high prices, but noted that his colleague at
Georgetown, George Walker, was expanding his import business. The
home company did not seem to be too much dismayed by very low profits,
but the debt problem continued to plague them. While Reid advised against
instituting legal proceedings – 'a very slow way of getting payment and an
alternative we seldom resort to whilst the Debtor appears to have an
inclination to pay' – the home company issued an ultimatum: no more
goods would be shipped unless they received interest on outstanding
debts.

Reid made some effort to diversify his trade, and avoid dependence upon
tobacco. In 1789 he was buying wheat and holding off tobacco purchases.
British ships were experiencing severe competition because so many were
being built by Northern merchants, and the tobacco trade was ceasing to be
profitable because so much was being grown in the Carolinas and Georgia.
In 1796 Smith, Huie & Alexander failed. James Dunlop became a trustee of
the estate and asked Reid to continue his exertion in collecting debts, but on
commission as there could be no hope of paying him a salary. Meanwhile
George Walker at Georgetown had been branching out on his own,
speculating in land in the District of Columbia, and engaging in
brickmaking. In December 1783 he wrote about a Negro who was a
bricklayer 'and good for nothing else except playing the fiddle'. Huie, Reid
& Co. were not best pleased by these activities, but grudgingly admitted

that if money was found to begin the public buildings 'we imagine a few years will produce a Town perhaps as large as Alexandria'.[13]

Ratification of Jay's Treaty raised hope that the everlasting debt question might be settled. Provost John Dunlop wrote to Henry Dundas that the treaty gave general satisfaction. 'It is peculiarly acceptable to me, who have now a propsect of getting something out of a property of £30,000 which I have for a long while considered as lost'. He hoped for appointment as one of the commissioners at Philadelphia, as he had passed five years of his early life in America and 'would have no objection to pass two or three years more in a good cause'. Perhaps his desire for the office was not unmixed with the thought that his prospect of recovering the £30,000 would be all the greater if he were on the spot.[14]

Unfortunately the debts were not easily settled. In August 1797 disappointment was expressed that the old claims were not being prosecuted as vigorously as had been expected.[15] A list of 'bad and doubtful debts' is found in a ledger kept by John Leitch of Glasgow dated December 1800. The sums are large and Leitch may have been acting on behalf of several companies.[16] In 1804 George Hamilton of Fairfield, Virginia, offered his services as collector of debts for Glasgow merchants, in place of William Drummond, deceased. 'A planter' he claimed' 'can do this better than a merchant.'[17]

Plagued by old debts, new competition, and uncertain markets the Glasgow merchants could not re-establish their former commercial hegemony on the Chesapeke. The evidence of direct trade with continental and English ports indicates that Glasgow was losing its position as the great entrepôt for the tobacco trade. The merchants and manufacturers were finding other outlets for their energies, but their fortunes elsewhere are not the concern of this chapter. Nevertheless the heritage in America could not be entirely erased. Men such as James Dunlop and George Walker shifted their interests to more profitable enterprises, adopted American nationality, and founded well-to-do families. The fortunes of men such as Francis Jerdone and William Allason, who broke away before 1776 from the tobacco merchants who employed them, has been noted in an earlier chapter. The Leitch ledger in 1798-1805 noted a number of 'new Virginia concerns', and some were still in the tobacco importing business.[18] Tobacco lords no longer dominated the Glasgow scene, but descendants of the young men whom they had employed in the colonies had merged into the mainstream of American life.[19]

Scottish merchants who had arrived in New York during the war and remained there after the peace, were in a good position to gather up the threads. Considerable quantities of goods had been imported during the war, and the long period of British occupation had meant that business was able to build on stable foundations. Neil Jamieson failed to make a success of it, but he was growing old and perhaps disheartened by the loss of his property in Virginia. A younger colleague, Colin (or Collin) McGregor, handled Jamieson's affairs after the latter's departure. This led to strained relations and a quarrel; but meanwhile McGregor had been building up extensive trading connections on his own account.[20] It is interesting to note that much of his early success was based on establishing personal links with fellow Scots in other colonies especially South Carolina.

McGregor came to New York in 1781, and a ledger which has been preserved begins on the day on which British troops evacuated New York: 'A Memorable but truly Melancholy date' says an inscription on the flyleaf. Despite his loyalist connections McGregor became attached, by interest if not by sentiment, to the new United States. When his brother contemplated emigration, Colin McGregor encouraged him to do so with the comment that 'bad as times are, this is certainly the *best* poor man's Country on earth'. In 1794 he deplored the bad relations which threatened war between Great Britain and the United States. Though the British might be stirred by dislike of the Americans 'the period approaches fast for opening the eyes of the people of Great Britain and Ireland, and they will soon see their real interests'. If war did come he would have to side with America. His property was all in that country and he wrote:

> I am determined to protect and defend it, and no natural prejudices shall influence my conduct, or cause me to swerve from opinions so justly and so well grounded.

Most of McGregor's import and export business was with Glasgow companies. In 1784 he seems to have been acting on behalf of Henry Riddell & Co. of Glasgow, but broke with them after they complained of 'the great losses sustained in their New York commerce'. There are references in his correspondence to 'adventures to Albany' but the nature of the speculative trade is not clear. He acquired considerable property, but failed in business at the end of the century and died in relative poverty in 1802.

A Glasgow man who made a great success of post-war trading was Robert Henderson.[21] In 1784 he formed a partnership with another Glasgow man, William Gardner, who had recently returned from South Carolina. Their object was to trade between Great Britain and the United States, as Gardner & Henderson & Co. in Glasgow and as Robert Henderson & Co. in America. A key man in their plans was another Glaswegian, David Lamb, who had remained in Charleston. In October 1784 Henderson moved from New York to Philadelphia, but he retained useful contacts with a number of Scottish merchants in New York and with one in Richmond, Virginia.[22] His principal business was the import of British goods, but he also purchased American produce for export or re-sale. Apart from astute management his success depended upon the range of goods and markets with which he dealt.

In the early days, Henderson's major problem was with his partner in Glasgow. Gardner's letters became less frequent, and Henderson had to rely upon Alexander Glen for information. Fortunately Glen was lively, well-informed, and his letters are a good source for Glasgow business in the post-war period. Gardner was in difficulties and though still in business in 1790, did not prosper. The partnership was dissolved, and in 1799 Gardner sold up his Glasgow business, moved to America, and when last heard of was engaged in speculative ventures in Kentucky and Louisiana. Henderson died suddenly in 1801, when on a visit to Saratoga Springs, by which time he was a very wealthy man.

In Charleston, South Carolina, Thomas Aiton was another prosperous merchant with important Scottish links.[23] His Charleston company, Thomas Aiton & Co., was associated with Cameron, Staley & Co. of Glasgow in which he was also a partner. There was also a branch in New York trading as William Stayley & Co. Aiton corresponded frequently with the Glasgow and New York companies, and his letterbook is an important source for transatlantic trade at the end of the century. Cotton and rice were his principal exports, and textiles and brandy the largest imports. He was not satisfied with his Scottish suppliers and advised the Glasgow company to purchase goods for export in England with the comment that 'the Scotch goods are in general much more substantial, but the English have the best charges.' Aiton frequently sent advice on the goods required but was consistently ignored. 'By heaven', he wrote, "it is a truth that we have seen goods of the same kind and quality with those sent out by our House in Glasgow charged near 50% less than ours were. What a fine chance for competition in selling.' He also experienced difficulty in obtaining credit, and even older firms were in difficulty. 'Money is scarce,' he wrote, 'and for the present mutual confidence appears to be entirely destroyed.'

Aiton found the Glasgow firm 'childish, stupid and unbusinesslike', and was at pains to remind his partners of the consequences for all if the Charleston house failed. 'What a prospect is before us – Disgrace, Bankruptcy and a jail.' Under the terms of the partnership the Charleston firm could not be closed down without the consent of Cameron & Stayley, but apparently the Glasgow firm acted unilaterally to sever the connection. The letterbook closes as Thomas Aiton was preparing to sue his partners.

An interesting example of a Glasgow merchant trying to retain a trading connection is found in the papers of Samuel Cary.[24] Cary had been a planter in Grenada who consigned his sugar to James Campbell of Glasgow. In 1791 he moved to Boston but retained control of some sugar interests, and Campbell hoped to retain his custom. There was little direct trade between Glasgow and Boston, but Campbell assured him that they would be able to correspond regularly by way of Liverpool. If Cary wished to make purchases in London, Campbell would not charge for the surcharge between Glasgow and London. The trade continued on these terms despite the coming of war in Europe and (in Campbell's words) 'the combination among the fanatical advocates for the abolition of the Slave Trade to discontinue the use of sugar'. In 1793 Campbell was on the verge of failure, suspended payment on bills, and reported an arrangement amongst his creditors to wind up his business. Relief came from somewhere, and in November 1793 Campbell said that his company was once more solvent, and hoped that Cary would continue to trust them with his business though advances would have to be limited to £2,000. Samuel Cary died in 1800, and it was now the turn of the company to lay down terms: they could not continue to carry the heavy debts owed by the estate but would refrain from pressing for settlement if the debt were reduced to £2,000. Nine years later the business association still continued despite a debt of £2,799 charged to Cary's estate.[25]

There are four large ledgers belonging to Thomas Buchanan of New York, who was related to George Buchanan of Glasgow and an heir to part of his estate.[26] He carried on a regular trade with Greenock, cotton being one of his principal exports. In the light of other evidence that Scots helped each other, it is no surprise that many of his American correspondents had Scottish names.[27]

So far the sources available for research have revealed little detailed information about new ventures in Scottish trade with America. The official records of imports and exports should provide statistical evidence, though the records for the import of cotton (which was not subject to duty) are imperfect. The papers of the Carron Iron Company contain many references to the export of ironware to the United States.[28] The papers of William Cadell & Co. contain a few references to trade with Philadelphia after independence.[29] Before his bankruptcy the company supplied Robert Morris with ironware from their foundry, and continued to trade with the company that acquired his assets. Apparently the trade was still in an experimental stage in 1785, as there were enquiries about the articles best suited for the American market. The reply indicated a good demand in Pennsylvania for nails and ironmongery, but a shipment of paper had sold badly and the Philadelphia company refused to take more.

The renewed migration from the Highlands caused even more alarm than the movement of earlier years. Now it was not only the Highland landlords who lost tenants but the King who stood to lose valuable subjects. In November 1784 George Dempster, who may have been asked to institute official enquiries, wrote a long letter on the subject to Henry Dundas.[30] He reported that three thousand people had emigrated during the summer of 1784, and he believed that a further hundred and fifty families had sold their possessions in the hope of emigrating but had been unable to obtain passages. He had travelled through the districts most affected, along the belt of land from Fort William to Tain by way of Inverness, and wrote

> I do not believe the people live worse than they did but on the contrary by means of the potatoes rather better. But they are too numerous for the country in its present state, which if nothing is done to alter it will soon be applied solely to the breeding of sheep and cattle. The people have got Ideas of living more comfortably, and believe it easier to effect elsewhere than at home, and in the present state of the Highlands it certainly is so.

He believed that the remedy lay in the development of towns on the coast, the encouragement of fisheries, and the allocation of land to the people for cultivation and house building. The way should be prepared by a commission, set up by the King or by Parliament, and the members should include Sir Adam Ferguson, Sir William Murray, and Adam Smith. It is an intriguing thought that if this suggestion had been acted upon the father of political economy might have applied his mind to town planning, land settlement, and government assisted industry.

During 1802 Edward Fraser of Reelig wrote a very long essay on the causes of emigration, which was clearly intended for publication but never printed.[31] He covered familiar ground, and advocated action to restrain conversion to sheep farming, steps to give crofters more security of tenure, and the promotion of fisheries. Another unpublished essay of 1803 was more emphatic in condemning the behaviour of landlords for their 'inconsiderate rage and temporary benefit in the universal adoption of the sheep farming system.' Allied with this was the raising of the rents, while the government had not helped by imposing a duty on whisky which was, to a Highlander, a necessity of life. These causes combined to make them easy prey to 'the delusive arts and allurements of interested speculators in the purchase of extensive wastes throughout different provinces of the United States, in Genesee and the back settlements of Carolina and Georgia, such as Tennessee, Kentucky, Ohio, etc.'[32]

As in the earlier wave of migration, movement was not confined to the poor or dispossessed, and some men of substance looked to a future in which they could play a more significant role than in their homeland. In 1793 a Catholic tacksman advised a friend to encourage his sons to learn farming and migrate to America 'where they may have good lands at small expence ... and need not be afraid of being tossed by the avarice of Landlords.' In the Highlands he thought that nothing but bankruptcy awaited tenants who could expect no consideration so long as they had a penny to pay their rents.[33]

Neither government concern nor the advice of well-wishers halted the upsurge of migration, and by the end of the century its scale was causing serious concern to the landowners. In 1803 John Grant wrote to Sir James Grant with information 'respecting our poor deluded brethern, the Highlanders, who have gone to America'.[34] They were even leaving 'the Domains of our much honoured chieftain', although 'no blame could be laid at the door of the Laird'. John Grant believed that the damage was being done by 'a set of designing rascals' who enticed people to migrate with promises of ease and plenty. 'This is not so', he concluded 'they are being led to misery'.

To obtain further information John Grant wrote to his son, a merchant in Baltimore. The reply, dated 30 May 1803, said that it had been many months since a shipload of Highlanders had arrived, though this had been a frequent occurrence in the preceding year. Of those who had arrived not 'one of a thousand of these deluded people' did not wish themselves home again after twelve months in America. They expected riches and liberty, but found nothing but a struggle to keep themselves alive. They generally went to the back settlements, where the land was good but thickly forested. It took ten years to bring land into full cultivation and during that long period life was hard.

John Grant's informant thought that the Highlanders were totally unprepared for this kind of existence, and even before settling were subject to disease. They usually arrived in the summer and 'of course mix with their own class, and the consequence is that they fall prey to their own ignorance and want of caution, and so perish in scores a day'. Large numbers of Scots and Irish died of fever in South Carolina every year. This information was clearly intended for dissemination among the Grant tenants who thought of emigration, but whether it was effective in persuading them to remain cannot be judged.[35] The renewal of war with France in 1803 made travel more hazardous, and the many interruptions to normal commercial relations between Great Britain and the United States after 1805 cut down the number of ships looking for emigrant passengers.

The migration stimulated the Earl of Selkirk to publish in 1805 his *Observations on the present state of the Highlands*. His diagnosis of its cause was more acute than that of John Grant. Entirely sympathetic with the landowners, he believed the change from paternalism to a desire to 'turn their estates to best advantage' could lead only to long-term improvements in material propserity; but in the meantime it left crofters without adequate means of subsistence, high rents, and little expectation of relief from indulgent chiefs. Under these circumstances emigration was likely to continue, and it was therefore of interest to the government to ensure that the benefits were not reaped by the republican United States. It would be advantageous to hold out to Highlanders going to British North America the promise of those privileges which they regarded most highly. These were freedom to settle together in chosen districts where they could preserve their own language, dress, and customs. If they were encouraged to remain a distinct people, they would be preserved from 'the infection of dangerous principles'.

Selkirk believed that the poor should be assisted to emigrate – to the right country – but in order to ensure that they chose the right destination, it was first essential to plant some of their own people in an advantageous situation. Traditionally Highlanders had gone to those parts of America where people from their own district were already settled. Unlike John Grant, he believed that they were usually well-informed before setting out. 'Continued and repeated communications between these settlers and their relations in Scotland' made emigrants well aware of the prospects and conditions in different parts of America. It followed that considerable inducements must be given to selected groups to settle in favoured locations in the British colonies, and their reports would then persuade others to follow.

Emigration of a different kind is recorded in papers of the Falconer family of New York.[36] William Falconer came from Banffshire and went to America as a young man in 1785. It is clear that though he came from a family with above average property and education, he followed the usual Highland pattern of going where he could find friends from the same district. In his case this was at Albany in New York, and one of the first letters from his father told him to enquire for 'any of the Strath Spey people', and a year later his mother wrote that it made her happy to know that he was 'so well content and satisfied with so many country folks from here around you'. William Falconer went into partnership with another Scot, Samuel Campbell, as a bookseller in Albany. The business did not prosper, but his letters were evidently cheerful enough to bring out his two brothers, Patrick and Robert. Robert was the most critical of conditions in America, but was also the most energetic and successful of the family. He went on to build up a prosperous business in New York City as a cotton exporter and general merchant.

The American career of Robert Leslie, one of the largest cotton and tobacco merchants in the south, lies wholly within the nineteenth century, yet the record of his early career is worth inclusion because it illustrates the way in which luck and opportunism opened the way to fortune for so many young Scots.[37] The story also provides information about James Dunlop, uncle of his namesake, the former factor for James and Henry Ritchie, and partner in Colin Dunlop & Co. Early in the nineteenth century Dunlop moved to London and carried on a very extensive Anglo-American business

Robert Leslie was distantly related to Dunlop but his family was poor, his mother kept a common lodging-house in Glasgow, and he was employed as a clerk in a cotton business. He led a lively social life, and association with a girl in the Gorbals produced an illegitimate child. His first stroke of fortune came when he was asked to verify the date of birth of John Dunlop's mother by consulting the parish register and was able to supply this information. He followed this up by asking Dunlop for employment in 1814. Dunlop gave him a minor job, Leslie moved to London, clearly made a good impression upon his employer, and in 1816 was sent on business to Antwerp and Paris. While he was making his way in London, he kept up correspondence with a Glasgow friend, George Reid, whose letters provide a lively commentary upon life among young male members of Glasgow's lower middle class, including the news that the girl in the Gorbals had another child on the way. Leslie suspected that it might not be his, but was terrified that the affair might become known to Dunlop and ruin his future prospects. He therefore preferred to send money through George Reid to keep her quiet.

Further alarm was caused when the great Mr Dunlop announced his intention of visiting his native city and calling on Mrs Leslie. Robert Leslie wrote in haste to his mother:

> I beg you will have my sisters and yourself clean – and your skin all covered, that is, have shoes and stockings on your feet – for here the very beggars have their feet covered – and your house as clean as possible.

She was to entertain him only in the front room, and avoid all mention of lodgers. Apparently the visit went off successfully – perhaps Dunlop was more tolerant of poverty than Leslie supposed – for in the following year he was given an important position in Dunlop's American business. Unfortunately the private correspondence ceases. We do not know what happened to Elizabetgh Calder, the girl in the Gorbals, and her two children, nor to the garrulous but dependable George Reid. Nor do we know whether the increasingly prosperous but not very likeable Robert Leslie sent money to relieve his mother.

Cultural contacts increased rather than diminished after independence. Whatever the tribulations of Scottish Loyalists many of the rising generation in the professional classes in Scotland were pro-American. Moreover it was at this time that Scottish philosophy established its ascendancy as Hutcheson, Reid, and later Dugald Stewart became the standard authors in almost all American colleges.

However the most distinguished post-war Scottish recruit for American academic life became a disappointed man. Charles Nisbet, minister of Montrose, was persuaded by John Witherspoon and Benjamin Rush to accept the presidency of Dickinson College in Carlisle, Pennsylvania.[38] Before setting out he was decidedly pro-American. He wrote to Governor John Dickinson, for whom the college was named, lamenting 'the great

Obloquy and Persecution to which I am exposed, by being known as a friend of America.' Soon after his arrival his opinion underwent a radical change, and in the subsequent years his dislike of all things American grew and intensified. He had ground for complaint. He had been led to believe by Benjamin Rush that the college was flourishing and would be the Princeton of the west. In fact it consisted of two rooms and a handful of indifferent students. It was perhaps more than the weather and sickness which made him write to Rush, less than a year after taking up his post; 'I find this climate disagrees with me, and that I cannot live or enjoy health in it.'

Nisbet was a friend and correspondent of David Erskine, Earl of Buchan, one of the most outspoken Scottish friends of America, to whom he made his acid comments: 'Of all the variety of Faiths we have in this country, good faith is by far the rarest'; 'It is a pity that Duplicity and Knavery should be so inseparable from the dealings of Americans'; 'What we want most is men of Uprightness, capacity and public Spirit'; 'God grant that the present taste for Revolutions may at least produce one in favour of common Sense, Religion, and good order in society.'

The Earl of Buchan was somewhat shocked by this denigration of a country that he had never visited but feverently admired. Some of his replies have been preserved.[39] 'Be persuaded my worthy Principal', he wrote in September 1786, 'that North America with all her failings, is a much more proper protectoress for you than this degraded Island where Religion, Liberty, and good manners are much on the decline.' In a letter of 1788 Buchan anticipated the 'Frontier thesis' and later isolationism:

> The Americans may lose in the Inland parts of the country the habits of Europe and may go through all the periods of improvement again after having lost their connection with the Mother Country and with Europe. In which case six or seven centuries would go far to make them an interesting people, but as it is they must not pretend to inveigle in the contests of other nations or aim at commerce and luxury.

Nisbet's letters to Alexander Addison, a Scottish clergyman in Philadelphia, contain many comments similar to those in his letters to Buchan. He was conscious of writing to one who, like himself, had chosen an American career without fully realising what life would be like in an equalitarian country in which refinement was rare. His dislike of democratic tendencies was evident when he wrote, 'The people are mere four-footed beasts and will be to the end of the world.' As for liberty: 'It is most impudent of Payne [sic] or any American to talk of the Rights of Man while there are 500,000 slaves in this country.'

A more contented academic from Scotland was John McLean who came out to practise medicine in New Jersey in 1795, but was soon after appointed professor of chemistry and natural history at Princeton, and shortly after added to his other duties the professorship of mathematics and natural philosophy. He dropped natural history but continued to combine the other three until 1812. McLean was born in Glasgow and admitted to the Faculty of Physicians and Surgeons in 1791. When he arrived he brought with him an introduction from the professor of materia medica at Glasgow for Caspar Wistar, a well-known Philadelpia doctor.[40] The letter stated that McLean had gone through 'a course of education of the most liberal kind', having studied at Glasgow, Edinburgh, London and Paris. In chemistry he was 'particularly eminent, especially in the French or Pneumatic Chemistry'. McLean played a major part in the development of scientific education at Princeton, received an M.D. from Aberdeen in 1797, and was elected a member of the American Philosophical Society in 1805. In 1812 he was persuaded to move to William and Mary as professor of natural philosophy and chemistry, but resigned after a year on grounds of ill-health. He died at Princeton in 1814.[41]

Independence did not stop the flow of American medical students to Edinburgh, and some were also beginning to find their way to Glasgow. By chance there is a fairly full record of one who came from America just after the turn of the century. John R. Lucas came to Edinburgh in 1802 to study medicine and act as tutor to Charles Baskerville, son of a wealthy Virginian planter. Between 1802 and 1804 he wrote twelve letters to William Baskerville reporting his son's progress and describing his own life and difficulties.[42] In 1803 his father died and Lucas found himself short of money. In order to support himself in Edinburgh he asked William Baskerville to sell off some of his late father's property, with the comment 'I had rather have a degree than the land'. He was convinced that he ought to complete the course at Edinburgh, rather than return home and seek instruction at Philadelphia. 'I shall be a much better physician than if I came home in the spring and graduated at Philadelphia . . . no person can ever call me a quack.' One difficulty was the high cost of living in Edinburgh. 'You can scarcely look at a man without paying for it.'

Lucas was strongly pro-British in the struggle with France; but to guard against the possibility of capture on land or sea by the French, he sent an urgent request for a certificate of citizenship from the Governor of Virginia. He was also troubled by the unpopularity of Americans at Edinburgh, the result, he thought, of the reputation gained a few years back by a group of Americans who had 'conducted themselves very unprudently and were very turbulent'. There may be some connection between this and a petition presented by American students at Edinburgh to Rufus King when he was American minister in London. They objected to the treatment of American prisoners captured as French privateers. King replied that he sympathised with the sufferings of the prisoners, but that the British had every right to treat as prisoners of war all persons fighting under the enemy flag.[43]

Another American, Robert W. Rutherford, came to Edinburgh to study in 1807, and wrote full but somewhat formal letters to his father.[44] He was well-connected and had many introductions. He met Dugald Stewart, which was 'a great honor', the Earl of Buchan 'a curious and eccentric character', the widow of Sir Alexander Dick who had been a friend of Banjamin Franklin, and Sir Hector Munroe, a distant relation of James Monroe. A cousin was M.P. for Jedburgh, and Robert Rutherford was able to witness an uncontested election at which, nevertheless, fifty-five voters sat down after the polling to 'an elegant dinner' (paid for, presumably, by the only candidate).

It would be possible to multiply examples of personal contacts as the two countries came to accept each other as independent nations. One anecdote may bring this chapter to a close because it illustrates the way in which traditional hostility – and even open war – could be mitigated by personal friendship. In 1813 Francis Jeffrey, editor of the *Edinburgh Review* and destined to a distinguished career as a Whig statesman, visited New York. The date may seem surprising for the United States and Great Britain were at war. But Jeffrey had come for a very good reason; he wished 'to claim the hand of the lady to whom he had been for some time engaged'.[45] He was already acquainted with James Monroe, Secretary of State, whom he had met in England, and wrote to him with the request that, though an enemy alien, he should 'not be confined very strictly to any place of residence'. He had a passport from his own government, and enclosed two letters to Monroe from Lord Holland. Monroe replied immediately giving him permission to travel to Philadlephia and Washington. Jeffrey returned thanks but added 'as I find your roads are not in the best possible condition for expeditious travelling, I am afraid I cannot expect to reach your capital for several days to come.' In the event the Scottish editor was unable to visit the American secretary of state, but the correspondence closed with mutual expressions of respect as Jeffrey left for Scotland, with his newly-married wife, by way of Boston and Halifax.

The *Edinburgh Review* was to enjoy an enormous reputation among American readers during the nineteenth century, and this episode in the life of its first and most distinguished editor is a fitting conclusion to this study of relations between Scotland and America during the preceding hundred and thirty years.

Chapter Nine

RETROSPECT

Do the sources for Scottish-American relations in the eighteenth century provide the foundation for broad generalisation? The detailed information that they contain is apparent in the preceding chapters, but abundance does not necessarily imply range or coherence. Accumulation may not enlarge understanding and one may end with nothing more than a number of disparate stories. The survey has revealed barren patches as well as lush pastures and, apart from the tobacco trade, it may be difficult to see more than brief lives and the records of short-lived enterprise.

It is pertinent to ask whether the categories of evidence which have been omitted or merely sampled could fill in more of the story. The records of colonial land grants, wills and litigation would certainly yield more information. There are also materials in the Public Record Office, port books, and customs records. The loyalist claims will yield more information about the state of the tobacco trade on the eve of the Revolution. The records of the churches may have a good deal more to yield, and Scottish legal records may provide more information about transportation and indentures.

These sources will facilitate research in depth on aspects of the Scottish-American relationship, but it is doubtful whether they will add to the general picture. The sources surveyed in this volume provide the framework for the subject, and no subsequent discovery is likely to alter it in any substantial way. It is possible that the records of a Glasgow tobacco company before 1750 are still hidden in a family attic or solicitor's strong room. There may be, somewhere, a large collection of immigrant letters. It is probable that some papers, diaries, or business papers are in private hands and have so far escaped identification. All these possibilities exist but it may still be claimed that a survey which has located so many sources deposited in public archives, state historical societies, museums, and university libraries, will not be radically changed by subsequent discoveries.

If this claim is accepted, what has been surveyed provides some interesting observations on the nature of historical evidence. It is skewed chronologically and by class. The records from 1700 to 1750 are scanty; between 1750 and 1775 they become abundant, thanks largely to the tobacco trade. There is ample material for business history, but little for social life in America. The annals of the poor are disappointingly thin. Even where the records are voluminous, the extent to which chance has determined their survival is a sobering thought for historians. Most of what we know about the great firm of John Glassford derives from the accident that the papers of Neil Jamieson, including many Glassford accounts and ledgers, were not destroyed during the confusion of the Revolution, but were preserved and eventually found a permanent home in the Library of Congress. Our knowledge of William Cunninghame's operations depends upon the happy accident that an Edinburgh lawyer kept long-forgotten records, eventually housed in the Scottish Record Office. More survivors' luck brought records of James and Henry Ritchie to the Library of Congress, because their principal factor, James Dunlop, remained in America after independence, made money from land speculation in the District of Columbia, and established a family that preserved his business records. It was also luck that a letterbook of the one factor who wrote highly personal accounts of his business problems (Alexander Hamilton) has survived because the assets of his Glasgow employer were acquired by John Glassford & Co.

Historians hardly dare to reflect upon the extent that their knowledge of the past depends upon chance survivals of this kind. The claim to scientific accuracy is qualified by the knowledge that, apart from government repositories, we have no more than samples of what is lost – and lost for ever. Then comes the tiresome question: with what assurance can we accept the evidence as truly representative of that which can never be known?

Any survey of sources must therefore acknowledge with humility the fragmentary character of the evidence; but too rigorous an insistence upon deficiencies in the record might end in the abandonment of all historical enterprise. Imagination and hypothesis must come to the rescue if the quest for historical truth is not to end in total agnosticism. These observations are of particular force when dealing with evidence provided by obscure men whose experience cannot be bolstered with massive evidence from record-keeping institutions.

Having made these disclaimers some reflections are permissible. There are first some facts which are indisputable. From the Act of Union to 1775 an increasing number of Scots found their way to America, and some became prominent in commerce, official employment, religion, medicine, and higher education. Of those who did not wield influence of this kind the most numerous were men employed in humbler capacities in commercial enterprise, or as schoolmasters, tutors, skilled tradesmen of various kinds, and Highland crofters. The impact of this Scottish migration was unevenly distributed. Very few went to New England; Virginia and Maryland attracted by far the largest number of lowland immigrants from the west and south-west; Charleston, South Carolina, was most-favoured by the sons of Lowland gentry. Highlanders went to Georgia, North Carolina, and northern New York. Philadelphia attracted a good many Scots, but the random elimination of evidence has worked adversely in that city, and left insufficient evidence of individuals to support generalisation about their geographical or social origin. The best that can be said is that infrequent references to Philadelphia in the Glasgow records suggests that the principal personal contacts were with Edinburgh and the east, while the reputation of Pennsylvania as a land of opportunity for the poor suggests that many of the immigrants came from humble backgrounds.

The Highlanders aimed to acquire land and settle in communities. In the early days of Georgia they were thought of as the ideal settlers to defend a frontier, but in other colonies they did not play this role. In North Carolina they were welcomed because the colony was poor and desparately wished to increase its population. The Highlanders never played a role in developing the Appalachian frontier comparable to that of men from Northern Ireland; but in northern New York the owners of vast tracts of wilderness saw settlement as the only way to increase land values, and Highlanders were the most readily available and most dependable source of manpower.

Apart from the Highland migration, Scottish movement was likely to follow the channels of trade and make for the more developed regions in the colonies. It is inconceivable that some lowland emigrants of farming stock did not make for more remote rural areas, but they have left no record. It was in the cities, the small market towns of Virginia and Maryland, and the areas of the developed cultivation of tobacco, rice, and indigo that Scots made their mark. Religious, medical, and educational influences usually conformed to the same patterns of trade. This concentration in the more advanced portions of colonial culture gave Scots an influence out of proportion to their numbers.

In social structure, religion, and educational objectives many American colonists found Scottish culture more attractive than English. If eighteenth-century Scotland was still a highly structured and deferential society, it did not suffer beneath quite the same dead weight of aristocratic and anglican privilege. If, as has been suggested, Scottish and colonial cultures were both 'provincial', they could find shared experience and opportunities in this status. Scottish universities were open to all. The social tone of the capital was set by ministers, lawyers, professors, and men of letters, not by titled men who lived on rents from inherited estates. In Glasgow the dominant élite was even more decidedly middle class. The tone of Aberdeen, with its episcopalian traditions and proximity to great landed estates, was slightly more aristocratic, but not so much as to make the 'provincial' American feel ill-at-ease. These affinities combined with the undeniable achievements in learning, science, medicine, and commercial enterprise to give Scotland a high reputation in colonial America. This respect was not greatly diminished by the unpopularity of tobacco factors who drove a hard bargain or, after 1765, by the supposed toryism of Scottish people. Those who were interested in Scottish philosophy found a marked coincidence between the abstract propositions of Hutcheson and their own practical needs.

This awareness of Scotland as an alternative English-speaking culture was the most significant aspect of the Scottish influence upon America; it is also the hardest to document. The importance of Scottish enlightenment thought in America has been rediscovered in recent years, but what may be more important is the influence of hundreds of forgotten ministers, schoolmasters, tutors, and merchants. This can be neither measured nor ignored.

Appendix A

PUBLICATIONS BY
EMIGRANT SCOTTISH DOCTORS

Medical

Chalmers, Lionel. *An essay on fevers,* Charleston S.C. 1767.

'On the Opisthotonos and Tetanus . . . sent to Dr John Fothergill' *Medical Observations and Inquiries, I,* (1757) 87–110.

An account of the weather and diseases of South Carolina, London 1776.

Colden, Cadwallader. *An account of the diseases and climate of New York,* possibly published New York 1720, but no copy now known. See F. Guerra. *American medical bibliography,* New York 1962.

An essay on the Iliac passion, Philadelphia 1741.

Observations on the fever which prevailed in the city of New York in 1741/2. Written in 1743. Communicated to Dr David Hosack by C. D. Colden. *American medical and philosophical Register,* I (1810–11) 310–30.

Remarks on the yellow fever of New York in 1741 and 1742 . . . written in 1743, communicated to the editors by his grandson *Medical Repository* XXIV, (1811) 1–9, 159–63. This may have been published previously in New York 1745.

Extract of a letter . . . to Dr Fothergill concerning the Throat Distemper. *Medical Observations and Inquiries, I,* (1757) 211–29.

A treatise on Wounds and Fevers, New York 1765.

Douglas, William. *A letter from one in the Country, to his Friend in the City; In relation to the Distresses occasioned by the doubtful and prevailing practice of the Inoculation of the Small pox,* Boston 1721.

The Abuses and Scandals of some late Pamphlets in Favour of Inoculation . . . in a letter to Alexander Stuart, M.D. & F.R.S. In London, Boston 1722.

A dissertation concerning inoculation for the small pox, Boston and London 1730.

A letter to Doctor Zabdiel Boylston; Occasion'd by a late Dissertation concerning inoculation of the small pox, Boston 1730.

An account of the throat distemper, New York 1740.

Garden, Alexander. 'An account of the Indian Pink' *Essays and Observations* (Edinburgh), III (1771) 145–53. Said to have been published in Charleston S.C. 1764.

Account of the use of the ashes of tobacco in the cure of dropsy . . . in a letter to Dr Hope. *Medical and Philosophical Commentaries,* Edinburgh, III, 1775–6, 330–2.

Hamilton, Alexander. *A defence of Dr Thomson's discourse on the preparation of the body for Small pox. . .,* Philadelphia 1751.

McLeane, Lauchlin. *An essay on the expediency of inoculation,* Philadelphia 1756.

Lining, John. 'A letter . . . to James Jurin M.D. Statical experiments made on himself for one year, accompanied with meteorological observations and six general tables'. *Philosophical Transactions XLII,* (1743) 491–8.

'A letter . . . to James Jurin M.D. . . . Serving to accompany some additions to his Statistical Experiments'. *Philosophical Transactions XLVIII,* (1745).

'A letter . . . to C. Mortimer M.D. Sec. R.S. concerning the weather in South Carolina; with abstracts of his meteorological observations in Charles-Town'. *Philosophical Transactions,* XLV, (1748) 336–44.

'Of the anthelmintic virtues of the Root of the Indian Pink, being part of a letter . . . to Dr. Robert Whytt, Professor of Medicine in the University of Edinburgh'. *Essays and Observations, Physical and Literary* (Edinburgh), *1,* (1754) 386–9.

'A description of the American yellow Fever in a letter to Dr. Robert Whytt'. *Essays and Observations, Physical and Literary* (Edinburgh) *II,* (1756) 370–95.

Middleton, Peter, *A medical discourse, or an Historical inquiry into the ancient and present state of medicine; the substance of what was delivered at opening the Medical School in the City of New York,* New York 1769.

Thomson, Adam. *A Discourse on the preparation of the body for Small pox,* Philadelphia 1750.

Scientific

Colden, Cadwallader. 'Plantae Coldenghamiae in provincia Noveboracensi sponte crescentes'. *Acta Socientatis regiae Scientiarum Upsaliensis, IV,* (1749), 81–136; *V,* (1751), 47–82.

An explanation of the First causes of Action in Matter and the Cause of Gravity, New York 1745.

Garden, Alexander. 'A description of a new plant Gardenia'. *Essays and Observations, Physical and Literary, II,* (1756), 1–9.

'An account of the *Gymnotus Electricus,* or electric eel'. *Philosophical Transactions, LXV,* (1775), 102–110.

SCOTTISH DOCTORS PRACTISING IN AMERICA AND AMERICAN DOCTORS EDUCATED IN SCOTLAND

This contains a list of names, from a wide variety of sources, of Scotsmen who are said to have emigrated from Scotland and practised medicine in America during the eighteenth century and of American doctors educated in Scotland.

It has been impossible to determine where all the emigrants were educated. For some it has been possible to find, in the Glasgow or Edinburgh university records, men of similar names attending classes at approximately the right time. These records have been added against a question mark – e.g. (? Monro 1740). The names for each colony or state have been recorded alphabetically.

The list of Americans said to have studied medicine in Scotland is easier to compile, for university records generally record place of birth. But there are no records providing this information for Edinburgh between 1748, when Alexander Monro primus's class lists cease, and 1755, when William Cullen's class lists start. No attempt has been made to give information about all the classes the students attended, only a single reference has been given to provide evidence that a student was at Edinburgh or Glasgow. The names in these lists have been arranged chronologically.

ABBREVIATIONS AND REFERENCES

DAB = Dictionary of American Biography, ed. Allen Johnson, New York 1928.

KB = Kelley, H. A. and Burrage, W. L. *American Medical Biographies,* Baltimore 1920.

LCP = Library Company of Philadelphia. Collections now at PHS.

MB = Edinburgh University matriculation books 1762–85, 1786–1803.

PHS = Pennsylvania Historical Society.

RCPE = Royal College of Physicians, Edinburgh.

RMS = Royal Medical Society.

SRO = Scottish Record Office.

Cullen. William Cullen, class lists 1755–65. Edinburgh University.

Walker. Professor Walker, class lists 1785–1800, in which he marks medical students in his class. Edinburgh University.

Gregory. Professor Gregory, class lists 1790–1800. Edinburgh University.

Hamilton. Professor Hamilton, class lists. RCPP.

Toner. J. M. Toner Papers, LC.

Waring. WARING LIBRARY, CHARLESTON, SOUTH CAROLINA.

ABRAHAMS, HAROLD J. *Extinct Medical Schools of Baltimore,* Baltimore 1969.

Addison, W. Innes. *A Roll of the Graduates of the University of Glasgow from 31 December 1727 to 31 December 1897,* Glasgow 1898.

The Matriculation Albums of the University of Glasgow . . . 1728 to . . . 1857, Glasgow 1913.

Alden, Ebenezer. *Early History of the Medical Profession in the County of Norfolk, Mass,* Boston 1853.

Anderson, P. J. *Fasti Academiae Mariscallanae Aberdonensis,* vol. II. Officers, graduates and alumni, Aberdeen 1889–98.

Blake, John B. *Public Health in the Town of Boston 1630–1822,* Cambridge Mass, 1959.

Bland, Theodorick. *The Bland Papers* ed. Charles Campbell, Petersburgh, Va, 1839.

Blanton, W. B. *Medicine in Virginia in the Eighteenth Century,* Richmond Va, 1931.

Bridenbaugh C. ed. *Gentleman's progress: The Itinerarium of Dr. Alexander Hamilton.* Chapel Hill 1948.

Clark, George Faber. *A History of the Town of Norton, Bristol County, Mass,* Boston 1859.

Coates, B. H. Life of Samuel Powel Griffit, PHS Memoires II, Philadelphia 1830, p. 5–12.

Cordell, E. F. *Medical Annals of Maryland 1700–1899,* Baltimore 1903.

Corner, Betsey. *William Shippen, Jr. Pioneer in American medical education,* Philadelphia 1951.

Daniels, George F. *History of the Town of Oxford, Mass, with genealogies,* Oxford Mass. 1892.

Dexter, F. B. *Biographical Notices of Graduates of Yale College,* New Haven Conn. 1913.

Eaton, Lilley. *Genealogical History of the Town of Reading,* Boston 1874.

Flexnor, James T. *Doctors on horseback,* New York 1937.

Forster, Edward Jacob. 'Medical Profession in Suffolk County, Massachusetts', in *Professional and Industrial history of Suffolk County,* 3 vols. Boston 1894.

Fothergill, Gerald. 'Emigrants from England'. *New England Historical and Genealogical Register, LXIV,* 1910, p. 325.

Haws, Charles H. *Scots in the Old Dominion,* Edinburgh 1980.

Hayden, Horace E. *Virginia Genealogies,* Wilkes Barre Pa. 1891

Jones, Elias. *New Revised History of Dorchester County,* Cambridge M 1966.

Judd, Sylvester. *History of Hadley, Hatfield, South Hadley, Amherst and Granby,* Springfield Mass. 1905.

Krumbhaar, E. B. Dr. William Hunter of Newport, *Annals of Surgery, CI,* 1935, 506–28.

Long, D. ed. *Medicine in North Carolina,* Raleigh N.C. 1972.

Malloch, Archibald. *Medical Interchange between the British Isles and America before 1801,* London 1946.

Norris, Richard C. The Preston Retreat, in *Founders' Week Memorial* ed. F. P. Henry, Philadelphia 1909, p.81–2.

Packard, F. R. *History of Medicine in the United States,* 2 vols. New York 1931.

Parker, E. L. *History of Londonderry NH,* Boston 1851.

Parramore, T. C. 'Doctors Whig and Tory'. *N. Carolina Med. J.,* 1966, 65–8.

Parramore, T. C. Personal Communication: information derived from a search of local records by Mr T. C. Parramore, 5012 Tanglewood Drive, Raleigh, N.C. 27612.

Quinan, J. R. *Medical Annals of Baltimore from 1608–*1880, Baltimore 1884.

Rush, Benjamin. *Autobiography* ed. G. W. Corner, Princeton 1948.
    Letters of Benjamin Rush ed. L. H. Butterfield, 2 vols. Princeton 1951.

Sibley, J. L. *Harvard Graduates: Biographical Sketches of those who Attended Harvard College . . . 1642,* Boston 1873.

Sydenham, Diane Meredith. *Practitioner and Patient: the Practice of Medicine in Eighteenth Century South Carolina.* Johns Hopkins PH.D. Thesis 1979.

Thatcher, James. *American Medical Biography,* Boston 1828.

Tilden William S. ed. *History of the Town of Medfield, Massachusetts 1650–*1886, Boston 1887.

Waring, J. I. *A History of Medicine in South Carolina,* Charleston S.C. 1964.

Whyte, Donald. *A Dictionary of Scottish Emigrants to the U.S.A.,* Baltimore 1972.

Wickes, S. *History of Medicine in New Jersey,* Newark N.J. 1879.

CONNECTICUT

Emigrants

Samuel Nesbett, educated Edinburgh, practised New Haven. (Connecticut Medical Society, *The Heritage of Connecticut Medicine,* New Haven 1942.)

Americans

Norman Morrison (d. 1761) (?Monro 1730).

Samuel Seabury (1729–96), Edinburgh 1752 (Dexter).

Edward Bridgewater, Edinburgh (Cullen 1759).

John Husband Osborne, Edinburgh (Cullen 1761).

William Shepherd, Edinburgh (Gregory 1790–1).

DELAWARE
Emigrants
None.
Americans
Henry Latimer (1752–1819), Edinburgh 1773 (M.B.).
Nathan Thomas, Edinburgh medical student, (Walker's lectures 1785).
George Munro (1760–1819), Edinburgh M.D. 1786.
Ebenezer Graham, Edinburgh (Gregory 1796–7).

FLORIDA
Emigrant
Henry Cunningham, from Fife, in E. Florida before 1771 (?Monro 1741).
Americans
None.

GEORGIA
William Bowler, surgeon with Highland regiment, settled Georgia (?Monro 1736).
James Cuthbert, from Inverness, possibly a physician (Abstract of Colonial Wills of the State of Georgia 34 & 35).
Thomas Hawkins, surgeon with Highland regiment, settled Georgia.
Americans
Joshiah Gibbon, Edinburgh M.D. 1776.
William Martin Johnson, Edinburgh 1784–5 (not in M.B.) (Rush Letters p. 87).
John Smith, Edinburgh M.D. 1787.
James Box Young, Edinburgh M.D. 1789.
James Bond Read, b. 1770 Edinburgh Member RMS. Leiden M.D. 1791.
Andrew Johnston, Edinburgh (Gregory 1799–1800).

KENTUCKY
Emigrants
None.
Americans
John Watkins, Edinburgh (Gregory 1790).
Ephraim McDowell (1771–1830), Edinburgh (Gregory 1793–4). John Bell's private surgery lectures (Flexner).
James Speed, (medical student Walker's lectures 1796).

MAINE
Emigrants
John MacKechnie (1703–1783), studied either Aberdeen or Edinburgh (?Monro 1726). Emigrated 1755, first to Boston and then to Maine (K.B.).

Alexander Ramsay (1754–1774), educated Dublin and Edinburgh (DAB).
Americans
None.

MARYLAND
Emigrants
James Anderson, (Toner).
James Bourman (b. 1764), surgeon who went from Scotland to Maryland as an indentured servant. (Fothergill).
George Brown (1689–1762), surgeon's mate on British ship, emigrated 1708 (Quinan).
Gustavas Brown (1744–1801), Edinburgh M.D. 1770, emigrated 1770.

Emigrants
George Buchanan (1697–1750), emigrated 1723 (Quinan).
James Davidson (1743–1811), Edinburgh 1768 (MB). M.D. King's College 1769, emigrated 1771.
Alexander Hamilton (1712–56), Edinburgh (Monro 1731).
John Hamilton (1692–1768), Edinburgh M.A 1719, *Medical Gazette,* March 31, 1768. ?Brother of Alexander.
Alexander Mitchell (1768–1804), Edinburgh 1788 (MB).
  – – – Ireland, Edinburgh with Gustavus Brown (Cordell).
William Murray (1708–69), b. Scotland, educated Barbados, emigrated 1735 (Cordell).
William Vans Murray d. 1759, emigrated after 1715 (Elias Jones).
Upton Scott, b. Ireland, (1722–1814), Glasgow M.D. 1753. May have been at Edinburgh (Cordell).
John Smith. Native of Scotland, resided in Charles Co., Maryland but left in 1775 for political reasons: went to Norfolk, Virginia (Quinan).
James Walker d. 1759, arrived in Maryland 1713. 1724 medical diploma from Aberdeen (Quinan).
George Walker d. 1743, arrived from Scotland 1713 (Quinan).
Henry Stevenson b. Ireland, (1721–1814), educated Ireland, England, Scotland (Toner under Steuart).
George Steuart (1695–1784), settled in Annapolis 1720 (Quinan).
Americans
James Leiper (1735–71), educated at Edinburgh (Toner).
James Murray (1739–1819), M.D. Glasgow 1765 and Edinburgh 1764 (MB).
Henry Reeder, Edinburgh (Cullen 1765–66).
Joseph Digges (1747–83), Edinburgh (Cullen 1765–6), M.D. Glasgow 1767.

Edward Gantt (1741–1837), Edinburgh (Cullen 1764–6), M.D. Leiden 1767.

Gustavus Richard Brown (1747–1804), Edinburgh M.D. 1768.

John Parnham (1740–1800), Edinburgh 1769–73 (MB).

Dennis Dorsey, Edinburgh M.D. 1776.

Ezekial John Dorsey d. 1822, Edinburgh M.D. 1776.

James Steuart (1755–1845), Edinburgh M.D. 1779.

John Tyler (1764–1841), London and Edinburgh (Toner, not in MB).

William Quynn (1760–84), Edinburgh 1783, died at Edinburgh (MHM, XXXI, (1936) 181–215.

George Buchanan (1763–1808), Edinburgh M.D. 1785.

Daniel Moores (1745–1802), Edinburgh M.D. 1786.

John Thomas Shaaf d.1817, Edinburgh 1788–90 (MB).

George Pitt Stevenson (1768–1819), Edinburgh M.D. 1789.

Robert Buchanan, Edinburgh (Gregory 1790).

John Weems, Edinburgh M.D. 1792.

John Irvine Troup, Edinburgh M.D. 1793.

John Cumming, Edinburgh (Gregory 1791–2), M.D. Glasgow 1793.

John Beale Davidge (1768–1829), Edinburgh (Gregory 1792–3), M.D. Glasgow 1793.

Perry E. Noel (1768–1813), Edinburgh M.D. 1794.

Robert Alexander, Edinburgh (Gregory 1794–5).

James Smith or Smyth (1773–1841), Edinburgh (Gregory 1796–7).

Arthur Pue, Edinburgh (Gregory 1796–7).

John Owen, Edinburgh (Hamilton 1797).

John Ewen, Edinburgh (Gregory 1797–8).

MASSACHUSETTS
Emigrants

Grancis Archibald, naval surgeon, settled Boston 721 (Alden).

Revd. John Campbell (c. 1690–1761), minister and doctor (Daniels).

William Douglas (1691–1752), M.A. Edinburgh 1705; Leiden 1711; M.D. Utrecht 1712.

James Halkerston d. 1721, may have attended St Andrews, naval surgeon, settled Boston 1721 (Blake).

William Hay (c. 1683–1783), said to have been educated in Scotland (Eaton).

Adam Johnstone d. 1806, (Clark).

Hugh Kennedy d. 1752, in Boston by 1720 (Forster 271–2).

Thomas Lowthain d. 1749, (Tilden).

Archibald Spencer, Edinburgh male midwife, (B. Franklin *Autobiography* ed. Labaree, New Haven 1964, p.240–298).

William Squire d. 1731, (Judd 443).

George Stewart d. post-1730, in Boston by 1714, army physician or surgeon (Forster 279).

James Tytler (1747–1804), Edinburgh 1764 (MB).

Americans

John Cuming (1727–88), Edinburgh c. 1750 (Sibley).

John Lowell (1734–76), Edinburgh (Monro c. 1754 and Harvard University Corporation Records XI, 39–40).

Joseph Edwards, Edinburgh (Cullen 1756–7).

Thomas Bulfinch (1728–1802), Edinburgh M.D. 1757, also in London.

John Jeffreys, Edinburgh (Cullen 1761).

Williams Smibert (1732–74), Edinburgh M.D. 1762.

Edmund Dana (1739–1823), Edinburgh (Cullen 1764).

John B. Swett (1752–96), Edinburgh 1779 (MB).

William Spooner (1760–1836), Edinburgh M.D. 1785.

William Jackson (1739–97), Edinburgh, medical student at Walker's lectures 1785.

Thomas Danforth, Edinburgh (Hamilton 1796).

Charles Windship, Glasgow M.D. 1797, Edinburgh (Gregory 1796).

Aberdeen Graduates who did not study in Scotland

John Jefferies (1745–1819), M.D. 1769.

Bela Lincoln (1733–74), M.D. Marischal 1765.

Peter Oliver b. 1749, M.D. Marischal 1790.

William Paine (1750–1822), M.D. Marischal 1775.

Charles Russell (1739–80), M.D. Marischal 1765.

NEW HAMPSHIRE
Emigrants

Robert Bartley, M.D. – to Londonderry N.H. c. 1790, educated Dublin and Edinburgh (Parker, p. 215).

Americans

Nathan Smith (1762–1829), Glasgow, Edinburgh, and London 1796–7 (DAB, but not in Glasgow or Edinburgh University Records).

NEW JERSEY
Emigrants

Ichabod Burnet (1684–1774), possibly educated Edinburgh (Toner).

John Maclean (1771–1814), Glasgow, matriculated 1783 Faculty of Physicians and Surgeons, Glasgow, M.D. King's College, Aberdeen 1797.

Alexander Rose (1713–80), educated Edinburgh, emigrated first to Pennsylvania then to New Jersey (Toner).

Americans

James Newell, educated Edinburgh c. 1745 (Toner).

Nosh Hart, Edinburgh (Cullen 1765–6).

NEW YORK
Emigrants

William Bruce, (?Munro 1743), medical officer, British army, settled in New York (DAB).

Dr Carrigan, Scottish physician (Toner).

Cadwallader Colden (1688–1776). Edinburgh M.A. 1705, London, and Paris.

Alexander Coventry, Glasgow 1783–4, Edinburgh 1784–5 (Diary, NYHS).

John Johnstone, (*Proc. N.J. History Society,* n.s. XV (1930) 347).

Archibald McLean, surgeon. (McLeane Papers, SRO).

Peter Middleton d. 1781, Edinburgh (Monro 1744), M.D. St Andrews 1752.

John Nicol, M.D. Edinburgh 1724. (Isaac Dubois *de sanguinis missionis usu et abusu* Leiden 1740, dedicated to John Nicoll M.D. Edin., of New York.)

William Wilson (1755–1828), M.A. Glasgow 1775, medical practitioner Claremont 1784.

Americans

John Jones, London, Edinburgh. M.D. Rheims 1751 (DAB).

James Jay (1732–1815), Edinburgh M.D. 1753.

James Smith (1741–1812), Edinburgh (Cullen 1762–3), M.D. Leiden 1764.

John van B. Tennant (b. New Jersey, d. 1770), Edinburgh (Cullen 1763), M.D. Leiden 1764.

Samuel Bard (1743–1821), Edinburgh M.D. 1765.

Samuel Martin, Edinburgh M.D. 1765.

Daniel Robert, Edinburgh c. 1768 (Rush p. 44).

William Moore, Edinburgh M.D. 1780.

Nicholas Romayne (1756–1817), Edinburgh M.D. 1780.

Benjamin Kissam, Edinburgh M.D. 1783.

John R. B. Rodgers, Edinburgh M.D. 1785.

William Hammersley, Edinburgh 1784, (medical student at Walker's lectures).

Richard Laurence, Edinburgh 1785 (MB).

Samuel Latham Mitchell (1764–1831), Edinburgh M.D. 1786, London, and Paris.

Richard S. Kissam, Edinburgh M.D. 1787.

David Hosack (1769–1835), Edinburgh M.D. 1791, and London.

Daniel Proudfit, Edinburgh (Gregory 1794–5).

Edmund Ludlow, Edinburgh (Gregory 1794–5).

Edmund Bainbridge, Edinburgh (Gregory 1794–5).

Walter W. Buchanan, Glasgow M.D. Edinburgh (Gregory 1797–8).

James S. Stringham (1755–1817), Edinburgh M.D. 1799.

Archibald Bruce (1777–1818), Edinburgh (Gregory 1799–1800).

Daniel Budd, Edinburgh (Toner).

NORTH CAROLINA
Emigrants

Archibald Campbell, from Tongue to N. Carolina in 1772, physician (Whyte).

William Cathcart, (?Munro 1729), (SRO, GD180, Cathcart of Genoch).

Thomas Cobham, came to N.C, 1766. Loyalist, surgeon in British army (Long).
Emigrants

James Fergus, (Long).

John Fergus (before 1758–1802). Edinburgh?, (Long).

Walter Ferguson C.A. 1763–89 (Parramore, personal communication).

James Giekie C.A. 1774–93 (Parramore, personal communication).

Nathaniel Hill (1769–1842), (Long).

William Houston N.D. (Parramore, personal communication).

Gabriel Johnston or Johnstoune (1699–1752), Edinburgh 1713–14, M.A., St Andrews 1720, Leiden 1721. Emigrated 1729. Governor of N.C. 1733. (DAB says that he had studied medicine).

Robert Lenox, settled Edenton c. 1755 (Parramore).

Gervais McGrath N.D. (Parramore, personal communication).

Alexander Morrison (1717–1777), b. Skye, settled in Carthage (Long).

Dr Smyth, first permanent resident of N. Carolina to have graduated in 1700 at Edinburgh (Long).
Americans

Alexander Gaston, doctor in New Bern 1767, Edinburgh (Cullen 1759).

James Dubois, Edinburgh (Gregory 1790–1).

Andrew Knox, Edinburgh (Gregory 1791–2).

John Pain, Edinburgh (Gregory 1791–2).

James Halsea, Edinburgh (Gregory 1793–4).

Simmons Jones Baker, Edinburgh (Gregory 1794–5).

Adam Struthers Hendens, Edinburgh (Gregory 1798–9).

PENNSYLVANIA
Emigrants

Charles McCarter, surgeon with continental army, settled Philadelphia (Toner).

William Crawford. Letter, Andrew Duncan to Benjamin Rush, 29 May 1783 (Rush MSS. LCP. PHS).

David Jameson, graduate of medicine from Edinburgh (not recorded) who migrated 1740 (Abrahams).

Lauchline Macleane (1727–78), born in Ireland. Edinburgh M.D. 1755.

John Stuart, educated Edinburgh. practised with L. Macleane .

Adam Thomson d. 1767, educated Edinburgh (Monro 1735) and friend of Alexander Hamilton.

James Watt, Glasgow M.A. 1790, M.D. 1796, minister of secession church, Pennsylvania 1794–5.

Americans

Phineas Bond (1717–73), Edinburgh 1742, M.D. Rheims.

John Redman (1722–1808), Edinburgh 1746 (His notes on A. Monro's lectures, National Library of Medicine, Bethesda). London. Leiden M.D. 1750.

Benjamin Morris, Edinburgh 1748, introduced to George Drummond by Joshua Crosby, Philadelphia. (Letter in SRO, GD 24/1/833).

Charles Morre (1724–1801). Edinburgh M.D. 1752. Arrived in Edinburgh 1748 with Banjamin Morris.

Cadwallader Evans. Edinburgh c. 1756 (Toner).

Ralph Asheton, Edinburgh 1758 (Packard). M.D. St Andrews (Corner).

George Glentworth (1735–92), Edinburgh (Cullen 1758–9). M.D. St Andrews (Corner).

William Shippen (1736–1808), Edinburgh M.D. 1761, and London.

John Morgan (1735–89), Edinburgh M.D. 1763, and London.

Thomas Ruston, Edinburgh M.D. 1764.

James Tapscott, Edinburgh M.D. 1765.

Hugh Williamson (1736–1819), Edinburgh, Cullen 1764–5. London, M.D. Utrecht 1766.

Adam Kuhn (1741–1817), Edinburgh M.D. 1767, Uppsala and London.

Benjamin Bush (1745–1813), Edinburgh M.D. 1768, and London.

William Logan, Edinburgh M.D. 1771.

Thomas Parke (1749–1835), B.M. Philadelphia 1770. London and Edinburgh 1771 (Journal, Pemberton Papers, PHS).

Ignatus D. Knowlton, Edinburgh M.D. 1773.

John Carson, Edinburgh 1774 (Letters introducing him to W. Cullen from J. Morgan, W. Shippen and B. Rush, Cullen Papers, Glasgow University).

John Sims, Edinburgh M.D. 1774.

Benjamin Duffield b. 1753, Edinburgh 1775 (MB).

George Logan (1753–1821), Edinburgh M.D. 1779. London.

Samuel Powell Griffitts (1759–1826). A.M. & M.D. Philadelphia, Edinburgh 1784, and London (Coates).

James Lyons, Edinburgh 1784–5 (Letter of introduction, Shippen to Cullen, RCPE), and London

Americans

Caspar Wistar (1761–1818), B.M. Pennsylvania State University, Edinburgh M.D. 1786, also London.

Benjamin Smith Barton (1766–1815), Edinburgh 1786 (MB), M.D. Kiel 1796.

Isaac Cathrall (1763–1819), educated London 1790, Edinburgh 1791 (MB), and Paris (Toner).

William Annan d. 1797, M.D. Glasgow 1791, Edinburgh (Gregory 1790–1).

James Ridel, Edinburgh (Hamilton 1792).

Thomas C. James (1766–1835), Edinburgh medical student (Walker's lectures 1792), also London.

Philip Syng Physic (1768–1837), Edinburgh M.D. 1792, London 1790.

John Cumming, Glasgow M.D. 1793.

Benjamin Dobel, Edinburgh (Gregory 1793–4).

William Boys, Edinburgh (Gregory 1794–5).

John Redman Coxe (1793–1864), Philadelphia M.D. 1789, Edinburgh (Gregory 1794–5), also London and Paris.

Adam Seybert (1733–1825), Philadelphia 1793, Edinburgh (Gregory 1794–5), also London.

Thomas T. Hewson (1773–1848), A.B. Pennsylvania, Edinburgh (Gregory 1795–6), also London.

Jonas Preston (1764–1836), graduated in medicine Philadelphia, went to Edinburgh, London and Paris (Norris). No record of his studying at Edinburgh.

Graduated at Aberdeen, but does not appear to have studied in Scotland:

Henry Norris, M.D. King's College 1786, recommended by Dr Richard Lynn and Dr Edward Ellion.

RHODE ISLAND

Emigrants

William Hunter (c. 1730–77), said to have been educated at Edinburgh Krumbhaar p. 507).

Dr James Keith, friend of Alexander Hamilton, met him on his journey to Boston (Bridenbaugh p. 102).

Thomas Moffat d. 1787, (?Monro 1732), M.D. Rheims.

Thomas Bodman, emigrated 1750 (Thatcher).

Americans

Robert Stewart, Edinburgh (Cullen chemistry 1765).

Benjamin Waterhouse (1754–1846), Edinburgh 1775–6 (MB).

Andrew Johnson, Edinburgh (Gregory 1799–1800).

SOUTH CAROLINA

General Reference: Waring.

Emigrants

Alexander Baron (1745-1819), Edinburgh M.D. 1768, settled Charleston.

Robert Brisbane, practised in S. Carolina with brother William.

William Brisbane (1736-71), from Glasgow, emigrated 1732.

Lionel Chalmers (1715-77), St Andrews M.D. 1756, emigrated 1737.

James Crockatt, (?Munro 1741), emigrated before 1763 (Smythe of Balhary, Scottish National Register of Archives).

Charles Fyffe, practitioner in Physic, S. Carolina (SRO, Hunter, Harvey, Webster and Will Muniments).

Alexander Garden (1730-91), M.D. Marischal College 1753, and Edinburgh (Anderson).

Francis Garden, Edinburgh M.D. 1768, brother of Alexander, came to S. Carolina and died soon after.

Robert Gibb. (Sydenham).

David Jameson, emigrated in company with Hugh Mercer in 1746.

John Lining (1708-60), (K + B).

Samuel Miller, (Cullen Papers, RCPE).

John Moultrie, may have studied at Edinburgh, emigrated 1728.

John Murray, (?Monro 1737-42), (SRO, Murray of Murraythwaite Muniments).

William Murray, *ibid*, cousin of John Murray.

David Oliphant (1720-1805), escaped after Culloden. In partnership with John Murray and later in practice with John Lining (?Monro 1741).

James Skene, M.D. Marischal College, 1766. Edinburgh (Cullen 1765).

Andrew Turnbull, educated London. Led expedition to Florida in 1768. In 1781 he took over Alexander Garden's practice in S. Carolina.

Robert Wilson, b. 1736, apprenticed to Dr Martin Eccles who was a member of RCPE, also studied London. Army service.

Americans

John Moultrie (1729-98), Edinburgh M.D. 1749.

Thomas Clayton, Edinburgh M.D. 1758.

James Clitherall, Edinburgh 1760-1, member of the Medical Society.

George Haig, Edinburgh (Cullen 1762-3), M.D.King's College 1764.

Nicholas Everleigh, Edinburgh (Cullen 1763-5).

Samuel Everleigh, Edinburgh (Cullen 1764-5).

Isaac Chanter, d. 1782, Edinburgh M.D. 1768.

Thomas Caw (1748-73), Edinburgh M.D. 1769.

Peter Fayssoux (1745-95), Edinburgh M.D. 1769.

John Farquharson, M.D. Marischal College 1769.

Charles Drayton, Edinburgh M.D. 1770.

Thomas Tudor Tucker, Edinburgh M.D. 1770.

William Roberts, Glasgow M.D. 1771.

Tucker Harris, Edinburgh M.D. 1771.

George Logan, Edinburgh M.D. 1773, and in London.

James Air, Edinburgh 1774-5, M.D. Leiden 1775.

Robert Peronneau, Edinburgh M.D. 1775.

Thomas Simons Dale (1749-1816), Edinburgh M.D. 1775.

Robert Pringle (1755-1811), Edinburgh (MB 1776-8).

Zachariah Neufville, Edinburgh M.D. 1778.

William Charles Wells b. 1757, Edinburgh M.D. 1780, also in London.

James Maxwell, Edinburgh (medical student at Walker's lectures 1786), M.D. King's College 1790.

Samuel Wilson (1763-1827), Edinburgh 1784-6, Glasgow M.D. 1786. (Waring Library, chemistry lecture notes Edinburgh 1784).

Levi Myres (1768-1822), Edinburgh 1785 (MB), Glasgow M.D. 1797, also on the continent.

Joseph Nicholas Wilson, Edinburgh M.D. 1788.

James Moultrie, Edinburgh M.D. 1788.

William Lehré, Edinburgh (Gregory 1790-1), Marischal M.D. 1791.

George F. Harnbaum Jr (1771-99), Edinburgh (Gregory 1790-1), Marischal M.D. 1791.

Thomas Marshall, Edinburgh (Gregory 1790-1).

Francis Kinloch Huger (1773-1855), Philadelphia M.D., medical student at Walker's lectures 1791. London.

William Chisholm, Edinburgh (Gregory 1791-2), Glasgow M.D. 1793.

Robert Wilson Jr, Edinburgh M.D. 1794.

George Hall, Edinburgh M.D. 1794.

Charles Rutledge, Edinburgh (Gregory 1794-5).

Jacob Williman, Edinburgh M.D. 1795.

Christopher Fuller, Edinburgh (Gregory 1796-7).

Edward Thomas, Edinburgh (Gregory 1796-7).

Sims White, Edinburgh (Gregory 1796-8).

Richard B. Scriven, Edinburgh (Gregory 1797-8).

James Hanscome, Edinburgh (Gregory 1797-8).

J. R. Poinsett, Edinburgh (Gregory 1797-8).

Robert MacKewn Haig, Edinburgh M.D. 1798.

Mahan Haig, Edinburgh (Gregory 1798-9).

Philip Tidyman, Edinburgh (Gregory 1797-1800). Göttingen M.D. 1800.

Alexander Baron Jr, Edinburgh M.D. 1799.

Andrew Balfour, Edinburgh (Hamilton 1799).

Thomas Akin, Edinburgh M.D. 1799.

Benjamin Bonneau Simons (1776-1844), Edinburgh (Gregory 1799-1800), Glasgow M.D. 1800. London and Paris.

VIRGINIA
Emigrants
James Bankhead, Edinburgh (Monro 1733).

David Black, d. 1782, (Blanton).

Archibald Blair, d. 1736, possible Edinburgh M.A. 1685 (Blanton).

John Brodie, M.D. possibly from Scotland, as he sent his son to Glasgow University.

John Murray Brown, native of Galloway (A. Brown, *The Cabells and their Kin,* Boston 1895).

John Brown, late of Coldstream, d. 1726, (Blanton).

William Brown, b. Haddington 1752, Edinburgh M.D. 1770. (Described as American). American father, Scottish mother (Blanton).

James Carmichael, Glasgow M.D. 1799, Edinburgh 1798 (Gregory).

Robert Couper, Glasgow M.D. 1782, tutor in Virginia for some years (Addison).

James Craik (1730–1814), studied at Edinburgh (DAB).

Robert Craik, d. 1754, brother of James Craik? (Toner), (?Monro 1733).

Robert Crichton, M.D. (Blanton), did not graduate at Edinburgh. (?Monro 1749).

Adam Cunningham, in Virginia 1728–35 (W. J. Bell, *The Colonial Physician,* p. 207).

James Currie, b. 1745, Glasgow M.A. 1769, M.D. 1770; Edinburgh 1767 (MB).

William Douglas, of Dover, County of Goochland, Virginia (Toner).

William Fleming, b. 1729, educated Edinburgh (Blanton), (?Monro 1746).

David Forbes, emigrated 1774, settled Fredericksburgh (Haws).

George French, emigrated shortly before Revolution, settled Fredricksburgh (Haws).

George Gilmer Sr (1700–57), educated Edinburgh. emigrated 1731 (Blanton).

George Graham, born England, educated Edinburgh (Blanton).

Roderick Gordon, ship's surgeon, resident King and Queen Country 1724–44 (SRO Miscellaneous Bundles RH 15).

James Henderson (1763–1829), educated Edinburgh (Blanton). A William Henderson graduated at Edinburgh 1784.

Robert Honeyman (1752–1824), M.A. Marischal College 1765, Edinburgh 1766 (MB). Emigrated 1772 (Blanton).

Alexander Jameson, University & King's M.D. 1742. 'Now of Hampton, James River, Virginia' (Anderson).

William Lynn, in Fredricksburgh before 1743 (Haws).

James McCaw, surgeon who emigrated from Wigtownshire 1765 (Blanton).

James Drew McCaw (1722–1846), Edinburgh (Gregory 1790) (Blanton).

Walter McClurg, (Blanton).

Emigrants

Alexander Mackenzie, in Virginia about 1740, *Medical Observations & Inquiries, vol* II 1762, p. 302.

Hugh Mercer (1725–77), M.A. Marischal College 1744, emigrated 1746.

Alexander Mitchell, physician from Ayr, he went to Virginia about 1790 (Whyte).

John Mitchell, born England? Edinburgh (?Monro 1729), letters to Professor Alston, Edinburgh University.

George Riddell settled Yorktown 1751, later moved to Williamsburg (Haws).

Andrew Robertson (1716–95), (Blanton).

John Spence (1766–1829), Edinburgh (Duncan 1784).

Andrew Somervail (1758–1833), (Blanton).

Adam Stephen (1718–91), Aberdeen 1740, Edinburgh (?Adam Steven, Monro 1743), (Blanton).

Alexander G. Strachan, b. 1749, educated Edinburgh, emigrated 1772 (Blanton).

John Strachey (1709–59), (Blanton p. 92).

George Todd, Orkney Archives, Sutherland-Graeme of Graemeshall Papers.

Mr Todd, possibly George Todd. Letter from Wm Cullen to Benjamin Rush, 1783, recommending Mr Todd (LCP, PHS, Rush Mss).

Michael Wallace (1719–67), indentured to Dr Gustavus Brown, 1734. Hayden p. 689.

Alexander Whitehead, M.D. Glasgow 1798, emigrated to Norfolk (Haws).

Walter Williamson, (Blanton), (?Monro 1745).

Robert White (1688–1752), educated Edinburgh, emigrated 1735 (Blanton).

Americans

James Taylor, Edinburgh (Cullen 1756–7).

Thomas Clayton, Edinburgh M.D. 1758.

William Marye, Edinburgh about 1758 (Blanton p. 86).

William Marshall, Edinburgh about 1758 (Blanton p. 86).

Samuel Colquhoun, Edinburgh (Cullen 1759–60).

James Feild, Edinburgh (Cullen 1757–61).

Theodorick Bland (1740–90), Edinburgh M.D. 1763.

George Peyton, Edinburgh (Cullen 1763'7.

William Bankhead, Edinburgh (Cullen 1762–3). Glasgow M.D. 1764.

James Blair, Edinburgh (Cullen 1760–7).

Lionel Dickson, Edinburgh (Cullen 1762–4).

Arthur Lee (1740–92), Edinburgh M.D. 1764, also in London.

George Gilmer, b. 1742, Edinburgh (Cullen 1760–5), Glasgow M.D. 1764.

—   Gilmer (brother of George). 'Mr Gilmer's sons are here'. (Bland p. 20). not in MB.

Corbin Griffin, Edinburgh M.D. 1765.

John M. Galt, Edinburgh 1767 (Blanton p. 86), not in M.B.

Americans

Ewen Clements, Edinburgh RMS 1768, Leiden M.D. 1769.

Moore Fauntleroy, d. 1802, Edinburgh 1768, M.D. Marischal 1764. M.D. University & Kings 1770.

Walter Jones, Edinburgh M.D. 1769.

Joseph Godwin, Edinburgh M.D. 1769.

Cyrus Griffin (1748–1810), Edinburgh 1769–70 (MB).

Archibald Campbell, Edinburgh M.D. 1770.

James McClurg(1743–1823), Edinburgh M.D. 1770, also London and Paris.

John Ravenscroft, Edinburgh M.D. 1770.

Thomas Griffin Tarpley, b. 1748, Edinburgh 1770–3(MB), Leiden M.D. 1773.

William Foushee, Edinburgh 1771–2 (MB).

Isaac Hall, Edinburgh M.D. 1771.

John Tayloe Griffin, Edinburgh M.D. 1774.

Philip Turpin, Edinburgh M.D. 1774.

Laurence Brooke (1758–1803) Edinburgh 1775–8 (MB).

William Boush, Edinburgh M.D. 1778.

Horace Buckner, d. 1820, Edinburgh 1776–7 (MB). Glasgow M.D. 1778.

John Taliaferro Lewis, Edinburgh 1777–9 (MB).

John Smith Shaw, d. 1811, Edinburgh M.D. 1777.

David Stuart, b. 1753, Edinburgh M.D. 1777.

William Spence, Edinburgh 1778 (MB), Glasgow M.D. 1780.

Philip Barrand, Edinburgh 1780 (Blanton p. 87).

William Graham, b. 1757, graduate of Edinburgh, M.A. and M.D. (not in (MB) (Toner). Blanton p. 86 describes him as an American who did not graduate. (A William Graham M.D. Edinburgh 1781 described as British).

John Ravenscroft, Edinburgh (A. Hamilton 1782) – no nationality given.

John T. Lewis, Edinburgh 1782 (Blanton p. 86, not in MB).

William Major Dixon, Glasgow M.D.1784, Edinburgh 1783 (MB).

John Bankhead, Edinburgh 1783 (MB).

Robert Cary Mitchell, Edinburgh. Member RSM 1784. Leiden M.D. 1786.

John Keigh, Edinburgh. Harveian Prize 1785, also London.

James Ramsay, Edinburgh 1783–6, 1787–8 (MB).

James Lyons, Edinburgh M.D. 1785.

James Skelton Gilliam, Edinburgh M.D. 1786.

Thomas Mann Randolph, Edinburgh (Medical student at Walker's lectures 1786).

John Tankard, Edinburgh 1785–6 (MB).

Augustus Smith, Edinburgh M.D. 1787.

Robert Walker, d. 1820, Edinburgh M.D. 1787.

John Peakie, or Peake, Edinburgh 1788 (Introduced to Cullen by letter from W. Brown Va., RCPE).

Alexander Schaw Feild, Edinburgh M.D. 1789.

Richard Feild (1767–1829), Edinburgh M.D. 1790.

Thomas Walker Gilmer, Edinburgh (Gregory 1790).

William Bird Lewis, Edinburgh M.D. 1790.

Robert Austin, Edinburgh (Gregory 1790).

David Corbin Ker, Edinburgh M.D. 1792.

James Moncure Daniel, Edinburgh (Gregory 1790), Glasgow M.D. 1791.

John Dalrymple Orr (1772–1816), Edinburgh (Gregory 1790–1).

Samuel Wilson, Edinburgh (Gregory 1790–2).

James Drew McCraw, Edinburgh M.D. 1792.

Daniel Conrad, M.B. Philadelphia, Edinburgh (Gregory 1791–2).

James Westwood Wallace, Edinburgh (Gregory 1791–2).

Francis Harris, Edinburgh M.D. 1793.

Carter Burwell Berkley (1768–1839), Edinburgh M.A., M.D. 1793.

Charles Minor, Edinburgh M.D. 1793

James Hyndman Purdie, Edinburgh (Gregory 1792–3), Glasgow M.D. 1793.

Robert Beverley Spratt, Edinburgh M.D. 1793.

Francis Peyton, Edinburgh 1793–4).

John Tennant, Edinburgh (Gregory 1793–4).

Samuel Brown (1763–1830), Edinburgh (Gregory 1792–3), Marischal M.D. 1794.

John Adams, Edinburgh (Gregory 1794–5).

Edward Fisher, Edinburgh (Gregory 1794–5).

Lewis Marshall, Edinburgh 1794–5).

David Walker, Edinburgh (Gregory 1794–5).

John Brockenbrough, Edinburgh M.D. 1795.

John Tazwell, Edinburgh (Gregory 1795–6).

William Tazwell, Edinburgh (Hamilton 1796).

James Greenhow, Edinburgh (medical student at Walker's lectures, 1796).

John Gilchrist, Edinburgh (Gregory 1796–7).

Robert Dowman, Edinburgh (Gregory 1796–7).

William Taliaferro, Edinburgh (Gregory 1796–7).

John Taliaferro, Edinburgh (Gregory 1796–7).

Alexander Whitehead, Edinburgh (Gregory 1796–8).

James Jones, Edinburgh M.D. also in France.

Bolling Stark, Edinburgh (Gregory 1797–9).

William B. Selden (1773–1849), Edinburgh (Gregory 1797–8).

William Thomson, Edinburgh (Gregory 1797–8),

Alexander Frazer, Edinburgh (Hamilton 1798).

John Watson, Edinburgh (Gregory 1797–9).

Bathurst Randolph, Edinburgh (Gregory 1797–9).

John Randolph Archer. Edinburgh (Gregory 1797–8).

Alexander Patrick, Edinburgh (Gregory 1798–9).

James French, Edinburgh (Gregory 1798–9).

John Hoges, Edinburgh (Hamilton 1799).

Samuel Clay, Edinburgh (Gregory 1799–1800).

David Fournoy, Edinburgh (Gregory 1799–1800).

James Scott, Edinburgh (Gregory 1799–1800).

John Bothwell Bott, Edinburgh M.D. 1800.

Richard E. Meade, Edinburgh M.D. 1800.

John Fitzgerald, Edinburgh M.D. 1800.

David Fauntleroy, Edinburgh 1800 (Blanton p. 87, not in MB).

Emigrants to America, no colony or state given.

Thomas Clarke, d. 1792, educated Glasgow (Thomas Clarke M.A. and M.D. Glasgow 1775), preacher and doctor, emigrated to America (Addison).

Samuel Adams, native of Scotland, came to America at time of American Revolution, having been surgeon in British army (Toner).

Americans, no colony or state given.

John Husband Osborne, Edinburgh (Cullen 1761).

Grant Elcock, Edinburgh 1763 (MB).

Benjamin Clifton, Edinburgh 1764 (MB).

James Virgo, Edinburgh 1765 (MB).

John Hyndman, Glasgow M.D. 1793.

Dr Brown, 1796. Edinburgh, London and Paris (Toner).

GUIDE TO THE SOURCES

The unpublished sources are arranged
1. In eight groups corresponding to the chapters in the text.
2. A select list of sources relating to Scottish participation in wars on American soil.
3. A list of additional sources in the United States which have been located but not surveyed in detail

In each group the sources are arranged by repository beginning with those in Scotland, followed by others in the United Kingdom, and then by those in the United States by state alphabetically.

The sources held by each depository are listed in approximate chronological order.

Arrangement by topic means that some sources are listed more than once. Cross references are provided when necessary.

Published sources follow the unpublished in each group.

Enquiries about sources listed in the National Register of Archives, Scotland, should be addressed to HM. General Register House, Edinburgh EH1 3YY, and *not* to the owner of the collection.

I. BACKGROUND AND BEGINNINGS
C. 1680–1707

MITCHELL LIBRARY, GLASGOW
Dunlop of Garnkirk and Tollcross
   Letters: from John Dunlop 1683, trading voyage to New York; 1701, from Archibald Dunlop, New York.

NATIONAL LIBRARY OF SCOTLAND
Dunlop
   Documents: *1688*–9, William Dunlop's affairs in South Carolina.

NATIONAL REGISTER OF ARCHIVES, SCOTLAND
Earl of Cromartie
   Letter: 1684, William Blaythwayt, Whitehall, to proprietors of East New Jersey.

SCOTTISH RECORD OFFICE
Eglinton
   Letters: 1686–7, William Dunlop, South Carolina.
Hume of Marchmont
   Letters: c. 1682, proposed settlement in South Carolina; one printed, *Hist. Mss. Comm.* XIV, App. III, 114. Letter: 1682, unsigned, writer

had 'interest in NY', proposes a settlement in America.

Leven and Melville

> Petition to the King: 1689, Francis Makemie Memorial to the King: Spanish hostilities in Carolina.

Abercairny

> Letter: 1685, from Amboy, New Jersey, about difficulty in getting possession of land (to the Earl of Perth).

John Macgregor

> Correspondence c. 1690: property in East New Jersey.

Miscellaneous (RH15)

> Titles of land in East New Jersey: 1683–5. Letter: 1689, enquiring whether servants could be found in Scotland (two or three hundred) for transportation to Virginia. List: 1696, twenty-eight men and women at Edinburgh awaiting transportation.

Court of Session Productions

> Journal 1699–1711: William Fraser, merchant in London, trading with Boston and Virginia.

PENNSYLVANIA, AMERICAN PHILOSOPHICAL SOCIETY, PHILADELPHIA

Montgomery Family

> Legal papers: William Montgomerie, who migrated to East New Jersey c. 1701. Letters: John Burnet, Edinburgh and John Burnet jr, Perth Amboy.

II.   SCOTLAND AND AMERICA
(excluding the tobacco trade), 1707–1760

KIRKCALDY MUSEUM AND ART GALLERY

Miscellaneous

> Indenture: 1735, service in Carolina.

NATIONAL LIBRARY OF SCOTLAND

Minto

> Letters: 1756–73, from Andrew Elliott, Lieutenant Governor of New York. Letter: 1764, General James Grant about East Florida.

Charles Strachan (later Fullerton)

> Letterbook: 1763–70, business in Mobile, Alabama.

McLeod of Geanies

> Letters: 1770–6, James MacLeod in Virginia.

Steuart

> Correspondence and papers: 1758–97, Charles Steuart, cashier and paymaster, American Board of Customs; account books 1776–96, letters from Loyalists. See also II Pennsylvania Historical Society: Steuart.

Russel & Aitken (solicitors)

> Letter: June 1774, from William Black, a Scottish stonemason

working in Virginia. Poor prospects but has a profitable job to do for
Lord Dunmore.

PERTH MUSEUM AND ART GALLERY

Literary and Antiquarian Society of Perth

Correspondence: 1741–3, about John Freeman and from William
Wallace of Virginia.

SCOTTISH RECORD OFFICE

Morton

Wreck of a Boston ship in Orkney, 1709.

Dalquharran

Instructions: 1715, to a collector of customs in Virginia.

Montrose

Letters: 1710–4, Robert Hunter, Governor of New York, to Duke of
Montrose.

Stair

Letters: 1712–5, Robert Hunter, Governor of New York, to the Earl of
Stair.

Hunter, Harvey, Webster & Will

Letter: 1716, John Dunbar – arrangements with those to whom he and
twenty gentlemen have been sold.

Clerk of Penicuik

Letters: 1716–20, James Clerk, trading to America. Letters: 1733–48,
from and about Sir Patrick Houston in Georgia.

Ross of Pitcalnie

Letters: 1719–48, John and Simon Dunbar.

Campbell of Barcaldine

Letter: 1734, from Georgia, conditions in the colony, need for
servants.

Broughton and Cally

Letters: 1718–36, on emigration to America.

Duff of Fetteresso

Legal papers: 1725–30, Helen Cuming, married to Robert Cuming in
New York.

Cunninghame Graham

Letters: 1741, about the collectorship of customs in Savannah,
Georgia.

Lindsay

Letters: 1729–52, from John Lindsay. Philadelphia, New York (where
he received a grant of 3,000 acres in 1733); proposal to settle over one
hundred families.

Abercairny

Letters: 1733, from John Borthwick, a transported convict, to John
Drummond. Also from George Marley and James Wedderburn.

Hamilton-Dalrymple
  Paper: William and John Kirkwood, who went to Boston, 1736. Letters: 1742, John Rutherford, on a visit to America. Letters requesting colonial appointments 1747, 1749, 1754–6.
Tods, Murray & Jamieson (solicitors) w.c.
  Papers: 1720–30, Alexander and Robert Nisbet, Charleston, s.c. Letters: 1795–7, James Mickie, Charleston, s.c. Shipping accounts: 1762–4, trade between Philadelphia and Leith. Crown grant of land in New York to William Hagart.
Miscellaneous RH15
  Papers 1725–45 relating to Dr Roderick Gordon and letters from him to his brother, Arthur Gordon of Carnoustie. He served as a ship's surgeon on voyages to Virginia and Maryland, settled in Virginia where he practised medicine, engaged in trade, and purchased a plantation.
Murray of Murraythwaite
  A very large collection covering the whole of the eighteenth century and the early years of the nineteenth century. The items of American interest are found mainly from 1748 to 1762 and include letters from Dr John Murray of Charleston s.c, letters from John Murray of Murraythwaite during his period as secretary of South Carolina, and from his brother William who practised medicine in South Carolina and was also in partnership with John in trading ventures and plantation management. Also a few letters from the late eighteenth century about estates in South Carolina. An invaluable source for medicine, office holding, business and social conditions in South Carolina.
Sharp of Houston
  Letter: 1739, James Glen.
Stewart of Dalguise
  Letters: 1725 and 1733, persons going to Georgia and Virginia. Letters. 1749–59, James Stewart, merchant in Charleston.
Fergusson of Craigdorroch
  Letter: 1759, Philip Morison, South Carolina.
Yule
  Marriage contract: John Greenless of Virginia and Mary Beveridge of Edinburgh, 1753. Pardon: 1777, Robert Mercer, for having signed the Association. (See below: *Mercer of Pittendreich*).
Sinclair of Freswick
  Letter: 1772, John Campbell, on practice of medicine in Maryland and Virginia.
Maclaine of Lochbuie
  Letter of credit: 1756, James Spalding (East Florida); agreement with

his father's creditors, 1770–2. Letter: 1773, Malcolm McLean, Boston, on apprenticeship. Letters: 1776–1776–9, Hector, Donald, and Archibald MacLaine.

Elibank
Paper: 1766, land owned by Lord Elibank in West Florida.

Ailsa
Two letters: 1767–9, on settlement in East Florida.

Leith-Ross
Letters: 1768–85, John Ross about his life in East Florida.

Dalhousie
Letterbook: 1746–52, James Glen, and other papers.

Beveridge
A collection of materials about James Glen made by James Beveridge.

Clerk of Penicuik
Letters: 1741–7, Alexander Gordon, secretary to James Glen, but severely critical of him.

Cathcart of Genoch
1. Letters: 1734–64, large collection from and about members of the Cathcart family in North Carolina; practise of medicine, landownership. See also II North Carolina State Archives: Cathcart; II North Carolina, University of: Cathcart.

Henderson of Fordell
Papers: 1763–75, General James Robertson's interests in Florida; also his land speculations in New York and Vermont.

Hannay
Letter: 1762, Alexander Duncan, N.C., settlement of his accounts with Michael Ancrum of Felesburgh.

Mercer of Pittendriech
Letters: 1769–74, Robert Mercer of New York; also his diary for 1770–4. Comments on non-importation agreements; treatment of Scottish merchants in Philadelphia; destruction of tea at New York. See above: *Yule*.

Miscellaneous Gifts and Deposits
Account book and papers: 1777–87, John Inglis, merchant in New York.

MASSACHUSETTS HISTORICAL SOCIETY, BOSTON
Scots Charitable Society, Boston
Records: eighteenth century, incomplete list of claimants and sums disbursed, accounts, post-war dispute over ownership of assets.

UNIVERSITY OF MICHIGAN, WILLIAM L. CLEMENTS LIBRARY
Fyffe Papers
Letters: 1757–75, William, Alexander, David and Charles Fyffe, South Carolina.

NORTH CAROLINA STATE ARCHIVES, RALEIGH
Thomas Pollock
Correspondence: 1717–37, as Governor of North Carolina; includes two letters to his kinsman Sir Robert Pollock.
Cathcart
Letters: to William Cathcart from Scotland, 1737–60. See also above SRO: Cathcart of Genoch and below.
London, John
Certificate of election as a burgess and guild brother of Glasgow during his visit c. 1770.

NORTH CAROLINA, UNIVERSITY OF, SOUTHERN HISTORICAL COLLECTION, CHAPEL HILL
Robert Hogg
Ledger: store at Wilmington, N.C. Many Highlanders among customers.
Cathcart
William Cathcart Correspondence: 1737–60. See also above SRO: Cathcart of Genoch and NORTH CAROLINA STATE ARCHIVES.
London, John
Diary N.D. but c. 1770. Microfilm of typescript in private hands. Records a visit to Scotland with unfavourable comments on cleanliness and food, but well received at Glasgow and met leading merchants.

PENNSYLVANIA HISTORICAL SOCIETY, PHILADELPHIA
Steuart
Letterbooks, 1751–63, of Charles Steuart, merchant at Norfolk. Va. Later Cashier and Paymaster of the American customs. See also above NLS: Steuart.

SOUTH CAROLINA, HISTORICAL SOCIETY OF, CHARLESTON S.C.
Robert Pringle
Letterbooks and other papers: 1737–70.
Robert Hogg
Business Papers: Hogg & Clayton, Charleston. S.C.
Alexander Fraser
Papers: Scottish merchant in Charleston S.C.
John Ernest Poyas
Day Book showing dealings with Scottish merchants in Charleston, S.C.

SOUTH CAROLINA, SOUTH CAROLINIAN LIBRARY, COLUMBIA
Glen
Official letters of James Glen; also letters about his property in South Carolina.

VIRGINIA COLONIAL INSTITUTE, WILLIAMSBURG
Lockhart Family
References to Robert Dinwiddie, as Governor of Virginia
Copies (also in SRA); originals in private hands.

Richard Corbin
Many letters from Robert Dinwiddie while Governor of Virginia. Includes also the diary of John Harrower (cf. Published Sources).

VIRGINIA HISTORICAL SOCIETY, RICHMOND

Peyton Family
Letters: the Scott family of Virginia; from Thomas Gordon, Provost of King's College, Aberdeen, to Elizabeth Scott, his daughter; also relating to Robert Eden Scott, later provost of King's College.

PUBLISHED SOURCES

Brock, Robert A. ed.
The Official Records of Robert Dinwiddie Richmond 1883.

Easterby, J. H.
History of the St. Andrew's Society of Charleston, South Carolina Charleston 1929.

Farish, Hunter D. ed.
Journal and Letters of Philip Vickers Fithian, 1733–4: a plantation tutor of the Old Dominion Williamsburg, 1957.

Rely, Edward Miles ed.
The Journal of John Harrower Williamsburg 1963.

McBean, William M.
Biographical Register of the St. Andrew's Society of the State of New York 2 vols, New York 1922.

Edgar, Walter B. ed.
The Letterbooks of Robert Pringle 2 vols, Columbia 1972.

Evangeline W. (with Andrews, Charles M.) Andrews, ed.
Journal of a Lady of Quality: being a narrative of a journey from Scotland to the West Indies, North Carolina and Portugal (Janet Schaw), New Haven 1923.

III THE TOBACCO TRADE

CUNNINGHAME DISTRICT ARCHIVES, KILMARNOCK

Cunninghame Family
Letters: 1764–6, Robert Reid, independent tobacco merchant in Virginia

GLASGOW, UNIVERSITY OF

Colquhoun Collection of Business Records
Cash book. 1754–7, Alexander Sharp & Co. A few items refer to trade with America.

MITCHELL LIBRARY, GLASGOW

Bogle Family
Papers: 1726–36; Robert, George and Matthew Bogle who were prominent in the tobacco trade in the early eighteenth century.

James Johnston of Bishopbriggs
    Ship's Log: 1766, *Betsy,* Glasgow to Virginia; 1779, a receipt for three slaves purchased at Savannah.

NATIONAL LIBRARY OF SCOTLAND

William Cunninghame & Co.
    Letterbooks (3): 1767–74, factors at Falmouth and Williamsburg, Va.

Alexander Houston
    Business papers: engaged in the West India trade; had dealings with tobacco importers but the only indication of their scale is a suit bought by James Ritchie and Co. in 1779.

Cadell of Grange
    Letters (3): 1773, protest to Parliament against a proposed steel mill in New England.

NATIONAL REGISTER OF ARCHIVES, SCOTLAND

Grant of Monymusk
    Observations: 1721, on preventing frauds in the tobacco trade, and replies of merchants.

NATIONAL REGISTER OF ARCHIVES, SCOTLAND. (COPIES IN STRATHCLYDE REGIONAL ARCHIVES)

Crighton-Maitland (Alexander Speirs)
    Correspondence: 1770–88, deals mainly with the period of the Revolution and after; also papers of companies associated with Speirs, and correspondence, 1804–5, on money owed by Americans to Speirs' estate.

PUBLIC RECORD OFFICE, LONDON

Treasury Records, Customs 14

SCOTTISH RECORD OFFICE

Hannay
    Papers: 1718, tobacco imported to Glasgow from Maryland.

Miscellaneous (GD) *1/455)*
    Cash Books: 1731/2, 1734/5, 1748/9, of a store in Westmoreland County, Virginia (possibly kept by William Campbell–the name 'John Conner' in one volume may be that of a clerk). Large sales from the store and purchases of tobacco. No indication of whether the storekeeper was independent or a factor. Customers include Richard Lee, William Lightfoot, John Bushrod, Aylett's Estate ('guardian Mr. Washington'–probably Augustine, father of George Washington), and other families of the Northern Neck of Virginia.

Exchequer Records
    These very full records include:
    1. All goods exported and imported from Scottish ports, 1707–1831.
    2. Exported items, e.g. woollens, linens, iron, haberdashery, hats, pipes, shoes, flax, pottery, ironware, books.

3. Listed separately: quantities of tobacco imported by individual merchants. Similar lists of wine imported. Other imports under 'general goods' and include sugar, rice, rum and spices.

4. Inquisitions and Extents: papers of crown debtors, goods forfeit to the crown, etc.

Melville Castle

Account: 1775, all tobacco imported into Scotland 1752–75.

Scottish Board of Customs and Excise

Collector's letters; Quarterly Accounts, Port Glasgow; Quarterly Accounts, Greenock.

John C. Brodie

Business letters and papers: William Cunninghame & Co 1761–89; includes the letterbook of John Robinson, factor at Falmouth, Va, 1767–74.

Oswald, Dennistoun & Co.

Cash book and journal: 1763–7; imports of tobacco, sugar and wine; ship owner and marine insurance.

Carron Iron Company

The early papers of this famous company contain many examples of orders for export to America being solicited from the leading tobacco importers.

Holmes McKillop & Co. (solicitors)

Business papers: 1753–64, George Kippen John Glassford, & Co., handling exports for the associated Glassford companies.

STRATHCLYDE REGIONAL ARCHIVES, GLASGOW

Mitchels, Johnston & Co. (solicitors)

Journal: 1772–9, and thereafter incomplete to 1816, of Baird Hay & Co.; partnership James Baird, John Hay, Ninian Menzies, and Peter Hay, trading in Virginia as John Hay & Co.

Neill Campbell

Indenture: 1758, with John Glassford for service as an apprentice to one of the factors in Virginia.

Mitchells, Johnston, Hill & Hoggan

Invoice: 1761–5, goods sent by Norman McLeod, merchant in Boston. Papers: 1779, lawsuit, James Ritchie & Co. v Alexander Houston & Co., concerning a shipment of tobacco.

William Colhoun

Letters: 1770, slave trade, Senegal to Virginia.

CALIFORNIA, HENRY HUNTINGTON LIBRARY, (MICROFILM, UNIVERSITY OF GLASGOW)

John Turner

Accounts and papers: factor for William Cunninghame at Rockyridge, Va.

MARYLAND HISTORICAL SOCIETY, BALTIMORE

Alexander Hamilton (tobacco factor)
Letters: 1760–70, 1784 – The first batch of letters contain much general information about the tobacco trade, and about the affairs of Lawson, Semple & Co. for whom Hamilton was factor. The later batch is noted in Section VII.

John Beall Borderley
Fee books: 1759–61, amounts (reckoned in pounds of tobacco) owing to the clerk of Baltimore County for 1759, included Archibald Campbell (50 lbs), Colin Dunlop & Co. (4,218½ lbs), William Dunlop (18 lbs), Alexander Lawson & Co. (137½ lbs).

NEW YORK, NEW YORK HISTORICAL SOCIETY

Neil Jamieson
Journals, ledgers, inventories, etc. – some relating to pre-revolutionary trade, others to Jamieson's attempts to re-establish business in New York during and after the Revolution

MICHIGAN, UNIVERSITY OF, WILLIAM CLEMENTS LIBRARY, ANN ARBOR (MICROFILM, SCOTTISH RECORD OFFICE)

Buccleuch Papers
Memorandum: 1766, by Archibald Henderson, formerly factor at Colchester, Va, on organisation of the tobacco trade. Prepared for Charles Townshend, Chancellor of the Exchequer.

MASSACHUSETTS, HARVARD UNIVERSITY, HOUGHTON LIBRARY, CAMBRIDGE

Arthur Lee
Papers: two letters from William Lee on the tobacco trade and the failure of Scottish banks in London in 1772.

VIRGINIA, PUBLIC LIBRARY ALEXANDRIA (COPY, STRATHCLYDE REGIONAL ARCHIVES)

Alexander Henderson
Letterbooks: 1758–65, factor at Alexandria (Glassford & Co.)

VIRGINIA, COLONIAL INSTITUTE, WILLIAMSBURG

George Yuille
Account book: 1754–7, factor for Yuille, Murdoch & Co. of Glasgow; also dealt with Wardbox & Anderson, Robert Bogle, Richard Oswald & Co. (all of Glasgow), James Buchanan (London), and Thomas Knox (Bristol).

Francis Jerdone
Business papers of Francis Jerdone. See also Virginia State Library and William and Mary College.

Lockhart Family
Several letter deal with the ship *Blandford* engaged in trade between Virginia and Port Glasgow; considerable information about freight carried for Scottish exporters. Copies of papers privately owned.

VIRGINIA HISTORICAL SOCIETY, RICHMOND
Carter Family
Letters (2): 1733, consignments of tobacco to Glasgow.
Thomas Adams
Papers: 1770, references to the state of the tobacco trade.
James Somerville
Accounts and memoranda: 1763–8, storekeeper at Hobshole and Fredericksburg; reference to William Allason, Lawson, Semple & Co., Arthur Morsom, and Archibald McCall. Papers: 1772–5, attempt to raise capital with Henry Mitchell, Thomas Hepburn and Patrick Lennon to conduct trade between Virginia to Leeward Islands, and St Eustalia, Dutch West Indies.

VIRGINIA, ROBERT E. LEE MEMORIAL FOUNDATION, STRATFORD
William Lee
Letterbooks: 1769- 95, references to the tobacco trade during his residence in London.

VIRGINIA STATE LIBRARY, RICHMOND
Francis Jerdone
Family Papers. (See also Colonial Institute, Williamsburg, and William and Mary College).
William Allason
Papers: Scottish merchant at Falmouth, Va. Agent for Baird, Walker & Co. of Glasgow, but also engaged in many other business activities. See published Sources: Allason.

VIRGINIA, UNIVERSITY OF, CHARLOTTESVILLE
John Smith
Papers: 1757–74, Virginia planter who sold tobacco to and purchased goods from Alexander Speirs & Co. through their factor, Alexander Banks, in Manchester, Va.

VIRGINIA, WILLIAM AND MARY COLLEGE, WILLIAMSBURG
Francis Jerdone
Factor for Alexander Speirs and Hugh Brown; became independent of them, purchased land, and established a family plantation. Letterbooks: 1756- 63, cf. Published Sources. See also Virginia State Library and Colonial Institute, Williamsburg.
Blow Family Papers
Letterbooks: 1770–2, Richard Blow. Example of a Virginian merchant ordering goods from Glasgow though not engaged in the export of tobacco.

WASHINGTON D.C. LIBRARY OF CONGRESS
Neil Jamieson
A very large collection: the business records of John Glassford's chief factor in America. Associated with this collection but separately

catalogued are the records of fifteen stores operated in Virgina and
Maryland by John Glassford & Co. This part of the collection also
includes the letterbooks of Alexander Hamilton, factor at Piscataway.

John and Henry Ritchie
Accounts and ledgers: dealing with pre-war operations in Virginia of
this Glasgow company.

Wilson Cary Nicholas
Papers: 1765–97, Robert Carter Nicholas (Williamsburg), acted as
attorney for Glasgow merchants including Dunlop and Montgomerie;
no relevant papers after 1774.

James Murdoch & Co.
Account books: 1773–5, two stores, attested copies of the accounts,
probably made to accompany his loyalist claims.

Edward Dixon
Ledgers and papers 1743–96, dealings with Allason, Scott & Co.
(purchase of textiles); settled accounts with bills drawn on John
Glassford & Co., William Gray & Co., Henderson, Dunlop & Cross
(all of Glasgow).

FURTHER ITEMS: 10.21, 10.22.

PUBLISHED SOURCES
Allason, William
Thomson, Edith E. B.
    'A Scottish Merchant in Falmouth in the Eighteenth Century' XXXIX
    (1931) Va MHB.

Dumfries
Truckell, A. E.
    'Early Shipping References in the Dumfries Burgh Records'
    *Dumfriesshire and Galloway Natural History Society: Transactions and
    Journal of Proceedings* 3rd series XXXIII 156–75, XXXIV 28–58.

Glasgow
Cleland, James
    The Rise and Progress of the City of Glasgow
    Glasgow 1820.
Gibson, James
    History of Glasgow
    Glasgow 1777.
Pagan, James
    Sketch of the History of Glasgow
    Glasgow 1847.

Hamilton, Alexander (tobacco factor)
Skaggs, David K. and McMaster, David
    'The Letterbooks of Alexander Hamilton: Piscataway Factor' *Md Hist*

Mg, IX 1966, 146–66 and 305–28, LXI 1967, 135–69.

Jerdone, Francis
'Letterbooks of Francis Jerdone' *WMQ* 1st Series XI 153–60, 236–42, XIV 144–5, XV 126–32.

IV THE HIGHLAND MIGRATION

ABERDEEN, UNIVERSITY OF
A & H Taylor Collection
Papers relating to to the Duff family. Many references to eighteenth-century emigrants.

NATIONAL LIBRARY OF SCOTLAND
Lee MS *3431* 177–83
Observations (anonymous) on emigration from Harris 1772.

Dundas Papers
Letter from George Dempster to Henry Dundas on emigration, 14 Nov 1784.

ACC *6954*
Letter from Alexander McNab advocating emigration 18 Oct 1793.

MS *6602 (bound with printed tracts* LC *2605)*
Anonymous essay on the state of emigration from the Highlands, 1803.

MS *9646*
Edward Fraser of Reelig, essay on emigration, 318 pp. Written about the end of 1802. Also some notes on emigration of the same date by Fraser in RHASS Papers, Adv Ms 73.2.15.

Liston Papers
Lady Liston's diary, 1796–1800, contains references to Highlanders in N.C.

NATIONAL REGISTER OF ARCHIVES, SCOTLAND
Marquess of Linlithgow
Lists: 1766, counties, sheriffs, taxable persons, towns, etc. in North Carolina.

Macleod of Macleod
Letter: 1771, about emigration to North Carolina planned by tenants.

SCOTTISH RECORD OFFICE
*Miscellaneous Gifts and Deposits (*GD I*)*
1. Robert Stewart, a Jacobite prisoner, bound to serve Edward Trafford in Virginia, 1716.
2. Certificate that Robert Stuart was assigned to William Gordon and had been sent by him to Scotland on business, 1717.

Society of Antiquaries of Scotland
Indenture: 1746, with signatures, binding 125 Highland prisoners to serve Samuel Smith of London for life. Smith assigns them to John

Hanburg for shipment to America to serve him for seven years.

Campbell of Barcaldine

Printed form of indenture: 1737, service in North Carolina; blanks filled with the names of John McLeod as master and William Campbell as apprentice for four years.

MacDonald

Letters: 1739, on a conspiracy to take 113 inhabitants of Skye for transportation to America. Formerly deposited in Scottish Record Office, but withdrawn by owner 1 Sept. 1977.

Seafield

Letter: 1775, from James Grant about ways of preventing emigration to America.

Lord MacDonald

List: probably 1802, tenants on MacDonald's land intending to emigrate to America; brief comments on reasons for emigration.

NEW YORK, COLUMBIA UNIVERSITY, NEW YORK

John Jay

Land grants: 1765, 1774, 1775, to disbanded soldiers of the 42nd Regiment.

NEW YORK, MONTGOMERY COUNTY ARCHIVES, FONDA

Kingsborough Patent

Biographical notes on settlers, many of them Highlanders.

NEW YORK, NEW YORK HISTORICAL SOCIETY

Livingston Papers

Advertisement, 1749, offering land in New York to settlers from Scotland.

Lawrence Papers

Grant of land to Donald Campbell (the Argyle Patent).

Beekman Papers

Agreement for lease of land: 1773, Beekman brothers with John Kelly and David McLeod, the latter to settle the land with families already in America or bought from Scotland. Correspondence about the grant and its settlement: on hundred families in a ship captured by John McLeod; Daniel McLeod; Daniel McLeod ready and willing to bring 400 persons from Scotland.

NEW YORK, NEW YORK PUBLIC LIBRARY

Margaret Lynn Lewis

Diary: 1730-c. 1780, daughter of the 'Laird of Loch Lynn' (Linnhe?), married John Lewis of Virginia; descriptions of life in Virginia; mother of General Andrew Lewis who fought under Washington.

George Chalmers

Papers: he went to Baltimore 1765, returned 1786 and appointed chief clerk at the Board of Trade; the papers deal with the Highlands,

1750–1801, economic conditions, and causes of emigration to America.

NEW YORK STATE ARCHIVES, ALBANY

New York Land Grants

Information about grants to Highland settlers.

NORTH CAROLINA, DUKE UNIVERSITY, DURHAM

Alexander McInnis

List of Highlanders settled in Richmond County. n.d.

NORTH CAROLINA, RECORDER'S OFFICE, FAYETTEVILLE

Records of Land Transfers, Cumberland Courts

NORTH CAROLINA, SECRETARY OF STATE'S OFFICE, RALEIGH

North Carolina Land Grants

NORTH CAROLINA, STATE ARCHIVES, RALEIGH

Colin Shaw

Correspondence 1784–89: information about emigration from Jura.

Angus Wilton McLean

'A History of the Scotch in North Carolina' – a 2 vol. unpublished typewritten manuscript.

Lachlan McNeil

Correspondence, 1784–5: two letters from McNeill in Breakuchie, Scotland, written to relatives in Cumberland County, North Carolina, dealing with family matters.

Cumberland County Collection

Includes numerous eighteenth-century wills and inventories of estates of Highlanders who lived in the county.

NORTH CAROLINA, UNIVERSITY OF, SOUTHERN HISTORICAL COLLECTION, CHAPEL HILL

MacAlester Family

Transcripts of several letters addressed to Alexander MacAlester; of special interest are those from his brother Hector, who had returned from North Carolina to Scotland. Originals in private hands; another set of transcripts in North Carolina State Archives.

Robert Hogg

Invoice book of Hogg and Clayton, Charleston, S.C. and sales book of their store at Wilmington. Most customers had Highland names.

James Hogg

Papers give detailed information about organised immigration from Caithness. Also some family letters.

Thomas Whiteside

Further information about the emigration organised by James Hogg.

PENNSYLVANIA HISTORICAL SOCIETY, PHILADELPHIA

Sir John Reid

Letter: 1773, on plight of a party of Highlanders in New York.

FURTHER ITEMS: X 4, 5, 6, 14, 15, 16.

PUBLISHED SOURCES
Jacobites and Transportation
Seton, Sir Bruce Gordon and Arnot, Jean Gordon
The Prisoners of the '45, edited from the State Papers
Edinburgh 1928.
MacLeod, Walter ed.
A List of Persons concerned in the Rebellion
Edinburgh 1890.
Hume, Edgar Erskine
'A Colonial Scottish Jacobite Family: the Establishment in Virginia of
a Branch of the Humes of Wedderburn' *Va MHB* XXXVIII 1930, 1–37,
97–124, 195–234, 296–346. See also XXIII 407–14.

Emigration (General)
Thom, William
A Candid Enquiry into the Causes of Migration from Scotland
Glasgow 1772.

Georgia
Bryant, Pat and Hemperly, Marion R.
Entry Claims for Georgia Landowners 1733–1750 Atlanta 1975.
Bryant, Pat
English Crown Grants in Georgia 1755–75, 8 vols, Atlanta 1972–4.
Beckemeyer, F. H. ed.
Abstracts of Georgia Colonial Conveyance Book 1750–61, Atlanta 1975.
Chandler, Allen M. (compiler)
The Colonial Records of Georgia 21 vols, Atlanta 1904–16. Reprinted
New York 1970. Especially Vols II and XXI. The originals of most
documents are in the Public Record Office, London.

North Carolina
'Scotus Americanus' *Information concerning the Province of North
Carolina addressed to Emigrants from the Highlands and Western Isles of
Scotland* Glasgow 1773.
Newsome, A. R. ed. 'Records of Emigrants from England and Scot-
land to North Carolina, 1774–5' *NC Hist R* XI (1934, 39–54, 129–43.

V RELIGION AND EDUCATION
ABERDEEN UNIVERSITY
James Beattie
Correspondence: 1787, from Benjamin Rush on Beattie's election to
the American Philosophical Society; 1800, from Peter Wilson (former
student) on his life and experiences in America (schoolmaster,
legislative assembly of New Jersey, professor at Columbia).

NATIONAL LIBRARY OF SCOTLAND
Cotton Mather
Letters: 1712–26 to John Sterling, Principal of Glasgow University, and to Robert Wodrow, 1726. Many have been published c.f. chapter 5, note 23.
Miscellaneous
Letters: 1726–29, to Robert Wodrow from Benjamin Colman and Samuel Mather.
Fettercairn Papers
Includes letters from America addressed to Myles Cooper, Loyalist and former president of King's College, New York.

SCOTTISH CATHOLIC ARCHIVES, COLUMBA HOUSE, DRUMMOND PLACE, EDINBURGH
Uncatalogued collection, which includes references to Catholic Highlanders migrating to America mainly after independence.

SCOTTISH RECORD OFFICE
Hamilton Bruce
Petition to the Society in Scotland for the Propagation of Christian Knowledge to support in Boston the ministry of John Squyre, 1717.
Seafield
Letter: 1726, from John Lang on his appointment as minister at St Peter's, New Kent, Virginia.
Society in Scotland for the Propagation of Christian Knowledge
Printed pamphlet, 1763, with references to the Society's work among Indians in New England; also a printed report, 1774, giving an account of these missions.
Abercairny
Letter, 1748, from Joshua Crosby of Philadelphia, expressing his preference for Edinburgh over English universities and hoping to raise money for the Royal Infirmary. Letters (15): 1760–75, Benjamin Franklin to Lord Kames. Eight printed in Jared Sparks, *Life and Works of Benjamin Franklin,* Boston 1836–40.
Church Assembly Papers
Appeals from South Carolina for a minister to be sent to the colony, 1704 and 1715, addressed to Moderator of the Presbytery of Edinburgh. Letters relating to the ministry of John Squyre in South Carolina, his experience of an Indian raid, and his removal to Boston, 1715–25.
Petition, 1724, from New York on behalf of the presbyterian congregation; description of the condition of the church. Petition, 1709, from presbyterians in Newcastle, Pennsylvania, asking for a minister. (These papers have been catalogued to 1741; the later papers may contain materials relating to the American Churches).

Society of Friends in Edinburgh

Papers include many references to American students studying in Edinburgh.

CONNECTICUT, YALE UNIVERSITY, NEW HAVEN

George Panton (in Knollenburg collection)

Papers of a Scottish episcopalian, 1769–80: ordination to serve in Church of England in America; tutor to a family in New York; chaplain to the British forces in New York; loyalist.

CONNECTICUT, YALE UNIVERSITY, BEINECKE LIBRARY, NEW HAVEN

Ezra Stiles

Memoir on Benjamin Franklin's success in obtaining D.D.'s from Scottish universities for American presbyterian ministers (1769). Also letters from Francis Alison, Philadelphia.

MARYLAND HISTORICAL SOCIETY, BALTIMORE

Alexander Hamilton (doctor in Maryland)

Letterbook, 1739–43, includes a letter approving of plans to raise money for the foundation of the Royal Infirmary in Edinburgh.

MASSACHUSETTS, AMERICAN ANTIQUARIAN SOCIETY, WORCESTER

Cotton Mather

Drafts of some letters to Scotland not found in the NLS collection.

NEW JERSEY, PRINCETON UNIVERSITY, PRINCETON

Samuel Davies

Notebook recording sums received and other information about a visit to Scotland soliciting funds for the College of New Jersey.

John Witherspoon

Letters about his appointment to the presidency of Princeton, and efforts to persuade him to accept, including many from Benjamin Rush. Many of them printed in Lyman H. Butterfield, *John Witherspoon comes to America* Princeton 1935. Also some notes by Witherspoon on preparations for his journey. List of books left by him to Princeton.

Hugh Simm

Letters and documents: 1768–84, came to America with John Witherspoon, studied divinity, schoolmaster, loyalist (Quartermaster, Loyal American Regiment).

John MacLean

Letters, biographical note: 1771–1814, Glasgow doctor, came to America in 1795; professor at Princeton 1796–1812 and at William and Mary, 1812–3. Notes on a course of lectures on chemistry given in the University of Glasgow, 1782–3. Lecturer not identified.

NEW JERSEY STATE HISTORICAL SOCIETY, NEWARK (COPIES IN THE PRINCETON COLLECTION OF WITHERSPOON PAPERS)

Witherspoon

Letters from Rush to Witherspoon about his appointment at Princeton.

NEW YORK, COLUMBIA UNIVERSITY, NEW YORK GENERAL MS COLLECTION

Myles Cooper

Letter to George Panton, 1778.

NEW YORK, NEW YORK HISTORICAL SOCIETY

John Sargent

Journal, 1809–19, of work at the New Stockbridge mission, perhaps intended for presentation to the S.S.P.C.K.

John Rodgers and Alexander Robertson

Minister and treasurer of the reformed Scots church in New York: unpublished memoir by Mary Darden Rodgers. Also Robertson's account book as treasurer.

PENNSYLVANIA HISTORICAL SOCIETY, PHILADELPHIA

Scots Church in Philadelphia

Minutes: 1768–91; dispute over the propriety of an appeal, after independence, to the associate presbytery of Glasgow.

Pemberton Papers

Notes: 1787, taken by Thomas Williamson of John Pemberton's visit to Scotland to win converts for the Quakers.

PENNSYLVANIA, PRESBYTERIAN HISTORICAL SOCIETY, PHILADELPHIA

Francis Alison

Notes for sermons or lectures; certificate of D.D. (Glasgow).

Associate Presbytery of Glasgow

Minutes on appointment to the presbytery of Pennsylvania 1791; another on the use of an organ in St Andrew's Church.

PENNSYLVANIA, UNIVERSITY OF, PHILADELPHIA

Francis Alison

Notes taken of his lectures on Moral Philosophy, Metaphysics, etc., by Jasper Yeates.

William Smith

Family and university papers.

VIRGINIA, COLONIAL INSTITUTE, WILLIAMSBURG

Augustine Smith

Letterbook: 1789–90, includes four letters to friends in Edinburgh with reminiscences of student days. Also a number of poems relating to Edinburgh.

WASHINGTON D.C. LIBRARY OF CONGRESS, PETER FORCE COLLECTION
University of Glasgow
Account of the plan of education, 1759.
PUBLISHED SOURCES
Scottish Philosophy (The works in this list are those which are known to have been widely read in America.)
Hugh Blair
Lectures on rhetoric and belles lettres
London 1783.
James Beattie
An Essay on the Nature and Immutability of Truth 2nd ed. enlarged
Edinburgh 1771.
Hutcheson, Francis
Inquiry into the Original of our Ideas of Beauty and Virtue
Dublin 1725 – and several later editions in London and Glasgow.
Hutcheson, Francis
Essay on the Nature and Conduct of the Passions and Affections
Glasgow 1729.
Hutcheson, Francis
Short Introduction to Moral Philosophy (the *'Compend')*
Latin: Glasgow 1742,
English: Glasgow 1747.
Hutcheson, Francis
System of Moral Philosophy 3 vols.
Glasgow 1755.
Hume, David
Essays Moral and Political
1st ed. (Anon) Edinburgh 1741,
2nd ed.   London   1748.
Kames, Lord
Essays upon Several Subjects concerning British Antiquities
Edinburgh 1747.
Kames, Lord
Essays on the Principles of Morality and Natural Religion
Edinburgh 1751.
Reid, Thomas
Enquiry into the Human Mind on the principles of common sense
Edinburgh 1764,
Essays on the Intellectual Power of Man
Edinburgh 1785,
Essays on the active powers of man
Edinburgh 1803.
Smith, Adam

Theory of Moral Sentiments
London 1776.
Religion: Congregationalist
Silverman, Kenneth
Selected Letters of Cotton Mather
Baton Rouge 1971.
Episcopalian
Manross, W. W.
The Fulham Papers in the Lambeth Palace Library: American Colonial Section
Oxford 1965.
Presbyterian
McCrie, Thomas ed.
The Correspondence of the Rev. Robert Wodrow 3 vols.
Edinburgh 1842.
Sprague, William D.
Annals of the American Pulpit 4 vols.
New York 1860.
Butterfield, Lyman H.
President Witherspoon comes to America
Princeton 1935.

VI SCOTLAND AND AMERICAN MEDICINE

EDINBURGH UNIVERSITY

Cadwallader Colden
Notes from the lectures of Wm Law. Regent at Edinburgh 1705. Materials for a new edition of Colden's *The principles of action in matter,* London 1751, with manuscript notes and corrections.
Dr Alston's
Letterbook containing letters from Dr Mitchell, Virginia. Account of Virginia and sending seeds and plants, 1738. Dr Alexander Garden, S. Carolina, describing the Indian pink and other S. Carolina plants and plant of work in vegetable poisons of S. Carolina, 1753. Dr John Lining, S. Carolina, on S. Carolina plants and their medical uses, 1754.
Lionel Chalmers
Letter from Lionel Chalmers, emigrant doctor to South Carolina, to Robert Whytt, professor of the theory of medicine, mentioning an outbreak of smallpox. N.D.
Benjamin Smith Barton
Letter to C. Stewart, printer in Edinburgh, about pressing fish, 1784.
Joseph Black
Letter from Dr John Morgan, Philadelphia, introducing Dr Rodgers, a prospective student of chemistry, 1784. Letter from Dr John Shore,

Petersburg, Va. introducing Dr Gibbons of Philadelphia, a medical student and concerning a species of plant as an antidote to spider venom, 1784.

American Physical Society (of Edinburgh)
Names of those who gave papers and transcriptions of their papers, 1794–7.

Chirurgo-Physical Society 1783–91
Dissertations read to the society, including one by John Pennington.

Dissertations
Dissertations of the Edinburgh Natural History Society, 1782–6, some by Americans e.g. Benjamin Smith Barton.

Class Lists
Alexander Monro, primus: anatomy 1720–44.
William Cullen: chemistry, 1755–62; materia medica 1761; clinical medicine 1763
Professor Walker: natural history 1782–1800.
Matriculation books 1762–1803 include lists of the medical classes, which are also separately recorded from 1783.
See also VI Royal College of Physicians, Edinburgh: Hamilton.

GLASGOW UNIVERSITY
William Cullen
Letters to Cullen from Arthur Lee (1764), Theoderick Bland (1764), John Morgan (1764, 1771, 1774), Benjamin Rush (1774, 1783, 1784), William Shippen (1774). Also some transcribed letters, 1783–9, from Benjamin Rush, Caspar Wistar, Samuel Miller; some of these are published, see Rush in Published Sources.

NATIONAL LIBRARY OF SCOTLAND
Pitfirrane Papers
Nineteenth-century copies of letters and 1755 journal on battle of Fort Duquesne. The letters of Dr Alexander and John Hamilton in Maryland to their brother Gavin, bookseller in Edinburgh.

Maxwell, MacMurdo and Newhall Family
Letters from Bolling Stark to his brother-in-law MacMurdo, that contain references of John Ravenscroft, studying medicine at Edinburgh 1763.
Letters from John Ravenscroft to his stepfather MacMurdo, while a student at Edinburgh 1762–70.

ROYAL COLLEGE OF PHYSICIANS, EDINBURGH
William Cullen
Letters to Cullen from William Shippen (1784), John Morgan (1786), Benjamin Rush (1786), Thomas Tudor Tucker (1786), Caspar Wistar (1786), William Brown (1788), Samuel Miller, Scottish doctor in

South Carolina (1789). For some from Rush to Cullen see Rush in Published Sources.

Alexander Hamilton (professor)
Midwifery class lists 1782–1800.

SCOTTISH RECORD OFFICE

In addition to those mentioned below there is information about Scottish doctors practising in the American colonies and in the United States in II SRO: Miscellaneous R. H. 15, Murray of Murraythwaite, and Cathcart of Genoch; II North Carolina State Archives: Cathcart; II North Carolina, University of Cathcart; v Princeton University: John Maclean; v Maryland Historical Society: Alexander Hamilton.

Smythe of Bathary
Papers: 1765–7, relating to the succession of Dr James Crockat, emigrant in South Carolina to property in Coupar Angus.

MacLaine of Lochbuie
Copy of will, 1772, of Archibald McLean, surgeon in New York, born Mull.

*Miscellaneous (*RH. *9)*
Marriage contract Charles Fyffe, practitioner in physic, South Carolina. N.D.

ABERCAIRNY

Letter, 1748, from Joshua Crosby, Philadelphia, recommending Charles Moore and Benjamin Morris, physicians, who intend to visit Edinburgh and discussing possibility of financial help from Philadelphia for Edinburgh Royal Infirmary.

Dalhousie
Letter: 1762, from W. H. Drayton of South Carolina – medical student at Balliol College, Oxford to Governor James Glen, concerning his financial affairs and his and his brother's progress in their medical studies. The brother, Charles Drayton, later completed his studies at Edinburgh.

Leven and Melville
Letter: 1778, from Dr Benjamin Rush relating that the funeral expenses of Captain William Leslie killed at battle of Princeton were generously given by General Washington, and giving wording comprised by Rush on the monument. Letter, 1794, from Benjamin Rush to Lord Balgowrie introducing Samuel Bayard American jurist.

Seafield
Letter: 1794, from Dr Benjamin Rush, Philadelphia, concerning enquiries about Alexander Grant, said to have died there.

NATIONAL REGISTER OF ARCHIVES (SCOTLAND)
Maxwell Stuart of Traquair
Letter: 1753, from Dr Peter Middleton, New York emigrant doctor.

INDIANA UNIVERSITY, BLOOMINGTON (MICROFILM IN NEW YORK ACADEMY OF MEDICINE)

Benjamin Rush

Manuscript diary of his time in Edinburgh 1768–69.

KENTUCKY, UNIVERSITY OF, BOWLING GREEN

Charles Meriwether

Papers of Charles Meriwether (1766–1843) who went to Scotland to study medicine.

MARYLAND HISTORICAL SOCIETY, BALTIMORE

Alexander Hamilton; physician (Delany Papers)

Letterbook: 1739–43, copies of six letters to Edinburgh to friends and relations and to Dr Robert Hamilton, a Glasgow physician, 1739–43. Letters to him from his mother in Edinburgh.

MASSACHUSETTS, BOSTON PUBLIC LIBRARY

Will Jameson

Letter, Edinburgh 1790, to Benjamin Smith Barton about making a collection of Scottish minerals for him and other matters.

MASSACHUSETTS HISTORICAL SOCIETY, BOSTON

Bulfinch

Letters of Thomas Bulfinch, jr. M.D. Edinburgh 1758, as student at Edinburgh, to his father and brother-in-law.

MICHIGAN, UNIVERSITY OF, WILLIAM L. CLEMENTS LIBRARY

Fyffe

Letters: 1757–75, from William Fyffe, emigrant doctor in South Carolina to his sister Elizabeth and father at Dron, near Dundee.

NEW JERSEY, PRINCETON UNIVERSITY, PRINCETON

Benjamin Rush

Benjamin Rush papers 1745–1813, containing many letters written by Rush while a medical student at Edinburgh 1767–8 in connection with the appointment of Witherspoon as principal of the College of New Jersey (Princeton). Published in the *Letters of Benjamin Rush* edited L. H. Butterfield, Princeton 1951.

MacLean Papers

John MacLean (1771–1814) b. Glasgow, M.D. ABERDEEN 1797. PROFESSOR OF CHEMISTRY AND NATURAL HISTORY, PRINCETON 1797–1812.

NEW YORK, NEW YORK ACADEMY OF MEDICINE

Bard Papers

Large collection of letters and papers of Samuel Bard (1741–1821) including letters to his father from Edinburgh where he was a student. Much of this has been published in Langstaff, J. B. *Dr. Bard of Hyde Park*, New York 1942.

NEW YORK, NEW YORK HISTORICAL SOCIETY

Alexander Coventry

Diary, begins 1783, of Alexander Coventry (1766–1830), M.D. Edinburgh 1783, who emigrated to New York.

Wilson Family Papers

William Wilson, physician, judge and postmaster – several letters from Thomas Rae, Berwick, Scotland (1787–1820).

NEW YORK, NEW YORK PUBLIC LIBRARY

Alice Colden Wadworth

'A sketch of my father's and mother's family' (MS). Gives information about Cadwallader Colden.

NORTH CAROLINA, UNIVERSITY OF, CHAPEL HILL

John Rutledge Papers

Contains material relating to Charles Rutledge of South Carolina who studied at Edinburgh 1794–6 but did not graduate.

Clithrall

Autobiography and diary of Mrs Eliza Clithrall, giving information about Dr James Clithrall of South Carolina who studied at Edinburgh, 1760–61 but did not graduate.

PENNSYLVANIA, AMERICAN PHILOSOPHICAL SOCIETY LIBRARY, PHILADELPHIA

Benjamin Smith Barton

Journals and notebooks 1785–1806 (photostats and transcriptions).

David Hosack

(1769–1835). Letters and papers including letter to James Gregory, Edinburgh on treatment of lock-jaw.

Arthur Lee

Autobiographical note.

John Morgan

Letters, 1763–84 to Sir Alexander Dick (photostats). The originals were at Prestonfield House, Edinburgh, but present location unknown.

Caspar Wistar

Papers including letter from T. C. Hope, Edinburgh, sending minerals from Strontian.

PENNSYLVANIA, COLLEGE OF PHYSICIANS, PHILADELPHIA

Joseph Parrish

'Biographical notice of Dr. Thomas Parke', in Ms Biographical Sketches and Memoirs of Members of the College of Physicians of Philadelphia.

John Morgan

Diary 1764, and letters of similar date.

Benjamin Rush
Miscellaneous papers
Caspar Wistar
Letters from William Cullen; material collected from life of Wistar by William Tilghman.
Joseph Carson
Scrapbook containing John Morgan's letters (1764–5) from Europe and letters between John Morgan and Benjamin Rush.

PENNSYLVANIA HISTORICAL SOCIETY, PHILADELPHIA
Library Company of Philadelphia
Benjamin Rush papers. Copy of letters from William Cullen to John Morgan, Philadelphia, 1768, introducing B. Rush. Letters to Benjamin Rush from William Cullen 1783, 1784, 1785, 1788. Ed. Dilly, London bookseller, 1770, 1771, 1774, 1784 mentioning American students in Edinburgh; Andrew Duncan from Edinburgh 1783, 1784, 1789, 1799; and Joseph Black, Edinburgh 1794, 1795. Many of these letters are published in the *Letters of Benjamin Rush* ed. L. H. Butterfield, Princeton 1951.

Benjamin Smith Barton
Papers 1778–1813.

George Logan
Papers, lecture notes at Edinburgh, Letterbook containing letters from Edinburgh to Charles Logan, 1775–9.

Samuel Powell Griffitts
Letters. Griffitts Correspondence, 1759–1825.

Caspar Wistar (in Vaux Papers)
Letter from Edinburgh to Thomas Wistar, 4 Feb., 1785.

Pemberton Papers
John Sims to Thomas Parke, Edinburgh 1772.

Gratz Collection
Correspondence between Benjamin Rush and John Morgan.

SOUTH CAROLINA HISTORICAL SOCIETY, CHARLESTON
Mary Pringle Anderson Collection
Letters of Robert Pringle in London to his brother Thomas of Symington, Edinburgh with mention of Dr Moultrie, South Carolina M.D. Edin. 1749.

Tucker Harris
Ms. biographical sketch of Tucker Harris (Virginian, M.D. Edinburgh, 1771) by G. Logan.

SOUTH CAROLINA, WARING HISTORY OF MEDICINE LIBRARY, CHARLESTON
John Lining
Letters: 1708–60, to the Royal Society, London.

Samuel Wilson
Samuel Wilson, M.D., Glasgow 1786; chemistry lecture notes, Edinburgh 1784.

Levi Meyers
Ms. biography of Levi Meyers, M.D., Glasgow 1787, by his daughter.

Moultrie
Manuscript account by M. van de Erre of James Moultrie of Charleston, Edinburgh 1788 M.D. Son of John Moultrie, first American to obtain Edinburgh M.D. 1749.

VIRGINIA HISTORICAL SOCIETY, RICHMOND

Miscellaneous Papers
Material relating to the following Virginians who studied medicine in Edinburgh: John Adams (1794‒6), John Randolf Archer (1797‒8), John Brockenbrough 1792‒5), Walter Jones (1763‒6). Letters from Virginian students in Scotland, J. Moncure Daniel, Glasgow 1791, Charles Minor, Edin. 1791‒2, Theodorick Bland, Edin. 1760‒3.

Arthur Lee
Arthur Lee (1740‒92) M.D. Edinburgh; letter from Glasgow to his brother.

James Henderson
Letterbooks of James Henderson (1783‒1829); emigrated to Virginia physician in America.

Jerdone
Jerdone Family Papers with references to Robert Honeyman (1752‒1822), naval surgeon, settled in Hanover County.

VIRGINIA STATE LIBRARY, RICHMOND

Ball, Gilmer, Tucker, Tazewell
Papers of families who had members who studied at Edinburgh at various dates.

VIRGINIA, UNIVERSITY OF, CHARLOTTESVILLE

Fitzhugh Papers
Correspondence of Dr John Spense with his wife Rose (Fitzhugh) Spense, of Dumfries, Va. relating in part to his time at Edinburgh (1784‒6).

John Taliaferro Lewis
Records of education at Edinburgh, 1777‒9.

Charles Minor
Medical diploma: Edinburgh M.D. 1793.

Richard E. Mead
A number of letters from Edinburgh 1798‒9.

VIRGINIA, WILLIAM AND MARY COLLEGE, WILLIAMSBURG

Campbell
Letter from Archibald Campbell (M.D. Edin. 1770) mentioning other

American students.

Tudor/Coleman Collection

Letters from Thomas Tudor Tucker at Edinburgh, 1768.

WASHINGTON D.C. LIBRARY OF CONGRESS

Joseph L. Toner

A great collection of information about early American doctors from a variety of sources.

Ruston

Letters from Edinburgh from Thomas Ruston M.D. Edinburgh 1765.

Walter Jones Papers

Letters from Edinburgh; M.D. Edinburgh 1768.

PUBLISHED SOURCES

Bard

Langstaff, J. B. *Dr. Bard of Hyde Park* New York 1942

Cullen

Thomson, John *Life and Works of William Cullen* Edinburgh 1832-59.

Rush

Butterfield, Lyman H. *Letters of Benjamin Rush* Princeton 1951.

General

Comrie, J. D. 'An Eighteenth century consultant' *Medical Life* XXXII 1925, 128-35. See also Appendix A.

VII SCOTS AND THE AMERICAN REVOLUTION

CUNNINGHAME DISTRICT ARCHIVES, KILMARNOCK

Cunninghame Family Papers

Letter: 1766, James Reid, describing the Stamp Act disturbance in Virginia.

MITCHELL LIBRARY, GLASGOW

Daniel Mackay

Journal (autobiographical): 1779-80, capture by an American privateer, experience as prisoner of war.

NATIONAL LIBRARY OF SCOTLAND

Stuart-Stevenson

Memorandum: 1775, by Alexander Speirs. Draft of a speech: 1777, on America, by Andrew Stuart, M.P.

NATIONAL REGISTER OF ARCHIVES, SCOTLAND

(COPIES IN STRATHCLYDE REGIONAL ARCHIVES, GLASGOW)

Crighton-Maitland

Papers: relating to his affairs during and after the Revolution. Also a letter from his sister, Judith Bell in Virginia, supporting colonial resistance. See III National Register of Archives, Scotland: Alexander Speirs.

PUBLIC RECORD OFFICE, LONDON (COPIES OF GLASGOW CLAIMS IN
STRATHCLYDE REGIONAL ARCHIVES)
Loyalist Claims
Voluminous records include much information about Scottish
claimants.

SCOTTISH RECORD OFFICE
Henderson of Fordell
A very large collection relating to the military service and property of
General James Robertson, 1761–86. Letterbook, 1780–3 of
Robertson as Governor of New York.
Abercairny
Letters (12): 1760–87, Thomas Stirling, on campaigns in America.

STRATHCLYDE REGIONAL ARCHIVES, GLASGOW
John Glassford
Rough notes of evidence to be given to the House of Commons on the
tobacco trade and consequences of a breach with the colonies.
Mitchells, Johnston, Hill & Hoggan (solicitors)
Papers: 1781–3, relating to the creditors of McCall, Smellie & Co.

MARYLAND HALL OF RECORDS, ANNAPOLIS
Maryland Provincial Convention
Petition: 1775, from Archibald Campbell and William Lilburn,
tobacco factors, against conviction for hoarding foods at their stores.
Maryland Commissioners of Confiscated British Property
Sales book; ledger; Intendent's letterbook: many references to property
formerly owned by Scottish merchants.
Maryland Committee of Observation
Proceedings: N.D. (1775 or 1776), case of the Revd. John Patterson,
accused of defaming the Provincial Convention.

MASSACHUSETTS, HARVARD UNIVERSITY, HOUGHTON LIBRARY,
CAMBRIDGE
Parrish
A collection of materials on southern Loyalists who went to the
Bahamas and other West Indian Islands.

NEW YORK, NEW YORK HISTORICAL SOCIETY
Forfeited Estates (New York)
Many entries refer to land confiscated from Scottish settlers.

NORTH CAROLINA STATE ARCHIVES, RALEIGH
Loyalists (North Carolina)
A large collection including some copies from the Public Record
Office, London.

VIRGINIA, WILLIAM AND MARY COLLEGE, WILLIAMSBURG
Blow Family
Letter: 1770, William Cunninghame of Glasgow, promising to observe

the terms of the Association.

WASHINGTON D.C., LIBRARY OF CONGRESS

James Dunlop

Papers: 1777–83, agent in America for James and Henry Ritchie; several instructions from the Ritchie's about purchases of tobacco wherever possible, 1777–83; reopening of trade in 1783. Also information about George Dunlop who was captured at Yorktown.

Gist Family

Papers: 1777–8, references to trade in tobacco 1777–8.

Daniel of St Thomas Jennifer

Report: confiscation in Maryland. Letter: criticising the policy of confiscation.

FURTHER ITEMS: X. 22, 23

PUBLISHED SOURCES

Loyalists

Egerton, H. E. ed. *The Royal Commission on the Losses and Services of American Loyalists* New York 1971.

MacDonald, Alexander

'The Letterbook of Captain Alexander McDonald' *New York Historical Society Collections, Vol* xv, New York, 1882.

McIntosh, Lachlan

Hawes, L. M. ed. *Lachlan McIntosh Papers in the University of Georgia Libraries* a thesis, 1968.

New York

O'Callaghan, E. D. ed. *New York Colonial Manuscripts* vol viii New York 1856.

New York

Paltsits, V. H. ed. *The Minutes of the Commissioners for Detecting and Defeating Conspiracies in the State of New York* 3 vols, New York 1972.

North Carolina

Clark, Walter ed. *State Records of North Carolina* vols xiii, xviii, Winston 1896.

Virginia

McIlwaine, H. R. ed. *Journal of the Council of the State of Virginia* Richmond 1931.

Virginia

Scribner, R. L. and Tarter, B. eds. *Revolutionary Virginia: The Road to Independence* 4 vols, Charlottesville 1978.

Witherspoon, John

Witherspoon, John *Thoughts on American Liberty* Philadelphia 1774; *An Address to the Natives of Scotland Residing in America* Philadelphia 1778.

VIII SURVIVORS AND NEW BEGINNINGS

HORNEL LIBRARY, KIRKCUDBRIGHT

Miscellaneous Letters

Letterbooks and accounts: 1781–9, shipments from Virginia to Glasgow and Liverpool. Letters: 1796–1815, William Muir, Virginia, to his aunt in Kirkcudbright.

MITCHELL LIBRARY, GLASGOW

Robert Henderson

Letters and papers, 1781–9. See also VIII New York Historical Society: Robert Henderson; VIII Pennsylvania Historical Society: Robert Henderson.

John Leitch

Ledger: 1797–8, many references to Glasgow companies trading with America, and to new partnerships in Virginia.

NATIONAL LIBRARY OF SCOTLAND

Cadell of Grange

Papers: 1775–1805, overseas trade including America; export of ironware to Philadelphia.

Ellice

Papers: the Ellice family owned land at Little Falls, New York; letters from agents and friends, 1798–1807.

Maxwell, MacMurdo and Newhall

Papers: 1761–86, 1754–1803, 1771–93, 1770–97, 1747–87, correspondence of George MacMurdo with his brother-in-law, business associates, Ravenscroft family and his sons in Virginia and Pennsylvania. Also general correspondence.

NATIONAL REGISTER OF ARCHIVES, SCOTLAND

Campbell-Preston of Ardchattan

Letter: 1791, James Campbell, advantages of living in America.

J. Ross Esq.

Papers: 1796–1819, John Marshall, estate owner in South Carolina.

W. S. B. Pollok-Morris

Letterbooks: 1783–1815, James Fairlie, information about Virginia, debts and trade after independence. Copies in Strathclyde Regional Archives.

SCOTTISH RECORD OFFICE

Dundas of Ochtertyre

Letters: 1783–9, George Dundas, giving details of his wife's property in Norfolk, Virginia, and of her claim before the commisioners for loyalist claims.

George Hamilton

Letter: 1803, purchase of an estate near Fredericksburg.

Patrick Home
   Papers: 1796–1801, sale of estate in Virginia.
Hamilton of Pinmore
   Correspondence: 1804, about debts in Virginia still unpaid.
James Dunlop of Garnkirk
   Papers: 1778–1803, partner in Colin Dunlop & Co.; sequestered
   property in Virginia.
George Craig
   Papers: 1782–1820, dealing with his estate in Pennsylvania.
Melville Castle
   Letter: c. 1806, Henry Glassford to Henry Dundas, complaining of
   inadequate sum proposed for settlement of Glasgow claimants.
   Memorandum: 1785, prepared for Henry Dundas by Patrick
   Colquhoun, on propects in the tobacco trade. Letter: 1795, from
   Provost John Dunlop of Glasgow, welcoming Jay's Treaty.
STRATHCLYDE REGIONAL ARCHIVES, GLASGOW
Baird, Hay & Co.
   Journal: 1772–1816, some references to John Hay & Co. with stores in
   Virginia and North Carolina.
MARYLAND HISTORICAL SOCIETY, BALTIMORE
Dunlop Family Papers
   A great deal of information about post-war trade, debt collection, and
   speculation in land in the District of Colombia.
Thomas Rutland
   Letterbook: 1784–7, contains letters to Robert Ferguson, Port
   Tobacco.
Alexander Hamilton (tobacco factor)
   Letters: 1784–98; receipts for ledgers now in GLC (Glassford papers).
MASSACHUSETTS HISTORICAL SOCIETY, BOSTON
Samuel Cary
   Correspondence: 1791–1814, he moved from Grenada to Boston in
   1791; continued to trade with James Campbell of Glasgow, who had
   formerly handled his sugar sales.
MICHIGAN, UNIVERSITY OF, WILLIAM L. CLEMENTS LIBRARY,
ANN ARBOR
Wilson-Livinston
   Letter: 1795, Thomas Bar of Berwick to his brother-in-law William
   Wilson, Clermont N.Y. About emigration to America.
NEW YORK, NEW YORK HISTORICAL SOCIETY
Robert Henderson
   Papers: 1784–1801. See also VII Mitchell Library, Glasgow and VIII
   Pennsylvania Historical Society.

Thomas Buchanan
Correspondence: 1747–8, trade and debts; ledgers 1800–17.

Neil Jamieson
Accounts and ledgers 1783–6. See also below Library of Congress.

Colin McGregor
Ledger, 1783–90. See also below New York Public Library.

Stuyvesant-Rutherford
Correspondence: 1780–84, Peter Stuyvesant and Myles Cooper, about the education of Stuyvesant's son 'Billy' in Scotland. Letters: 1807–8, Robert W. Rutherford to his father, John Rutherford of New York, whilst studying at Edinburgh. Full and informative on University life and Edinburgh society. Also an account of an election at Jedburgh where a cousin, James Rutherford, was elected.

King Papers
Letter: 1798, from American students at Edinburgh, asking Rufus King (then American minister in London) to intercede on behalf of Americans captured as French privateers and held as prisoners in Scotland. King replied that he could do nothing to help.

Falconer Family
Letters and papers: 1785–1856, records of a family originating from Strath Spey. William Falconer emigrated to America, 1784, and became a bookseller; he was followed by his brothers, Robert and Patrick. Robert was the most vigorous. and also the most dissatisfied with American conditions; but became wealthy as exporter of cotton to Scotland (Typescripts)

NEW YORK, NEW YORK PUBLIC LIBRARY

Colin McGregor
Papers: 1783–95, many of the earlier papers deal with the affairs of Neil Jamieson; others with McGregor's independent trading ventures. See also above New York Historical Society.

Francis Jeffrey
Letters: 1813, to James Munro, about his visit to New York.

NORTH CAROLINA, DUKE UNIVERSITY DURHAM

Robert Leslie
Correspondence: 1800–17, a young Glasgow man, employee of James Dunlop; letters mainly from friends in Glasgow.

Baskerville
Letters: 1802–4, John R. Lucas to William Baskerville of Virginia. Lucas was studying medicine at Edinburgh and also acting as tutor to Baskerville's son.

PENNSYLVANIA, DICKENSON COLLEGE, CARLISLE

Charles Nisbet

Letters (10): 1784–95, when President of Dickenson College, to Benjamin Rush and Earl of Buchan; highly critical of college and of American society and politics.

PENNYSLVANIA, HISTORICAL SOCIETY PHILADELPHIA

Robert Henderson

Letterbooks and other papers 1790–4. See also above Mitchell Library, Glasgow, and New York Historical Society.

Earl of Buchan (David Erskine)

Letters: 1786–8, to Charles Nisbet; 1791, to George Washington (enclosing a snuff box made from the oak under which William Wallace sheltered after the battle of Falkirk).

PENNSYLVANIA, UNIVERSITY OF PITTSBURGH

Charles Nisbet

Letters (56): 1784–1803, to Alexander Addison in Pittsburgh.

SOUTH CAROLINA, SOUTH CAROLINIANA LIBRARY, COLUMBIA

Thomas Aiton

Letterbook: Feb-June 1802, trade with Glasgow.

VIRGINIA HISTORICAL SOCIETY, RICHMOND

James Henderson

Letterbook: 1807, describing a visit to Scotland; numerous references to members of his family in Virginia and to estate of John McCredie of Richmond, Va.

VIRGINIA, UNIVERSITY OF, CHARLOTTESVILLE

Daniel Grinnan

Papers: 1784–1815, Virginian attorney who acted on behalf of the Glasgow creditors of William Gray; also winding up the estates of other Glasgow concerns. Informative letters from Walter Colquhoun of Virginia and Glasgow, and from Walter Fleming of Glasgow.

WASHINGTON D.C., LIBRARY OF CONGRESS

Neil Jamieson

Letters, 1783–6, on his business affairs in New York. Correspondence with Scots merchants in Virginia. See also above New York Historical Society.

Dunlop Family Papers

Post war trade, debt collection 1780–1800.

Huie, Reid & Co.

Papers, accounts, ledger and inventory: 1784–90, active in Dumfries, Virginia; associated with Huie, Alexander & Co. of Port Glasgow (some of their records are catalogued under that name).

James Ritchie
Instructions: 1784, to factors for resuming trade, conduct of business, direct sales in Virginia to French agents, etc.

Robert Ferguson (with Glassford Papers)
Letterbook 1787. Much information about new conditions by a former Glassford factor.

Thornton
Papers of William Thornton, Edinburgh 1781, M.D., Marischal College, Aberdeen 1784. Gave up medicine and became one of the principal architects of the new federal buildings in Washington D.C.

PUBLISHED SOURCES

Tobacco Trade after 1783
Skaggs, David K. and McMaster, David eds. 'Post-Revolutionary Letters of Alexander Hamilton, Piscataway Merchant' *Md. Hist. Mg.* LXIII 1968, 22–54, LXV 1970, 18–35.

Emigration after 1783
Bell, Whitfield J. 'Scottish Emigration to America: A Letter of Dr. Charles Nisbet to Dr. John Witherspoon, 1784' *WMQ* XI (1954), 276–89.
Selkirk, the Earl of,
Observations . . . on the present state of the Highlands
Edinburgh 1802.

General
Joyce, John, 'Letter on Life in Virginia, 1785' *Va MHB* XXIII (1915) 407–14. Includes material on Scots in Norfolk, Va.

IX SCOTS AND THE WARS IN AMERICA

The preceding lists have not included sources which deal exclusively with military or naval events. Scots made notable contributions to the forces of the Crown, and at home much of the information about life and conditions in America was derived from men who served in that part of the world. It is therefore appropriate to include a selection from sources even though no reference has been made to them in the text.

ABERDEEN UNIVERSITY

Duff of Braco
Letter: 1775, William Braco Gordon, criticising General Gage and other comments on the campaign.

GLASGOW UNIVERSITY

Bannerman
Letter: 1775, Captain W. S. Laurie, battle of Bunker Hill and account of Boston.

NATIONAL LIBRARY OF SCOTLAND

Halkett
Letters: 1772–95, mostly to Sir John Halkett (including twenty from

Sir William Erskine), on the war in America.

Liston

Journal: 1777, describing war in America.

Erskine Murray

Letters (copies): 1776, on war in America.

Nisbet

Papers: 1756-92, William Molleson, controller of the army accounts, financial administration of the British army in America.

Stuart Stevenson

Letters: 1776-7, Major Charles Cochrane, on war in America.

NATIONAL REGISTER OF ARCHIVES, SCOTLAND

Robertson-Aikman of the Ross

Letter (part): 1757, John Forbes, on affairs of the wing under his command.

MacNeal of Lossit

Commission: 1757, to Joshua Loring to build boats for service on Lake George or at Woods Creek. Letter: 1777, Captain MacNeal on British army plans.

Duke of Atholl

Papers: 1757-63, various matters relating to the Black Watch (42nd) regiment in North America.

MacPherson-Grant of Ballindalloch

Papers: 1757-9, General James Grant; military campaign against Cherokees; 1760-75 governor of East Florida; 1771-93, estates in Florida.

Adam of Blair-Adam

Letters: 1775-85, Lord North and other correspondents, on the American War.

MacPherson-Grant of Ballindalloch

Papers: 1775-83, General James Grant. Voluminous papers, letters and letterbooks.

Earl of Dundee

Letters: 1777-80, Major Patrick Fergusson, military affairs, campaign in South Carolina; also an account of his death, 1780.

Douglas Hume

Letters: 1777-80, Lord Dunglass, on war in America.

Campbell-Preston of Ardchattan

Letters: 1775-6, Duncan Campbell, situation in New York. Letters: 1776-80, Charles Campbell captive, imprisonment, commentary on military events.

SCOTTISH RECORD OFFICE

Mackay of Bighouse

Letters: 1758-61, from Allan Campbell (42nd Highlanders), 1758 to 1759; from Major Alexander Campbell 1759-61 (4 letters).

Cunninghame of Thorntown
Papers: 1763–1802, John Peebles, captain in 42nd Highland Regiment.

Ross of Kilravock
Letters and papers: 1757–9, Major James Clephane of Simon Fraser's Highland Regiment.

Campbell of Barcaldine
Letters: 1757–9, Allan Campbell, on Ticonderoga and Crown Point.

Hunter, Harvey, Webster & Will
Journal: 1765. of a detachment of the 42nd Regiment in the Ohio valley.

Broughton and Cally
Letters: 1779–82, includes defence of Kirkcudbrightshire coast against Paul Jones.

Campbell of Ballieveolan
Orderly book of 74th Regiment at New York, 1783.

Cunningham of Thornton
Papers relating to Captain John Peebles, 42nd Regiment, 1776–1802.

Leven and Melville
Letters and papers of Captain William Leslie, 17th Regiment, 1771–9. Includes a letter from Benjamin Rush saying that the expenses of Leslie's funeral had been paid by George Washington.

Robertson of Kindeace
Notebook of operations, 1779–81, kept by an officer of the 76th Regiment.

Gilchrist of Ospisdale
Papers relating to the 71st Regiment 1777–85, and correspondence on military matters.

Campbell of Barcaldine
Letters from Alexander Campbell, 1774–6: Bunker's Hill, New York. And from Patrick Campbell, 71st Regiment, 1776–82.

Dundas of Ochtertyre
Letters: 1773–93, Dr David Dundas and his wife, general comments on the war. Letters: 1780–1, Captain Ralph Dundas of H.M. Sloop *Bonetta;* news of war from Charleston, S.C., conduct of the Edinburgh regiment, naval operations. Also a letter about his share in tobacco seized on the James River in Virginia.

Drummond Castle
Papers relating to Lord Drummond's part in the abortive peace negotiations at Philadelphia, Jan-Feb 1776.

MacLaine of Lochbuie
Letters from and about members of the family serving with the Royal Highland Immigrants 1773–80 and, 1783– 1783–4, about British

evacuation of New York. Many other letters relate to the 84th Regiment.

Seafield

Letters and papers of Capt. John Grant, Commissary General and Paymaster of the Ordnance in America 1772–88. Letter from Simon Lovat of Fraser about raising his regiment, 1775. Many other letters from officers serving in America 1777–80.

NEW YORK, NEW YORK HISTORICAL SOCIETY

John Bremner

Journal: 1756–64, of a soldier in the 55th (Lord Howe's) Regiment; very detailed accounts of military life and battles.

Captain Alexander McDonald

Letterbook: 1775–89, describes his part in raising the 84th (Royal Highland Immigrant) Regiment.

X FURTHER SOURCES

In the course of the survey of the sources for the study of Scottish-American links in the eighteenth century information was collected from a number of libraries and archives in the United States about holdings which could not be examined in detail. A list of these sources is given below in alphabetical order of the states where they are to be found.

ALABAMA STATE DEPARTMENT OF ARCHIVES & HISTORY MONTGOMERY

A small amount of material relating to early Scottish traders in Alabama, their relations with the Indians, etc. Names include Lachlan McGillivray, John Barnard, and Robert Grierson.

ALABAMA, MOBILE PUBLIC LIBRARY

Forbes Company (Panton Leslie & Co.); Papers, ca. 1790–1840.

Papers of a large trading company of Mobile, Ala., which was active ca. 1790–1840. All of the people involved in the beginnings of the company were of Scottish descent.

GEORGIA STATE DEPARTMENT OF ARCHIVES AND HISTORY, ATLANTA

Oglethorpe's Regiment.

Lists of personnel of Oglethorpe's Regiment, Rangers, Independent Companies, Car's boatmen, Highlanders. Typed alphabetical list of names, with occasional notes of where they had land. (51 pp.)

'Loyal Judith'

List (6/5/1741) of Highlanders shipped on the 'Loyal Judith' and the amount of money due them for one years provisions (21/9/1741). Also list of men at Darien capable of bearing arms and of women and children and their ages.

Moore, Francis.
Text of journal regarding arrival at St. Simons of a party of Indians and Highlanders. (3 pp.)
KENTUCKY, FILSON CLUB, LOUISVILLE
Kennedy, ?.
Letter, ca, 1818–19, to a friend in Scotland, in reply to a letter of 15/8/1818 requesting information that is necessary for those who wish to visit or remain in the western country. Mentions opportunities for poor people; lack of king, priests and nobility; good climate, rich land, transportation, scarcity of good money; cheap merchandise, freedom of religion etc.
McConnell, William.
Papers 1782–1813. Includes Dr. Benjamin Bell's opinion and advice for treatment of McConnell's asthma, Edinburgh, 24/9/1788.
MAINE HISTORICAL SOCIETY, PORTLAND
Mowat, Capt. Henry.
Papers (including some copy-letters), 1734–98, of Capt. Henry Mowat, a Scottish sailor.
MASSACHUSETTS HISTORICAL SOCIETY, BOSTON
Edinburgh University.
A number of references to or papers relating to Edinburgh University; for example a diploma awarded to Thomas Jefferson, 1787.
Coffin, Mrs. Francis.
Two letters, 1802–3. from Mrs. Francis Coffin, an American staying in Edinburgh, to a friend in the United States, commenting on the capital's social life and on its attractions for tourists.
MICHIGAN, UNIVERSITY OF, WILLIAM L. CLEMENTS LIBRARY, ANN ARBOR
Minto, Walter.
Includes degree certificate of LL.D. from Aberdeen University, membership certificates of the Edinburgh Orange Society and the American Philosophical Society and three letters from Benjamin Rush. They are concerned with Rush's son, who was boarded with Minto while attending Princeton University.
MINNESOTA HISTORICAL SOCIETY, ST PAUL
Fur trade project, 1967–68.
Papers relating to a project for the identification of sources of information on the fur trade between Montreal, Minnesota and western Canada, 1770–1820. The project involved a trip to Scotland and England to visit repositories, and the papers include correspondence and data sheets relating to this visit.

NEW JERSEY HISTORICAL SOCIETY, NEWARK
Scottish landholders in New Jersey, eighteenth century.
Letters, indentures and other documents.

NEW YORK STATE ARCHIVES, ALBANY, AND ALBANY INSTITUTE OF
HISTORY AND ART
Although there was a large colony of Scots and Scotch-Irish in the
Albany area, there appears to be few surviving manuscripts which
relate to continuing transatlantic contacts. However, there are a
number of items connected with their activities in the United States,
particularly in connection with the petitions 1739–63 necessary to
secure the Argyle Patent. In addition, the names of local Scots can
readily be ascertained from the records of the Albany Scottish
organisations.

NEW YORK, ROCHESTER UNIVERSITY
MacKenzie, Donald
Diary – Account book, 1801–7, of Donald MacKenzie, who emigrated
to the United States from Inverness in 1804.

NORTH CAROLINA, UNIVERSITY OF, SOUTHERN HISTORICAL
COLLECTION, CHAPEL HILL
London, John
Diary of a visit to Scotland (c. 1770); full and critical comments. Copy
of an original in private hands; log of a voyage from Greenock, Scotland
to Wilmington, N.Ca., in 1803.

NORTH CAROLINA, DUKE UNIVERSITY, DURHAM
Hook, John
Letters, papers and merchant records, 1752, 1770–1823, of John
Hook, a wealthy Scottish merchant and tory, and of the merchant firm
of Hook's son-in-law.
Ross, William
Family and business correspondence, 1738–1875, of William Ross, a
merchant of Washington, North Carolina, and of his father-in-law,
John Simpson, a Scottish merchant who came to Washington in the
early 1780s.

PENNSYLVANIA, CUMBERLAND COUNTY HISTORICAL SOCIETY
Nisbet, Charles
A small collection of assorted papers (lecture notes, a record of a land
purchase) relating to Charles Nisbet, a Scot who was first president of
Dickinson College.

VIRGINIAN HISTORICAL SOCIETY, RICHMOND
McCredie, Andrew & William
Powers of attorney & affidavits, 1753, authorising John Boyd, William
Cunninghame, Allan MacRae and John Mitchell to represent the
McCredies' (of Glasgow) interest in the estate of Thomas McCredie.

Buchanan, Andrew

Power of attorney, 1784, concerns the payment of the debts of the Glasgow firm of Buchanan and Simpson, and the sale of its land and slaves in Virginia.

Anon. Diary, May 1783 – July 1785.

Kept by a person serving as a midshipman in a British man-of-war and later as a medical student at Edinburgh University.

Parker family

Papers, 1759–1835 (microfilm), includes correspondence from Patrick Parker (Edinburgh).

Roberton, Wyndham

Papers, 1740–1925 (microfilm), correspondents include Arthur Robertson (Glasgow) and William Robertson (Edinburgh).

Sandeman, William; Insurance Policy, 1801.

Issued to William Couper on goods during a voyage from Dundee to Norfolk, Va.

WASHINGTON, CHILTON, WILLIAM SCOTT; 12044 23rd AVE., SEATTLE, WASHINGTON, 98125

28. Hamilton Letters, 1801–23.

20 letters between Hugh and George Hamilton in Scotland and Virginia.

Papers owned by William S. Chilton.

WISCONSIN STATE HISTORICAL SOCIETY, MADISON

29. Edinburgh – University.

Medical degree from the University of Edinburgh, awarded to Ebenezer Campbell, 22.6.1742.

BIBLIOGRAPHY

I. GUIDES AND INDEXES

Raimo, John W. ed. *A Guide to Manuscripts relating to America in Great Britain and Ireland,* published for the British Association of American Studies by Mansell Publishing, 3 Bloomsbury Place, London WC1A 2QA and by Meckler Books, 520 Riverside Avenue, P.O. Box 405, Sangatuck Station, Westport, Connecticut 06880.

Scottish Record Office Office. *List of American Documents* Edinburgh 1976. Raimo lists all the documents noticed in the Scottish Record Office List, and some additional items. In some cases the call number of the box, folder, or bundle may have been altered, and it is advisable to consult the lists and indexes in the Scottish Record Office. Raimo's Guide does not (with a few exceptions) include items listed in the following older guides, all of which may be obtained on microfilm from Microfilm Ltd, Bradford Road, East Ardsley, Wakefield, West Yorkshire WF3 2JN, England.

Andrews, Charles M. *Guide to the Materials for American History, to 1783,* in the Public Record Office of Great Britain, 2 vols Washington D.C. 1912, 1914.

Andrews, Charles M. and Davenport Frances G. *Guide to the Manuscript Materials for the History of the United States to 1783,* in the British Museum, in Minor London Archives, and in the Libraries of Oxford and Cambridge, Washington D.C. 1908.

Paullin, Charles O. and Paxson, Frederic L. *Guide to the Materials in London Archives for the History of the United States since 1783,* Washington D.C. 1914.

For materials in the United States consult the multi-volume *National Union Catalog of Manuscripts* Library of Congress, Washington D.C. 1961– A cumulative index was published in 1964, and since then there have been indexes for each volume; but there is no cumulative index for the whole series.

Hamer, Philip *Guide to Archives and Manuscripts in the United States* Washington D.C. 1961 gives brief descriptions of the holdings in 1300 repositories and 20,000 collections.

Many of the state archives publish guides to their holdings. A list of addresses is given in Frank Freidel ed. *Harvard Guide to American History* Cambridge, Mass. 1974 vol. I 98–100. In addition a number of universities and private libraries publish

233

lists of their holdings or lists on specified topics. The repositories in the list of sources which follows will indicate those which have yielded important materials for the study of Scottish-American relations. There are in addition a large number of county or city historical societies.

II. GENERAL WORKS

Donaldson, Gordon *The Scots Overseas,* London 1966

Ferguson, William *Scotland: 1689 to the Present,* Edinburgh 1968.

Gipson, Lawrence H. *The British Empire before the American Revolution,* 14 vols, 1936–69.

Haws, Charles *Scots in the Old Dominion,* Edinburgh 1980.

Payne, Peter L. ed. *Studies in Scottish Business Enterprise,* London 1969.

Shepperson, George F. 'Writings on Scottish American History', *WMQ* XI 1954.

Slaven, Anthony *The Development of the West of Scotland: 1750–1960,* London 1975.

Wertenbaker, Thomas J. *Norfolk, Historic Southen Port,* 2nd ed. rev. 1962.

III. EARLY TRADE AND SETTLEMENT to 1750

Anderson, R. 'The Aberdonian Abroad' *Aberdeen University Review* IX 36–46, 130–8.

Bulloch, J. M. *The House of Gordon* 3 vols, Aberdeen 1903, 1907, 1912.

Campbell, Roy H. 'The Anglo-Scottish Union of 1707: the Economic Consequences' *Economic History Review* XIV 1963–4 468–77.

Insh, George P. *Scottish Colonial Schemes* 1620–1686, Glasgow 1922.

Piotrowski, Thaddeus M. *The Scots and their Descendants in Manchester, New Hampshire* Manchester 1976.

Pomfret, John E. *The Province of East New Jersey* Princeton 1962

Skene, W. F. *Memorials of the Family of Skene* Aberdeen 1887.

Smith, Abbot E. *Colonists in Bondage: white servitude and convict labour in America, 1607*–1776 Chapel Hill 1947.

Smout, T. C. 'The Development and Enterprise of Glasgow', *Scottish Journal of Political Economy* VII 1960, 194–212.

'The Glasgow Merchant Community in the Seventeenth Century' *Scottish Historical Review* XLVII 1968, 63–71.

Taylor, A. & H. *The House of Forbes* Aberdeen 1937.

Wertenbaker, T. J. *Norfolk: Historic Southern Port,* Durham N.C. 1931.

Early Scottish Contribution to the United States Glasgow 1945.

Whitehead, William A. *East New Jersey under the Proprietory Governments* 2nd ed. Newark 1875.

Coakley, R. Walter 'The Two James Hunters of Fredericksburg'. *Virginia Magazine,* LVI (1948&, 3–21.

IV. THE GLASGOW TOBACCO TRADE

Barker, T. C. 'Smuggling in the Eighteenth Century: the evidence of the Scottish tobacco trade' *Virginia Magazine of History and Biography* LXII 1954, 387–99.

Devine, Thomas M. *The Tobacco Lords: a study of The Tobacco merchants of Glasgow* Edinburgh 1975.

Hamilton, K. 'The Failure of the Ayr Bank' *Economic History Review* 2nd series VIII 1955–6, 405–18.

Price, Jacob M. 'The Rise of Glasgow in the Chesapeke Tobacco Trade' William and Mary Quarterly, XI 1954, 179–99.

'The Beginnings of Tobacco Manufacture in Virginia' *Virginia Magazine of History and Biography* LXIV 1956, 3–29.

France and the Chesapeke 2 vols, Ann Arbor 1793.

Capital and Credit in British Overseas trade: the view from the Chesapeke, 1700–1776 Cambridge, Mass. 1980.

Sheridan, Richard 'The British Credit Crisis of 1772 and the American Colonies', *Journal of Economic History* XX 1960, 161–86

Soltow, J. H. 'Scottish Traders in Virginia, 1750–75' *Economic History Review* 2nd series XII 1959–60, 83–98.

V. THE HIGHLAND MIGRATION

Adam, Margaret I. 'The Highland Migration of 1770' *Scottish Historical Review* XVI 1919, 280–93.

'The Causes of the Highland Emigration of 1785–1803' *Scottish Historical Review* XVII 1920, 73–89.

Chalker, Fussell M. 'The Highland Scots in the Georgia Lowlands' *Georgia Historical Quarterly* LX 1976, 1.

Flinn, Michael ed. *Scottish Population History from the Seventeenth Century to the 1930s* Cambridge 1977.

Graham, Ian C. C. *Colonists from Scotland* Ithaca 1956.

Gray, Malcolm *The Highland Economy 1750–1850* Edinburgh 1957.

Grimble, Ian *Emigration in the Time of Rob Donn* 1714–8, Edinburgh 1963. Also in *Scottish Studies* VII 1963 part 2.

Ives, Larry E. *British Drums on the Southern Frontier* Chapel Hill 1974.

MacDonald, Ewen J. 'Father Roderick MacDonnell: Missionary at St. Regis and the Glengarry Catholics' *Catholic Historical Review* XIX 1933, 265–74.

McLean, John P. *An Historical Account of the Settlements of Scotch Highlanders in America prior to the peace of 1783* Cleveland 1900.

Flora MacDonald in America Lumberton N.C. 1909.

Mason, John 'Conditions in the Highlands after the "Forty-five"' *Scottish Historical Review* XXVI 1947, 134–46.

Merrens, Harry Roy *Colonial North Carolina in the Eighteenth Century: a study in historical geography* Chapel Hill 1964.

Meyer, Duane *The Highland Scots of North Carolina* Chapel Hill 1957.

Mix, David E. E. *Catalogue of Maps and Surveys in the Offices of the Secretary of State, State Engineer and Surveyor and Comptroller in the New York State Library* Albany 1859.

O'Callaghan, E. B. 'Early Highland Migration to New York' *Historical Magazine* 1st series, v 1861, 301-4.

Philipson, Nicholas and Mitchison, Rosalind eds *Scotland in the Age of Improvement: Essays in Scottish History in the Eighteenth Century* Edinburgh 1970.

Wood, J. David "Scottish Migration Overseas' *Scottish Geographical Magazine* LXXX 1964, 164-76.

Youngson, A. J. *After the '45: the Economic Impact on the Scottish Highlands* Edinburgh 1973.

VI. RELIGION AND LEARNING

Ahlstrom, S. 'The Scottish Philosophy and American Theology' *Church History* XXIV 1955, 257-72.

Anderson, P. J. 'Aberdeen's Influence on American Universities' *Aberdeen University Review* v 27-31.

Clive, John and Bailyn, Bernard 'England's Cultural Provinces: Scotland and America' *William and Mary Quarterly* X1 1954, 214-51.

Collins, W. L. *President Witherspoon: a Bibliography* 2 vols, Princeton 1925

Hamony. R. 'Jefferson and the Scottish Enlightenment' *William and Mary Quarterly* XXXVI 1979.

Hook, Andrew *Scotland and America: a Study of Cultural Relations 1750-1835,* Glasgow 1975.

Kraus, Michael 'Charles Nisbet and Samuel Stanhope Smith: Two Eighteenth Century Educators' *Princeton University Library Chronicle* VI 1944, 17-36.

McAlister, J. L. 'Francis Alison and John Witherspoon: Political Philosophers and Revolutionaries' *Journal of Presbyterian History* LIV, 1976

Montgomery, T. H. *A History of the University of Pennsylvania to 1770* Philadelphia 1900.

Parkinson, Sarah W. *Charles Nisbet: first President of Dickinson College (Carlisle)* n.p. 1908.

Pears, Thomas C. 'Francis Alison' *Journal of the Presbyterian Historical Society* XXVIII 1950, 213-25.

Pryde, George S. *Scottish Universities and the Colleges of Colonial America* Glasgow 1957.

Ritchie, Carson T. A. *Frontier Parish* Aberdeen 1976.

Robbins, Caroline 'When it is that Colonies may turn Independent: An Analysis of the Environment and Politics of Francis Hutcheson, 1694–1746 *William and Mary Quarterly* XI 1954, 21–51.

Rouse, Parke jr. *James Blair of Virginia* Chapel Hill 1971.

Schlenther, Boyd S. 'Scottish Influences, Especially Religious in Colonial America' *Records of the Scottish Church Historical Society* XIX 1976, 133–54.

Sloan, D. *The Scottish Enlightenment and the American College Ideal* New York 1971.

Stohlman, Martha L. L. *John Witherspoon: Parson, Politician, Patriot* Philadelphia 1976.

White, Morton *Philosophy of the American Revolution* New York 1978.

Wills, Garry *Inventing America: Jefferson's Declaration of Independence* New York 1978

VII. SCOTLAND AND AMERICAN MEDICINE

Some additional titles are listed in Appendix B.

1. General Works

Bell, Whitfield J., jr. *The Colonial Physician and Other Essays* New York 1975.

Blanton, W. B. *Medicine in Virginia in the Eighteenth Century* Richmond Va 1931.

Bridenhaugh, C and J. *Rebels and Gentlemen* New York 1962

Carson, Joseph *History of the Medical Department of the College of Philadelphia* Philadelphia 1869.

Cordell, E. F. *Medical Annals of Maryland* 1799–1899, Baltimore 1903.

Flexnor, James T. *Doctors on Horseback* New York 1937.

Kelly, H. A. and Burrage, W. L. *Cyclopedia of American Medical Biography* Philadelphia 1912.

Dictionary of American Medical Biography New York 1928.

Krans, M. 'American and European Medicine in the Eighteenth Century *Bull. Hist. Med.* VIII 1940, 679–95.

Malloch, Archibald *Medical Interchange between the British Isles and America before 1801* London 1946.

Long. D. ed. *Medicine in North Carolina* Raleigh N.C. 1972.

Packard, F. R. *History of Medicine in the United States* 2 vols, New York 1931.

Packard, F. R. 'How London and Edinburgh Influenced Medicine in Philadelphia in the Eighteenth Century' *Ann. med. Hist.*, n.s. IV 1932, 219–44.

Quinan, J. R. *Medical annals of Baltimore from* 1608–1180, Baltimore 1884.

Shryock, R. H. *Medicine in America: Historical essays* Baltimore 1966.

Shryock, R. H. *Medicine and Society in America* 1660–1860, New York 1975.

Smith, R. W. Innes *English Speaking Students of Medicine at the University of Leyden* Edinburgh 1932.

Thacher, J. *American Medical Biography* 2 vols, Boston 1828.

Thomson, W., and Craigie, D. *An account of the Life. Lectures and Writings of William Cullen* vol. I Edinburgh 1832; vol II Edinburgh 1859.

Toner, J. M. *Contribution to the Annals of Medical Progress and Medical Education Before and During the War of Independence* Washington 1874.

Viets, H. R. *A Brief History of Medicine in Massachusetts* Boston 1930.

Waring, J. I. *A History of Medicine in South Carolina* Charleston S.D. 1964.

Wilson, J. Gordon 'The influence of Edinburgh on American Medicine' *Proc. Inst. Med. Chicago* VII 1929.

2. Biographies

Bell, Whitfield J., Jr. *John Morgan, Continental doctor* Philadelphia 1965.

Bell, Whitfield J., Jr. 'Benjamin Smith Barton, M.D. Keil' *J. Hist, Med.* XXVI 1971, 197–203.

Berkeley E. and D. S. *Dr. Alexander Garden of Charlestown* Chapel Hill N.C. 1969.

Berkeley E. and D. S. *Dr. John Mitchell, the Man who Made the Map* Chapel Hill N.C. 1974.

Bridenhaugh, C. ed. *Gentleman's Progress: the Itinerarium of Dr. Alexander Hamilton* Chapel Hill 1948.

Corner, Betsy *William Shippen, Jr., Pioneer in American Medical Education; a Biographical Essay* Philadelphia 1951.

Hosack, Alexander E. *Memoir of the Late David Hosack* Philadelphia 1861.

Hosack, David *Biographical Memoir of Hugh Williamson, M.D., LL.D.* New York 1821.

James, Mrs. Thomas Potts *Memorial of Thomas Potts Junior* privately printed 1874.

Langstaff, J. B. *Dr. Bond of Hyde Park* New York 1942.

Rush, Benjamin *Autobiography* ed. G. W. Corner, Princeton 1948.

Thacher, James *American Medical Biography* Boston 1828.

Rush, Benjamin 'Memoirs of the Life and Character of John Redman, M.D.' *Philadelphia Medical Museum* v 1808.

VIII. THE REVOLUTION AND AFTER

Brown, Wallace *The King's Friends: the Composition and Motives of the American Loyalist Claimants* Providence 1965.

Crispin, Barbara 'Clyde Shipping and the American War' *Scottish Historical Review* XLI 1962, 124–34.

Devine, T. M. 'Glasgow Merchants and the Collapse of the Tobacco Trade' *Scottish Historical Review* LII 1973, 50–74.

Evans, E. G. 'Planter Indebtedness and the Revolution in Virginia' *William and Mary Quarterly* 3rd Series XIX (1962), 511–23.

Evans, E. G. 'Private Indebtedness and the Revolution in Virginia' *William and Mary Quarterly* XXVIII 1971, 347–74.

Fagerstrom, D. I. 'Scottish Opinion and the American Revolution' *William and Mary Quarterly* XI 1954.

Fingerhut, E. R. 'Use and Abuses of the American Loyalist Claims' *William and Mary Quarterly* XXV 1968, 245–58.

Leyburn, J. G. 'Presbyterian Immigrants and the American Revolution' *Journal of Presbyterian History* LIV 1976.

Low, W. A. 'Merchant and Planter Relations in post-Revolutionary Virginia, 1783–9' *Virginia Magazine of History and Biography* LXI 1953, 308–18.

Robertson, M. L. 'Scottish Commerce and the American War of Independence' *Economic History Review*, 2nd series IX 1956–7, 123–31.

NOTES

Notes to Chapter One

1. Scots Charitable Society, papers in the Mass HS. The records are incomplete.
2. The Standard work on early Scottish colonial venture is George Pratt Insh *Scottish Colonial Schemes 1620*–1686, Glasgow 1922. As the present work is confined to settlements that subsequently became part of the United States it will not deal with Nova Scotia or Darien.
3. *Ibid.* ch. VI *passim.*
4. *Ibid.*
5. In addition to the work by Insh ch. V *passim,* see William A. Whitehead *East New Jersey under the Proprietory Government,* Newark 1846, and *Contributions to the Early History of Perth Amboy,* New York 1856.
6. Henry Goodwin Smith *The History of the 'Old Scots' Church of Freehold,* Freehold N.J. 1895, 20.
7. There is a fuller treatment of James Blair in ch. V below.
8. T. C. Smout "The Development and Enterprise of Glasgow, 1556–1707" *Scottish Journal of Political Economy,* VII (1960) 194–212, and "The Glasgow Merchant Community in the Seventeenth Century *Scottish Historical Review.* XLVII (1968) 53–71.
9. T. C. Barker "Smuggling in the Eighteenth Century: the Evidence of the Scottish Tobacco Trade" *Va MHB,* LXII (1954) 387–99.
10. *Register of the Privy Council of Scotland,* 1st, 2nd, & 3rd Series Edinburgh 1877–1970.
11. SRO, Exchequer Records.
12. SRO, Court of Session Production, William Fraser, merchant of London, trading with North America, especially Virginia and Boston, 1699–1711.
13. SRO, GD 158; Historical Manuscripts Commission, *14th Report* Appendix III, 113–15.
14. GD 103.
15. SRO, Abercairny Muniments GD 24; Historical Manuscripts Commission, *10th Report* Appendix, 137.
16. SRO, Henderson of Fordell GD 172, contains papers relating to Perth's estate 1782–6, and Hannay Papers GD 214 contain a memorial from James Drummond of 1786. The Perth claim was exceedingly complex. The original grantee, James Drummond, 4th Earl of Perth, followed James VII and II into exile and by him was created Duke of Perth. His son was implicated in the 1715 rebellion and debarred from succession to his father's Scottish titles, but before his attainder he had transferred his Scottish estates to his son. One issue was whether the New Jersey land grant was also transferred or had become forfeit. The last direct heir died in 1760, and the estates were inherited by a distant cousin, James Drummond, who assumed the title of Earl of Perth; but this was contested

by another descendant. This dispute then became entangled with the further question of the status of the Perth property in New Jersey during and after the Revolution.

17. Miscellaneous Bundles RH15 131/1–3.

18. A study, based on these records, has been completed by Elizabeth Menzies 926 Kingston Rd., Princeton, N.J. 08540, together with an investigation of the family backgrounds of settlers whom it has been possible to identify.

19. MLG. Papers of Dunlop of Garnkirk and Tollcross. Research into the Dunlop family is complicated by their fondness for certain names. There is a John and James in every generation, and Archibald, Colin and William appear frequently.

20. NLS, Ch. 8546–8. Dunlop Papers. William Dunlop petitioned the King in 1689 about hostilities commenced by the Spanish in Carolina, S.R.O. Leven and Melville Muniments.

21. MLG, Dunlop Papers D16.

22. MLG, Shawfield Papers. Extracts were published in the *Glasgow Herald,* 3 June 1959.

23. The records are in the Dumfries Burgh Museum.

24. SRO, GD/95/10/Item 38.

Notes to Chapter Two

1. Howard F. Barker "National Stocks in the Population of the United States". *Annual Report of the American Historical Association for 1931,* vol. I ch. IV.

2. The estimate depended upon establishing a list of distinctive Scottish names, discovering the proportion of these names to the whole population of Scotland, and assuming that the same proportion would apply in America. But most of the distinctive names were from the Highlands and the north-east, while in Virginia, Maryland, and South Carolina the majority of immigrants were from the lowlands. The 'distinctive' names may therefore account for a lower proportion of the whole than in Scotland. There is no statistical base for the number of Scots in Georgia. The figure depends upon the assumption that the number would continue southward the increasing proportions observed from Maryland to North Carolina.

3. Wallace Brown *The King's Friends: The Composition and Motives of the American Loyalist Claimants,* Providence R.I. 1965, 259.

4. *Ibid.,* 250.

5. T. C. Smout *A History of the Scottish People,* London 1969, 258–9.

6. Julian P. Boyd ed. *The Papers of Thomas Jefferson,* VI 432–3, to Wilson Cary Nicholas, 31 Dec. 1783.

7. 'Scotus Americanus' *Information concerning the Province of North Carolina addressed to Emigrants from the Highlands and Western Isles of Scotland,* Glasgow 1773.

8. SRO, Sinclair of Freswick Muniments, John Campbell to William Sinclair, 1772.

9. It has been estimated that by 1900 twenty five per cent of the students at Glasgow were from working-class families (W. H. Mathew 'The Origin

and Occupation of Glasgow Students, 1740–1839' *Past and Present*, (1966) 33). The calculation is slightly suspect, both because of the difficulty in defining 'working class' and because of the large number who attended without matriculation. Boys from poor families were interested in getting a degree – many others were not – so their proportion among matriculated students was likely to be high. Nevertheless the major point stands: a higher proportion of boys from poor homes attended Glasgow university in 1800 than in most twentieth-century British universities.

10. T. M. Devine *The Tobacco Lords*, Edinburgh 1975. The count is taken from Appendix I, 177–84. For general comments on the education of merchants see *Ibid.*, 8–9.

11. Alexander Carlyle *Autobiography*, Edinburgh 1861, 74, Devine *op. cit.*, p. 8.

12. Rosalind Mitchison 'Two Northern Ports' *Scottish Studies*, VII (1963) 75–82. The other port was Thurso, which never shared in this law-made prosperity. A sample shows six rice ships docking at Kirkwall in one quarter of 1761, and four in one quarter of 1762. This article is based on the Customs Account in the SRO which are complete for the two ports from 1744. In 1745–9 American ships accounted for 47 per cent of all ships entering Kirkwall so the trade was already firmly established by that year.

13. SRO, GD/18/5288 Clerk of Penicuik Muniments.

14. SRO, GD 199 Ross of Pitcalnie Muniments.

15. SRO, Miscellaneous RH 15/1/95.

16. Many letters and other materials relating to the Humes of Wedderburn in Virginia were used by Lieutenant Colonel Edgar Erskine Hume in 'A Colonial Scottish Jacobite Family – the Establishment in Virginia of a branch of the Humes of Wedderburn' *Va MHB*, XXXVIII (1930), 1–37, 97–124, 195–234, 292–346. George Hume wrote frequent letters to his brothers, sisters, and other relations in Scotland. Letters were often entrusted to William Hunter, Merchant of Fredericksburg, whose nephew lived near Wedderburn. The letters are very informative about conditions in Virginia. In addition to letters from George Hume there are letters to and from other members of the Hume family. This name is sometimes spelt 'Hume' and sometimes 'Home'.

17. SRO, GD 267 1/3 Home of Wedderburn Muniments.

18. Lieutenant Colonel Edgar E. Hume accepts the claim of the Virginian Humes that they were heirs to Wedderburn, and, through the failure of two other branches of the family, peers of Scotland and of France.

19. SRO, GD 18 5360/3–9 Clerk of Penicuik Muniments.

20. Pat Bryant *English Crown Grants in Georgia 1735–75*, Atlanta 1972.

21. E. Merton Coulter *A Short History of Georgia*, Chapel Hill 1933, 151.

22. SRO, GD 237 Box 10 Bundle 1. Tods, Murray and Jamieson Collection. The documents are in poor condition. The collection includes a marriage contract of 1724 between John Lloyd of Charleston and Sarah Collins. Business transactions are mentioned with several other Scottish merchants: William Robertson, Hugh Campbell, William Snow, John Skinner, and James Stewart.

23. SCHS, holds transcripts of his letterbooks for 1737–45. These have been

published: Walter B. Edgar ed. *The Letterbook of Robert Pringle,* 2 vols.
Columbia S.C. 1972.

24. Walter B. Edgar 'Studies in the Society's History and Archives CV–CVII'
Journal of the Royal Society of Arts, CXXII (1973–4), 95–8, 171–2. A
portrait of Pringle, painted by an unknown artist in London, is reproduced
on p. 96.

25. SRO, GD 219 Murray of Murraythwaite Muniments. This voluminous
collection is an important source for the colonial history of South Carolina.

26. SRO, Stewart of Dalguise Muniments. He said that two-thirds of the
merchants in Charleston were Scots – an exaggeration but an indication of
their importance in the commercial development of South Carolina.

27. William L. Clements Library, University of Michigan. Sixteen letters from
the brothers to their father and sister. Also one from Ann, William's wife.
William's letters are the most numerous and important. The letters cover
1757 & 1775. For Charles Fyffe see William M. MacBean *Biographical
Register of the St. Andrews Society of New York,* New York 1922, vol. I,
232.

28. UNC, Robert Hogg – sales ledger of a store at Wilmington.

29. SCHS, Fraser Papers. The Collection of this society also include a
merchant's day book kept by John Ernest Poyas of Charleston for 1764–6.
Scottish partnerships with whom he did business include Corrie and Scott;
Robertson, Jamieson & Co; Hogg and Clayton; Mackenzie, Thompson &
Co. There is also mention of a Captain John Scott.

30. SRO, GD 180/624, Cathcart of Genoch Muniments. Letters to John
Cathcart of Genoch from William Cathcart and John Rutherford; letters
from William Cathcart to Robert Cathcart (his nephew), 1760–9; letters
from Gabriel Cathcart to Robert Cathcart. UNC holds microfilm copies of
the correspondence of Dr William Cathcart (originals in private hands),
and the NCSA holds some letters from Scotland to Dr Cathcart.

31. NLS MS 5025–46, Steuart Papers, 1758–89; PAHS, Charles Steuart letters
and papers 1762–3, 1789.

32. CIW. Diary of the Rev. Robert Rose, 1747–51; there is a genealogical
account of his descendants compiled by Christina Rose. *The Rev. Robert
Rose: family in Scotland and Virginia,* San José, Calif., 1972 (privately
printed).

33. VA HS, Peyton family papers. There is a brief notice of John Scott in
Lorenzo Sabine, *Biographical Sketches of Loyalists of the American
Revolution,* 2 vols. Boston, 1864. Sabine says that he was reputed to be a
man of marked ability, gay, witty, a fine orator, and 'the handsomest man
of his day' (p. 268). He gives no source for these observations.

34. R. E. Scott appears in a short (5 lines) entry in the *Dictionary of National
Biography.* None of his papers are preserved at Aberdeen. The VAHS papers
were inherited by Mrs Peyton from her mother, Elizabeth Gordon Scott.

35. SRO, GD 136/416/1–4, Sinclair of Freswick Muniments. John Campbell to
William Sinclair, 26 July 1772.

36. SRO, GD 25 Sec 9 Ailsa Muniments.

37. SRO, GD 188/12/5, Leith-Ross Muniments. John Ross was a member of the
'Parliament' of East Florida, and a certificate of his election is included in
the collection.

38. SRO, GD 172 Boxes 42 and 48 R. O. Henderson of Fordell Muniments. The land leased in Charlotte county had been granted to two officers in 1775.
39. Museum and Art Gallery, Perth. Freeman Papers.
40. NLS, Acc. 5340 Box 1 FS McLeod of Geanies Papers. The two brothers cannot have seen much of each other, for William told an extraordinary story of a visit to James, in which the latter failed to recognise him, and treated him as an imposter.
41. SRO, GD 1/787/1−3 Mercer of Pittendreich Muniments.
42. SRO, GD 203 Lindsay Muniments.
43. In addition to Colonial Office papers in the Public Record Office in London, there are several sources of information about Glen.
    (i) South Caroliniana Library, Colombia, S.C. Many letters on official business, some letters from Scotland after his retirement, to James Drayton, who managed his South Carolina estates.
    (ii) SRO, GD 45 Dalhousie Muniments. Letterbook 1746−52 (a most important source for South Carolinian history during this period) also some copies of the *Edinburgh Almanack* and *Daily Journal* with hand-written notes by Glen (some referring to South Carolina), accounts referring to Glen's estate prepared by his nephew and heir, David Erskine. These papers are in the Dalhousie Muniments because Glen married the Countess of Dalhousie.
    (iii) SRO, GD 215 Beveridge Papers. A collection of materials relating to Glen made by James Beveridge of Linlithgow; includes photographs of his plantation, town house, slave quarters and other buildings in South Carolina.
44. The information in this and the two preceding paragraphs is drawn from the letterbook of 1746−52.
45. SRO, GD 18/5023 Clerk of Penicuik Muniments.
46. NCSA, correspondence of Thomas Pollock 1717 and 1737.
47. The authority for the life of Dinwiddie is John R. Alden *Robert Dinwiddie: Servant of the Crown,* Williamsburg 1973. There is a published collection of his letters, dealing almost exclusively with official business, by R. A. Brock *The Official Records of Robert Dinwiddie,* Virginia Historical Society, Richmond 1883. The Lockhart family papers (in private hands: copies in Colonial Institute, Williamsburg and Strathclyde Regional Archives, Glasgow) contain some information about the family. The Richard Corbin Papers at the Colonial Institute, Williamsburg, contain many letters from Corbin to Dinwiddie.
48. SRO, GD 110/988 Hamilton-Dalrymple Muniments.
49. SRO, GD 24/1/464 Abercairny Muniments.
50. See below for the account of John Borthwick.
51. The remark formed part of his advice on the appointment of a school-master (above p. 17). For a lively picture of a tutor's work see Hunter D. Farish ed. *Journal and Letters of Philip Vickers Fithian, 1773−4;* a plantation tutor of the old Dominion, Williamsburg 1957. The introduction contains some general comments on Scottish tutors in Virginia.
52. YUL, Knollenberg Collection. There are further notes on Panton in ch. V.

53. SRO, GD 24/1/464 Abercairny Muniments.
54. CIW, John Corbin Papers. Published as *The Journal of John Harrower* ed. Edward Miles Rely, Williamsburg 1963.
55. SRO, GD 248/564/3 Seafield Muniments.
56. NLS, McMurdo Maxwell Papers, George Clapham to McMurdo 28 Feb 1774.
57. David Duff's frustrated ambition to move from humble schoolmaster to affluent parson was less unrealistic than it may seem. Many Scottish tutors seem to have taken anglican orders and obtained parishes. See ch. v below.

Notes to Chapter Three

1. Ian Charles Cargill Graham *Colonists from Scotland,* published for the American Historical Association, Ithaca 1956, 118–19. Charles H. Haws, *Scots in the Old Dominion,* Edinburgh 1930, chs. 6 and 7, gives a general account of Scottish merchants in Virginia and details of many individuals.
2. James Robinson, factor at Falmouth, was a partner in William Cunninghame & Co.; William Reid, William Henderson, John Hamilton, James Dougall, and David Walker (all factors or storekeepers) were also partners in companies headed by Cunninghame; Charles Cruickshank and Archibald Moncrieff, factors in Maryland, were partners in Speirs, French & Co.; Neil Jamieson of Norfolk was a partner in two of the several partnerships associated with John Glassford.
3. William Cunninghame wrote at great length, and in great detail, two or three times a month to his principal factor, John Robinson of Falmouth; John Glassford wrote frequently to Neil Jamieson in a hand which only those long familiar with it could decipher.
4. Thomas M. Devine *The Tobacco Lords: a study of the Tobacco Merchants of Glasgow and their Trading activities c. 1740–90,* Edinburgh 1975, has a list (Appendix I, p. 177 ff) of all regular importers of tobacco who were registered burgesses or guild brethren of Glasgow. This includes 164 names. SRA holds a list, compiled by Mr Richard Dell, of all co-partnerships and their individual members active in Glasgow in the middle years of the eighteenth century.
5. The leading authority on this, and all other aspects of the trade, is Jacob M. Price. See especially his *France and the Chesapeke: a history of the French Tobacco Monopoly 1674–1791, and of its relationship to the British and American Tobacco Trades,* 2 vols, Ann Arbor 1973 and *Capital and Credit in British Overseas trade; the view from the Chesapeke, 1700–76,* Cambridge, Mass. 1980. The French contract and its effect upon the Glasgow merchants is described p. 604–17. See also Devine *op. cit.,* 64–8. Devine points out that though the French trade was of obvious significance it did not take more than one-third of the exports in most years.
6. Devine *op. cit.* The success of Glasgow merchants is attributed to direct purchase, the ability to sell whole cargoes in bulk (under the commission system a merchant was bound to get the best price, and often broke up the consignment in order to do so), and, above all, to cost efficiency. They frequently cut prices to levels which were deemed uneconomic in London but 'were able to compensate for their lower returns from selling tobacco

by practising economies of scale, by their income from retail of goods to planters and by cheaper operating costs' (Devine, 68). The merchants did not hold large quantities of tobacco, but sometimes played the market by holding stocks in warehouses on the Clyde until they judged that the European prices were at a satisfactory level. R. H. Campbell, 'The Anglo-Scottish Union of 1707. II, The Economic Consequences'. *Ec. Hist. R.* 2nd series XVI, (1963–4) discusses this and other aspects of the trade.

7. J. H. Soltow 'Scottish Traders in Virginia 1750–1775' *Ec. Hist. R.* 2nd series XII, (1959–60).

8. Devine *op. cit.*, ch. 6 *passim.*

9. PRO, A.O. 12. Petitions and Compensations of American Loyalists, 1785–9, (xerox copy in MLG).

10. T. C. Barker, 'Smuggling in the Eighteenth Century: the evidence of the Scottish Tobacco Trade' *Va HMB*, LXII (1954), 387–99.

11. Quoted in Devine *op. cit.*, 85.

12. Jefferson was acquainted with one factor, Andrew McCaul, and the tone of the correspondence between them indicates a very friendly relationship. On at least one occasion, after his return to Glasgow, McCaul purchased books on Jefferson's behalf. Jefferson was also acquainted with Neil Jamieson.

13. Graham *op. cit.*, 124.

14. This supposition is based on the evidence that when Neil Jamieson, formerly the wealthiest merchant on the Chesapeke and a Loyalist, tried to resume contacts with Virginia his correspondents had Scottish names but had not been mentioned previously in his voluminous papers. See below ch. VII *passim.*

15. Devine *op. cit.*, ch. III *passim.*

16. According to James Pagan *Sketch of the History of Glasgow,* Glasgow 1847, 90, the first partnership for ropemaking was formed in 1696, leather tanning began soon after 1707, green bottle making in 1730, the Delftfield pottery in 1748, the making of flint glass or crystal in 1777. Examples of Delftfield work are now extremely rare, and few survive in Scotland. It is surprising that the first distillery in the Glasgow area was not established until 1786.

17. K. Hamilton 'The Failure of the Ayr Bank' *Ec. H. R.* 2nd series VIII (1955–6), 405–18. The effects of the 1772 financial crisis are discussed in Richard Sheridan, 'The British Credit Crisis of 1772 and the American Colonies,' *Journal of Economic History,* XX 161–86.

18. In MLG.

19. The list was compiled by Richard F. Dell, Archivist of the Strathclyde Region, using the following sources: Glasgow Burgh Court Register of Deeds, 1660–1775; Glasgow Burgh Court Register of Probative Writs, 1721–65; Port Books of Port Glasgow and Greenock. Information was also derived from James Gibson *History of Glasgow* Glasgow 1777, John Cleland *The Rise and Progress of the City of Glasgow* Glasgow 1820, and James Pagan *Sketch of the History of Glasgow* Glasgow 1846. Other tobacco importers were listed, but identified by a single reference. Many merchants may have speculated in the trade from time to time, or been in it for only a ʌort period.

20. va HS, Carter Family Correspondence.
21. A. E. Truckell 'Early Shipping References in the Dumfries Burgh Records' *Dumfriesshire and Galloway Natural History and Antiquarian Society: Transactions and Journal of Proceedings,* 3rd Series, XXXIII, 156–75, XXXIV, 28–58. These two articles contain the details of all voyages, merchants, ships, and masters 1750–62.
22. Devine *op. cit.,* Appendix II.
23. PRO Treasury, Customs 14; SRO Records of the Board of Customs and Excise – Collector to Board CE 60/1/3–15, Collector's Quarterly accounts Pot Glasgow E. 504/28 and Greenock E. 504/15.
24. Names familiar in the tobacco business include Alexander Speirs, William French, John Ingram, George MacFarlane, Hugh Milliken, William Gordon, John Glassford, David Dalyell, George Oswald, George Buchanan, and Colin Dunlop.
25. SRO, E. 371 An inquisition on tobacco imported in the ship *Jenny* by Matthew Bogle and dated 27 May 1752 is evidence of his continued interest in the trade. There is also evidence of trade from other Scottish ports with America, e.g. an inquisition dated 22 Feb 1754 on tobacco imported in the *Delight of Montrose* by Thomas Douglas, Robert Dunbar, Robert Dickie, James Smith jr, and Thomas Christie, merchants of Montrose.
26. SRO, GD 51 1/354/1–33. Items 1 and 2.
27. Maryland Hall of Records, Annapolis. There was also an inspection law in Virginia.
28. There are many such items in the Neil Jamieson and Glassford papers in LC. The journals, ledgers, and inventories in the Glassford papers relate to fifteen stores in Maryland and Virginia. In va HS, there are accounts of William Cunninghame & Co's Falmouth Store. The LC also holds an account book (in poor condition) of James and Henry Ritchie showing debts due to their Hobshole, Virginia, store in August 1775. This collection also includes store inventories, a ledger for 1761, and a daybook for 1765–6. The records of Alexander Speirs & Co. (in private hands; copies in SRA) include account books relating to pre-war transactions and debts.
29. Maryland Hall of Records, Chancery Court, Maryland County Court Records, claims for Confiscated British Property. Many cases and claims relate to debts contracted before 1776. The claims by Glasgow merchants are numerous.
30. In the Henry Huntingdon Library, San Marino, California.
31. Principal sources for the organisation in Scotland are the John C. Brodie Collection (containing the papers of William Cunninghame & Co.), Alexander Speirs & Co. (copies in SRA, and John Glassford's letters in LC collection of Neil Jamieson Papers.
32. William L. Clements Library, University of Michigan, Buccleuch Muniments. The SRO holds microfilm copies RH/98. Reel 6.
33. In the Public Library of Alexandria, Virginia; copy in SRA.
34. A virulent form of typhus; probably communicated by rats or other vermin that came ashore with the goods.

35. The unsatisfactory storekeeper was Mr Orr at Alexandria; his successor was Mr Riddell.
36. Materials for the notes on Neil Jamieson come from W. M. McBean ed. *Biographical Register of the St. Andrews Society of New York* and from his own papers.
37. Copies of selected letters are in SRA.
38. Alexander Blair, Fredericksburg; Robert Mundell, Port Tobacco; Adam Fleming, Cabin Point. The principal stores of John Glassford & Co. were at Alexandria, Cabin Point, Colchester, Dumfries, Falmouth, Fredericksburg, and Norfolk in Viginia; Bladensburg, Upper Marlboro, Lower Marlboro, Leonardtown, Newport, Piscataway, Port Tobacco, Georgetown, and Rock Creek in Maryland. In addition to these the John Glassford Papers in LC refer to stores owned by Simson Baird & Co. (later merged with James Brown & Co.), Bogle, Scott & Co., Jamieson, Johnstone & Co., Glassford & Henderson, John Pagan & Co., Glassford, Gordon & Monteith.
39. SRO, John C. Brodie Collection, GD 247, Box 58. Bundle P and Box 58. Bundle O, letterbook of John Robinson, Falmouth, Va.; Henry Huntington Library, San Marino, California, accounts and papers of John Turner, Rockybridge, Va.; VA HS, papers of Andrew Cochrane, Falmouth; Accounts of John Robinson; letters addressed to Walter Colquhoun, Falmouth; accounts of the Falmouth store with Col. Charles Carter and John Chiney 1765–9, and other accounts 1764–72,; judgements in Virginia Courts in favour of Cochrane, Cunninghame & Co. 1756–73, in favour of Cochrane, Dreghorn & Co., 1763–6 and 1781.
40. The papers are in private hands; copies are held in SRA.
41. LC holds the following Ritchie papers for the pre-war period in a ledger for 1761, a daybook 1765–6, and an account book 1771–7. The post-war papers of the company are of considerable interest and will be reviewed in Chapter VII.
42. MD HS; there are other Hamilton papers in LC, see below. Papers produced for the bankruptcy of Jamieson, Semple & Lawson are in the SRO, Court of Session Productions CS. 96.
43. Hamilton's letterbooks as factor for James Brown & Co. are in the Glassford papers in LC: Hamilton assumed responsibility for the Glassford properties in Maryland, after Neil Jamieson's departure from Norfolk 'Alexander Hamilton's Letterbooks 1774–5' *Md. Hist. Mg.* LXI, 146–66, 305–28; lxii, 135–69; lxiii, 22–53. There are further references to these letters in chapters VI and VII.
44. Cunninghame District Archives, Kilmarnock. Letters from Robert Reid are included in the Cunninghame family papers.
45. SRA, TD 200/43.
46. MD HS, Alexander Hamilton Papers. Agreement dated 1 January 1770.
47. Cunninghame District Archives, Cunninghame Family Papers.
48. Robert E. Lee Memorial Foundation, Stratford Hall, Virginia. Letterbooks of William Lee, 1769–95.
49. VA HS, Thomas Adams Papers.
50. Letterbooks of William Lee 1769–95, Robert E. Lee Memorial Foundation, Stratford Hall, Virginia.

51. *Ibid.*
52. Houghton Library, Harvard University, Arthur Lee Papers.
53. There are several collections of Jerdone papers. 1. Letterbooks for 1756–63 at WMC. 2. Business papers in the CIW. 3. Family papers in VA SL. Portions of the 1756–63 letterbook are printed in *WMQ,* 1st series, XV, 126–32; there are also items from another letterbook, which seems to have disappeared, in *ibid.,* 1st series XI. 153–60, 236–42, XIV, 144–5.
54. Houghton Library, Harvard University, Arthur Lee Papers 23 June 1772.
55. For information about his papers, see note 53 above.
56. He also corresponded with friends and relatives in Scotland: Alexander Dunlop of Glasgow, Captain Hugh Crawford of Greenock, Thomas Caverhill of Jedburgh, and another Thomas Caverhill of Glasgow whom he referred to as his cousin.
57. VA SL, Allason Papers: letterbooks 1770–89, 1785–93; papers from 1774 onwards. WMC: Blair, Bannister, Homer and Whitney Papers. LC: William Allason Papers: bills of exchange drawn in 1759, invoice for goods supplied to Lord Dunmore 1774–5, and a letter from his brother, David, at Falmouth. See Edith E. B. Thomson 'A Scottish Merchant in Falmouth in the Eighteenth Century' *Va MHB,* XXXIX (1931), 108–117, 230–38, and W. A. Low 'Merchant and Planter Relations in Post Revolutionary Virginia 1783–1789' *ibid.,* LXI (1953), 308–18.
58. Two Robert Arthurs, father and son, were tobacco importers in Glasgow, Richard Oswald belonged to the Glasgow merchant family, with business in London and Glasgow, and John Barns & Co. was a small Glasgow firm trading with Virginia.
59. UVA, John Smith Papers. The company traded in Virginia as Speirs, Bowman & Co.
60. WMC, Blow Family Papers, letterbook of Richard Blow, 1770–72.
61. Originals in private hands in London; copies in CIW.
62. James King and William Luard (beef), James Aiken (barley), John King (cooperage), William King (candles), Thomas McGill & Co. (ship's fitters), Hugh Morris (ship's stores), Patrick Dougal (ship's stores), and the Port Glasgow Ropework.
63. SRO, GD 58. Carron Iron Company. The records are very full and are contained in many letterbooks. A full analysis of the contents would occupy a volume in itself. For the purpose of this survey two letterbooks (1760 and 1787–9) have been sampled.
64. The correspondence in the later volumes sampled is briefer and less informative. The volume of trade was large, but there was clearly no longer any need to go into details or ask for custom.
65. SRA, TD 132/1–72. Records deposited by Holmes McKillop & Co. (Solicitors).
66. SRO, GD. 1 618/1. Another major figure in the entrepôt trade was Alexander Houston of Glasgow, but his business seems to have been concerned exclusively with imports from and export to the West Indies, and the sale of West Indian sugar in Europe. NLS, Mss. 8793–8800, 8895–8. However Alexander Houston & Co. had some dealings in tobacco, though it does not figure in these records. In 1779 James Ritchie & Co. brought suit against Alexander Crichton, a partner in Alexander

Houston & Co., for failure to deliver some tobacco which Ritchie had contracted to sell. Ritchie claimed £1,000 for the estimated loss of profits so the consignment must have been a large one.

Notes to Chapter Four

1. It is not possible to present any figures that give an accurate picture of the migration between 1730 and 1775. For the years 1774 and 1775 information does exist (its character is discussed below). The record in Donald Whyte *A Dictionary of Scottish Emigrants to the U.S.A.* (Baltimore and London 1972), is of little use for the earlier years. The sources in this survey include a large number of names not recorded by Whyte.

2. Sir Bruce Gordon Seton and Jean Gordon Arnot eds. *The Prisoners of the '45, edited from the State Papers,* Edinburgh 1928, 26.

3. Abbot E. Smith *Colonists in Bondage: White Servitude and Convict Labor in America,* 1607–1776, Chapel Hill 1947.

4. Duane Meyer *The Highland Scots of North Carolina,* 1732–1776, Chapel Hill 1957, ch. II, considers the evidence and the way in which it became enshrined in so many histories of the period.

5. The Revd. Walter Macleod ed. *A List of Persons concerned in the Rebellion,* Edinburgh 1890, 359. William Ferguson observes that 'far from being a "Scotch rebellion", as it seemed to most Englishmen, the '45 was more like a Scottish civil war, a considerable portion of Cumberland's army being Scottish'. *Scotland: 1689 to the Present,* Edinburgh 1968, 153.

6. In the lists printed by Walter McLeod *op. cit.,* the following names appear more than fifteen times: Cameron (33), Drummond (19), Farquharson (25), Fraser (51), Gordon (71), Grant (57), MacDonald (60), MacGrigor (17), Mackenzie (32), MacLachlan (19), MacPherson (28), Ogilvie (27), Robertson (41), Ross (29), Stewart (104). At the other end of the scale there were fewer than ten Campbells, Duffs. Grahams, McAlisters, MacEwens, MacLeans, Macintoshes, MacIntyres, Mackays or Macleods. Twenty-one other clans also provided fewer than ten.

7. *Ibid.,* appendix I. Seton and Arnot eds, *op. cit.,* list 3,471 prisoners but these include some who were arrested on suspicion, some deserters from the British army, and some English jacobites who joined at Manchester.

8. Duane Meyer *op. cit.,* 44–53. Working from the statistical surveys of the Revd. Alexander Webster *Account of the Number of People in Scotland,* Edinburgh(?) 1755, and Sir John Sinclair *The Statistical Account of Scotland,* 21 vols. Edinburgh(?) 1791–99, he gives an increase of the Highland counties from 266,085 in mid-century to 303,612 in its last decade, an increase of 14%. This increase was irregularly distributed from 41.3% in the parish of Nairn, 23.5% in Argyll, 13% in Ross (including Lewis), to decreases in the Highland portion of Dunbartonshire, the Elgin parish of Duthel, the Banff parish of Kirkmichael, and six parishes in Perthshire. Most of the decreases seem to have been in areas from which it was comparatively easy to move to lowland towns, while the highest increases were recorded in the more remote districts. Ian Grimble in 'Emigration in the time of Rob Donn, 1714–78,' *Scottish Studies,* VII (1963), 129–53, discounts the effect of population increases in Sutherland

but stresses the break-up of patriarched society and the mutual obligations that it entailed. He draws attention to the contrast between the lands of Lord Reay, which enjoyed social harmony from 1768 to 1797 under the rule of a mentally deficient chief, and those of the Countess of Sutherland where factors pressed hard upon the people.

9. Hector St John Crevecour *Letters of an American Farmer.* London, 1732 (and many later edition). The 'History of Andrew the Hebridean' is part of letter III. 'What is an American?'

10. 'Scotus Americanus' *Information concerning the Province of North Carolina addressed to Emigrants for the Highlands and the Western Islands of Scotland,* Glasgow, 1773. For a fuller account of this pamphlet see p. 82–3.

11. John Patterson MacLean *An Historical Account of the Settlement of Scotch Highlanders in America prior to the Peace of 1783,* Cleveland and Glasgow 1900. Reprinted Baltimore 1960.

12. Maclean refers to the *Scots Magazine, Edinburgh Evening Courant,* and the *Caledonian Mercury.*

13. Maclean relied for this information upon a petition presented by Lieutenant Donald Campbell, who also implied that Lachlan Campbell would have had his land if he had been prepared to bribe the governor. Maclean provided little information about emigration to Georgia, though this was the earliest in time.

14. PRO. Treasury 47. Bundles 9–12. The names of emigrants to North Carolina were abstracted from these lists by A. R. Newsome and published in *The North Carolina Historical Review* XI (1934), 39–45, 129–43. The information which follows is derived from this publication.

15. NLS. Lee MS. 3431, 177–83.

16. The Scottish Catholic Archives are housed at Columba House, Drummond Place, Edinburgh. Preliminary enquiry indicates that there is material of interest to immigration historians, though it is more likely to be abundant after than before the Revolution. The references to America in the General Assembly papers to 1741 are very infrequent; it is possible that more requests for ministers will be found after 1770 in the wake of the great migration.

17. SRO, GD 1 53/73. About 700 taken at Preston were transported to the West Indies.

18. SRO, Collection of the Society of Antiquaries of Scotland, GD 103 2/382–3.

19. Seton and Arnot eds. *op. cit.,* 27.

20. Bryant, Pall and Hemperley, Marian R., *Entry Claims for Georgia Landholders.* Atlanta, 1975, 162.

21. *The Colonial Records of Georgia,* compiled by Allen M. Chandler, Atlanta 1904–16; AMS reprint New York 1970. Material relating to the Highland settlers is in vol. 2, *Minutes of the Common Council of the Trustees,* and vol. 21, *Original Papers, Correspondence of the Trustees, General Oglethorpe and Others.* Most of the documents are from the PRO. The instructions to Hugh Mackay are in vol. 2, 110.

22. *Colonial Records of Georgia,* vol. 21, 11–12.

23. *Ibid.,* vol. 21, 13–4. One story circulated by those opposed to the scheme was that in Georgia men were yoked four and four to a plough, and so served in place of horses.

24. Eventually headrights were claimed for 163 who arrived in Georgia. This displeased the trustees who had contracted for 110 plus 50 women and children; and these were to be 'free men and servants' not 'Gentlemen grantees of 500 acres'. Twenty of those who embarked were servants of Patrick and John Mackay. (Patrick and John claimed for thirty). Eventually it was agreed that the excess was 31 and their passages were to be paid for by labour or public works or provisions surplus to their own requirements. *Ibid.*, vol. 2, 164.

25. *Ibid.* The Earl of Selkirk, writing over sixty years later, made the same point in his *Observations on the present state of the Highlands.* By then he was able to identify those parts of the United States to which emigrants from different Highland districts had followed early migrants from their clans.

26. *Ibid.*, 336. The records do not show a large number of McLachlans in Georgia.

27. Larry E Ives *British Drums on the Southern Frontier,* Chapel Hill 1974, 50ff.

28. John Prebble *Mutiny: Highland regiments in revolt, 1743–1804,* London 1975, contains information about this incident. However he is probably incorrect in saying that few Highland soldiers survived war and disease after their first commander, Aeneas Mackintosh, returned to Britain in 1743.

29. The following volumes have been edited by Pat Bryant and Marion R. Hemperley: *Entry claims for Georgia Landowners 1733–*1750 (1975), *English Crown Grants, 1755–*1775, and one volume for each parish (except where otherwise noted): *St. Andrew* (1972), *St. Matthew* (1972), *Islands in Georgia* (1972), *St. John* (1972), *St. David, St. Patrick, St. Thomas, St. Mary* (Four in one volume, 1973), *St. Matthew* (1974), *St. Paul* (1974), *St. George* (1974).

30. Duane Meyer, see Note 4, is the most authoritative study.

31. Duane Meyer *op. cit.,* 81, expresses misplaced surprise that a highland county should have been named for 'butcher' Cumberland. Campbells would have been among the first to honour the victor of Culloden. After the Revolution Campbelltown was renamed Fayetteville.

32. Duane Meyer *op. cit.,* 89–90, drawing upon material from the manuscript volumes i–xxxvii of the North Carolina Land Grants, Secretary of State's Office, Raleigh, and Records of Land Transfers in Cumberland County, Recorder's Office, Fayetteville, N.C. 312 private purchasers with Highland names were identified in Cumberland County.

33. SRO, GD 170/3339. Campbell of Barcaldine Muniments.

34. NCSA. Transcripts of papers in private hands. Other transcripts are in UNC, where it is stated that the originals are in the possession of Mrs A. P. MacAllister of Hendrsonville, N.C. The Name appears as MacAlester, MacAllister, and McAllister.

35. 'Scotus Americanus' *op. cit.* (See note 10 above).

36. UNC, Invoice book of Hogg and Clayton, Charleston, S.C., and sales ledger of the store at Wilimington. The persons trading with the store were predominantly Scottish and included Farquhar Campbell, John Lyon, Samuel McCree, John Rainie, Hugh Waddell, William Campbell, Robert

Cochrane, William Dry, Duncan, Ancrum & Shaw, Arthur and Archibald McLaine, Thomas Henderson, David Ross, John Kirkwood, Thomas Cunningham, Robert Johnston, Neil Mackay, Allen McDougal, Martha Dalrymple, Archibald Bell, John McPherson, John McDonald, Andrew McIntyre, Alexander Colvin, William McLaing, Mary McLeanan, Archibald McNeale, Robert Rowan, Neil Hendrey, Samuel Campbell, the two McAllister brothers – Alexander and Hector – mentioned above, and Jean Colvin who married Alexander.

37. UNC, James Hogg Papers.
38. There is also information about this incident, and the names and former residences of the emigrants, in the Thomas Whiteside Papers in UNC.
39. See ch. VII. As late as 1803 James Hogg was sending money to his two sisters in Scotland, and some later family letters are included in the collection.
40. NCSA, Colin Shaw Correspondence 1784–89.
41. There is a list of Scottish Highlanders settled in Richmond County (Gum Swamp, Beaver Dam, Ives Creek, and Leith's Creek) in the Alexander McInnis Papers, Duke University, Durham, N.C. Another small collection is the McMillan Family Papers, UNC, Southern Historical Collection. Letters refer to the estate of Captain Iver McMillan of Campbelltown, Argyll, who left money to be divided between the heirs of his brother Ronald, who had settled in Wilmington, N.C.
42. NLS, Mss. 5696–5704. Liston Papers (additional).
43. NYHS, Diary (anonymous) 1821–4. The references to North Carolina occupy only four pages in the three volume diary, which displays lively observation and some literary skill.
44. I am grateful to Mr. David Wilson of the University of Cambridge for this reference.
45. In the 1851 letter quoted above these were given as Cumberland, Bladen, Robeson, Richmond, Montgomery, Moore, and Barnett.
46. NYHS, R. R. Livingston Papers.
47. PA HS, Letter to an unknown recipient dated 1 June 1773.
48. NYHS, Lawrence Papers. The location was from the head of South Bay, southward to the boundary of land petitioned for by Ebenezer Lacey and his associates, eastward to the New Hampshire line, and westward to mountains and vacant land. This was the Argyle Patent (see p. 73). It will be recalled that this was largely recognition of the fact that Lachlan Campbell, Donald's father, had been cheated out of the land promised to him and his party of Highlanders.
49. I am grateful to Mr David Fraser, who spent the year 1978–9 at the University of Syracuse on a scholarship award by the St Andrews Society of New York, for drawing these sources to my attention.

Notes to Chapter Five
1. NLS, Adv. Mss. 27.6.2., Cotton Mather to John Wodrow, January 1722.
2. In all colonies the Bishop of London had diocesan responsibility; the commissary was, in effect, head of the Anglican Church in a colony, but he could not ordain priests and could only recommend clergy for preferment.
3. William Wilson Manross *The Fulham Papers in the Lambeth Palace Library's American Colonial Section,* Oxford 1965, 160–1.

4. The Scotts of Aberdeen and Overwharton parish, Virginia, are the subject of a report in ch. II. Other Aberdeen men in the Virginian church included James Thomson, Marischal 1706-10 or 1711-15. St Mark's parish, Culpepper County, 1740-72. Bishop Meade *Old Churches in Virginia,* Philadelphia 1872 II, 77-8, says that he was a graduate of Edinburgh, but he seems to have assumed that all Scots clergy were Edinburgh graduates unless otherwise identified. James Thomson, Marischal 1745-8. Went to Virginia as a tutor 1767, returned to Britain to take orders, and was then rector of Leeds parish, Fanquier County, until 1812. Christopher McRae, Marischal, graduated 1753. Littleton parish, Cumberland County, 1773-6 and 1785.

   These clergy are identified by Dr James Gammack, *Aberdeen University Review,* x, 147-8. The list is certainly incomplete. The most influential of them was Archibald Campbell, who kept a school attended by George Washington, John Marshall, James Madison, and James Monroe. A seventeenth-century Aberdonian, James Keith of Hamilton parish, Fauquier County, was John Marshall's grandfather.

5. John Harrower's diary (see p. 43) provides an alternative account of an indentured tutor.

6. The word 'Associate' was used to describe the ministers who 'associated' outside the regular presbyteries.

7. *Act of the Associate Presbytery for renewing the National Covenant of Scotland, and the Solemn League and Covenant of the Three Nations,* Edinburgh 1744, 109.

8. Some observers detected the influence of still older Scottish dissenting traditions in the explosion of rhetoric which ushered in the Revolution. In 1774 a Scottish visitor to Princeton reported that he had heard 'forty boys repeat Orations at the . . . commencement, every one of them full of the old Cameronian resisting sentiments.' NLS Charles Steuart Papers, James Parker to Steuart, 3 Nov 1774.

9. For the Glengarry highlanders see Sister Mary Christine Taylor S.S.J., *A History of the Foundation of Catholicism in Northern New York,* New York, 1976, 79; Martin J. Becker *A History of Catholic Life in the Diocese of Albany 1609*-1864, New York 1973, 21; Ewen J. MacDonald 'Father Roderick MacDonell, Missionary at St. Regis and the Glengarry Catholics' *Catholic Historical Review,* XIX (1933), 265-74.

10. Douglas Sloan *The Scottish Enlightenment and the American College Ideal,* New York 1971.

11. Quoted in Sloan *op. cit.* See also Thomas H. Montgomery *History of the University of Pennsylvania,* Philadelphia 1900, for a full account of William Smith's work in establishing the curriculum; also Edward P. Cheyney *History of the Univesity of Pennsylvania,* Philadelphia 1940. The events which brought John Witherspoon to Princeton and the consequences for American higher education are examined later in this chapter. For further information about Smith see p. 111-2.

12. Henry F. May *The Enlightenment in America* New York 1976 9, 293-4, 342-50.

13. Garry Wills *Inventing America: Jefferson's Declaration of Independence* New York 1978. Morton White *Philosophy of the American Revolution* New York 1978, emphasises the influence of Hutcheson, but makes only three

passing references to Reid. The dates of publication of the major Scottish works are significant and seem to have been overlooked by some previous writers on the enlightenment in America. Hutcheson's first work (which made his reputation) was the *Inquiry into the Original of our Ideas of Beauty and Virtue*, published in Dublin in 1725, and went through several later editions in London and Glasgow. His *Essay on the Nature and Conduct of the Passion and Affections* was published in 1729. The *Short Introduction to Moral Philosophy* or *Compend* was published in Latin in 1742, in English in 1747, and the three volume *System of Moral Philosophy* posthumously in 1775. Lord Kames published his *Essays on the Principles of Morality and Natural Religion* in 1751. Thomas Reid's *Enquiry into the Human Mind*, which contained the essence of ideas developed in later essays, appeared in 1764. American readers therefore had ample opportunity of studying those works, and the burden of proof would seem to lie with those who minimise their influence.

14. Alison, born in 1701, came to America as a tutor in 1735 in the family of Samuel Dickinson of Maryland. He was ordained by the presbytery of New Castle in Delaware, and opened an academy at New London, Pennsylvania in 1743, which later moved and became the nucleus of the University of Delaware. His pupils at the academy included three signers of the Declaration of Independence – Thomas McKean, George Read, and James Smith – and Charles Thomson, secretary of the Continental Congress.

15. Morton White *op. cit.*, 133. The evidence cited above suggests that the immediate source of Wilson's quotations may have been Alison's lecture notes, copies of which would certainly have been available.

16. Morton White *op. cit.*, 98 n; John Adams *Diary and Autobiography*, vol. I, 2. For a discussion of Hutcheson's contribution to revolutionary thought see Caroline Robbins 'When is it that Colonies may turn Independent: an analysis of the environment and politics of Francis Hutcheson', 1694–1746,' WMQ XI, (1954) 213–51.

17 The quotations all come from *Essays on the Principals of Morality and Natural Religion*, Edinburgh 1751.

18. The quotations in this and the preceding paragraph are from *Essays upon Several Subjects concerning British Antiquities*, Edinburgh 1747, Appendix to the Essay on 'Succession or Descent'.

19. In 1785 an Irish visitor, John Joyce, wrote that the Scots who remained in Norfolk were 'very desirous of having a dissenting clergyman placed there, as they have no worship of any kind, their Church being destroyed with the town, which had been a most beautiful edifice.' (Va MHB XXII 407). If this pre-revolutionary Scottish church existed it escaped the notice of T. J. Wertenbaker in his *Norfolk*, Chapel Hill 2nd ed. rev. 1962, despite his careful use of the records. Perhaps a small place of worship was magnified by recollection into 'a most beautiful edifice.'

20. Manross *op. cit.*

21. See Carson, T. A. Ritchie *Frontier Parish*, Aberdeen 1976.

22. NLS, Adv. Mss. 27.6.2.

23. NLS, ADV. MSS. 27.6. The letters to Principal Stirling are reprinted in Kenneth Silverman *Selected Letters of Cotton Mather*, Baton Rouge 1971.

Silverman also reprints one letter to Stirling held by the University of Virginia and another held by The American Antiquarian Society. The NLS letters from Mather to Wodrow are in Silverman and others in Thomas McCrie *The Correspondence of the Rev. Rober Wodrow*, 3 vols. Edinburgh 1842. Finally a letter from Mather to Sir John Maxwell of Pollock, rector of Glasgow university, is reprinted in Silverman.

24. SRO, Church of Scotland General Assembly Papers 24/1 fos. 210–13, 24/2 fos. 224–7, 32 fos. 531–40, 45. fos. 189–94.

25. Silverman *op. cit.*, 135–7.

26. Samuel J. Baird *History of the New School Presbyterians*, Philadelphia 1868, 42.

27. *Ibid.*, 54. The present location of this letter (if it has survived) is unknown.

28. Cf G. W. Pilcher ed. *The Reverend Samuel Davies Abroad: The Diary of a Journey to England and Scotland, 1753–55*, Urbana 1967, 89–103, and a list of correspondents and donors given in the Appendix.

29. William D. Sprague, *Annals of the American Pulpit*, vols III and IV, New York 1860. For the use of Sprague's work as a source see below.

30. SRO, CH1/2/49 fos. 43–48

31. Glasgow University Library. Letters from Francis Hutcheson to Thomas Drennan of Belfast. Many years later Hugh Simm, who went out to America with John Witherspoon, said that Witherspoon had had many requests to obtain more ministers from Scotland (Princeton University, Hugh Simm Papers).

32. SRO, GD95.12.2. Records of the SSPCK.

33. There is a copy in the SSPCK records in the SRO, GD95.13.29.

34. NYHS. John Sargent succeeded his father or grandfather. The older John Sargent was born in 1709, educated at Yale, and ordained in 1735. In 1743 he published. – *The Causes and Danger of Delusions in Affairs of Religion* also *A Letter to Dr. Colman: containing a proposal of a Method for the Education of Indian Children*, which is regarded as a notable contribution to educational theory. He died prematurely in 1749. There is a reference to him in the Ezra Stiles Papers at Yale University; but his employer is named as the Society for Propagating the Gospel among the Indians. The Society in Scotland must have assumed responsibility for the New Stockbridge mission after the Revolution.

35. As one might suppose Boyd was not listed as a 'distinguished minister', but referred to in a footnote *op. cit.*, III, 29.

36. *Ibid.*, III, 136. No reference has been found in Scottish records to a settlement in New Hampshire, but sources on the spot are used by Thaddens Piotrowski in *The Scots and their Descendants in the Manchester, New Hampshire, area*, Manchester 1976.

37. Sprague ch. IV, 73.

38. With the NYHS.

39. NYHS holds an account book of the church kept by Robertson. It is largely a record of collection and petty expenditure.

40. PA HS. Minutes of the Scots congregation in Philadelphia 1768–91. There were three other Scots churches which may have been short-lived.

41. Presbyterian Historical Society, Philadelphia, Miscellaneous Papers.

42. YUB. Ezra Stiles Collection. With miscellaneous papers for 1769.

43. Francis Alison was given a D.D. by the University of Glasgow in 1756. In the Alison papers in the Presbyterian Historical Society there is a note describing the degree as conferred upon his son. Francis Alison Jr.; if so, the University was giving its most distinguished degree to an unusually young man. It seems probable that the elder Alison was the recipient.

44. Seafield Muniments. G.D. 248/5648. John Lang to 'My Lord' (possibly Lord Findlater) 7 Feb 1725/6.

45. As the Bishop of London's 'Commissary' was his personal representative in the colony, James Blair's commission had lapsed with Bishop Robinson's death in 1723. There was some delay before Blair was reappointed by Bishop Gibson, Manross, *op. cit.* 169, 181

46. *Ibid.*, 42, 43, 44.

47. *Ibid.*, 194, 199, 206. Much earlier a correspondent from Maryland had said that it would be better for parishes to remain vacant than to go filled with young men from Scottish universities, *ibid.*, 29., 26 May 1781.

48. NYHS. Charles Inglis Papers. Letters dealing exclusively with church affairs have been transferred from this collection to the Church History Society, 606 Ruthervue Place, Austin 5, Texas.

49. YUL, Papers of George Panton.

50. Ritchie *op. cit.*, 191.

51. On 31st July 1778 Myles Cooper wrote to Panton saying that he had written on his belhalf to the Archbishop of Canterbury and the Bishop of London. Columbia University Library, Columbia General Ms. Collection.

52. Each has an article in the *Director of American Biography.* For Seabury see also J. P. Lawson *History of the Scottish Episcopal Church,* Edinburgh 1844 326–8, 330–2.

53. SRO, CH 10.1.3.

54. There is a diary of this visit in the PAHS, Pemberton papers.

55. YUB. Stiles Collection.

56. There are also a few papers of Francis Alison in the Presbyterian Historical Society, Philadelphia. They consist of a sermon (with typescript), no date, Of the Rights of the Supreme Power; some notes headed 'Civil and Religious Liberty' (the portion preserved is an argument against innate ideas).

57. LC, Peter Force Collection. Ontology was a branch of metaphysics. Pneumatology in its original meaning was the study of "spirits" – that is of non-material aspects of personality and thus a forerunner of modern psychology. It is probably used in this sense though it came later to mean the chemistry of gases and this branch of study was pioneered at Glasgow.

58. MD HS, letterbook of Dr Alexander Hamilton, 1739–43. This Alexander Hamilton should not be confused with the statesman or with the tobacco factor.

59. SRO, GD 24/1/833.

60. The University of Pennsylvania has a large collection of William Smith's papers. These deal with family and university affairs. There are also several manuscript sermons.

61. In a chapter devoted to the study of Scottish influences in America it is unnecessary to pursue William Smith's later career. Briefly, he gave

cautious support to the Revolution, but took little part in controversy. He remained provost, but after the war was bitterly disappointed in his failure to become a bishop in the Episcopal Church. His later years were clouded with depression and there were accusations of intemperance.

62. Princeton University Library has many letters exchanged between Witherspoon and Rush, and one letter to Rush from Richard Stockton. The New Jersey Historical Society has five letters from Benjamin Rush to Witherspoon. Most of the letters in both collections were published by Lyman H. Butterfield, *John Witherspoon comes to America* Princeton *n.j.* 1935. At Princeton there is also an *Edinburgh Almanack* for 1768 with notes on the end papers, including 'memoranda of things to be done and persons to be seen in London prior to departure for America; a memorandum of things to be done at Philadelphia; a memorandum of things to remembered in America'. There is also a note that James Robertson, weaver, wished to be informed 'if there by any encouragement for him to remove his family (wife, four daughters, and one son) to America', and names of others who wished to migrate.

63. The list is in PUL.

64. Douglas Sloan, *op. cit.*

Notes to Chapter Six

1. Benjamin Bell his grandson. *The life, character and writing of Benjamin Bell,* Edinburgh 1868.

2. Elias Jones. *New Revised History of Dorchester County.* Cambridge MD 1966.

3. SRO, Murray of Murraythwaite Muniments.

4. University of Michigan, William L. Clements Library, Fyffe Letters.

5. Appendix B.

6. Appendix B.

7. Appendix A.

8. Appendix A.

9. Appendix A.

10. Cadwallader Colden to William Douglas, 1728. *The letter and Papers of Cadwallader Colden,* vol. I. New York Historical Society Collections, New York 1917, p. 272.

11. William Douglas to Cadwallader Colden, 17 Feb. 1735/6. *op. cit.* vol. II, 1918, p. 146.

12. 'Early letters of Arthur Lee', *Southern Literary Messenger,* XXIX, (1854), 71–2.

13. SRO, Dalhousie Muniments. Letter from W. H. Drayton of South Carolina, at Balliol College, Oxford, to Governor James Glen, 1762, referring to his and his brother Charles' medical studies.

14. W. I. Addison, *A roll of the Graduates of the University of Glasgow from 1727 to 1897,* Glasgow 1897. *List of Graduates in Medicine in the University of Edinburgh from* MDCCV *to* MDCCC LXI, Edinburgh 1867. Table I summarises the American students in Scotland for each five-year period 1745–1800.

15. The names of all identified American students studying in Scotland are listed in Appendix C.

16. Glasgow University Archives 19057. List of Students in Anatomy and Botany 1790–1800.

17. Samuel Bard to his father, 22 June 1762, quoted in J. B. Langstaff, *Dr. Bond of Hyde Park*, New York 1942, p. 24.

18. Samuel Bard to his father, 29 Dec. 1762, in Langstaff *op. cit.*, p. 37.

19. W. J. Bell, Jr., 'North American and West Indian Medical graduates of Glasgow and Aberdeen'. *J. Hist. Med.*, xx, (1965), 411–14.

20. B. Rush. *'Autobiography'*, ed. G. W. Corner, Princeton 1948, pp. 42, 44.

21. *General list of the members of the Medical Society of Edinburgh,* Edinburgh 1823.

22. Edinburgh University, Chirurgo-Physical Society 1783–91. Dissertations read to the Society.

23. *The Laws of the Royal Physical Society,* Edinburgh 1819, with lists of members.

24. Edinburgh University, American Physical Society Dissertations 1794–7.

25. W. B. Blanton, *Medicine in Virginia in the eighteenth century,* Richmond Va., 1931, p. 91.

26. W. J. Bell, Jr., *John Morgan, Continental Doctor,* Philadelphia 1965, p. 67.

27. Edinburgh University, Prof. John Walker. Natural History Class Lists 1782–1800.

28. *Laws of the Society Instituted at Edinburgh* MDCCLXXXII *for the Investigation of Natural History,* Edinburgh 1803, with list of members from its foundation.

29. Edinburgh University, Edinburgh Natural History Society, Dissertations 1782–5.

30. *History of the Speculative Society 1764*–1904, Edinburgh 1905.

31. 'Early Letters of Arthur Lee', *op. cit.*, p. 76.

32. W. J. Bell, Jr. *op. cit.*, p. 67.

33. B. Rush, *op. cit.*, p. 49.

34. S.R.O., Leven and Melville Muniments. Letter 1778 from Benjamin Rush, Philadelphia, to Lord Leven.

35. SRO, Society of Friends in Edinburgh Archives.

36. PaHS. James Pemberton to John Pemberton, 8 August 1783. Pemberton Papers XXXIX, 89.

37. Rush. *op. cit.*, p. 49.

38. D. M. Lyon, 'A student of 1765–70. – A glimpse of eighteenth century medicine,' *Edinburgh Medical Journal* XLVIII (1941) 206–7, gives account of Ravenscroft expenses at Edinburgh.

39. W. J. Bell, Jr. 'Thomas Parker M.B. physician and friend'. *op. cit.*, p. 78.

40. W. J. Bell, Jr. *John Morgan, Continental Doctor,* Philadelphia 1965, p. 67.

41. MASS HS, letter from Thomas Bulfinch, 20 Dec. 1756, to his father Bulfinch Papers.

42. Thomas Bond to Benjamin Franklin, 6 July 1771, in William Pepper. The medical side of Benjamin Franklin, *University of Pennsylvania Medical Bulletin* XXIII (1910) 333–5.

43. Benjamin Franklin to Thomas Bond, in Pepper. *op. cit.*, pp. 336–9.

44. William Quynn, Letter to his father 12 Nov. 1783, in D. MacKay Quynn and Wm. Rogers Quynn. 'Letters of a Maryland Medical Student in

Philadelphia and Edinburgh', *Maryland Historical Magazine* XXXI (1936) 181–215.

45. MASS HS, Letter from Nathan Smith to John Warren, 2 May 1797. Warren Papers, vol. 3.

46. Benjamin Rush to John Morgan, 27 July 1768 in Joseph Carson, *History of the Medical Department of the University of Pennsylvania*, Ms Scrapbook in College of Physicians of Philadelphia, vol. II, 27.

47. PA HS, Thomas Parke, Journal No. 2, 22 Oct 1771 in the Pemberton Papers, LVII, 98.

48. W. J. Bell, Jr. 'Philadelphia Medical Students in Europe'. *op. cit.*, p. 54.

49. Samuel Bard, Letter to his father, 4 Feb. 1764, Langstaff *op. cit.*, p. 55.

50. PA HS, George Logan to Charles Logan, 2 March 1778. Letterbook, *op. cit.*,

51. *Ibid.*

52. Thomas Parke Journal No. 2, 22 Oct 1771. Pemberton Papers, *op. cit.*, LVII 98.

53. *Ibid.*

54. George Logan to Charles Logan, 2 March 1778, *op. cit.*, PA HS.

55. *Ibid.*

56. VA MSS. 2 M6664a.

57. William Quynn. Letter to his father, Edinburgh, 15 Dec. 1783. D. Mackay Quynn and William Rogers Quynn. Letters of a Maryland Medical Student in Philadelphia and Edinburgh. *op. cit.*, p. 195–7.

58. 'Early letters of Arthur Lee'. *op. cit.*, p. 73.

59. W. J. Bell, quoted from 'Philadelphia Medical Students in Europe, 1750–1800' *op. cit.*, p. 49.

60. George Logan to Charles Logan, 2 March 1778 *op. cit.*

61. L.C. Ruston Papers, letters home from Edinburgh by Thomas Ruston, 1763–5.

62. Thomas Quynn to his father. Edinburgh 9 Feb 1784. D. Mackay Quynn and William Rogers Quynn. *op. cit.*, p. 198–9.

63. 'Early letters of Arthur Lee'. *op. cit.*, p. 80.

64. *Letters of Benjamin Rush*, ed. L. H. Butterfield, Princeton 1751 pp. 33–8, 45–8.

65. MD HS Alexander Hamilton to P: J: D-d (Provost John Drummond) (1741). Dulany Papers.

66. Benjamin Franklin to Sir Alexander Dick, 2 June 1765, in Pepper, *op. cit.*, p. 214–15.

67. S. Griffin to Levi Bartlett, April 4 1794. W. J. Bell, Jr. 'Medical Practice in Colonial America', *Bull. Hist. Med.* XXXI (1957 444.

68. E. Berkeley and D. S. Berekeley. *Dr. John Mitchell, the man who made the map of North America*, Chapel Hill N.C. 1974.

69. PA HS Library Company of Philadelphia Collection. Banjamin Smith Barton to Benjamin Rush, 24 Jan 1787. Rush Mss., XXVII, 2.

70. *Ibid.* Daniel Coxe to Benjamin Rush, 16 May 1791. Rush MSS. XXVII 11.

Notes to Chapter Seven

1. An analysis of loyalist claims on the British government after the war shows that of the 1,144 claims made by persons not born in America, 470

were made by Scots, 290 by English and 280 by Irish. In addition there
were some with Scottish names among those who were merely identified as
having been born in Great Britain, Wallace Brown *The King's Friends,*
Providence, R.I. 1965, ch. 14 *passim.* In Virginia 'all the evidence confirms
that Scots made up the backbone of Virginian Loyalism'. *Ibid.,* 181.

2. In November 1774 James Parker wrote to Charles Steuart, 'The Glasgow
    factors seem to be the great object of their resentment. The case is
    plain – to them they owe money.' NLS Charles Steuart Papers. Emory G.
    Evans argues convincingly against the thesis that indebtedness was a major
    factor in Virginian opposition to Britain in 'Planter Indebtedness and the
    Coming of the Revolution in Virginia' *WMQ* 3rd Series XIX (1962)
    511–33. He concludes that indebtedness was 'no more than an
    unconscious and unarticulated conditioning element that helped to make
    Virginians more receptive to rebellion and independence.' (533).

3. Wallace Brown *op. cit.,* p. 205.

4. Thomas M. Devine, *The Tobacco Lords,* Edinburgh 1975, 115–20.

5. *Ibid.,* 111.

6. *Ibid.,* 116–7. The prominence of the merchant who failed also attracted
    attention to their difficulties. Both Andrew and James Buchanan had been
    Provosts of Glasgow. The former planned and developed Buchanan Street,
    now the city's finest thoroughfare.

7. Cunninghame Papers, Cunninghame District Archives, Kilmarnock. Reid
    was associated with James McCall & Co but was not a salaried factor.

8. A very faint addition in the margin of the letter seems to imply that
    tobacco held by the inspectors at Hobshole was seized but returned after
    two days.

9. Reid enclosed a copy of the oath but it has not survived.

10. NLS Charles Steuart Papers. Charles Steuart was the owner of a slave
    named Somerset whom he brought with him to England but whom he
    came to regard as unsatisfactory. His attempt to send him as a slave to the
    West Indies led to the most famous case in the annals of the British anti-
    slavery movement. Somerset's cause was taken up by Granville Sharp. In
    1772 Lord Chief Justice Mansfield decided that no man could be held as a
    slave in England and that Somerset was therefore free. The doctrine that
    slavery being contrary to natural law could not exist without positive law
    to sustain it was of great importance in later controversies in the United
    States. There is much information about the case in NLS Charles Steuart
    papers.

11. WMC, Blow family papers.

12. David K. Skaggs and David McMaster 'The Letterbooks of Alexander
    Hamilton, Piscataway Factor." *Md. Hist. Mg.,* LXI, 146–66, 305–28;
    LXIII, 22–25. Hamilton was factor for James Brown & Co., but after the
    war he also assumed responsibility for Glassford's interests on Maryland.

13. See p. 274–5.

14. See ch. III.

15. See ch. VII.

16. Maryland Hall of Records. Campbell was employed by Glassford, Lilburn
    by Buchanan, Hastie & Co.

17. SRO, Sinclair of Freswick Muniments.
18. MD HR. Undated proceedings by the Committee of Observation in August 1775.
19. MD HR. Journal of Proceedings: Commissioners of Confiscated British Property, 1781–2; Sale Book of Confiscated British Property 1781–5; Sale Book of Confiscated British Property 1784; Intendant's Letterbook (No. 10) (1782; Ledger of the Commissioners of Confiscated British Property.
20 LC.
21. The details can be found in H. R. McIlwaine ed. *Journal of the Council of State of Virginia,* Richmond 1931.
22. LC.
23. LC, James Dunlop Papers. This James Dunlop should not be confused with that of his uncle, James Dunlop of Garnkirk, who was a partner in Colin Dunlop & Co. and, before the war, the owner of much property in Virginia and Maryland.
24. NLS, Ms 8258ff. 34–6,, Stewart Stevenson Papers. Evidence was also given at the same time by John Glassford before the House of Commons. He answered questions about the quantity and value of tobacco imported, the Stamp Act and its effects in America, debts owed to British merchants, and the commercial consequences of a breach between Britain and the colonies. SRA, TD 80/2. The document consists of rough notes on his evidence, perhaps taken down by a clerk or secretary.
25. The papers are in private hands but there are copies in SRA. Speirs died in 1782 and most of the papers preserved consist of those which passed into the hands of the trustees of his estate. The most important item is a letterbook (11th Oct. 1781 to 12th May 1789); the early letters, written by Speirs himself, are voluminous; there are also letters in another (and more legible hand) relating to business transactions of Speirs, French & Co.; after late 1782 all the letters are of this type and lack the personal touch that Speirs gave to his own correspondence. In addition to the letterbook the principal items are: Day Book, 1777–82; Ledger 'B', 1773–30 May 1780; Legder 'C', 1 June–5 April 1785; 'State of the private affairs of Alexander Speirs: abstracts from accounts for 1770, 1771, 1773, 1782, 1785, 1788'; Sederunt Book for Trustees, 14 Dec. 1782–5 April 1785; Sederunt Book for Patrick Colquhoun & Co., a partner in this company. Emory G. Evans argues that resistance to the repayment of debts in Virginia was due largely to the influence of Patrick Henry, and that by 1797 British creditors were able to win most of their suits in the state courts ('Private Indebtness and the Revolution in Virginia', *WMQ* Series XXVIII (1971) 349–74). But the sources suggest that though the courts may have been fair it was extremely difficult for creditors to gather satisfactory evidence.
26. The great bulk of the Jamieson papers in L C were surveyed in III. There is also a small collection of Neil Jamieson papers (accounts and ledgers) in the NYHS. The first document is with the Jamieson papers in NYHS; the second in the LC collection.
27. Several members of the Corbet family were in business in Glasgow in the eighteenth century, but none is recorded as having died in Virginia during the war. Letters to Neil Jamieson from his son-in-law, James McDowell,

introduce the kind of gossipy news which is rare in the correspondence of Glasgow merchants. For instance on 2 April 1784 he told him that he had a new grandson, and that there was a forthcoming parliamentary contest between Clay Campbell and Jack Crawford, 'C. C. will not bribe but J. C. has no other means but hard cash as Glasgow and Dumbarton are against him – Renfrew is the casting borough'.

28. U va, Daniel Grinnan Papers.

29. LC.

30. PRO, T. 79; copies of Glasgow claims in SRA. These were used extensively by Wallace Brown in *The King's Friends* to substantiate his general account of the Loyalists.

31. Skaggs and McMaster *op. cit.*, LXV. 35, Hamilton to Matthew Blair, 21 Oct. 1784

32. Walter Clark ed. *State Records of North Carolina*, Winston 1896, XIII, 478, 535, 553, 650; XVIII, 75.

33. An annotated list of these loyalist materials, including many county records, is available from NCSA.

34. J. H. Easterby *History of the St. Andrew's Society of Charleston, South Carolina*, Charleston 1929.

35. The figures are abstracted from William M. McBean *Biographical Register of the St. Andrew's Society of the State of New York*, 2 vols. New York 1922.

36. The few papers relating to the Scots Charitable Society are in the Massachusetts Historical Society.

37. SRO. GD 170.

38. *Ibid.*

39. James Murray is well represented in the sources. Papers relating to his career in North Carolina are in NCSA; papers relating to his life in Boston (from which the following extracts are taken) are in MASS HS; and there are several letters from him to Charles Steuart in NLS. See also James H. Stark, *The Loyalists of Massachusetts*, Boston 1910, 254–60.

40. Cadwallander Colden, David Colden, Sir William Johnson, John MacDonald, Duncan Campbell, Benjamin French (?), Daniel McAlpin, Peter McLarin, and Roderick McKenzie.

41. E. D. O'Callaghan *New York Colonial Manuscript.* ed. New York 1856, VIII, 682–3. Thomas Gunnersal, an assistant to the British commissary general, said that, after being warned by him and others, Johnson decided to leave his home and set out for Canada with 130 highlanders and 120 others.

42. Printed in *New York Historical Society Collections* vol. 15 (1882). According to MacBean's *Biographical Register of the St. Andrews Society of the State of New York* he was chief of the MacDonalds of Ardnamurchan.

43. Presbyterian vols. III and IV, New York 1860.

44. For Witherspoon see ch. V above.

45. For a recent account of McIntosh see Harvey H. Jackson, *Lachlan McIntosh and the Politics of Revolutionary Georgia*, Athens, Georgia, 1979.

46. Copies in SRA.

Notes to Chapter Eight

1. SRO, GD 51, Melville Castle Muniments.

2. It is perhaps indicative of the attitude of many prominent merchants that

Colquhoun refers to 'provinces' rather than 'states'. The full implications of independence had yet to be grasped.

3. LC, Neil Jamieson Papers. There are earlier references to this collection in chs. III and VII. For a general review of conditions during and after the war, see M. L. Robertson, 'Scottish Commerce and the American War of Independence' *Ec. Hist. R.* 2nd Series IX, (1956–7), 123–31.

4. McCullum was a close friend of James Fairlie, whose papers are reviewed below, and succeeded in establishing himself. In 1798 a company called Daniel McCallum & Co. was active in Virginia. In a similar vein a young man starting his career was advised to seek opportunities in Virginia. 'Most of the Mercantile people having left Virginia there will in a little time be a very great opening for people of that profession. NLS Charles Steuart papers 43, Jan. 1782.

5. There is one intriguing illustration of difficulties attending the resumption of trade. John Lawrence wrote from Virginia to ask whether Jamieson had any records of a store managed by a Mr Corbet. 'A little time before Mr Corbet died, I am informed that in one of his drunken fits he burned the Books and Accounts that he had kept of his transactions on our account.'

6. LC, with the Glassford papers.

7. The son's name was Jordan, so he was probably the son of Colonel Jeremiah Jordan mentioned above.

8. There is a copy in SRA, from papers in private hands.

9. Fairlie went on to Jamaica only to find that his company had failed. 'It is a most melancholy consideration to me at any advanced period in life that after doing business for so many years, I should find myself without sixpence.' However he seems to have remained in Jamaica until 1804, when he returned to Kilmarnock.

10. LC, Dunlop Family Papers; also in the Md HS, Dunlop papers 1788–1808, including ledgers for 1793–1811 giving details of tobacco supplied to Buchanan & Dunlop; Somervell, Dugail & Co.; and James Ritchie & Co.

11. LC, James Ritchie Papers.

12. LC, Huie, Reid & Co. Papers 1784–9; Smith, Huie, Alexander & Co. Papers 1784–96; Day Book, Dumfries 1786–7; Account Book beginning 6 December 1785; Inventory of goods and land at Dumfries, 1 September 1788; Account Book, 1790.

13. W. McBean, *Biographical Register of the St. Andrews Society of the State of New York*, New York 1922, vol I, 260 says that George Walker was a member in 1787. He was a native of Clackmannan, a surveyor in Virginia, a merchant in Philadelphia, and then resident in Georgetown. In 1798 he wrote a public letter in the *Washington Gazette* attacking the Commissioners for the District.

14. SRO, GD. 51 Melville Castle Muniments, 17 August 1795.

15. NYHS, Letters of Thomas Buchanan to Robert Ferguson 20 June 1798.

16. SRA, John Leitch Ledger 1798–1805. The larger debtors were Hanson Randolph of Virginia (£119), 'French Funds' (£1052), Alexander Yuille (£125 and £420, the property of George Yuille & Co.), Alexander Donald (£407, also property of George Yuille & Co.).

17. SRO, GD 142, Hamilton of Pinmore Muniments.

18. SRO. Companies frequently mentioned are David McCallum & Co., Andrew Dick, Robert Gordon & Co., Findlay, Bannatyne & Co., George Yuille & Co., Buchanan & Dunlop, R. Craig, Corbett, Russell & Co., Leitch and Smith, John and James Ritchie, Milliken & Barr.

19. In addition to the sources specifically mentioned in the text the following contain some references to trade between Scotland and Virginia or Maryland after 1783.
   SRA: Baird, Hay & Co., Journal 1772–1816. Contains a few references to John Hay & Co., with stores at Southampton, Va., Gray's Creek, Va., and Cross Creek, N.C.
   MD HS: (1) Letterbook of Thomas Rutland 1784–7. A merchant at Annapolis, exporting iron, slaves, and tobacco. Some letters to Robert Ferguson at Port Tobacco. (2) Dunlop Papers. Ledger 1793–1800. Many dealings with individuals or companies with Scottish names.
   LC: Dunlop Family Legal Papers: sale of land in June 1798 by Thomas Dick of Bladensburg to John Laird of George Town (formerly confiscated, purchased by William Ferguson and assigned by him to Dick; sale of land in 1802 in the District of Columbia to James Dunlop and Joeph Carleton.

20. NYHS, Colin McGregor's Ledger 1784–90; NYPL, Colin McGregor Papers. Many deal with attempts to look after Neil Jamieson's interests, but there are also numerous letters to and from other persons. He usually signed himself 'Coll. McGregor' and was for that reason often described as 'Colonel McGregor', but it does not appear that he ever held military rank. Light is thrown on the first stage in McGregor's American career by a letter to George McMurdo of Dumfries early in 1781. It introduced Colin McGregor as a promising young man who was going out to America. McMurdo had many friends in Virginia and it is possible that some of them had moved to New York. NLS, Maxwell-McMurdo Papers, April 1781.

21. NYPL, Henderson Letterbook 1790–4; PA HS, Henderson Papers. The latter is a much larger collection. Most of the letters in the 1790–4 letterbook in the NYPL are in the hand of Henderson's nephew, David Bell, whose spelling and grammar was often weak.

22. Humphrey McAusland, Cochrane McLure and Alexander Riddell of New York; William Nimmo of Richmond. His Glasgow correspondents (in addition to Gardner) were Alexander Stewart, Alexander Glen, and Alexander Smith.

23. SCL. Thomas Aiton Letterbook Feb-June 1802. A typescript (slightly edited for style and minor details) is available.

24. MASS HS, Samuel Cary Papers.

25. John Campbell & Co was one of the Glasgow companies with which Colin McGregor corresponded.

26. NYHS, Thomas Buchanan & Co. Ledgers 1800–17.

27. Duncan Campbell, Alexander McDonald, Grant & Mitchell, Archibald Galbraith, Stewart, Galloway & Co., Dougall Campbell, Hugh Monro, James McDonald, Alexander McDonald, George Reid, William and Robert Bruce, Murdoch, Masterton & Co., Murdoch, Yuille, Wardrop & Co.

28. SRO, G58.

29. NLS, Cadell of Grange Papers Box 31.
30. NLS Dundas Papers, 14 Nov. 1784.
31. NLS MS 9646; also some notes by Fraser in RHASS PAPERS. ADV MS. 73.2.15.
32. NLS MS 6602 (bound with printed tracts LC 2605).
33. NLS Acc. 6945. Alex. McNab of Inishowen to Archibald MacRae of Ardintoul, 18 Oct. 1793.
34. SRO, Seafield Muniments. John Grant to Sir James Grant, 1 August 1803.
35. Another indication of alarm amongst landowners in a list, (SRO, GD 221/25/67), probably prepared in 1802, of persons on Lord Macdonald's estates in Skye who intended to emigrate, and adding notes on their reasons for doing so. Some were discharged soldiers without employment, others had been turned out of land.
36. NYHS, Falconer Family Papers (typescripts), 1785–1856.
37. Duke University, Durham, N. C. Robert Leslie Papers.
38. Dickinson College Library, Charles Nisbet Letters; University of Pittsburgh Library, Letters from Charles Nisbet to Alexander Addison.
39. PA HS, Letters from David Erskine, Earl of Buchan. For Buchan see Andrew Hook *Scotland and America, 1750*–1835, Glasgow 1975, 20, 25, 83–4, 140, 234–5, 237–9.
40. PUL, John McLean Papers.
41. PUL has a copy of lecture notes on chemistry delivered at Glasgow in 1782–3. This would have been too early for McLean himself to have attended the lectures, but he may have acquired them from a former student. McLean's chemistry had certainly progressed far beyond that, but if he was the owner of the notes (as seems likely) it may be possible to trace a link between Joseph Black and the development of chemistry teaching in America.
42. DUL, William Baskerville Correspondence, 1802–4.
43. NYHS, Rufus King Papers.
44. STUYVESANT-RUTHERFORD PAPERS
45. NYPL, Francis Jeffrey Papers.

INDEX